GRAND TOURS AND COOK'S TOURS

GRAND TOURS

AND

COOK'S TOURS

A HISTORY OF LEISURE TRAVEL, 1750 TO 1915

Lynne Withey

WILLIAM MORROW AND COMPANY, INC.

NEW YORK

Library of Congress Cataloging-in-Publication Data
Withey, Lynne.
Grand tours and cook's tours : a history of leisure travel,
1750 to 1915 / Lynne Withey.—1st ed.
p.   cm.
Includes bibliographical references and index.
ISBN 0-688-08800-7
1. Voyages and travels—History.   I. Title.
G96.W58   1997
910'.9—dc20   96-20860   CIP

Printed in the United States of America

First Edition

1   2   3   4   5   6   7   8   9   10

BOOK DESIGN BY MISHA BELETSKY

For Claude

PREFACE

NEARLY A decade ago, when I was trying to settle on a topic for my next book, a friend suggested that I take up the history of travel. At the time, it sounded like the perfect subject. It would be a logical sequel to the book I had just finished on Pacific exploration; it would finally get me to delve into the history of the nineteenth and twentieth centuries after years of writing about the eighteenth; and it would give me yet more vicarious outlets for my incurable wanderlust, and yet more excuses to indulge my passion for reading travel literature. I had covered the Pacific with James Cook; now I could do the grand tour with Boswell, Goethe, Wordsworth, Mark Twain, Edith Wharton, and dozens of others. The trick, of course, would be defining the boundaries. After all, the history of travel extends back to the beginning of recorded history and takes in the entire world. Even in the optimistic glow that surrounds one at the beginning of a new project, I knew it would be necessary to focus; and yet the idea of taking on a broad sweep of history with a huge cast of characters provided much of the appeal.

From the outset, I decided to focus on people who traveled mainly for the fun of it—thus excluding explorers, pilgrims, traders, emigrants, and others who traveled on business or out of necessity—and on those who ventured some distance from home. By concentrating on pleasure travel, I limit my scope to the modern period, as relatively few people undertook long journeys merely for recreation before the eighteenth century. By concentrating on long journeys, I distinguish *travel* from the broader category of vacation trips (leaving out of my story the development of seaside resorts, for example), because one of my main interests is recording how travelers responded to cultures quite different from their own. Within this framework, I expected to describe the expansion and changing nature of travel, which I loosely characterized in my own mind—following the example of many other writers—as a gradual shift from "travel" to "tourism."

The more I delved into the subject, however, the more it became apparent that such a shift is a moving target. There is an old joke among historians about the English middle class, which always seems to be rising no matter what era one chooses to study; I've come to feel the same way about travelers and tourists. In a now classic essay, "From Traveler to Tourist: The Lost Art of Travel," Daniel Boorstin dated the decline of the traveler and the rise of the tourist from around the middle of the nineteenth century, when railroads began to revolutionize transportation and the first travel agents invented the package tour, thus bringing leisure travel within the reach of the middle and working classes. Paul Fussell, writing about the adventurous traveler-writers of the 1920s and 1930s, men like Graham Greene and Robert Byron and D. H. Lawrence, saw the years between the World Wars as "the final age of travel," declaring that "tourism is all we have left." Not so for William W. Stowe, however, who concludes his recent book on nineteenth-century American travelers with an afterword recalling his own "grand tour" of Europe in the mid-1960s, characterizing himself and his contemporaries as "lineal descendants" of travelers like Mark Twain and Henry James. Today, he adds, it has all changed—not because today's young travelers have suddenly become "tourists," but because changes in the travel industry have made it possible for them to tour Asia, or Africa, or South America as easily as his generation toured Europe.¹ Indeed, a friend who spent several months in the mid-1970s traveling by bus across Iran, Iraq, Afghanistan, and India once remarked to me that there was a fairly standard circuit through those countries, a kind of latter-day "grand tour" popular with young travelers—until war and revolution put much of the region off-limits.

Regardless of the timing one chooses, there is in all these formulations both a sense of loss and a judgment that the authentic experience of travel has become more and more difficult to achieve in the face of encroaching tourism. The notion of "travel," as Boorstin points out, implies effort—in old English the word was the same as "travail," meaning work—and independence, both highly valued qualities in Western culture. "Tourism," on the other hand, a term that came into the language in the early nineteenth century, meaning simply the act of making a tour, has taken on negative connotations, implying mass movement, following the herd, going where one is told to go and thinking what one is expected to think.²

While these are scholars' interpretations of travel history, with their modern-day tendency to read back into the past our contemporary concerns about overcrowding and desecration of beautiful places, travelers themselves have displayed the same tendencies. Edward Gibbon complained that Switzerland was overrun in 1784, while Wordsworth, to his chagrin, found himself the object of admiring hordes by the 1830s—long before steam transit and travel agents created opportunities for mass travel (although Wordsworth lived long enough to fight, unsuccessfully, against the railroad's encroachment on his beloved Windermere). As long as people have been traveling, it seems, they have been regretting the proximity of what Henry James called "one's detestable fellow pilgrim," looking back nostalgically to an earlier time when favorite destinations were less crowded, when one could truly be a "traveler" rather than a "tourist."³ That earlier time, obviously, lies in the mind of the beholder, leading at least one historian to point out that the traveler/tourist distinction is not really a matter of historical timing, but rather harks back to a sort of "golden age" when one could travel free of the trappings of the modern tourist industry and the hordes it serves.[4]

I have chosen to write primarily about what most people would label "tourism," but in an effort to rescue tourists from their detractors and to acknowledge the fact that, just as "travel" and "tourism" have coexisted at least as far back as Gibbon, there are elements of both the traveler and the tourist in most everyone who ventures forth from home. The original, nonpejorative definition of tourist implies, above all else, the notion of traveling for pleasure; the tourist is one who makes a circuit, traveling over a particular itinerary (whether prescribed in advance or not, whether with a group or not), for the sake of the journey itself. Rather than equating tourism with mass, mechanized travel, I prefer to consider it rather more broadly, as leisure travel—a distinctly modern phenomenon but one that predates railroads and travel agents by several decades. In this sense, I would argue, tourism originates with the "grand tour," which had its origins in the sixteenth century but reached its heyday in the late eighteenth. Although limited mainly to the sons of wealthy families and intended primarily for educational purposes, by the middle of the eighteenth century the grand tour had become common enough among Britain's upper classes, and combined pleasure and instruction to such an extent, that it constitutes the first significant example of leisure travel on a large scale.

This book begins, then, at the point when the grand tour became something of a cultural institution, around the middle of the eighteenth century, and traces the history of pleasure travel up to World War I, after which the automobile and the airplane changed the nature of travel so dramatically, and encouraged such vast growth in the numbers of people traveling, that it would require at least another book or two to do justice to the story. I am interested especially in the growth of travel as a business—changes in transportation, the rise of travel agents, the beginnings of government and business efforts to entice tourists to their regions, for example—but also in individuals' experiences of travel. As a result, this book interweaves the history of tourism as an industry with the changing experiences of an increasingly large and diverse array of individual travelers. Throughout my story, there is a third theme as well: As travel becomes more commonplace, so does criticism of other travelers. Increasingly, travelers take pains to distinguish themselves from the masses, to style themselves as "travelers" rather than "tourists." Usually such criticism had been thinly veiled class snobbery, as well-to-do travelers found themselves sharing favorite destinations with less wealthy, less sophisticated men and women. They responded by attempting to differentiate themselves from the average tourist, seeking out new, usually more distant (and therefore more expensive and more exclusive) destinations, traveling first-class, patronizing luxury hotels and resorts. As one segment of the travel industry promoted mass tourism, inventing packaged tours and advertising budget train tickets and hotel accommodations, another segment catered to the rich, providing a constantly escalating standard of luxury for those who could afford to insulate themselves from run-of-the-mill tourists.

It is a long and complex story, and inevitably I have had to make some choices in order to keep this book within reasonable bounds. Because of my interest in the experience of travel, and particularly in how travelers responded to their encounters with other cultures, I have focused on journeys of some distance—although not necessarily great distances by today's standards. At a time when one can fly from London to Paris in an hour or from New York to London in five, when the global marketplace is rapidly erasing distinctions among cultures (at least on a surface level), it is useful to remember how vastly different France seemed to British travelers in the nineteenth century, for example, and also how much time and effort it took to travel even two or three hundred miles. On the other hand, because I am concerned with leisure travel and with the growth of mass tourism, I have confined my scope to destinations that could readily be visited by travelers using standard means of transportation: Europe, the United States (until the late nineteenth century, only the eastern United States at that), and those parts of the Middle East and Asia made accessible by the reach of European imperialism.

Finally, there are the necessary choices about which individual travelers to include. At times it has seemed as if everyone who left home in the nineteenth century wrote a book about it. Most of my

travelers were British or American, for the simple reason that those
nationalities predominated among pleasure travelers, at least among
those who traveled considerable distances and wrote about their experiences. In the eighteenth century, most of them were also men,
although, perhaps surprisingly, women began to travel in great numbers after about 1815. I have tried to include a range of types of
people, from famous travelers to the more ordinary folk who chanced
to leave behind an account of their journeys; but, inevitably, those
who wrote about their travels were more likely to be either writers
by trade or well known for some other reason. Choosing themes and
characters has been a little like planning a long journey, with some
of the same frustrations—how much one would like to detour here,
pause a few days there, see every village and church and lovely view
along the route—and so I can only conclude by saying that I have
tried to select judiciously and to be, as an eighteenth-century traveler
might have put it, both instructive and entertaining.

ONE OF THE GREAT pleasures of writing this book was working
in the Archives of the Thomas Cook company. The staff there, especially Edmund Swinglehurst, Joy Hooper, and Jill Lomer, were
extraordinarily helpful in guiding me through their extensive collections, which are truly a treasure trove for anyone working on the
history of travel. Mr. Swinglehurst's own writings were also an invaluable source, as were his comments on early drafts of my manuscript. I owe special thanks also to the staff at the Bancroft Library
at the University of California, Berkeley, and to Roy Ritchie and
Peter Blodgett at the Huntington Library, for their assistance in fer-
reting out sources on travel in the western United States.

As always, friends and colleagues have been a constant source of
support and encouragement over the many years I have spent writing
this book. I am especially grateful to Claude Kolm, Lee Ann DuRard,
Michael Hindus, Harvey Ginsberg, and Timothy Seldes for their critical comments on earlier drafts of the manuscript.

CONTENTS

CONTENTS

ONE

GRAND TOURS

CHAPTER 1

YOUNG GENTLEMEN

ON TOUR

J AMES B OSWELL, one of the most celebrated travelers of the
eighteenth century, was simply a rebellious youth of twenty when
he left home for the first time, seeking escape from his father, his
legal studies, and what seemed to him the stultifying provincial life
of Scotland. Like many privileged young men of his generation, Boswell occupied the years between university and career with an extended tour of continental Europe, a rite of passage intended to
supplement a young man's formal education and provide him with
some experience of the world—a sort of mobile finishing school for
young men. For many of these young men, Boswell included, this so-
called "grand tour" also provided a socially acceptable form of escape, a way of sowing wild oats, in the parlance of a later time.
Historical hindsight demonstrates that Boswell was a far more tal-
ented and perceptive observer than most young grand tourists, but
at the time he was very much like them: young, rich, well educated
in the classical tradition of the time, immature, a bit rebellious, yet
perfectly well aware of the social role expected of him as an adult.

3

If he was perhaps more seriously at odds with his family than most of his contemporaries, and more inclined to agonizing self-doubts (many of them committed to paper), he nevertheless serves as a quite typical and highly entertaining guide to the young gentleman's grand tour.[1]

The son of a prominent Edinburgh judge and heir to the estate of Auchinleck, near Glasgow, Boswell was expected to follow his father into the law after completing his undergraduate studies at Edinburgh College. Young Boswell, however, found literature more to his liking, and took to spending most of his evenings at the theater. When he became intimate with a Roman Catholic actress and began reading religious tracts that she and her priest gave him, Alexander Boswell—whether more appalled by the young woman's profession or by her religion is hard to say—packed his son off to the university at Glasgow, where he could continue his legal studies away from the nightlife of Edinburgh and closer to the Auchinleck estate. After five months in Glasgow, Boswell rebelled and ran off to London, apparently with the intention of joining the Catholic Church and becoming a monk.

Unable to travel to London himself to reason with his son, Alexander Boswell asked a friend, the Earl of Eglinton, to look after young James. Eglinton complied, although not in quite the way that the elder Boswell might have hoped. The best way to rid a headstrong young man of religious delusions, Eglinton believed, was to distract him with the pleasures of city life; he took Boswell to parties and the theater and introduced him to women and notable men like the Duke of York and Laurence Sterne. As Boswell's biographer later put it, Eglinton "salvaged him from Romanism by making him a Deist and a rake." Eglinton also suggested that Boswell seemed better suited to a career in the military than the law, prompting James to write his father asking that he purchase a commission in the Foot Guards, a regiment permanently stationed in London. This was enough to bring Alexander Boswell to London to escort his son home.[2]

Alexander vetoed the Guards scheme, recognizing it for what it was—a ploy to stay in London—and insisting instead that James return to his legal studies, this time under his father's supervision.

4

For two years James lived at home in open rebellion against his father, spending as much time as possible writing, attending the theater, and engaging in affairs with various women. He did manage to learn enough to pass the examination in civil law, however, and finally his father agreed to let him go to London and use whatever influence he could muster to obtain a commission. In November 1762 Boswell returned to London with a modest allowance from his father. Securing a commission proved difficult, however, and after several months Boswell was no closer to a career decision. His father renewed the pressure to come home and take up the law. Once again, father and son reached a compromise: James would spend a year in Holland studying law and then take a few months to travel on the Continent. The two men had rather different ideas about a proper itinerary and fit subjects of study for a Continental tour, however, so toward the end of his year in Holland, James was arguing with his father again. This time, Alexander offered his son a choice between touring the German courts and traveling through Flanders to Paris, with the goal in either case of observing court life and politics in other nations. James, on the other hand, dreamed of going to Italy. But his father thought Italy and France, other than Paris, a waste of time—the former because of its "intoxicating" effect on young travelers and the latter, as he told James, because "there is nothing to be learned by travelling in France."[3]

Alexander Boswell's attitude, that travel was worthwhile only if educational, was a common one at the time. Even the grand tour, with its primarily educational goals, was suspect among many people, who questioned the value of turning young men loose in unfamiliar surroundings with nothing more than a tutor and some servants as chaperons—and with good reason, as gambling and whoring were common enough pastimes among grand tourists. Others simply thought the educational value of travel was wasted on the young.[4] Notwithstanding the critics, however, by the middle of the eighteenth century the Continental tour, which had its origins among the British aristocracy in the sixteenth century, had expanded to become a common experience among the sons of wealthy professional and mercantile families—men like Horace Walpole, son of Robert Walpole, the British prime minister, who toured the Continent in the early 1740s with his friend the poet Thomas Gray; Edward Gibbon, dispatched to Switzerland in 1753 to study with a Protestant minister after his father discovered that his son had surreptitiously converted to Catholicism; William Beckford, heir to a man who had made his fortune raising sugar in the West Indies and retired to live the life of a country squire in England; and Tobias Smollett, who first traveled to the Continent as a young man in the 1740s and returned with his family in 1763, this time seeking a more healthful climate to relieve the symptoms of tuberculosis.[5]

These were just a few of the thousands who made the grand tour in the eighteenth century. The numbers ebbed and flowed as periods of war made any nonessential travel inadvisable; the Seven Years' War (1756–63), in particular, cut off British access to the Continent. From 1763 until the French Revolution, however, the number of people crossing the Channel increased dramatically, with only a brief decline in the late 1770s and early 1780s, when France and Britain were once again at war. In 1785, an acquaintance in Switzerland told Gibbon that 40,000 English men and women were touring the Continent that year, while a newspaper report about a year later claimed that 3,760 English tourists had arrived in Paris during one six-week period. Small numbers by modern standards, to be sure, but perceived as a remarkable increase by contemporaries, demonstrating (according to the report on Paris tourists) that "the rage for travelling" had reached "an amazing pitch of folly." Even as far east as Dresden and Vienna, not the most popular stops on a grand tourist's itinerary, the British consuls, whose jobs included looking after visiting Britons, remarked on the inundation of tourists.[6]

Throughout the eighteenth century, grand tourists were almost exclusively male and predominantly British, although there were some notable exceptions—among them Lady Mary Wortley Montagu, who accompanied her husband during his stint as ambassador to Constantinople from 1716 to 1718 and left him twenty years later to pursue a peripatetic life on the Continent; and Johann von Goethe, already famous in the mid-1780s as the author of *The Sorrows of Young Werther,* who slipped away from the court at Weimar to travel in Italy, seeking escape from his fame and the formalities of court life.[7] The grand tour was largely a British invention, mainly

6

because Britain, as the wealthiest nation in the world, had a sub-stantial upper class with enough money and leisure to travel. (Philip Thicknesse, who traveled extensively through France and Spain in the 1770s, remarked that those who believed the French had no in-terest in traveling were wrong; it was the cost of travel and govern-ment restrictions on leaving France that kept them home.) In addition, many educated Britons felt isolated from the rest of Europe and from the sources of Western history and culture. To become a fully educated member of elite society, they believed, one had to see the ruins of classical Rome as well as the churches and palaces and art collections of the great Continental capitals.[8]

By the time Boswell set off on his travels, the grand tour had settled into a more or less fixed pattern. Although the first major guidebook to European travel, Thomas Nugent's *Grand Tour* (first published in 1749), gave equal weight to France, Italy, Germany, and the Netherlands, devoting one thick volume to each country, in fact the grand tourists of the late eighteenth century confined them-selves mainly to France and Italy, concentrating on a handful of cities: Paris, Geneva, Rome, Florence, Venice, and Naples, with brief stops in some of the smaller Italian cities. This had not always been the case; in the sixteenth and early seventeenth centuries, the reli-gious controversies of the Reformation made Italy a potentially dan-gerous place for British travelers, and young tourists typically spent most of their time in France, often devoting several weeks or months to language study in one of the provincial towns before going to Paris.[9] While the French capital remained an essential part of the grand tourist's itinerary, Italy was its heart. For Western Europeans, Italy was the source of all that was important in their culture, both ancient and modern: home of the Romans, whose language formed the core of upper-class British education and whose government and art remained models for emulation, and of the great Renaissance artists, considered by the British to be the finest exemplars of modern aesthetic taste. As Boswell's mentor, Samuel Johnson, put it, "A Man who has not been in Italy, is always conscious of an inferiority, from his not having seen what it is expected a man should see."[10]

By the time Boswell set off on his tour, Italy was gaining popu-larity for less exalted reasons as well. The Italians' reputation as a gregarious and uninhibited people, the presumed easy availability of women, even the brilliant colors of the landscape and the warm climate exercised a powerful attraction for northern Europeans. Certainly the pleasures of the senses were always part of the grand tourists' motives—at least if the cautionary literature warning of the temptations facing young travelers is any indication—but the traditional purpose of the grand tour was educational, focused on visiting historical and cultural sites and observing what were loosely known as the manners and customs of foreign nations. Toward the end of the eighteenth century, however, the sensual pleasures of the Mediterranean climate and culture were more readily acknowledged as one of the main reasons to visit Italy. When Boswell wrote, "I'm determined to try all experiments with a soul and body," he had in mind the pleasures of the flesh more than the intellect.[11]

Goethe, traveling two decades later, seeking escape from what seemed to him an unbearably rigid court society, claimed to feel the weight of responsibility and routine fall away as soon as he crossed the Alps. Unlike Boswell, he was attracted not to greater sexual license but to freedom from the notion of work as an end in itself. Italians, he remarked, worked "not merely to *live* but to *enjoy* themselves: they wish even their work to be a recreation." He was not uncritical of the Italian approach to life—living for the moment left many cold and hungry in winter, he observed—but was profoundly influenced by his encounter with a radically different approach to everyday life. Both men were somewhat ahead of their time in acknowledging so clearly Italy's appeal to the senses as well as the intellect, but by the early decades of the nineteenth century, the Mediterranean, and Italy in particular, would become a mecca for northern Europeans seeking respite from both cold winters and rigid social conventions.[12]

ALTHOUGH GRAND TOURISTS had to contend with conditions that seem primitive by contemporary standards, by the late eighteenth century travel was actually quite well organized compared to what it had been a few decades earlier. Roads improved substantially in the second half of the century, regular coach and cross-Channel ferry routes were established, and a few entrepreneurs began providing services designed specifically to aid the tourist. One could, for example, arrange for transportation across much of the Continent from either London or Paris. The few guidebooks available in the seventeenth and early eighteenth centuries—weighty tomes like Nugent's *Grand Tour,* which was mainly a description of the European capitals, and essays offering moralistic advice to young travelers— were supplemented by a new genre of books written in the guise of travelers' accounts but devoting much of their attention to practical advice on itineraries and places to see.[13]

Even so, a Continental tour was not something to be undertaken lightly in the eighteenth century, nor was it for anyone on a schedule or a budget. Grand tourists had to be prepared to adjust itineraries and endure frequent delays, as well as cope with seemingly arcane bureaucratic regulations. The British traveler's ordeal began with the Channel crossing. Although, in theory, ferries sailed on regular schedules by the 1760s, rough seas or contrary winds could delay sailings for hours or even days. The crossing from Dover to Calais, the shortest route, took at least three hours and more commonly five or six; passages requiring double that time were not unknown. Travelers often found themselves sitting in port, waiting for rough weather to subside, or, once across the Channel, anchored offshore until conditions allowed their ship to enter harbor.[14]

Once onshore, the traveler had to go through customs formalities and then arrange for transportation onward, as few wanted to stay more than a night or two, if that, in Calais, Boulogne, or Ostend, the main ports of entry to the Continent. Customs inspectors, in the opinion of British travelers who suffered their whims, could be maddeningly thorough in their search through every trunk, bag, and hatbox, and capricious in levying duty. Bribes were routine. Tobias Smollett, always quick to complain about being cheated while traveling, resigned himself to greasing the palms of customs officials. Taking a principled position is admirable, he remarked, ''but requires a great share of resolution and self-denial.'' Luggage was subject to inspection again at the gates of every major city. To avoid long lines at Calais and further delays en route to Paris, travelers were advised to leave their bags in the care of a reliable innkeeper at the port,

9

who would see to its inspection, deliver overnight bags to clients' rooms, and have all luggage not needed immediately sealed by customs agents, freeing it from further inspection along the road to Paris. Even this practice did not always work, however; Smollett was annoyed to discover that his books were seized at Calais and dispatched to Amiens, at his expense, to be examined for material "prejudicial" to France.[15]

Clearing customs was just one example of the annoyingly complex bureaucratic regulation of travel, itself a product of the complexity of European politics. Of the frequently visited countries on the Continent, only France and the Netherlands were unified nations with centralized governments and legal systems. The German states included a bewildering array of principalities ranging in size and importance from Frederick the Great's Prussia to tiny fiefdoms barely larger than a good-sized country estate in England; Switzerland was a loosely knit federation of cantons and free cities; and "Italy" was an assortment of separate states and kingdoms, some independently controlled and others, at various times, under the jurisdiction of the Hapsburg Empire. Boundaries and alliances shifted frequently over the course of the eighteenth century as a result of wars and shifting political alliances, creating confusion about borders, customs, passports, currency, even measurement. A mile in Italy was not the same as a mile in England, nor was it consistent from one part of Italy to another.

Passports were not required to enter France in the eighteenth century, although experienced travelers and guidebook writers generally recommended obtaining one from the French consul in London as a precaution. In Italy, the situation varied among the numerous states and cities, and regulations changed frequently. Naples, for example, had a strict policy throughout most of the eighteenth century requiring visitors to obtain visas from the Neapolitan ambassador in Rome. As a precaution, British travelers were advised to carry two all-purpose passports, one signed by an Italian prince, ambassador, or cardinal, and the other by an English consul resident in Italy. One could, as an alternative, obtain a passport from the British secretary of state and have it stamped or "viséd" by the appropriate foreign officials, but such documents were hard to come by, requiring a per-

sonal recommendation from a banker or high government official
and payment of a substantial fee. Not until the second half of the
nineteenth century was the British passport system routinized to the
point where British documents largely replaced those issued by foreign governments for British travelers. Even then, passports were
not required to enter and leave Britain, but simply to establish one's
identity abroad. The modern system did not come into effect until
World War I, when it was deemed necessary for security reasons.[16]

The multiplicity of currencies in circulation—perhaps the worst
case was Switzerland, where each canton issued its own money—
was mitigated somewhat by the widespread practice of accepting
major forms of hard currency, especially the French louis d'or and
the sequin (used in Rome, Florence, and Venice) throughout much
of Europe. British coins were also accepted in a few large cities on
the Continent. Even so, keeping track of different currencies and
maintaining a supply of ready cash was no simple matter for the
traveler. One popular eighteenth-century guidebook devoted several
pages to tables of exchange rates and conversion of common mea-
sures. Most travelers carried letters of introduction from their bankers to foreign banks, requesting that they supply the traveler with
money by drawing against his British account. It was not always
easy to find bankers willing to accept bills, however, and commis-
sions were generally high.[17]

Arranging transportation on the Continent was somewhat less
complicated than getting across the Channel, although by no means
free of frustrations. Transportation services were quite well developed throughout Europe, and major roads were good in France and
the Netherlands, although less so in the German and Italian states.
The traveler arriving in Ostend or Calais had three choices. He could
purchase or hire a private carriage and horses, an expensive undertaking possible only for the very wealthy. More practically, he could
rent a carriage—anything from a simple two-seat chaise to an elaborate coach—and travel "post," which meant hiring horses and
driver at designated stations spaced along the main roads at intervals
of six or seven miles. The posting system was well developed by the
1760s, with detailed rules about the number of horses and men required for different types of coaches and the intervals at which horses

had to be changed. Guidebooks listed every post station along the major intercity routes. These books, called *Livre de Post,* also included detailed maps, part of a series produced by French government engineers beginning around mid-century. Most posting stations doubled as inns, offering travelers the convenience of dining while waiting for fresh horses to be harnessed to their carriages. The system offered the comfort of private travel without the expense and responsibility of maintaining one's own coach and horses, although there were some disadvantages. Fresh horses were not always readily available; more than one traveler wrote of being told that all available horses were being kept in reserve for some prince or nobleman who was expected to pass through shortly. Travelers also complained of being overcharged and rudely treated. Even so, posting was the mode of choice for most well-to-do travelers.

The less wealthy, or those who preferred not to be encumbered by a carriage, could avail themselves of public transit, most commonly the *diligence,* a large, cumbersome conveyance that resembled three coaches hitched together with a platform across the top for luggage and additional passengers. The diligence, which could carry up to thirty people, traveled between major cities in France on regular, if slow, schedules; four or five miles an hour was about average. By the late eighteenth century, daily service was available between Calais and Paris, while coaches departed Paris five times a week for Lyons, and twice a week for Bordeaux. In the 1780s, it took three or four days to go from Calais to Paris (compared with two in a private carriage) and five from Paris to Lyons or Bordeaux. Traveling by diligence could be crowded and uncomfortable—springs weren't introduced until the late eighteenth century—and meant long days on the road, often starting before dawn, but fares were cheap and schedules reasonably reliable. Similar services existed outside France but usually employed smaller, humbler conveyances— in rural Switzerland and Germany, simple wagons with benches and crude coverings—and did not offer schedules as extended or as frequent as those in France. Boswell described the German equivalent, called a *postwagen,* as "a remain of barbarity of manners . . . just a large cart, mounted upon very high wheels, which jolt prodigiously."[18]

Many British grand tourists avoided the diligence because they disliked traveling at close quarters with strangers, especially foreign strangers. Arthur Young, a student of agricultural practices who traveled on the Continent in the 1780s, was appalled that his fellow passengers entertained themselves by singing for most of the trip, leading him to remark that he "would almost as soon have rode the journey blindfold on an ass." Smollett complained about the slow pace, the crowded conditions, and the necessity of eating French food; diligence passengers had no choice in where they ate meals or spent the night. ("I hate the French cookery, and abominable garlick, with which all the ragouts, in this part of the country, are highly seasoned," he remarked while staying in Lyons.) For the open-minded, however, the diligence offered a quick way to become acquainted with the natives, and those who could not afford posting had little choice.[19]

An even cheaper alternative was the *vetturino* system (*voiturin* in French). In Italy and Switzerland, where diligence service was limited, it was often the only alternative to posting. Vetturinos were self-appointed guides who contracted with travelers to provide transportation, lodging, and meals along a specified route for a single price. Traveling with a vetturino was even slower than traveling by diligence—six or seven days from Lyons to Turin instead of three and a half to four, for example—and unless one's party was large, it meant being thrown among strangers, as vetturinos typically put together groups of six to twelve. It also meant eating and sleeping wherever the vetturino chose, often spending twelve hours or more on the road; because the vetturino charged by the trip, rather than the day, it was in his best interests to get his passengers to their destinations in the shortest possible time. In northern Italy, Goethe complained that "travelling with *vetturini* is an exhausting affair; the only thing to be said for it is that one can always get out and walk." As the small, uncomfortable wagons often used by vetturinos made little better than three miles an hour, walking was indeed a reasonable alternative.[20] On the positive side, the traveler had all his basic needs seen to for a single and generally inexpensive price, although guidebooks warned travelers to bargain with the vetturino. This mode of travel was common in Italy, where the language barrier provided an extra incentive. (Most British travelers spoke at least some French, but fewer understood Italian; and while French was a universal language among Europe's upper classes, it was less widely spoken in Italy.) By the late eighteenth century, it was even possible to hire the services of a vetturino before leaving home, through an agent in London.[21]

ONCE PAST THE formalities at Calais, most grand tourists headed straight for Paris. From the moment they arrived in the French capital, British visitors felt themselves in an utterly foreign world. Paris was smaller and more densely populated than London, its narrow streets clogged with "infinite Swarms of inhabitants and more Coaches than Men," as Thomas Gray put it. Many buildings lacked latrines, and as a consequence residents habitually dumped the contents of chamber pots and other refuse into the streets below. Pedestrians had to keep their wits about them to avoid being run over by vehicles or dirtied by the mud and garbage that littered the streets. Horace Walpole expressed an extreme point of view when he called Paris "the ugliest beastliest town in the universe," but most British visitors thought Paris a filthy, noisy, congested city. They might grant the magnificence of buildings like the palaces of the Louvre and the Tuileries, the cathedral of Notre Dame, or the church and hospital of the Invalides, and grand public spaces like the Luxembourg Gardens, the Champs Elysées, the Place Louis XV (now Place de la Concorde), Place des Victoires and Place Vendôme, but even then national pride encouraged unfavorable comparisons. Philip Thicknesse, for example, offered backhanded compliments to the Place des Victoires and the Luxembourg and Tuileries gardens, calling them "very fine" although not in the same league as the residential squares and gardens of London; while William Jones thought Notre Dame compared unfavorably with Westminster Abbey and the cathedral at Canterbury.[22]

Criticism of Paris could not be entirely attributed to British chauvinism, however, as French visitors also deplored the city's filthy streets and cramped buildings—among them Voltaire, who wished for more open spaces, public markets, fountains, and grand monuments. He much preferred London (or more specifically, that part of London rebuilt after the great fire of 1665) to Paris. The only part of Paris that merited unqualified praise was the tree-lined promenade along the old ramparts of the city. Walking or riding along the boulevards on warm evenings, perhaps stopping at one of the many coffeehouses lining the route, was a popular pastime among Parisians, one that visitors to the city enjoyed as well.[23]

By the mid-1780s, when Paris was in the midst of a building boom, visitors found more to admire in the newly planned residential neighborhoods north of the boulevards and the neoclassical architecture of many new churches and other public buildings, among them the magnificent circular domed Halle aux Bleds (grain market), the Church of Sainte Geneviève (now the Panthéon), and the Théâtre Français (now the Odéon). Construction of new bridges across the Seine and demolition of the houses that jammed both sides of old bridges like the Pont Neuf made navigating the central city easier. Most ambitious and impressive was the expansion of the Palais Royal (a former royal residence then owned by the king's cousin, the Duc d'Orléans) into a vast rectangle of shops opening onto a covered promenade surrounding a public garden. Completed in 1784, the Palais Royal quickly became the most popular gathering place in Paris, where residents and visitors alike might shop, attend the theater, view a fine collection of paintings, have their portraits sketched, or take refreshments at the Café de Chartres (now the three-star restaurant Grand Véfour)—a favorite haunt of Thomas Jefferson's during his years in Paris.[24]

Most grand tourists devoted several weeks to Paris. They might take up residence in one of several small hotels, although many preferred to rent furnished lodgings, which provided more space and privacy and were more economical for a long stay. These domestic arrangements, like nearly everything else in Paris, came in for a certain amount of criticism. Accustomed to carpeted, furniture-filled rooms, the British often found Parisian houses cold and cheerless with their large rooms, stone floors, and sparse furnishings. Most of the travelers missed their slabs of meat and simple, unadorned potatoes and vegetables—Smollett complained that the meat was "boiled or roasted to rags"—although some acknowledged that the quality of the French meat and poultry was excellent and the variety in styles of cooking far surpassed what they had been used to at home. Arthur Young, who took quite the opposite position from Smollett on French food, thought French-style vegetables with sauces much superior to "our greens boiled in water," while Philip Thicknesse applauded the French custom of eating small quantities of meat and drinking nothing stronger than wine (and then only with dinner) as much healthier than English culinary practices. Even Smollett had to admit that French breakfasts of petits pains and pâtés of butter were "exquisite."[25]

Once suitably lodged, the British visitor's first task was acquiring a Parisian wardrobe. Despite deep ambivalence about French culture, British visitors conceded (implicitly, at least) Paris's place as the fashion capital of Europe, and, not wanting to appear conspicuous as foreigners, they took pains to dress in the French style.[26] Preliminaries accomplished, visitors typically spent their days visiting churches and other public buildings, royal palaces, and homes of noblemen, paying particular attention to their art collections. In the eighteenth century, works of art were nearly all in private homes (apart from the paintings and sculpture that were an integral part of churches and other public buildings), although they were generally accessible to people with the appropriate credentials who requested permission to see them. In France, much more than in Britain, "the appearance of a gentleman, and particularly a stranger, is a ticket to go any where," as Thicknesse put it, even to the palace at Versailles, permanent residence of the royal family in the latter part of the eighteenth century. At Versailles, "the appearance of a gentleman" meant being well dressed and carrying a sword, but those lacking swords could rent them at the palace.

Many tourists did in fact make the journey to Versailles—which most criticized as overly formal and cold—both to see the art collections and gardens and to be presented to the king and queen. Approved visitors could wander freely through the public rooms of the palace, although etiquette specified that one could not approach the royal family and their attendants too closely. In Paris itself, the Louvre palace, although no longer occupied by the royal family, still housed much of the splendid royal art collection. Paris's significance as an art center owed much, Gibbon thought, to the fact that the French nobility lived mainly in Paris, thereby concentrating the nation's wealth in its urban homes, while the British upper class put more of its money and energy into its country estates. If all the art and architecture spread across England were concentrated in London, he argued, "we should be astonished at our own riches."[27]

The Parisians themselves were a target of endless, and mostly hostile, comment. The British thought them loud, boisterous, rude, lazy, indelicate, and interested only in pleasure. Smollett accused the French of "gay dissipation"; Samuel Johnson called them "a gross, ill-bred, untaught people." (The feelings of contempt were mutual; Parisians often accused the British of rude and drunken behavior, especially at meals.) Gambling was a favorite social pastime, and young men were cautioned to be careful about being taken in by card sharps, who would befriend them only to cheat them out of their money, and by "artful women," who would entice them into compromising situations.[28]

French women drew the sharpest criticism from British travelers, who disapproved of their makeup, their powdered wigs, and their easy sociability, all of which made them seem little better than prostitutes to the more prudish of British visitors. Even the usually temperate Gray was a bit shocked to see that women's faces were "dyed in Scarlet up to the Eyes." British visitors, of course, had little access to everyday French life, and therefore came away with a skewed picture of French society. Although some had introductions to families that gained them invitations to social gatherings, most encountered the French people in the shops and streets or in formal situations like the presentations at Versailles. It became easy for the British, already negatively disposed to the French because of differences in politics and religion, to attribute obvious differences in appearance, dress, and manner to loose morals and a superficial attitude toward life.[29]

Apart from Paris, France held few attractions for eighteenth-century travelers. Mary Wortley Montagu liked Dijon, although she thought it much too expensive, and Smollett spent several weeks in Nice, where he hoped to recover his health; but most grand tourists traveled in search of high culture, which meant focusing one's attention on the major cities. Provincial France was seen mainly as territory to be traversed en route from Paris to Italy. The usual route passed through Burgundy and across the Alps, often with a stop in Geneva. A longer and more difficult route followed the Rhone River to the Mediterranean, where travelers had a choice between a badly maintained, often steep and winding road along the coast and a sea journey in an open boat from Marseilles or one of the other French ports to Genoa or Livorno. Avoiding the Alps was the chief advantage of this route, along with the chance to see several fine examples of Roman ruins in Provence—but at the cost of some very rough traveling. Some tourists, Boswell included, skirted France altogether in favor of a tour through the Netherlands and Germany. Although gaining popularity in the eighteenth century, mainly because of close ties with the British monarchy, the German states still had limited appeal for travelers because they were considered backward and primitive, centers neither of art and culture, like Italy, nor of courtly manners and polite breeding, like France. Boswell spent most of his time in Berlin and Potsdam, the two most important Prussian cities, attending fashionable parties and angling (unsuccessfully) for an audience with Frederick the Great.[30]

If the German states were seldom exciting, Geneva—a popular stop en route to Italy—was downright dull, in Boswell's estimation. Switzerland was "a phlegmatic nation," he complained (borrowing the phrase from Joseph Addison, who had toured the Continent at the beginning of the century). In Geneva, where the town gates closed at 5:00 P.M., there were no fashionable courts and no glittering parties, but merely a prosperous, respectable bourgeoisie, "exactly like an English country town," thought Mary Wortley Montagu.[31]

Geneva may have lacked excitement, but it interested British tourists as the birthplace of Calvin. Even more important for those of a literary or philosophical bent, both Voltaire and Rousseau lived nearby. In an era when people with the right introductions could call upon strangers at will, visiting these intellectual giants was part of the itinerary of many Britons making the grand tour. Boswell, who was even more enamored of famous men than most of his contemporaries, simply presented himself at Voltaire's home one afternoon during the usually acceptable calling hours. Although the great man was ill and confined to bed, Boswell found plenty of other company there to entertain him, and in due course Voltaire himself joined the group. The next day Boswell wrote a charmingly ingratiating note to Voltaire's sister, who managed the household, asking to be permitted to spend the night on his next visit. The ploy succeeded perfectly, and he spent two nights under Voltaire's roof, arguing politics and religion well into the night.[32]

Rousseau, on the other hand, lived a reclusive life in Môtiers, a tiny village near Neuchâtel, with his housekeeper, Thérèse Levasseur. (She was in fact his mistress, though this fact was not generally known at this time).[33] He seldom received visitors, although this did not deter Boswell, who was determined to add Rousseau to his list of conquests. Notwithstanding his letter of introduction from a man who had befriended Rousseau at a critical point in his life, Boswell decided to write his own letter, gambling that a direct, forthright approach might carry the day. "I am a Scots gentleman of ancient family," he opened. "Now you know my rank. I am twenty-four years old. Now you know my age. . . . I am travelling with a genuine desire to improve myself. I have come here in the hope of seeing you." He apologized for his French, acknowledged that Rousseau seldom received visitors, expressed sympathy for his frequent illnesses, and asked for an interview "as a man of singular merit" and as one who had been profoundly influenced by Rousseau's writings. The strategy worked. Rousseau replied that he couldn't resist meeting Boswell, even though he was ill and in no mood for visitors. Boswell dressed with as much care as if he were to be presented at court—scarlet coat and waistcoat trimmed with gold lace, buckskin breeches, a fur-trimmed green overcoat and lace-trimmed hat held under his arm to give an "air of being solid." Apparently he made a favorable impression, because Rousseau invited him to return three times and agreed to correspond with Boswell as he continued his tour through Italy.[34]

FROM GENEVA, the Italy-bound traveler had to confront the Alps—for many, the most difficult and unpleasant part of the entire grand tour. The most common route took travelers south from Ge-

neva (or east from Lyons, for those who bypassed Geneva) to Cham-
béry in Savoy (now part of France), then southeast to the little hamlet
of Lanslebourg, where the carriage road ended. At that point, carriages had to be taken apart and hauled by pack animals twelve
miles over the Mont Cenis pass to Susa, just across the Italian border.
From Susa it was then a relatively easy thirty-mile journey to Turin.
The other major Alpine passes, including the Simplon, St. Gotthard,
and St. Bernard—all more familiar to twentieth-century travelers
than the Mont Cenis route—were less popular because they were
more difficult to reach from Lyons and Geneva, the usual jumping-
off points for a trip into Italy. None was accessible for wheeled vehicles. The St. Gotthard pass, one guidebook remarked, "to a lover
of rude and picturesque nature, will be highly interesting," while the
Mont Cenis route was described as "nothing terrible . . . at least from
May to October."[35]

Even so, crossing the pass was an ordeal for most travelers, who
had to be carried by porters in what Boswell called "the Alps machine"—a kind of litter suspended between two logs and carried by
four to eight men. Young and robust as he was, it did not occur to
him to walk the twelve-mile distance, nor did most of his contemporaries eschew the sedan chair in favor of hiking, although Gibbon
felt some guilt at the spectacle of men being employed as little more
than beasts of burden. The ascent from Lanslebourg to the top of
the pass (about six miles) generally took about four hours. Most travelers paused at the top to visit a monastery; Boswell, who made his
crossing on a Sunday, stayed long enough to attend mass and dine
with the priest, "an immensely ignorant" man, in his estimation.
The descent into Italy, another six miles but even steeper, was faster—frighteningly fast, according to some travelers, who entertained
visions of pitching headlong into oblivion as their porters rushed
nimbly down the mountain trails. Gray wrote his mother that "the
men perfectly fly down with you, stepping from stone to stone with
incredible swiftness in places where none but they could go three
paces without falling." Some adventurous travelers going over the
pass back to Lanslebourg in winter went down on sledges.[36]

Gray and a few others, among them Joseph Addison, enjoyed
their travels through the Alps. As Gray wrote to one of his friends,

he remained unimpressed with the works of art he had seen, "but those of Nature have astonished me beyond expression." Most eighteenth-century Europeans, however, found the mountains distasteful and even frightening. These negative feelings stemmed in part from the practical difficulties of travel in mountainous regions, which was almost always tedious and could at times be dangerous, but there were aesthetic reasons as well. Prevailing tastes valued order and symmetry and, above all, the visible manifestations of human creativity in taming nature and shaping civilization. It was no coincidence that travelers most interested in seeing the monuments of Roman civilization, the works of Renaissance painters, the courts of European capitals, or the salons of French intellectuals looked upon mountains as misshapen, chaotic heaps of rock. Men like Addison and Gray were ahead of their time in finding a wild sort of beauty and (in Gray's case, at least) evidence of God's creative hand at work in such panoramas.[37]

The alternative to enduring the Alpine crossing was even worse. Traveling down the Rhone from Lyons to Marseilles could be pleasant—most people went by boat—if boring. Once past the main ports of Marseilles and Toulon, however, the road along the Mediterranean coast was hardly better than a footpath, and the crude bridges spanning the rivers along the route were often washed out. According to Smollett, bridges over the Var River near Nice, which marked the border between France and the Kingdom of Sardinia, were regularly destroyed in disputes between the two jurisdictions. He had to pay guides to carry himself, his family, and their luggage across the river. In theory, it was easier to travel by sea, especially beyond Nice, where the road deteriorated and bandits still sometimes threatened travelers even as late as the 1760s; but the crude boats in common use on the Mediterranean coast, along with changeable weather conditions, made the sea route unpredictable at best. Typically one hired or took passage in a felucca, a shallow-bottomed, open boat equipped with both sails and oars. Large enough to take a small carriage on board, feluccas were nevertheless fairly primitive craft, with benches for seats and a simple awning over the stern as the only protection from wind and rain. They were versatile and easily maneuverable but unsafe in stormy seas, so travelers who chose to travel by boat often made unscheduled stops in ports along the way. (The "normal" time required, according to Smollett, was something between fourteen hours and two and a half days.) He and his family completed the trip from Nice to Genoa in two days, stopping overnight at San Remo, where they put up at what was supposed to be the best inn on that stretch of the Italian coast. In fact, Smollett complained, they found small, dirty, overpriced rooms, bad food, and a single crude common room shared with "watermen and muleteers."[38]

He had little to complain about in comparison with other travelers' problems. Addison took the better part of a week to get from Marseilles to Genoa by boat. After sitting out two days in San Remo because of bad weather, he set off again only to be forced back to Monaco by contrary winds. Rough seas drove him ashore again the next day, at which point he gave up on boats and took the land route (much worse than the road over Mont Cenis, he concluded) the rest of the way. Boswell experienced a similarly tortuous journey when he decided to return to France via the coast route after his sojourn in Italy. (He should have known better, having read Addison's account of his travels.) On their first night out, Boswell's party stopped at Vado, a village about thirty miles north of Genoa. The next day was too stormy to sail. Boswell considered going on by land, but was told that it would take him four days to reach the French village of Antibes (a distance of about 120 miles), while it was only a day's trip under sail. After a day in port the felucca was able to leave Vado, but had to put ashore again after sailing only about five miles. Too impatient to wait out another delay, Boswell left his servant Jacob and the luggage in the boat and set off alone, on foot, to a village where he could hire a horse. Despite visions of robbers and murderers, he rode on until 1:00 A.M., when he roused the owners of a village inn to provide him a bed. The next morning he watched helplessly as his felucca sailed past the little port, unable to make its way ashore to pick him up. Boswell spent the next three and a half days traveling by horseback over rough tracks to Antibes, arriving two days after his servant and luggage—and demonstrating, in the process, why most people preferred to travel by sea, delays and all.[39]

*   *   *

TURIN, THE first stop for most travelers to Italy, was a pretty but dull city meriting only a brief visit for most travelers, although Boswell—entranced at finally reaching Italy—lingered there for a month. Armed with a letter of introduction to one of the city's fashionable ladies, he lost no time in seeking out the pleasures he expected Italy to offer. In Italy, he believed, one might be permitted to do as the Italians do, or at least as he thought they did, and that meant every woman who struck his fancy was fair game. Boswell was supported in this notion by the first Italian men he met, who assured him that he might have any woman he liked. "Manners here were so openly debauched," he concluded, "that adultery was carried on without the least disguise." Unfortunately for Boswell's intrigues (mostly in boxes at the opera), the women he encountered thought otherwise; three countesses spurned him in rapid succession, no doubt seeing through his overblown professions of passion and his haste to make a conquest. As an Italian sitting near Boswell at the opera one evening remarked, "A traveller expects to accomplish in ten days as much as another will do in a year."[40]

The "musts" for the grand tourist in Italy were Rome, Florence, Naples, and Venice, more or less in that order of priority. Most tourists visited a number of smaller cities along the way, but there was no standard itinerary through the Italian states. From Turin, there were two major routes south and east: to Genoa (the main port of entry for those arriving by sea) and then on to Florence and Rome, perhaps stopping in Pisa, Livorno, and Lucca en route; or east to Venice and then south, possibly with stops in Milan, Parma, Verona, Vicenza, Padua, Ferrara, and Bologna. Most took one route south and another homeward, varying the interim stops according to season and interest.[41]

Among the cities north of Florence, only Venice merited more than a few days from most travelers, who were both fascinated and repelled by this fabled seaport that seemed, by the late eighteenth century, to have decayed into a state of faded elegance. Once-magnificent buildings were run-down and dingy; every canal was an open sewer, turning the city into a "stinkpot," as one visitor observed. Even Goethe, who could find beauty in the poorest of Italian villages, deplored the use of canals as garbage dumps and the "disgusting sludge" that accumulated in the squares and pathways on rainy days. Yet the city was full of life, with its diverse array of people drawn from all over Europe and the Mediterranean world. There were cultural attractions, in the opera, notable collections of paintings, and the studios of contemporary artists—Canaletto and his imitators were especially popular in the early and mid-eighteenth century—but those who liked Venice seemed to enjoy simply strolling about the city observing the people and the constantly changing life of the streets. John Moore remarked on the "mixed multitude of Jews, Turks, and Christians; lawyers, knaves, and pick-pockets; mountebanks, old women and physicians; women of quality with masks; strumpets barefaced; and in short, such a jumble of senators, citizens, gondoliers and people of every character and condition" who frequented the Piazza San Marco every night. William Beckford was delighted by the profusion of nationalities—Turks, Arabs, Orientals, Russians, Greeks, and Slavs—making the piazza, with its "confusion of languages," a veritable Tower of Babel. Besides its international population, attracted by Venice's commercial opportunities, the city's residents included thousands of courtesans, earning Venice a reputation as "the brothel of Europe."[42]

Whether they traveled south from Venice or opted for the route to Genoa and then south along the coastal road, saving Venice for the journey home, travelers headed for Florence and Rome had to cross the Apennine Mountains at some point. Hardly a barrier of Alpine proportions, the Apennines could still be a formidable challenge. In general, roads in Italy were much poorer than in France, and the mountain routes, difficult at best, could become impassable in bad weather, forcing travelers out of their carriages to continue their journeys by mule or on foot. Adding to the discomfort, mountain villages offered primitive accommodations. The noted musician Charles Burney complained of a "wretched inn or pigsty, half stable and half cowhouse, with a fire but no chimney, surrounded by boors and muleteers, all in appearance cut-throat personages, with no kind of refreshment but cold veal and stinking eggs"—better, perhaps, than the mustard and crows' gizzards offered to Beckford by two "hags" in a tiny village "suspended on the brow of a bleak mountain."[43]

After days of jolting over bad roads and substandard accommodations, travelers found Florence a welcome sight. With its lovely setting straddling the Arno River, it was one of the most popular of European cities, especially among the British. A sojourn of several weeks was not uncommon, and by the end of the eighteenth century, a substantial number of British expatriates were living permanently in Florence, forming the core of a British community that would flourish in the first half of the nineteenth century. Having been one of the most important centers of Renaissance culture, Florence was full of treasures for eighteenth-century tourists, who had been educated to admire Renaissance painting as the pinnacle of artistic achievement. As in Paris, art collections were all in private hands, the most important ones at the Uffizi and the Grand Duke's Pitti Palace. Evenings in Florence, as in other Italian cities, were often devoted to the opera, which was as much a center of social life as a place to listen to music. One British visitor, critical of the Florentines' custom of playing cards in their boxes during performances, was told that music added to the pleasure of a card party. It was far more difficult for visitors to gain entrée to local society than in Paris, a point that annoyed some—one was never invited to dinner in Florence, Arthur Young complained—but the city was so popular with tourists that they spent much of their time socializing with each other. When Boswell arrived in Florence, he found at least a dozen Englishmen acquainted with him either personally or by reputation.[44]

By comparison with the journey to Florence, traveling on to Rome was a fairly simple matter, although Beckford complained of his slow pace over roads that seemed not to have been repaired "since the days of the Caesars." A brief stop in Siena was usually all that detained tourists en route to what was, for most, the single most important destination on the grand tour. At a time when education beyond the primary level invariably meant training in the classics, when every educated man was expected to know Latin and Greek, Rome was considered the source of all that was important in Western civilization. Those brought up in this classical tradition ap-

25

proached the city in a state of high anticipation. Beckford was not alone in straining for a sight of its monuments for miles before he could reasonably expect to see anything. When the city skyline finally came into view, at twilight, he thought it looked "still so wonderous classical" that he half expected fauns and satyrs to emerge from the fields alongside the road. For Goethe, viewing the monuments that had become so familiar to him from books and from the etchings hanging on the walls of his childhood home was deeply satisfying, because it allowed him to put together into a coherent whole those aspects of the classical tradition that he had understood only "in fragments and chaotically." Gibbon later claimed that a walk through the ruins of the Forum had inspired his great work, *The Decline and Fall of the Roman Empire* (published in six volumes between 1776 and 1788). Addison toured the city using Horace and Virgil as his guidebooks.[45]

To do justice to the classical Roman monuments required a month, Lady Mary Wortley Montagu thought, while a popular guidebook recommended six weeks as a minimum to see the ancient monuments along with Rome's more modern attractions, adding that one could easily spend a year there profitably. Rome's popularity among tourists had, by the early eighteenth century, spawned a small army of tour guides, both Italians and foreigners who had settled in Rome. The most famous among them was Johann Winckelmann, a Prussian who became Europe's leading authority on classical art and was named the Vatican's chief supervisor of antiquities in 1763.[46]

Boswell signed on with one of several British guides for a six-day "Course in Antiquities and Arts," which had the advantage of covering the major sights while still leaving him plenty of time for other pleasures. Goethe, on the other hand, felt only contempt for the "birds of passage," as he called those who raced through the wonders of Rome. One must study Rome slowly, he thought. "One is, so to speak, reborn and one's former ideas seem like a child's swaddling clothes. Here the most ordinary person becomes somebody, for his mind is enormously enlarged even if his character remains unchanged." Boswell may have lacked Goethe's patience, but he was not unmoved by Rome's monuments. Visiting the Forum called forth images of Cicero addressing his fellow Romans, while a subsequent visit to Cicero's house inspired him to speak Latin. He and his guide thereafter spoke only Latin to each other during their tour of ancient sites. Beckford, who thought even five years wouldn't be enough to see all Rome had to offer, eschewed formal tours altogether in favor of wandering about the city "just as the spirit chuses."[47]

Modern Rome had its attractions too, of course. Like other Italian cities, Rome had important collections of Renaissance art (especially those owned by the Vatican) as well as a lively community of contemporary artists. Many grand tourists succumbed to the temptation to have their portraits painted, often on the site of some famous classical monument. A few made serious purchases of art, in Rome as well as in other cities on their tour; many private art collections in Britain were launched with paintings shipped home from grand tours. There were the more vulgar pleasures too, as the flood of tourists to Rome supported a substantial cadre of prostitutes. Having failed at bedding countesses, Boswell was a frequent customer, whimsically justifying his behavior: "I remembered the rakish deeds of Horace and the other amorous Roman poets, and I thought that one might well allow one's self a little indulgence in a city where there are prostitutes licensed by the Cardinal Vicar."[48]

Apart from the classical monuments, the Vatican itself was Rome's biggest tourist attraction. St. Peter's Cathedral dominated the city skyline, and the Church owned one of the finest art collections in Europe; in addition to those treasures, the Church itself and its pervasive influence throughout Rome (and indeed all of Italy) inspired a great deal of curiosity and comment—much of it negative—from visitors. Attending mass at St. Peter's was on everyone's list of things to do, as was witnessing the ceremony of the veil, when young girls committed themselves to the life of the convent. Not surprisingly, the Protestant British saw in these ceremonies the specters of ignorance and coercion, at best influencing girls too young to know their minds and at worst forcing them against their wills into a stultifying life. Gray had the good fortune to be in Rome when a new pope was being chosen, a process he followed with great curiosity, while Boswell, always eager to meet famous men, managed to secure an audience with the pope.[49]

Most visitors drew a sharp contrast between modern and ancient

Rome. The signs of decay were not so palpable as in Venice, but modern Rome nevertheless seemed but a poor successor to the grandeur of the classical city. The Vatican, to be sure, boasted enormous wealth, but elsewhere the signs of poverty were overwhelming. Even the famous monuments were decaying from years of neglect, so much so that Gray and Walpole, visiting in 1740, thought Rome would hardly be worth seeing some years hence. "Between the ignorance and poverty of the present Romans, every thing is neglected and falling to decay," Walpole wrote; "the villas are entirely out of repair, and the palaces so ill kept, that half the pictures are spoiled by damp."[50]

British visitors typically blamed Rome's decay on the Catholic Church, arguing that the Church absorbed too much of the country's wealth in its showy display and too many of its men and women in unproductive work at monasteries and convents. Strolling near the Colosseum, Beckford was seized with "a vehement desire . . . to break down and pulverize the whole circle of saints' nests and chapels, which disgrace the arena." The "lazy abbots" praying near the ancient ruins were "such as would have made a lion's mouth water; fatter I dare say, than any saint in the whole martyrology, and ten times more tantalizing. . . . Heavens! thought I to myself, how times are changed! Could Vespasian have imagined his amphitheatre would have been thus inhabited?" With its frequent holy days and festivals (about 120 a year in the 1770s), the Church encouraged what foreign visitors believed to be the natural laziness of the Romans, thus contributing to the legions of beggars who wandered the streets and clustered around the entrances to every church and public building, badgering tourists with offers of unwanted services and demands for money.[51]

If Rome seemed, at times, to be a city of beggars and ne'er-do-wells, Naples was even worse. Travelers commonly reported tens of thousands of unemployed, a problem they attributed to the immense wealth and influence of the Church hierarchy, as well as to a glut of unproductive lawyers, priests, and monks. Even so, Naples was a popular destination among grand tourists, one devoted almost exclusively to the pleasures of the senses. Apart from visits to the archaeological excavations at Herculaneum and Pompeii (begun in 1738 and 1755, respectively), most of those arriving in Naples after weeks of visiting galleries and Roman ruins dispensed with educational touring and simply enjoyed themselves. As Goethe put it, "In Rome I was glad to study: here I want only to live, forgetting myself and the world, and it is a strange experience for me to be in a society where everyone does nothing but enjoy himself." He criticized travelers who accused the Neapolitans of laziness, pointing to many who appeared to be idle but really weren't, like sailors lounging about the port while waiting for a fair wind. Northern Europeans, Goethe believed, had to work "feverishly" all the time to store up enough reserves for winter and bad weather; it was hard for them to understand the more relaxed attitude of southern Italians, where food was more easily grown and shelter could be more simply constructed. As a result, Italy had shoddier standards of craftsmanship, little manufacturing, and lower levels of achievement in art and culture than in the northern countries, but with compensating advantages: People could satisfy their needs with only modest exertion, leaving plenty of time to devote to pleasure.[52]

Even the appearance of Naples suggested hedonism, with its brilliant displays of flowers and fruits and the brightly colored homes and clothing of the city's residents. Northerners might think such bright colors "barbaric or in bad taste," wrote Goethe, but in Naples they seemed entirely appropriate, "for nothing can outshine the brightness of the sun and its reflection in the sea. The most brilliant colour is softened by the strong light, and the green of trees and plants, the yellow, brown and red of the soil are dominant enough to absorb the more highly coloured flowers and dresses into the general harmony." Goethe and many other visitors to Naples in the late eighteenth century enjoyed the hospitality of William Hamilton, the British ambassador there from 1764 to 1800. Hamilton became a near-legendary fixture in Naples, noted both for his gracious entertaining and for his beautiful wife, Emma, a blacksmith's daughter forty years his junior, who later became famous in her own right as the mistress of Admiral Horatio Nelson. In Goethe's eyes, Hamilton had fully absorbed the Italian ethos, giving himself up to the pursuit of pleasure with native abandon. "After many years of devotion to the arts and the study of nature," he wrote, Hamilton "found the acme of these delights in the person of an English girl of twenty with a beautiful face and a perfect figure. . . . In her, he has found all the antiquities, all the profiles of Sicilian coins, even the Apollo Belvedere . . . as a performance it's like nothing you ever saw before in your life.''[53]

The seemingly carefree life of Naples was only the most obvious example of those qualities that made Italy so appealing to men like Goethe and Boswell. There were others, however, who saw only poverty, squalor, and laziness, made more egregious when juxtaposed against the physical remains of the wealth of the Roman Empire, Renaissance Florence, or sixteenth- and seventeenth-century Venice. These differing attitudes were partly a matter of temperament; a man like Smollett hated everything that wasn't British, while others like Goethe, Boswell, and Gray displayed an immense curiosity about cultures different from their own. Smollett and others like him went through Italy complaining constantly about terrible roads, dirty inns, bad food, and the common practice of extorting high prices from travelers who had no choice but to pay, while others recorded such incidents but attached only minor importance to them. ("It was not for good eating or convenient bedchambers [that] we came to this country,'' one traveler observed.) Smollett was older than most grand tourists, and obviously quite set in his ways, but there were plenty of much younger men, like Horace Walpole, who found little on their travels to unseat their sense of British superiority.[54]

These different reactions also reflected the beginnings of a change in sensibility: Goethe was one of the early voices of romanticism, which would have a profound influence on popular attitudes and would, among many other things, contribute toward making Italy even more popular among travelers a generation or two later. Even Boswell, traveling almost a quarter century before Goethe, displayed something of this change in attitude. For nearly all eighteenth-century British travelers, however, regardless of temperament, Italy and the Italians evoked more positive reactions than France and the French. (Even Smollett's complaints were mostly about conditions of travel, not people.) The difference can be attributed in part to travelers' continuing fascination with Italy as the seat of the Roman Empire and so, in effect, as the cradle of Western civilization; but perhaps more important for eighteenth-century travelers was the fact that Italy was a friendly state (or, more accurately, collection of states) while France was not. France was Britain's great rival for world domination, and so, quite naturally, British travelers looked for evidence of its weakness. Italy, on the other hand, posed no threat, for it seemed obviously to be a land in decline. Italy's greatness lay in the past, which was precisely its appeal for the eighteenth-century grand tourist.

CHAPTER 2

TOURING IN SEARCH

OF THE

PICTURESQUE

S IX YEARS after he returned from his Continental travels, Boswell persuaded Samuel Johnson to join him on the tour of the
Scottish Highlands. The two men had talked of such a tour for years,
according to Boswell, who had even discussed the prospect with Voltaire during his sojourn in Geneva. Voltaire "looked at me as if I
had talked of going to the North Pole," Boswell recalled, "and said,
'You do not insist on my accompanying you?' 'No, sir.' 'Then,' he
replied, 'I am very willing you should go.' "[1]

The Scottish Highlands seemed remote indeed to those living in
England and continental Europe, not least to Johnson himself. Boswell had to talk him out of taking pistols and ammunition along,
assuring him that the remote Highland roads were not threatened by
robbers.[2] Although united with England under a single crown in
1707, Scotland in the 1770s was still very much a foreign country to
the English, with its own established religion (Presbyterian rather
than Anglican), cultural traditions, and language (although English
had supplanted Gaelic in Lowland Scotland by Boswell's time).

From London to Edinburgh was a ten-day journey. Getting from Edinburgh to the Highlands, where Boswell and Johnson were bound, could take the better part of a week, over roads hardly better than cart tracks.

Isolated from the more populous Lowlands, this region had long been largely independent from the rest of Scotland, ruled by clan chiefs who challenged British rule at several points in the first half of the eighteenth century by supporting the exiled Stuarts' bids to reclaim the throne. In the last of these attempts, in 1745, Charles Stuart, grandson of the former King James II (and better known as "Bonnie Prince Charlie"), landed on the west coast of Scotland, raised substantial support among the Highland clans, and marched south to within 130 miles of London. British troops chased Charles and his supporters back into Scotland, crushing what remained of the Highland forces in a brutal battle on Culloden Moor, near Inverness, in April 1746. The battle and subsequent suppression of clan rule in the Highlands were still very much a part of recent historical memory when Johnson and Boswell set out on their journey. Although the rule of the chiefs had been broken, clan traditions remained strong, and there were many villages in the north where English was still little understood.[3]

It was just this quality of remoteness and difference that inspired Boswell and Johnson to undertake their journey through the Highlands, especially the islands off the west coast. "To find simplicity and wildness, and all the circumstances of remote time or place, so near to our native great island, was an object within the reach of reasonable curiosity," Boswell explained.[4] For the first part of their journey, however, he took pains to show Johnson the more sophisticated side of his native country. During several days in Edinburgh, he struggled with a kind of national inferiority complex, introducing Johnson to the city's intellectual and social elite while admitting that it was not so refined or lively as London's. Then they traveled north up the east coast, enjoying the hospitality of country gentlemen along their route, much as if they were on a jaunt from London. Even so, Johnson noticed striking differences in food (much of which he didn't like), legal practices, speech patterns, even building styles (windows weren't hinged, but moved up and down, a considerably inferior system, in his opinion).[5] He was much taken with the ruins of ancient Scotland, among them a Druid temple near Banff, the ruins of Elgin Cathedral, and Gordon castle. They quoted Shakespeare to each other on the heath where, according to tradition, Macbeth met the witches; called on the Thane of Cawdor; and visited Macbeth's castle, where, wrote Boswell, "I had a most romantic satisfaction in seeing Mr. Johnson actually in it."[6]

At Inverness, they gave up their carriage and took to horseback—there were no roads suitable for carriages beyond another day's travel—and turned west, riding along Loch Ness and then on to the west coast, crossing over to Skye, the first of the islands on their itinerary. They toured Coll and Mull as well, returning to the mainland at Oban and continuing south along the west coast to Glasgow and finally back to Edinburgh. Soon after leaving Inverness, the pair began to see some of the "simplicity and wildness" that so intrigued Boswell. Near Loch Ness, they noticed a rude little dirt hut with only a hole in the sod for a window and a peat fire in the center of the floor for warmth. The elderly woman who lived there spoke just a few words of English, but invited the two curious visitors into her home. "Mr. Johnson was pleased at seeing for the first time such a state of human life," observed Boswell, although Johnson in his own account of the journey wrote disdainfully of the poverty, the bad roads, the barren landscape, and the lack of civilized comforts throughout the Highlands.[7] The land, especially, struck him as intolerably monotonous, lacking trees, fences, or any sign of cultivation. "What is not heath is nakedness," he wrote; ". . . an eye accustomed to flowery pastures and waving harvest is astonished and repelled by this wide extent of hopeless sterility." Such landscapes offered little inducement to the traveler, he believed, as one could imagine such views well enough in the comfort of one's home. (The Victorian literary critic Leslie Stephen, an avid mountain climber, once remarked, "It would be difficult to imagine a human being more thoroughly out of his element than Dr. Johnson on a mountain.") For Johnson, tours dedicated simply to viewing landscape were "useless labours, which neither impregnate the imagination, nor enlarge the understanding."[8]

Given this point of view, Scotland held little interest for Johnson.

He considered it a country without any sort of intellectual tradition. Its language had no written form; its history and stories were handed down by "illiterate" bards. To a man for whom the written word was the very essence of civilization, a nation without a written literary tradition was by definition savage. Although a written form of Gaelic (or Erse, as it was usually called among the English and Lowland Scots) was in common use by the eighteenth century, Johnson declared that there could not possibly be more than five hundred lines of written Gaelic more than one hundred years old. Moreover, the Gaelic language itself was a primitive tongue, in Johnson's opinion—"the rude speech of a barbarous people, who had few thoughts to express, and were content, as they conceived grossly, to be grossly understood."[9]

Johnson's main interest in touring the Highlands, like Boswell's, was to see "primitive" people in their native habitat. Curiosity about people and their cultures—especially remote, exotic people—was widespread among intellectuals in the late eighteenth century, as were theories about the underlying causes of physical and cultural differences. Traversing the steep paths of northern Scotland, Johnson ruminated on the reasons that the Highlanders seemed so much a people apart from the lowland Scots and the English. The mountainous terrain itself explained much of the difference, he believed; such remote regions were inevitably the last to be conquered and therefore slower to become "civilized," because (so Johnson argued) contact with other people is the source of civilization. He attributed the standard stereotypes about Highlanders—they were "thievish," had "primitive manners," feuded constantly with their neighbors— to their isolation.[10]

Johnson was disappointed in his expectations of observing a primitive society, however, for civilization was clearly making inroads into the Highlands—a result, he believed, of the English suppression of the clans nearly thirty years earlier. (Over dinner one evening, according to Boswell, Johnson boasted that the Scots had none of the advantages of civilization until they encountered the English. "We have taught you,' said he, "and we'll do the same in time to all barbarous nations—to the Cherokees—and at last to the orangoutangs.")[11] There were occasional scenes from the past: the old woman in her hut near Loch Ness, and a village a little farther west populated entirely by the MacRae clan, where not a single person could speak English. Boswell described this experience as "the same as being with a tribe of Indians. . . . Some were as black and wild in their appearance as any American savages whatever," while one woman was "as comely as the figure of Sappho." He and Johnson behaved as European explorers of "primitive" lands had learned to do, distributing little gifts of tobacco and white bread (which the villagers claimed never to have seen), with pennies for the children. But Johnson, less given to enthusiasm than Boswell, thought they had come "too late to see what we expected, a people of peculiar appearance, and a system of antiquated life. The clans retain little now of their original character, their ferocity of temper is softened, their military ardour extinguished, their dignity of independence is depressed, their contempt of government subdued, and their reverence for their chiefs abated." Only their language and poverty remained, and those were diminishing too, under the influence of English schools and a new awareness of money which, Johnson thought, would make the Highlanders more industrious and therefore more prosperous. "A longer journey than to the Highlands must be taken by him whose curiosity pants for savage virtues and barbarous grandeur," he concluded.[12]

Despite their comments about savages and barbarous customs, Johnson and Boswell were not exactly roughing it. Throughout their journey, the two men spent most of their time with the Highland gentry. At Dunvegan, for example, on the remote northwest coast of the island, they enjoyed the hospitality of the McLeod family. Recently returned from England, the McLeods understood "southern elegance" and "English economy," Johnson noted approvingly. In those few cases where the pair stopped at simple country inns, Boswell was often surprised at the quality of the food and the polite manners of the innkeepers; this was not what he had expected in the rude and barbarous Highlands.[13]

Johnson's book on the Highland tour drew harsh criticism from Scots whose national pride was understandably wounded by his attacks on their intelligence and character. English reviewers were more often favorable, although many rose to the defense of their northern neighbors; one writer called Johnson's book "petulant," while another thought him extraordinarily rude to accept the hospitality of the Scots and then declaim so harshly against their country. Most critics focused on what they deemed his unfair treatment of the Scots as a people, but some also took him to task for his negative remarks about the land itself, arguing for the beauty of a landscape that had seemed bleak and forbidding to Johnson.[14]

Touring Scotland just three years after Johnson, the English minister William Gilpin reacted very differently. If Johnson and Boswell spent most of their time observing the Scottish people, with only a passing glance at the landscape, with Gilpin it was the reverse. To be sure, he commented on the bloody history of Scotland and agreed with Johnson that suppression of the Highland chiefs in the 1740s had been the key to ending the often violent rivalries among clans. Unlike Johnson, however, he attributed the rapid decline of violence in Scotland to the natural virtue of the Highland people, who had been corrupted by the "force of clanship." The English action was therefore merely a catalyst, not the driving force of change, as Johnson would have it. But mostly Gilpin wrote about the Scottish landscape, criticizing Johnson for his "peevishness" in knocking Highland scenery.[15]

Given the proclivities of the three men, it was hardly surprising that they differed so remarkably in their reactions to Scotland. Johnson and Boswell were interested in men, history, and language; Gilpin, in nature, landscape, and art. His journey to Scotland in 1776 followed tours of Wales and the English Lake District, all focused on the natural beauty of the regions and their potential as subjects for artists. Gilpin's books about his travels (published in the 1780s) proved enormously influential in shaping English tastes in landscape and art and in popularizing travel to the regions he had visited. His first book, *Observations on the River Wye, and Several Parts of South Wales, etc. Relative Chiefly to Picturesque Beauty,* published in 1782, unleashed a horde of tourists on the Wye Valley. Subsequent books on the Lake District and Scotland (published in 1786 and 1789) did much the same for those regions.[16]

Gilpin was not exactly a maverick in his appreciation of scenic beauty in the 1770s and 1780s. His response to Scotland and the

37

other regions he visited was indicative of a broad change in tastes, which drew travelers increasingly to regions for their natural features rather than their historic or cultural significance, a shift that was well under way by the time Gilpin made his journey to Scotland. As early as the 1760s, travel to the northern regions of Britain, including Scotland, was on the increase, so much so that Lord Breadalbane (one of the Scottish gentry visited by Johnson and Boswell) could write in 1773 that the tour of the Highlands was becoming *"le bon ton."*[17] Gilpin's importance lay less in revolutionizing taste than in popularizing an aesthetic change already in process, primarily by advising his readers about where to travel, what to look for, and how to observe and appreciate what they saw.

THE DIFFERING reactions of Johnson, Boswell, and Gilpin were not merely idiosyncratic, but reflective of important intellectual and aesthetic changes that began in the late seventeenth and early eighteenth centuries before reaching their fullest expression around the end of the eighteenth. Simply put, Europeans of the early modern period were accustomed to thinking of man as the center of the world and nature as something to be shaped or exploited for his purposes. Gradually this attitude changed toward one that valued the natural world and found beauty in it.[18] Most travelers before the middle of the eighteenth century (and many in the later decades as well) were interested primarily in the human world; the artistic and historical monuments of earlier times, as well as the politics and society of other nations, were the usual subjects of observation. Even those who traveled in rural areas, like Johnson and Boswell in Scotland, were mostly interested in the evidence of human activity.

Before the middle of the eighteenth century, few people found beauty in wilderness settings; land untouched by the hand of man seemed forbidding and even sometimes dangerous. Boswell, for example, noted that he could have visited the Highlands by himself, but it wouldn't have been the same without a companion to add some life to the landscape. "A landscape or view of any kind is defective," he wrote, "... without some human figures to give it animation."[19] Cultivated fields, houses, villages, fences, and, as Johnson noted, even trees made a landscape more welcoming to the eighteenth-century eye, both for the sake of variety and for the evidence of human habitation they offered. Vast open spaces, dense forests, or rocky terrain, on the other hand, were likely to be criticized as monotonous and unpleasant. Mountains and oceans, far from being objects of beauty, inspired feelings of trepidation among early travelers (as we have seen with the grand tourists). Toward the end of the eighteenth century, however, a growing number of travelers began, like Gilpin to find beauty, solace, even spiritual inspiration, in nature.

These changing attitudes had their roots in religious beliefs, but were influenced also by the changing conditions of life in Europe and North America, especially in urban and industrializing areas. Christian doctrine, going back to Augustine, held that God had produced the irregular and barren features of the earth after the original creation, in his wrath at Adam's fall; thus it was possible to believe in the perfection of God's creation while detesting some of the earth's physical forms, which were meant to be ugly and horrifying. In the late seventeenth and early eighteenth centuries, however, a new generation of theologians began to argue that the earth in all its varied forms was part of God's original design and that the greatness of God was manifest in nature. Among the first to develop this point of view was Bishop Thomas Burnet, who made the grand tour in 1671. Profoundly moved by his experience of traveling through the Alps, yet disturbed by what he called "those wild, vast, and indigested Heaps of Stones and Earth," Burnet began, even before completing his travels, to work out a theory reconciling traditional notions about order and symmetry in nature with the inescapable majesty of the Alps. His book, *The Sacred Theory of the Earth,* first published in 1681, maintained the traditional view that the world's irregular features came after the Creation, but argued that God's presence was evident in all of nature, from the most tranquil pastoral settings to the craggiest Alpine passes. Burnet's book created a storm of controversy when it was published, but by the end of the seventeenth century, the belief that God was visibly manifest in all forms of nature had gained widespread acceptance. Early visitors to Wales, for example, often cited Burnet's theories in their accounts of their travels.[20]

The belief that God was manifest in all of nature helped create an intellectual climate in which an appreciation of natural landscape could develop. Much more influential, by the second half of the eighteenth century, were the ideas of a group of secular intellectuals who challenged the assumption that an increasingly sophisticated, urbanized civilization should be considered a positive good, arguing instead for the virtues inherent in a simpler way of life. Associated primarily with the French *philosophes,* especially Rousseau, these arguments found a large and sympathetic audience throughout Europe in the late eighteenth century. Their most dramatic manifestation was perhaps the notion of the "noble savage," which led many Europeans to idealize so-called "primitive" peoples like American Indians and the inhabitants of newly discovered South Pacific islands. Johnson and Boswell's interest in touring Scotland to observe people in a lesser state of civilization owed something to this set of ideas; so, on a much cruder level, did the attention lavished on the South Pacific islanders and other "primitives" brought home to London and Paris by explorers in the 1760s and '70s. At a more basic level, however, the association of simplicity with virtue encouraged a greater appreciation of the natural landscape. As forests and open land diminished in the face of urban expansion, nature came increasingly to be seen as something to be prized rather than feared.[21]

Rousseau's ideas were widely disseminated through his writings, especially the novels *Emile* and *La Nouvelle Heloïse.* The latter, published in Paris in 1761, was quickly translated into English and went through several editions. Set in the villages of Vevey and Clarens, on the shores of Lake Geneva near Lausanne, the novel is a moral tale about Julie ("the new Eloise"), the man she loves, and the man she marries for family's sake. It is a story of love, duty, and sacrifice, idealizing the virtue inherent in a young woman whose life is bounded by the rural villages in which she was raised. For decades after the novel first appeared, travelers visited Vevey and Clarens looking for sites associated with the fictional Julie's life. (Local residents were not above capitalizing on their popularity as a tourist attraction, apparently. A French visitor to Clarens in the 1780s encountered a young man with a copy of *La Nouvelle Heloïse* in hand, ready to guide tourists to sites mentioned in the novel.)[22]

The Romantic poets also helped shape these changing tastes in the late eighteenth century. Like Rousseau, many of them enjoyed great popularity in their own time, unwittingly encouraging travelers to seek out the scenes associated with their writing. In Germany, for example, Goethe's poetry as well as that of some of his contemporaries helped popularize travel to the Alpine regions. A generation later, Schiller's play *Wilhelm Tell* (published in 1804) drew thousands of visitors to the villages in eastern Switzerland associated with the legendary Tell: the marketplace at Altdorf where he supposedly shot the apple from his child's head, the cave along the lake where his chapel had stood, the village where he was born. In Britain, Wordsworth and the other Lake Poets helped promote tourism to the Lake District, less for their descriptions of specific scenes than for their own celebrity value; a visit to the Lakes was hardly complete without a pilgrimage to Wordsworth's home.

Yet the development of a general appreciation of nature does not fully explain how travelers came to find beauty in such rugged landscapes as those of the Scottish Highlands or the Alps. Rousseau and Goethe, for all their idealization of nature, disliked mountains. Like any good grand tourist, Rousseau crossed the Alps just once, to get to Italy; he chose the more gentle landscape around Lake Geneva as the setting for his novels. Goethe, writing in the late 1780s, thought the very idea of climbing mountains "profane and barbaric," describing the Alps as "zig-zags and irritating silhouettes and shapeless piles of granite, making the fairest portion of the earth a polar region."[23] And although Wordsworth devoted most of his 1790 walking tour of Europe to the Alps, most of his other friends thought the very idea of such a tour "mad and impracticable," so much so that Wordsworth decided not to tell his family about his plans until he was safely on the French side of the Channel. Later he wrote his sister, "I expect great pleasure on my return to Cambridge, in exulting over those of my friends who threatened us with such an accumulation of difficulties as must undoubtedly render it impossible for us to perform the tour."[24]

Understanding what particular kinds of natural landscapes appealed to late-eighteenth-century travelers brings us back to Gilpin and to the habits of observation he encouraged among his readers, as well as to others who influenced changing aesthetic tastes during this period. Gilpin himself, for all his appreciation of the Scottish Highlands, thought that mountains, though beautiful in themselves, were improved with "the drapery of a little wood to break the simplicity of their shapes, to produce contrasts . . . and to give that richness in landscape, which is one of its greatest ornaments."[25] Variety, for Gilpin and his contemporaries, was essential to natural beauty; a scene that combined different elements of nature to create visual interest without appearing too orderly or too highly structured was more beautiful than a view, say, of unbroken mountains or forest.

The most beautiful scenes in nature were those Gilpin called "picturesque," a term he defined quite literally as "that kind of beauty which would look well in a picture." Gilpin didn't invent the term. Thomas Gray, for one, had used it as early as 1740; touring the Lake District in the 1760s, he translated every view into terms appropriate for a painting.[26] Nor was it purely a British concept, notwithstanding a certain chauvinistic quality to Gilpin's praise of what he considered the uniquely beautiful qualities of the British landscape. In France, "voyage pittoresque" became a standard label for travel books as early as the 1780s. (The term originated with a guide to works of art in Paris, published initially in 1755—literally a "voyage pittoresque" through Paris—but was widely used in the first half of the nineteenth century for books describing the scenery of regions as disparate as rural France, California, and Chile.)[27] Gilpin's contribution was to mold vague concepts into a coherent aesthetic theory and apply it to specific locations, popularizing those regions among travelers in the process.

Gilpin's influence owed a great deal to a growing appreciation of landscape painting among his contemporaries. Traditionally considered inferior to history painting and portraiture, landscape painting began to earn greater respect and appreciation by the middle of the seventeenth century with the work of Dutch, French, and Italian painters like Jacob van Ruisdael, Claude Lorrain, Nicolas Poussin, Gaspard Dughet, and Salvator Rosa. British travelers to Italy especially admired the work of Rosa and his French contemporaries; many brought paintings home to Britain, where they became prominent features of collections in stately homes throughout the country.

In the second half of the eighteenth century, landscape painting became a major theme in British painting with the work of Thomas Gainsborough, who was much influenced by the Dutch landscape painters, and Richard Wilson, who worked more in the style of the French painters (and was often referred to as "the English Claude").[28] These painters not only helped shape aesthetic tastes by defining those elements of nature worthy of the artist's endeavor, but also accustomed their audiences to view natural settings much as if they were the subjects of paintings. Many travelers became so habituated to this mode of seeing that they identified different types of scenery with the styles of different painters—rugged, mountainous scenes invariably called to mind Salvator Rosa, for example, while Claude and Poussin were considered more delicate and restrained. To describe a scene as "worthy of the pencil of a Claude" became a stock phrase in travelers' accounts.[29]

"Picturesque" scenes were by definition unthreatening and human in scale; indeed, the addition of a person or two, perhaps a house or part of a village, only added to the appeal of the setting. To eighteenth-century eyes, untamed nature remained forbidding, yet had an undeniable kind of beauty. When Addison wrote that the Alps "fill the mind with an agreeable kind of Horror," or the Duchess of Northumberland described her visit to a castle in Scotland as "a scene of glorious Horrour and terrible Delight," they were not contradicting themselves, but employing what became an increasingly common way of describing nature in its wild, untamed state.[30] Such scenes were often described as "sublime," a term that entered travelers' vocabulary as far back as the late seventeenth century but was first given specific definition in Edmund Burke's book *An Inquiry into the Origin of Our Ideas of the Sublime or Beautiful,* published in 1756. Burke defined the sublime as a companion to, yet distinct from, the beautiful. The attributes of beauty, according to Burke, were smoothness, smallness, gradual variation, and delicacy of form and color; the sublime, in contrast, he characterized in terms of roughness, darkness, vastness, power, solitude, and infinity—in short, the qualities in nature that had once terrified but gradually came to delight travelers.[31] Like the notion of the picturesque, the language of the sublime was a European, not merely a British, phenomenon. A French traveler writing in the 1780s, for example, described the mountains and waterfalls around Lauterbrunnen as "les plus sauvages, les plus sinistres, et les plus majestueusement fracassés."[32]

Throughout most of the eighteenth century, however, sublime scenery remained something of an acquired taste, which helps explain why so many advocates of nature didn't like mountains, and why Wordsworth's friends thought he was crazy to devote his European tour to hiking in the Alps. (Wordsworth himself described the high Alps as the "most sublime and beautiful part of Switzerland," but he and his companion encountered few other tourists on the high mountain paths.)[33] In time, however, the concept of the sublime lost its connotation of horror, and the various terms used to describe the natural landscape—picturesque, beautiful, romantic, sublime—lost much of their precision, becoming more or less interchangeable terms. In a jumble of adjectives typical of the late-eighteenth-century traveler, Arthur Young described a scene on Lake Keswick as "a full view of most romantic terrible craggy rocks, inclosing a noble cascade . . . in the most picturesque manner imaginable. . . . Nothing can be fancied more grand, more beautiful, or romantic." And then there was the scene at a waterfall in Scotland, when Coleridge and Wordsworth overheard two tourists exclaiming about the "majestic" vista—much to Coleridge's delight, as he and Wordsworth had been debating the precise meanings of words like "grand," "majestic," and "sublime" only the day before. "Majestic," Coleridge thought, was just the right word to describe the scene before them. His delight was soon crushed, however, when the couple went on to describe the falls as "sublime and beautiful."[34]

The overuse of terms like "picturesque" and "sublime" was in itself a sign of how pervasive the changing attitudes about nature had become and how deeply they influenced travelers' choices about where to go and what to see. By the time Wordsworth returned to the Alps in 1820, to retrace his 1790 journey—this time with his sister, wife, and three friends, touring the high Alps had become almost commonplace. They walked over the Simplon pass in the company of several others, on an excellent paved road, newly constructed by Napoleon; they encountered other foot travelers in village inns, and even ran into people they knew from England in obscure corners of Switzerland.[35]

THE INFLUENCE of changes in taste on travelers' habits was apparent throughout Europe, beginning as early as the mid-eighteenth century. (The same kinds of changes prevailed in North America as well, but that is a subject for a later chapter.) In Switzerland, for example, Interlaken became popular as a summer resort with prosperous families from Bern by the 1750s. Excursions from there to the Staubbach waterfall drew travelers to Lauterbrunnen and nearby Grindelwald, turning those villages into small resorts by the 1780s.[36] Chamonix, at the base of Mont Blanc in Savoy (now part of France), gained notoriety when a Swiss scientist, Horace-Bénédict de Saussure, offered a prize in 1760 for the first person to discover a route to the summit of Mont Blanc. Like Rousseau and Goethe, Saussure wasn't interested in mountains for their intrinsic beauty but rather as a means to an end—in his case, scientific experimentation. Curious about how atmospheric conditions changed at high altitudes, he wanted to climb Mont Blanc himself, after someone else had shown the way.

Saussure's challenge went unmet until 1786, when a local doctor, Michel-Gabriel Paccard, and his guide, Jacques Balmat, finally claimed the prize. In the meantime, Chamonix gained favor with tourists (mostly French and Swiss, but also a few British) drawn by the beauty of Mont Blanc and the glaciers around it—"les sites sublimes de la Savoie," in the words of one French writer from the 1780s. Climbing the lower slopes of Mont Blanc became so popular that a number of local men supplemented their income by guiding travelers on the region's mountain paths and ice fields. In the 1780s, their business had expanded so much that they created a guildlike organization with its own rules about the number of guides and the type of equipment required for various kinds of expeditions. The publicity surrounding the conquest of Mont Blanc (a feat duplicated by Saussure himself the following summer, to much fanfare) added to Chamonix's popularity.[37]

In Britain, similar changes in taste encouraged travel closer to home, sometimes as an alternative to the Continental tour.[38] At least one early visitor to the Lake District, Richard Cumberland, argued for a sort of "see England first" strategy, upbraiding his countrymen who "penetrate the *Glacieres,* traverse the *Rhone* and the *Rhine* in preference to the English lakes," which "exhibit scenes in so sublime a stile . . . that if they do not fairly take the lead of all views in Europe, yet they are indisputably such as no English traveller should leave behind."[39] The more remote regions of northern England, Scotland, and Wales became especially popular with travelers as early as the 1760s, in striking contrast to the preferences among earlier travelers within Britain, who had confined themselves for the most part to the southern half of the country, making only a quick pass at most through the hills and moors of the far north. Daniel Defoe, for example, who toured England in the 1720s and published a widely read book about his travels, *Tour Thro' the Whole Island of Britain,* praised the pastoral landscape of southern and central England while describing the Lake District as "a land of unhospitable terror, barren and bleak." The Lancashire hills, just south of the Lake District, were even worse, since they lacked the useful ores of other mountainous regions. Guy Miege, in a book called *The New State of England* (1691), admired England because it was "generally a flat and open Country, not overgrown with wild and unwholsom Forests, nor dreadful high mountains," while Celia Fiennes, an enthusiastic traveler who spent years visiting just about every corner of England in the late seventeenth and early eighteenth centuries, complained of the barrenness of the Lake District.[40]

By the end of the century, travel within Britain got an extra boost from the unsettled political conditions on the Continent, as the French Revolution and the subsequent Napoleonic Wars made it unsafe for English travelers to cross the Channel for the better part of twenty years, until Napoleon's defeat at Waterloo in 1815. War, combined with changing aesthetic tastes and the British addiction to travel, created a tourist boom in northern England and Scotland—especially in the Lake District, which was by the 1790s the single most popular tourist destination in the British Isles. Thomas Gray was one of the first travelers to turn Defoe's tour on its head, favoring north and west over south and east. After visiting the Lake District in 1767 and again in 1769, Gray wrote a long essay describing in detail what he considered to be the finest views in the region. Finally published in 1778 (seven years after Gray's death) as an appendix to Thomas West's *Guide to the Lakes,* the first guidebook to the region, the essay helped popularize a particular set of scenes and a specific way of viewing them.[41]

Gray recommended vantage points at moderate elevations, allowing sufficient perspective on the expansive scenery of the lakes without making the objects below look "poor and diminutive." His favorite was a view of Lake Grasmere with the village of Grasmere on a promontory jutting into the lake, the parish church at its center, with meadows along the periphery extending to the water's edge. In the foreground, a farmhouse sat at the bottom of a lawn, surrounded by woods extending halfway up the mountains in the background. The lake itself, with its varied shoreline, and the mountain range in the distance completed the scene: "one of the sweetest landscapes that art ever attempted to imitate."[42] Thus, even before Gilpin defined the picturesque, Gray approached natural scenery as if each view were a picture. The better to appreciate these scenes, he carried with him a small convex mirror mounted on a piece of black felt, known as a "Claude-glass" after the painter Claude Lorrain. To use the glass, one stood facing away from the view, holding the mirror in front to catch the reflection of the scene, a technique that supposedly sharpened the image and softened the colors. Such glasses became an indispensable part of tourists' baggage.

Travelers who wanted to be sure of taking in the greatest number of views in the most efficient manner could rely on West's guide, which mapped out a specific route, including a series of viewpoints (or "stations," as he called them) and detailed instructions about how to find them. He advised visitors to begin their tour in the southern part of the district, if possible, thereby building up from merely "pleasing" scenery to the more spectacular terrain of the northern lakes. West recommended carrying two Claude-glasses, one on a black backing for sunny days and the other on silver foil for cloudy days, as well as a telescope. He also urged visitors to travel between early June and late August. This highly directed approach to seeing the Lakes proved enormously popular; West's book went through seven editions by the end of the century and another three by 1812. West himself died soon after the book's publication, but a local schoolmaster, William Cockin, revised and reissued subsequent editions, beginning in 1780. At least two competing guides published in the late 1780s and 1790s did not diminish the popularity of West's volume, as the number of tourists and the market for guides continued to expand.[43]

The appeal of the Lake District for these early visitors lay in a combination of its "sublime" and "picturesque" qualities. The wildness of the scenery, itself appealing, was enhanced by its variety, as lakes, mountains, trees, and the occasional rustic cottage together created effects that none of the elements alone could provide. Arthur Young, for example, praised a view of Windermere—a "scene with an elegance too delicious to be imagined"—as a "beautiful sheet of water . . . dotted with no less than ten islands," all visible from a single vantage point, some high, others low, some with clumps of trees, others with scattered trees, "a more beautiful variety no where to be seen." Similarly, the poet Robert Southey liked the view of a tiny village surrounded by forest and mountains, with a river and an ancient bridge in the foreground, the bridge "as rude in construction as the cottages." The scene had "all the elements which the painter requires; nothing can be more simple than the combination, nothing more beautiful."[44]

The village's rustic quality was a major part of its appeal for Southey, as well as for other tourists. Remote from the population centers of England until the transportation improvements of the mid-eighteenth century, with limited agricultural and commercial resources until the advent of tourism, the Lake District appeared to many visitors as the perfect example of the Rousseauean ideal of virtuous simplicity, with its quaint villages and charmingly unlettered people. That these qualities were badges of poverty did not seem to occur to most tourists. William Hutchinson, touring the Lakes in the 1770s, described one young woman he encountered as "full of youth, innocence, and beauty;—simplicity adorned her looks with modesty, and her down-cast eye; virgin apprehension covered her with blushes . . . and as she turned her eyes for an instant upon us, they smote us with all the energy of unaffected innocence." Such people and their surroundings were just as picturesque, in their way, as the lakes and mountains; Hutchinson's traveling companion responded to the young woman by pulling out his sketching pad and pencil. Another traveler, Joseph Budworth, praised the beauty and innocence of a woman he encountered at an inn in such flattering terms that curious tourists called upon her for years to come.[45]

The tendency to view landscape as a series of well-composed pictures inspired prescriptive guidebooks like West's and encouraged travelers like Young to urge that trees be trimmed in forested areas and steps cut into rocky paths to provide better views and rest stops for weary walkers.[46] Eventually, however, the popularity of picturesque travel threatened to reach absurd proportions, and as a result, tourists searching for the perfect views, armed with their guides and maps and Claude-glasses, became a subject for satire by the 1790s. In one of the more gentle commentaries, the heroine of Jane Austen's *Northanger Abbey,* while walking near Bath, tries so hard to absorb what her more sophisticated companions tell her about picturesque aesthetic conventions that by the time they reach the object of their walk and gaze down at the city, she is prepared to dismiss the panoramic view "as unworthy to make part of a landscape." Later, while visiting her friends' magnificent country home, she silently laments their absence when she makes her first foray through the grounds, for without them "she should not know what was picturesque when she saw it." In *The Lakers,* a play satirizing tourists in the Lake District, the main character—an amateur botanist and writer of gothic novels named Miss Beccabunga Veronique—paints landscapes that bear little relationship to their ostensible subject, as she removes houses and adds trees to create picturesque effects. Justifying her techniques, Miss Veronique remarks, "If it is not like what it *is,* it is like what it ought to be." And *The Tour of Dr. Syntax in Search of the Picturesque,* by William Combe, spoofed the pretensions of a bored minister who leaves home in search of scenery and diversion. Busily sketching at Windermere, he remarks that a single bird, a lone fisherman, and a boy playing by himself won't make good pictures; but put them with something else and they become more interesting. Finally he ends up sketching the animals in a farmer's barnyard, nicely clustered and therefore "picturesque."[47]

Over time, tourists became more interested in manufactured amusement than in the scenery itself, however packaged and framed. Hutchinson rode in a barge on Ullswater, maintained by the Duke of Portland, which carried six brass cannon; when fired, they set off a series of echoes, reverberating off the cliffs along the edge of the lake. The effect was stunning, according to Hutchinson, because the gradual diminishing of the echoes was followed by the sound of waterfalls, and then more echoes, and so on, seven times. Between cannon blasts, guests on the barge were entertained with French horns, which also echoed across the water, seeming to imitate the sounds of bassoon, clarinet, and organ by turns. Such special effects were initially intended to enhance the sublimity of the scene, but soon took on more of the qualities of a carnival. These noisy boat trips spread from Ullswater to Windermere and Derwentwater as well, and from the estates of a handful of gentlemen to innkeepers and other commercial proprietors. Regattas featuring boat races and mock naval battles became popular on Derwentwater in the 1780s, giving the lake "all the rustic calm of a battlefield," in the words of one modern writer. On one of the smaller lakes, in a bizarre form of horse racing, horses were taken out on the lake in a boat with a plug in its bottom. The plug was pulled, forcing the horses to swim for their lives; the first one to make it to shore won. To add to the entertainment, water spaniels chased ducks.[48]

With the growing popularity of the Lakes and the expansion of commercial forms of entertainment came complaints about overcrowding and desecration of pristine scenery. As early as the 1790s, visitors bemoaned the presence of other tourists, concerned that their numbers would put an end to the region's quiet seclusion—the very quality that made it appealing. Wordsworth, who had spent his childhood in the Lake District and moved back permanently in 1799 after a decade of traveling on the Continent and living in southern England, was among the most severe critics of the commercialization associated with tourism. "The Brothers" (published in 1800) opens with a complaint: "These Tourists, heaven preserve us! needs must live/A profitable life: some glance along,/Rapid and gay, as if the earth were air,/And they were butterflies to wheel about/Long as the summer lasted." Like his contemporaries, Wordsworth did not want to cut off tourism altogether, but rather limit it to people who were prepared to appreciate the region's beauty in a contemplative way (preferably on foot). In that spirit he offered his own "Guide to the Lakes," first published anonymously in 1810 as an introduction to a book of paintings by Joseph Wilkinson, an amateur artist. Words-worth expanded and published the "Guide" separately in 1820, with subsequent editions following in 1822, 1823, and 1835. In the 1840s, it was incorporated into a more extensive guidebook, which became the standard for tourists to the region well into the 1860s.[49]

By writing a guide, Wordsworth hoped to be able to shape how people perceived and understood the natural beauty of the region. In contrast to earlier travelers and writers, who had focused on the picturesque qualities of the region in the literal sense, Wordsworth treated landscape as an integral part of the region and its history. Disturbed by the numbers of people he saw following prescribed tours, so busy adjusting their Claude-glasses that they couldn't ap-preciate the scene independently, he intended his book as a guide for the "*Minds* of Persons of taste," those capable of an independent appreciation of natural beauty. There was a certain elitist quality to Wordsworth's *Guide,* since persons of taste were generally also per-sons of wealth, but the parallel was not exact; he also deplored the influx of moneyed city folk—not, as many others complained, be-cause they ran up prices, but because they built conspicuous houses that clashed with the natural setting and tampered with nature by constructing seawalls along lakeshores and creating gardens filled with plants not native to the area.[50]

In attempting to reserve the Lakes for people of his sensibility, however, Wordsworth was fighting an uphill battle. His own poetry helped promote the popularity of the region, to the point that he himself became one of the region's top attractions by the 1830s. One summer his wife complained to a friend that breakfast was the only time she and her husband had to themselves. "Soon afterwards we may look for Tourists, who by hook or by crook make their way to us." The visitors' book at the Wordsworths' home, Rydall Mount, records twenty-five hundred names for the years 1830–37; in the 1840s, the Wordsworths' neighbor Harriet Martineau (who also wrote a guidebook) thought they were receiving about five hundred people a year.[51] By the end of the nineteenth century, the *Atlantic Monthly* could label the Lake District as "Wordsworth Country" (in an article titled "The Wordsworth Country on Two Shillings a Day"). The very thought would no doubt have appalled the poet, although he would have approved of this author's approach to seeing the Lakes: traveling light, much in the style of Wordsworth's own youthful journey to the Alps, carrying only a knapsack stuffed with a change of underwear, socks, needles and thread, a towel, sponge, soap, toothbrush, comb, some food, a flask of whiskey, a map, a guide to Britain, and—of course—a volume of Wordsworth's poetry.[52]

FOR A TIME, travelers who found the Lake District too commercial could venture north into Scotland with reasonable confidence that they would find pristine natural beauty unsullied by crowds. Despite observations by people like Lord Breadalbane about the increasing popularity of travel in the Highlands, the remoteness of the country and limited accommodations for travelers saved Scotland from turning into another Lake District, at least until the 1820s. The sheer size of the country helped, too, as travelers spread themselves out over a much larger area.[53] As late as the beginning of the nineteenth century, although the main roads were quite good throughout Scotland as far north as Inverness, many of the more appealing areas, from a traveler's point of view, were accessible only by foot or horseback. North of Inverness, a region seldom visited by travelers, there were no carriage roads at all. Even on the main routes, coach and posting services were rare beyond Edinburgh and Glasgow, limiting travel to those with private carriages willing to go to the trouble and expense of hiring horses by the day or longer. Inns were widely scattered and not generally up to English standards, which could be an even more serious deterrent to travelers lacking the connections of a Boswell or Johnson. One guidebook published at the end of the eighteenth century advised travelers to acquire a "strong roomy carriage" and then construct a large box inside; the top could be used as a table and the bottom as storage for wine and other provisions. Carry bed linens, towels, blankets, and pillows as well, the author advised, and then one would not have to worry about finding accommodations in remote locations. Even under the best of conditions, it took about four days to cover the two hundred-plus miles between Edinburgh and Inverness until the 1840s, when a good system of public coaches was well established.[54]

For those with the time and money to make the journey, however, Scotland offered even more rewarding views than northern England and Wales. In part this was the nature of the country itself, and in part simply the fact that Scotland was far less developed commercially. Gilpin thought Scotland's most impressive feature was its vast expanse of land "intirely *in a state of nature*"—that is, without the stone walls or other signs of civilization that so often broke up the English landscape. To many travelers, Scotland's scenery was grander as well, appropriately viewed after developing one's powers of appreciation on tours of England or Wales.[55]

The standard tour of Scotland, as it developed in the late eighteenth century, took travelers in a loop from Edinburgh north to Stirling, then on to Perth and Dunkeld (generally considered the gateway to the Highlands); west along Loch Tay to Inveraray, on the west coast; and finally south to Loch Lomond, Glasgow, and the valley of the Clyde. By the end of the century, a detour from Stirling to Callender, Loch Katrine, and the mountain pass known as The Trossachs became increasingly popular. Those with sufficient time and an interest in seeing the more remote parts of the Highlands might trace a wider circuit similar to Johnson and Boswell's itinerary, following the northeast coast all the way to Inverness, then continuing southwest along Loch Ness to Fort William and back to Glasgow, perhaps with a side trip to some of the Inner Hebrides, of which Mull, Iona and Staffa were the most popular.[56]

A great part of Scotland's appeal to turn-of-the-century tourists, besides its scenic beauty, lay in its long and colorful history, still visible in the ruins of centuries-old castles and the remnants of an ancient culture that survived in Highland villages. The late eighteenth century saw a revival of interest in medieval history and art; "Gothic" style, once scorned as a barbarous aberration from classical aesthetics, became popular again, and educated Europeans began to see in the history of the medieval period evidence of a simpler, more virtuous way of life epitomized in the novels of Rousseau. Because of its distance from the centers of trade and power and its strong sense of a separate cultural identity, Scotland was a treasure trove for travelers in search of history.

Where Johnson and others of his generation had disdained the Scots as a barbaric and bloodthirsty people, later travelers idealized them as independent and proud, fighting for their independence from English encroachment. In the area around Loch Lomond, visitors followed the trail of William Wallace, who led the Scottish resistance to English rule at the end of the thirteenth century. When Edward I finally succeeded in crushing the Scottish rebellion, Wallace eluded pursuit for months before he was finally captured and taken to London for trial and execution. A patriot and martyr to the Scots, Wallace became a folk hero to English (and American) visitors as well. Throughout the country, visitors sought out the castles that had been home to rival Scottish rulers, many of them with literary associations: the well-preserved castle at Stirling and the even grander one at Blair Atholl, which had such extensive grounds that a complete tour required hours of walking; the ruined castle of Duncan, the murdered king made famous in Shakespeare's *Macbeth;* and the nearby site of Birnam Wood (though lacking trees by this time, much to the disappointment of James Plumptre, who quipped, "I suppose it never returned from its march with Malcolm's Soldiers to Dunsinane"). Farther north were Cawdor Castle and the heath where Macbeth's witches danced, Taymouth Castle with its fancifully reconstructed Druid Temple (built in 1750 by Lord Glenorchy), and the ruined cathedral at Elgin.[57]

In the remote areas of the northern Highlands, encounters with kilted, Gaelic-speaking villagers brought history to life and lent a certain authenticity to the traveler's experience. As Dorothy Wordsworth wrote after an otherwise disappointing excursion, "The highlander upon the naked heath, in his Highland dress, upon his careful-going horse, with the boy following him, was worth it all." Another day, toward nightfall, the Wordsworths encountered a young boy calling cattle home for the night, in Gaelic. "His appearance was in the highest degree moving to the imagination: mists were on the hillsides, darkness shutting in upon the huge avenue of mountains, torrents, roaring, no house in sight to which the child might belong; his dress, cry, and appearance all different from anything we had been accustomed to,'' she wrote. ''It was a text, as Wm. has since observed to me, containing in itself the whole history of the Highlander's life—his melancholy, his simplicity, his poverty, his superstition, and above all, that visionariness which results from a communion with the unworldliness of nature.''[58]

Some travelers, of course, carried their search for the authentic historical experience to extremes. In a sequel to *Dr Syntax*, William Combe satirized those antiquarian-minded tourists in his tale about ''Dr. Prosody,'' who insists that his servant dress up in a full suit of armor while serving dinner in a castle and later exhumes graves on the island of Iona, convinced he has discovered evidence that will prove the authenticity of Ossian's poems. Outraged villagers are ready to attack until they realize he is merely a harmless ''antiquarian madman.''[59]

By the second decade of the nineteenth century, visitors began planning their itineraries to include scenes associated with the enormously popular writings of Sir Walter Scott. His books, published between 1802 and 1831, fused history, folk traditions, and an eye for descriptive detail in a style that made him one of the most beloved of contemporary writers. Scotland was already a popular travel destination by the time Scott was born in 1771, but his books contributed significantly to the remarkable increase in Scottish tourism in the early nineteenth century and did much to direct travelers to particular locations. Scott's first two books, *The Minstrelsy of the Scottish Border* (1802–1803) and *The Lay of the Last Minstrel* (1805), celebrated the folk tradition of southern Scotland, where Scott lived most of his life.[60]

Much more significant, however, was *The Lady of the Lake* (1810), the first of Scott's works to receive widespread recognition. Its setting—The Trossachs and Loch Katrine, about thirty miles north of Stirling—became one of the most popular destinations in Scotland during the early 1800s. Earlier travelers had rarely visited this region, despite its great beauty, because it was accessible only by foot or horseback. (William and Dorothy Wordsworth, who thought nothing of hiking thirty miles, were a source of great curiosity for one local man, who rarely encountered strangers and couldn't understand why anyone would come so far to see what seemed rather ordinary to him.) By the 1820s and '30s, however, The Trossachs and Loch Katrine were at the top of every traveler's list—including Americans', who began to visit Europe in growing numbers after 1815—and many of them toured the region with *The Lady of the Lake* in hand. The book tells the story of Ellen, a beautiful young woman, and her father, Douglas, an exiled king, who live simply and self-sufficiently in a small cottage hidden in the forest near Loch Katrine, cut off from the rest of the world by nearly impenetrable mountains. When a lost hunter stumbles across Ellen rowing her little boat on the loch, he is captivated by her beauty and innocence, a match for her sublime surroundings. Only later does he learn the story of Ellen and her father's true identities. Ellen's tale, so saccharine to later generations of schoolchildren forced to read it, had enormous appeal to the generation that admired *La Nouvelle Heloïse* and was beginning to discover the folk heroes of Scottish history. (The book sold about twenty thousand copies in its first year, a huge number for that time.) Moreover, Scott's descriptions of the setting were so detailed that they left readers with a sharp mental picture of Loch Katrine, and so accurate that many travelers used the book as a guide.[61]

Like Wordsworth, Scott himself became a tourist attraction. He was in fact far more popular in his own time than Wordsworth, as thousands of people visited his home at Abbotsford, south of Edinburgh. Like Wordsworth, he too regretted the influx of tourists to scenes he cherished, complaining in 1810 that he lived in an age when "every London citizen makes Loch Lomond his washpot."[62] In fact, however, early-nineteenth-century visitors to Scotland did not encounter the same degree of overcrowding that was already, in the opinion of contemporaries, spoiling much of the Lake District, largely because of its distance from southern population centers. But the fundamental tension between travelers' appreciation of unspoiled natural beauty and the pressures created by the growth of tourism was present there, as it was in the Lake District, Wales, certain regions within the Alps, and other areas that became popular around the turn of the century as a result of the growing interest in what one modern writer has called "scenic tourism."[63] It was only a matter of time before visitors to Scotland would also begin complaining that too many tourists were spoiling the very beauty they had come to see. Royal patronage—King George IV visited Scotland in 1822 and Queen Victoria in 1837—did even more than Scott for the popularity of his native land, and improvements in transportation later in the nineteenth century finally removed the barrier of distance.

Scott's popularity extended well beyond the borders of the British Isles. The American writer William Cullen Bryant encountered German tourists along with Americans and Britons at Loch Katrine in 1845, and the French lionized Scott when he visited Paris in the 1820s.[64] The aesthetic and intellectual changes of the late eighteenth and early nineteenth centuries, which had such a profound impact on travelers' destinations and their responses to the places they visited, crossed the boundaries of nationality and language. Scott, Wordsworth, Goethe, Schiller, all were part of the common intellectual baggage of upper-class men and women throughout Europe and North America. When peace finally returned to Europe in 1815 after more than two decades of revolution and war, and it became possible to travel freely on the Continent once again, these changing tastes would influence a new kind of "grand tour"—one that emphasized natural beauty and scenes associated with modern writers to a much greater degree than ever before.

CHAPTER 3

THE GRAND TOUR

REVISITED

W HEN NAPOLEON was defeated and sent into exile on the island of Elba in 1814, it was as if the floodgates to the continent had opened. Barred from France, Switzerland, and Italy for the better part of twenty years, Britons hastened to cross the Channel, impelled by curiosity about changes wrought by the Revolution and Napoleonic rule in addition to the traditional motives for touring the Continent. The first wave of postwar tourism was cut short when Napoleon escaped from Elba in March 1815, but his defeat at Waterloo three months later inaugurated an extended period of peace.

Among those who took advantage of peace to travel on the Continent was the twenty-eight-year-old poet George Gordon, Lord Byron. Restless by nature and distracted by a scandal over his separation from his wife, Byron decided to leave England, perhaps forever, in 1816. He visited Belgium (touring the battlefield at Waterloo), sailed up the Rhine, settled down for several months in Geneva (where he spent much of his time with the poet Shelley), and finally made his way to Venice, where he lived for three years.

Like many postwar travelers, Byron had been to the Continent before, although not on the usual sort of grand tour. In 1809, fresh from Cambridge and itching to travel but shut out of France and Italy because of the war, he had persuaded a friend, John Cam Hobhouse, to join him on a voyage to Greece and Turkey. They sailed to Lisbon and then across the Mediterranean, stopping at Gibraltar, Malta, Sardinia, and finally Patras, on the west coast of Greece, where they embarked upon an overland adventure that would take them into the remote and little-known kingdom of Albania, across Greece to Delphi, and finally to Athens. After lingering for two months in Athens, the pair took ship for Smyrna (today Izmir), and spent four months touring Asia Minor. Then Hobhouse went home and Byron returned to Greece for another eight months.[1] In nearly two years of travel, Byron encountered only a handful of British visitors, although Lord Elgin had already shipped a substantial quantity of sculpture from the Parthenon to England (later earning Byron's scathing criticism). Greece in the early nineteenth century was an impoverished country with little evidence to remind visitors of the achievements of its ancient civilization. What remained was largely neglected; even the famous temple at Delphi was buried in silt, much to Byron's disappointment.

Italy in 1816 was a different story. After several months in Venice, Byron wanted to visit Rome but hesitated because, as he put it, "at present it is pestilent with English. . . . A man is a fool who travels now in France or Italy, till this tribe of wretches is swept home again." He was not entirely exaggerating. An estimated 2,000 English tourists visited Rome in 1818—a small number by modern standards, but enough to make their presence felt in a city that was then much smaller than it is today. A visitor to Paris that same year claimed that there were at least 30,000 English in that city. "In two or three years the first rush will be over, and the Continent will be roomy and agreeable," Byron thought, but in fact the number of travelers to the Continent continued to increase over the next several decades. By the early 1830s, about 5,000 English tourists visited Rome at Christmas, the most popular season; in the early 1840s, the number of visitors to Florence reached about 11,000, about half of them English and most of the rest American. "So many people travel that one is apt to ask who can be left at home,'' James Fenimore Cooper wrote while touring Italy in 1828.[2]

Ironically, Byron himself contributed to the trend he so detested. The first two cantos of his long poem *Childe Harold's Pilgrimage*, based on his travels in southern Europe, established his reputation as a poet when they were published in 1812. He drew upon his travels in Switzerland and Italy for the third and fourth cantos, published in 1817 and 1818, which proved even more popular. Thousands of travelers used *Childe Harold* as a kind of guidebook to the Continent (much like those who toured Scotland with *The Lady of the Lake* in hand). Like Scott and Wordsworth, Byron unwittingly contributed to the overcrowding of his chosen retreats; and like them, he himself became part of the attraction. After his years in Venice, Byron moved from one city to another in northern Italy, finally settling in Genoa, where he became one of the city's chief "lions," a term British travelers used to label sightseeing attractions (including human ones). He received few visitors, but that didn't stop people from trying to gain an audience with him. His support for Greek independence in the early 1820s helped make it a popular cause in Britain, and his death in Greece, in 1824, while organizing an attack against the Turks, further elevated his reputation as a romantic hero. After his death, Byron's home in Genoa, as well as scenes associated with his poetry, remained popular tourist attractions for decades.

TRAVELERS TO THE Continent after 1815 tried to re-create the old grand tour, following the well-worn routes to Paris and Italy, but their numbers, backgrounds, and tastes all set them apart from pre-war travelers. They were no longer predominantly the wealthy young men of Boswell's generation; for the first time, women began traveling in large numbers, and in addition, there were more family groups and more people of merely upper-middle-class means. Wordsworth, for example, returned to Switzerland in 1820 with his wife, sister, and another couple, revisiting the scenes of his youthful tour. James Fenimore Cooper, en route from Southampton to Le Havre, was surprised to meet a young Englishwoman traveling with only a maid and footman, a practice she assured him was perfectly respectable. Cooper himself, traveling with his wife, five young children, and a nephew acting as his secretary, was among the growing number of Americans already displaying a remarkable similarity to their British ancestors in their propensity to travel, inspired by much the same kind of interest in the historical and cultural heritage of the European capitals that had motivated the eighteenth-century grand tourists. The Americans' numbers were small compared with the legions of British travelers—two thousand to eight thousand Americans sailed across the Atlantic annually from the 1820s to the 1850s, including business as well as pleasure travelers—but they increased dramatically in the second half of the century.[3]

Although postwar visitors shared their predecessors' interest in the art and culture of the European capitals, they brought to their travels different sensibilities, which influenced their choice of destinations and their perceptions of what they saw. Travelers' adulation of writers like Byron, and their propensity to use literary works as guidebooks and elevate authors' homes and scenes from their works to the status of tourist attractions, were among the important changes in styles of travel. An appreciation of the natural landscape, in part fostered by writers like Byron and Wordsworth, was another. The Alps became an experience to be savored rather than dreaded, and Switzerland a place to linger or even to make the object of a special trip. The Rhine region of Germany gained favor for the same reasons. Classical monuments remained part of the standard itinerary, but were often overshadowed by Renaissance and modern painting, as well as by the increasingly popular masterpieces of Gothic architecture.[4]

Although years of restrictions on travel and curiosity about changes on the Continent sparked the immediate post-1815 spurt in travel, the sustained increase in numbers during the 1820s, '30s, and '40s owed more to the growing prosperity of a rapidly industrializing Europe, which gave more people the money to travel and encouraged the improvements in transportation that made it easier. The industrial revolution fostered a remarkable increase in productivity with resulting gains in overall national wealth and a shift in production from agriculture to manufacturing, which helped distribute wealth more broadly through the population rather than concentrating it in the hands of the landed aristocracy. Britain, already the wealthiest nation in the world in the eighteenth century because of its leading position in world trade, became even wealthier as it began to industrialize in the late eighteenth and early nineteenth centuries. Between 1750 and 1850, Britain's gross national product per capita increased two and a half times; over the course of the nineteenth century, real income quadrupled. Other nations in Europe also enjoyed increases in productivity and income, but having been slower to industrialize and less prosperous to begin with, they lagged far behind Britain. In the 1850s, for example, per capita annual income in Britain was about £33, compared with £21 in France and a little over £13 in Germany. The United States, although slower to industrialize, experienced sustained economic growth from the 1820s through 1850s (with the exception of a banking crisis and depression in the late 1830s and early 1840s), resulting in a steady increase in personal income. By mid-century, its per capita income exceeded even that of Britain.[5]

This growing prosperity was not evenly distributed throughout all levels of society, nor was it a steady upward trend throughout the century; the middle and upper levels of society benefited more than the lower levels, and economic growth was more rapid in the second half of the nineteenth century than in the first. Even so, in the three decades after the Napoleonic Wars, more people had the means to travel than ever before, especially among the British. Added to the traditional reasons that the British traveled—a sense of insularity, an interest in the culture of Continental capitals, a desire to escape northern winters—and the interest in travel fostered by previous generations of grand tourists, it was no wonder that the French writer Théophile Gautier observed in 1840 that "the English are everywhere except in London."[6]

Not that travel was yet possible for the masses or even the average middle-class family. Before the era of railroads, a Continental tour still required a good deal of time and money. Two or three months was generally the minimum devoted to such tours, and six months to a year was more common, especially among Americans, for whom the cost of passage to Europe was substantial (about $300 round-trip for first-class cabins throughout the first half of the nineteenth century) while daily expenses were modest (about $2 or $3 per day for top-quality food and lodgings). Americans, in effect, felt compelled to amortize high transportation costs over several months. As a result, the early American travelers were for the most part wealthy families and successful writers like Cooper, though there were also students sent to study in Europe (mostly at German universities), clergymen sent by congregations to study or restore their health, and social reformers on lecture or fund-raising tours. European travelers, too, were still largely drawn from the "leisure class"—those who had independent means or had the sort of professional jobs that they could set aside for a time. (Until the late nineteenth century, professionals, bankers, and civil service officials had much more leisurely schedules than their modern counterparts; a five- or six-hour day was common, in contrast to shopkeepers and factory workers, who typically worked a ten- to twelve-hour day.)[7] But there were many more such people by the early nineteenth century, as men who made money in manufacturing or professions adopted the ways of the gentry.

ALTHOUGH THE BASIC modes of travel remained little changed from the prewar days, better roads and improvements in shipping made getting from one place to another faster and more reliable. The first steamships crossed the Channel in 1816; by 1821, French-owned steamers shuttled between Dover and Calais on regular schedules, cutting the time required for the crossing to about two hours in good weather.[8] In the United States, the Black Ball Line introduced the first regularly scheduled transatlantic service with biweekly sailings in 1818. At least four other companies followed suit in the next few years. Although these services used sailing vessels, requiring about three weeks for the eastbound crossing and five for the westbound, they made it easier for Americans to cross the Atlantic by providing reliable, predictable transportation. Competition among the lines helped keep fares down as well. Steamships were first used on the transatlantic route in 1838; by mid-century, both American and British companies offered regular service by steamer, cutting the typical travel time between New York and Liverpool to nine or ten days.

During the 1840s and '50s, the design of sailing ships improved dramatically, so that the fastest clipper ships rivaled the early steamers in speed.[9]

Getting to London and the Channel ports from the British provinces also became quicker and easier. Turnpike companies proliferated, constructing new intercity roads using improved methods of paving. Better design, notably the introduction of spring-based suspension in the middle of the eighteenth century and the invention of the elliptical spring in the first decade of the nineteenth, resulted in more comfortable coaches with larger passenger capacity. Frequency of service increased as well, with eight times as many coaches operating between major urban centers by the mid-1830s. On average, travel time between major cities dropped by half between 1770 and 1830, with even more dramatic reductions on some routes: A journey from Edinburgh to London in the 1750s, for example, required ten days in summer and at least twelve in winter; by the 1830s, it took just under two days. A trip from Bath to London that had required three days in 1750 could be done in twelve and a half hours in the 1820s. London to Brighton, once a two-day trip, was cut to just over five hours. Long-distance travel was further simplified with the introduction of stopovers on long routes at no extra charge, transfers from one line to another on a single fare, and, on routes to coastal towns, coordination of arrival and departure times with Channel steamers.[10]

Once across the Channel, travelers found similar improvements. In the second half of the eighteenth century, the major French roads were generally considered superior to those in England—the result of a centralized road-building program launched in the 1750s.[11] Napoleon built even more new roads and improved existing ones in many parts of France, Switzerland, and Italy so he could move armies and equipment faster and more efficiently. Long after he was in exile, his engineering achievements benefited peacetime tourists. Especially notable was the Grande Route Militaire across the Jura Mountains to Geneva and over the Simplon Pass to Italy, the first road across the Alps accessible to wheeled vehicles. For travelers headed to Milan or Florence, it chopped ninety miles off the Mont

Cenis route. Besides making the journey to Italy faster and easier, Napoleon's road made a remarkably beautiful stretch of Alpine scenery much more readily accessible. While most British travelers deplored Napoleon's political and military ambitions, they appreciated his achievement in breaching the Alps. "This passage of the Simplon alone is sufficient to immortalize his name," one woman wrote. "It is quite the eighth wonder of the world."[12] By the end of the 1830s, travelers' choices multiplied as carriage roads were completed over several other Alpine passes, including the St. Bernard, St. Gotthard, and Brenner.[13]

Napoleon's engineers also began to widen the road along the Mediterranean coast between Nice and Genoa, although long stretches remained inaccessible to wheeled vehicles until the late 1820s. When the road was finally completed in the 1830s, its lovely scenery and mild winter weather made it the route of choice between France and Italy. The beginning of regular steamship service from Marseilles to Genoa, Livorno, Civitavecchia, and Naples in the 1830s offered yet another possibility, attractive since it was much faster (about eighteen hours to Genoa, for example, compared with three days by carriage).[14] Even so, many travelers continued to prefer the land route for its scenic beauty, among them the American scientist Benjamin Silliman, who described the Nice–Genoa road as "one of the most varied and picturesque in the world." Charles Dickens, traveling by ship in the 1840s, was so taken with the view from deck that he later sailed back to Nice and hired a carriage to drive to Genoa just to see the countryside at closer range.[15]

A network of public coaches covered nearly all of France by the 1820s, and one could even arrange through service directly from London to Paris, with the Channel crossing, meals, and lodging included in a single price. As a faster alternative to the French diligence (described by Cooper as "a moving house"), postwar travelers could reserve places in the *malle-poste* or mail coach. Maintained by the government to carry the mails, these carriages made only the briefest of stops to change horses (where they had first priority) and allow passengers to consume hasty meals. Each carriage could accommodate two or three passengers, who paid about double the diligence fares for the privilege of getting to their destinations more quickly—thirty-four hours from Paris to Lyons, for example, compared with about sixty by diligence.[16]

Those who could afford it still generally traveled post, however, hiring horses at the posting stations spaced several miles apart on all major roads. Many engaged couriers to travel with their parties, arranging for horses, meals, and lodging en route. The posting system in France was well organized and regulated, with clearly specified charges, although travelers sometimes complained of being cheated, usually by being forced to hire more horses than were legally required to pull their particular type of carriage. The privacy of traveling post appealed especially to British travelers, who hated the prospect of spending hours jammed into a coach among chatty strangers. The French liked to travel with their dogs, a habit that struck the British as bizarre, and they made matters worse by insisting on keeping the windows closed. The British, on the other hand, loved dogs but thought them better left at home, and believed in the therapeutic value of fresh air, no matter how cold. They also thought Continentals' hygiene left something to be desired. A closed coach full of Frenchmen and their dogs was an experience to be avoided—"a very purgatory of heat, closeness, confinement, and bad smells," wrote William Hazlitt (who was admittedly prone to dramatize his troubles) in 1824. "Nothing can surpass it but the section of a slave-ship, or the Black-hole of Calcutta."[17]

An American traveling by coach in both Britain and France was struck by the differences. The British coach, "an elegant piece of machinery," was better built than the lumbering French vehicles; the horses were of better quality, the coachmen better dressed, and the overall speed about double that of the diligence. Inside, the atmosphere was solemn and dignified—"the passengers quiet, clean, and glum, sitting bolt upright with an umbrella standing between their legs, and ever and anon passing the hand along that side of the thigh next a fellow passenger to prevent contact with him"—in utter contrast to the French coach, in which "there was much drinking of wine, eating of cakes, . . . infinite fun and laughter." Such raucous behavior was distasteful to many British travelers, although the American traveler, twenty-year-old William Preston, preferred

French gregariousness to the more reserved style of the British. Other Americans also remarked that the French diligences did not live up to their negative reputation.[18]

As one traveled farther south and east, transit services were generally more limited, despite significant improvements in the 1820s and '30s. In Italy, most travelers continued to rely on vetturinos well into the nineteenth century. Even as late as the 1830s, diligences and mail coaches served only a few major cities, and the posting system was neither as comprehensive nor as well regulated as those of France and Britain.[19] Travelers often complained that Italian postilions demanded more than the official fees for horses, despite posted regulations. When one British visitor, John Mayne, asked a postilion why they always demanded more than the posted prices, the man replied that it had been twenty years since the English had visited Italy, so they ought to help make up for lost revenue. Mayne found the incessant bargaining so frustrating that he gave up his carriage at Florence and hired a vetturino to take him on to Rome.[20]

Postwar travelers to the Continent also found a broader range of accommodations available to them. New inns were established in major cities, although most travelers still preferred to rent furnished lodgings, especially in Paris, Florence, and Rome, where they were likely to stay for weeks at a time. The fashionable quarters of these cities were filled with spacious town houses, whose owners were often happy to rent part of their homes to visitors; in Paris, such lodgings became even more plentiful after the Revolution, as hard-pressed members of the aristocracy needed help to make ends meet. The British thought the notion of sharing one's home with strangers curious, but were happy to take advantage of it. Besides offering a greater measure of privacy and comfort, furnished lodgings were remarkably cheap by British and American standards. Once settled in Rome or Florence, travelers found it possible to live luxuriously for a fraction of what they would spend in London or New York. Even Paris, considered the most expensive of Continental cities, was far less costly than London. Cooper and his family, for example, rented a large country house outside Paris for $100 a month and a grand apartment in Florence with a large drawing room and dining room, two huge bedrooms and several smaller ones, a study and servants' quarters, for $60 a month, less than half the cost of a modest house in London. (A fringe benefit was purchasing wine produced by the family that owned the building—"much better wine than half the claret that is drunk in Paris"—for four cents a bottle.)[21] By mid-century, the prospect of living like aristocracy on a middle-class income, along with the blurring of social distinctions that naturally occurred when people were removed from their everyday surroundings, encouraged many socially ambitious upper-middle-class families to settle on the Continent for extended periods of time. And for the budget traveler, Italy could be cheap indeed. The young American writer Bayard Taylor and three friends rented a three-room furnished apartment in Florence for $10 a month, taking their meals in cafés and trattorie for about 25 cents a day.[22]

By the 1820s, so many British travelers were visiting Paris that some proprietors began catering to British tastes. Landlords, mindful of earlier travelers' complaints about the French preference for large, sparsely furnished rooms with bare tile or parquet floors, added carpets, upholstered furniture, and washbasins to rental lodgings, while inns and pastry shops began serving British-style food and drink. Not all travelers appreciated the changes, which came, ironically, at a time when increasing numbers of British travelers were developing an appreciation for French food. One Englishwoman thought the food at French inns was fine, except when they tried to produce British cooking. Another, returning to Paris in 1829 after an absence of thirteen years, was dismayed, upon going in search of her favorite French pastry shop, to find it displaying plum cakes and puddings, with a young woman behind the counter speaking broken English. It was all part of what she saw as the rise of "Anglophilia" in Paris—admirable, perhaps, in its new appreciation of English poets, but unfortunate if it meant a blurring of distinctions between French and British food. For her part, she was glad to have seen France "while France was still so French!"[23]

THE SURGE IN travel after 1815, especially among those who could not afford to spend a year or more on their Continental tours, helped create demand for a new kind of travel book—one that eschewed reflections on art and life in foreign capitals for practical advice. By the 1820s, the modern travel guide made its first appearance, with its lists of sightseeing attractions and its detailed, point-by-point descriptions of routes, methods of transport, and accommodations.

Mariana Starke, probably the first person who could be called a professional guidebook writer, produced nine editions of her popular *Letters from Italy* between 1800 and 1839. The earlier editions, written in the tradition of the eighteenth-century travel account, were largely descriptive, although even then she included more practical advice than other guidebooks of the time—too much, according to some of her critics, who thought she should call her books travelers' guides rather than *Letters from Italy*. She did just that in a completely new version, commissioned and published in 1820 by John Murray, one of London's leading publishers—known especially as Byron's publisher, but also a specialist in travel literature. Titled *Travels on the Continent: Written for the Use and Particular Information of Travellers*, Starke's new book was based on her travels in 1817 after a twenty-year absence. She began with a preface designed to reassure her readers that the Continent was indeed safe for British visitors—countering rumors that demobilized soldiers roamed the roads in southern France, the Alps, and remote parts of Italy, plundering the unwary.[24]

More comprehensive than previous editions of Starke's book, this version included chapters on France and Switzerland in addition to her extensive treatment of Italy, along with brief sections on Germany, Austria, Portugal, Spain, Holland, the Scandinavian countries, and Russia. Each chapter described the routes between major towns and advised on accommodations and cultural attractions. For Paris and the Italian cities, Starke described the major art galleries, listing every painting and rating its degree of interest by assigning one to four exclamation points (a device first used in a 1787 guide to France by Thomas Martyn).[25] A series of appendices provided practical details: post stations along major routes with the distance between each and brief comments on sights along the way; inns, restaurants, and shops in major towns; theaters, doctors, post offices, currency exchange rates, special passport requirements, and a host of other details. A visitor to Rome, for example, could find information about where to hire an Italian teacher or a dancing master; buy furs, pearls, ladies' shoes, English books and writing paper, local and foreign wines, and firewood; or stable a horse and carriage.[26]

Among the many travelers who used Starke's guide was her publisher's son, also named John, who toured the Continent in 1829. He found it accurate on Italy, where the author herself had traveled extensively, but the treatment of other countries, where Starke had much less experience and relied heavily on information from others, was so riddled with errors as to render the book all but useless. The few other guidebooks available were flawed for other reasons—they covered limited areas, were out of date, or, in some cases, unavailable in English.[27] By the time Murray returned to London, he had decided to write his own guidebook. It would be the first of a long series, which set the standard for the modern travel guide and proved enormously profitable for his family's publishing firm.

Because Murray believed guidebooks should be based on detailed, firsthand experience, he launched his enterprise with a book on northern Europe and the German states, where he had spent much of his own Continental tour. His *Hand-Book for Travellers on the Continent,* published in 1836, covered Holland, Belgium, Prussia and the other northern German states, as well as the Rhine as far south as Switzerland. A year later, he added *A Hand-Book for Travellers in Southern Germany,* which included Bavaria, Austria, and the Danube as far as the Black Sea. A guide to Switzerland, Savoy, and Piedmont appeared in 1838. Murray wanted to strike a happy medium between overly general, superficial guides (like Starke's) and those written by local enthusiasts who told the reader more than he wanted to know. He had no pretensions to originality or literary style, but aimed to produce a simple, straightforward, practical guide based primarily on his own observations but supplemented by the works of others where appropriate. He skipped the detailed history and description characteristic of many earlier guides, and made no attempt to be comprehensive, concentrating instead on "matter-of-fact descriptions of what *ought to be seen,*" not everything that "*may be seen.*"[28]

Judging from the success of his guides, Murray understood his audience well. His books followed a common format, beginning with an introductory chapter that included a capsule history and description of the region (including comments on the "manners" of the people); practical information on transportation, currency, passport and customs requirements, inns, and major sights; and a brief homily on the proper frame of mind for travelers (one should learn something about the language and customs of the country, plan ahead, maintain one's patience and good temper, and above all, leave one's prejudices at home—especially "the idea of the amazing superiority of England, above all other countries, in all respects"). Next came a list of suggested itineraries for varying lengths of time, usually three weeks to six months, followed by detailed chapters on each subregion, outlining specific routes, indicating the miles between each post town along the way, the major sights, and recommended inns. Thus travelers could get all the essential practical advice in one forty- or fifty-page summary, save themselves the trouble of mapping out an itinerary by reviewing Murray's suggestions, and then turn quickly to the detailed sections on the areas they planned to visit, skipping over any irrelevant parts. The books' compact size (approximately 4½ by 7 inches) made them easy to carry.

Murray's genius in creating his series lay in taking the uncertainty out of travel: He told his readers where to go, how to get there, and what to see. If better roads and the invention of steam helped make travel faster, Murray helped make it more predictable. He and his father also displayed the publishing acumen that had made their firm one of the most successful in London, first by perceiving the need for a new kind of guide and then by standardizing it, with common titles (all were called *Hand-Book for Travellers in . . .*), organization of material, format, and cover. The distinctive red bindings became the handbooks' trademark, making them instantly recognizable. Eventually the handbooks would become so popular that some readers would accuse them of dictating travelers' habits, but in their early years, the books filled an obvious need in a rapidly expanding market.

About the same time that Murray began work on his first handbook, a young German bookseller, Karl Baedeker, was at work on a similar volume. Like Murray, Baedeker was the son of a printer, but his own interests at first ran more to the bookselling side of the business. As a student at the University of Heidelberg, he had worked part-time for a bookseller; later he worked for a bookseller in Berlin before returning to Essen, his hometown, to join the family business. In 1827, after a brief apprenticeship, he moved to Coblentz, at the intersection of the Rhine and Moselle rivers, where he opened his own bookstore. A year later, Baedeker bought a small publishing firm that was about to go bankrupt. The firm's assets included a guide to the Rhine between Mainz and Cologne by August Klein, which had sold well in the late 1820s and early '30s, as the introduction of steamship service on the Rhine in 1828 and the appeal of picturesque travel helped boost the region's popularity. When he ran out of stock in the early 1830s, Baedeker decided to revise the book himself (Klein had died some years earlier) and reissue it. The new version appeared in 1835.

In subsequent years, Baedeker noticed English tourists along the Rhine carrying Murray's handbook. Many came to his shop looking for Murray's guides or asking about other books on the region. That along with the success of Klein's book encouraged him to publish his own guides. His first, on the Rhine region (published in 1839), was much broader in scope than the revised version of Klein's book. Like Murray, he followed with other guides, first to Germany and Austria (1842) and then to Switzerland (1844). Baedeker freely admitted that he got the idea for his series from Murray and copied his format, general organization, and the term "handbook." In 1854 he also adopted the red covers. Baedeker added the system of rating attractions with stars, later adopted by Murray as well, and devoted more care to his maps. British travelers who read German generally thought Baedeker's guides superior, both for their maps and for their high degree of accuracy.[29]

The first American-published guidebook to Europe, directed specifically to American travelers, appeared at about the same time as Murray's and Baedeker's guides. *The Tourist in Europe,* published in New York in 1838, was aimed at less-than-wealthy travelers, arguing that one could tour Europe for "scarcely a greater sum than is often wasted in unsatisfactory pleasures."[30] It was a rather sketchy outline of the popular routes through Britain and the Continent, with recommendations for hotels and sightseeing as well as a detailed list of typical expenses. Short on details, as the author readily admitted, it offered little competition to Murray's handbooks, which became popular with American as well as British tourists.

Murray continued his series with a guide to Scandinavia and Russia (1839), pursuing his personal interest in northern Europe and his sense that there would be a market for a book aimed at those inclined to "quit the more beaten paths of southern Europe, and explore the less known, but equally romantic, regions of the north."[31] (Already there were travelers looking for spots not yet overrun with tourists.) Not until 1842 did he take on Italy. Starke had died in 1838, shortly before the last edition of her book appeared, and it was time for a new version. Murray did not attempt the job himself, but hired Sir Francis Palgrave to write a handbook for northern Italy (published in 1842) and Octavian Blewitt to prepare two additional volumes on central and southern Italy (1843 and 1853). Murray himself tackled Greece (1840) and France (1843).

Because Germans didn't travel as much as the British and tended to stay closer to home, Baedeker's market was much more limited than Murray's. As a result he turned to translations in 1846, with a French edition of the Rhineland handbook. An English translation appeared in 1861. After that point, most new handbooks appeared simultaneously in French and English as well as German.[32] Murray, on the other hand, had a huge ready-made market and never saw the need to translate his guides. The different travel habits of Germans and British probably also account for the fact that Baedeker launched his business with guides to his own country and the adjacent, culturally similar, Austria and Switzerland—his first guide to France didn't appear until 1855—while Murray started with books on foreign countries, adding handbooks to regions within England only in 1849.

The popularity of Murray and Baedeker's guides—Murray published ten different guides, some in multiple editions, by 1850—was in itself an indication of the expansion of travel in the early nineteenth century. The range of material covered in the guides and the inclusion of two- and three-week itineraries suggested the possibility, new in postwar Europe, of taking relatively short trips and visiting out-of-the-way places. In practice, however, the tradition of the grand tour died hard. Paris and Italy, the favorite destinations for generations, remained popular. Postwar grand tourists might linger in Switzerland or cruise down the Rhine, as scenery took its place alongside the cultural monuments of the great cities as a proper object of sightseeing, but otherwise, the basic outlines of a Continental tour changed little. Americans imitated the British tradition, following much the same itineraries with the obvious addition of Britain itself.[33]

PARIS CONTINUED TO be the first major destination for most travelers to the Continent, its significance heightened in the immediate postwar years by curiosity about changes wrought by the Revolution. For those who had visited before 1789, the physical changes were striking, especially in the area around the Louvre and the Tuileries. Napoleon launched an ambitious building program: He restored and extended the Louvre palace; demolished buildings between the Louvre and Tuileries to make way for a road and a triumphal arch (planned but not actually built) at the entrance to the latter; began construction of the Rue de Rivoli, a broad street lined with uniformly designed buildings linking the Louvre with the Place de la Bastille; and started work on the Arc de Triomphe at the western end of the Champs Elysées. On the eastern side of the city, he commissioned a fountain in the form of a giant elephant, with water spouting from its trunk, on the site of the Bastille. (Never completed, the momument fell apart in the 1840s and was replaced by the present column.) Napoleon also initiated several important public works: widening streets, rebuilding the quays along the Seine, building canals in an attempt to alleviate Paris's chronic water shortage, establishing a system for numbering buildings, and extending the limited sewer system.[34]

Despite Napoleon's ambitious program, however, old Paris with its congested, filthy streets still overshadowed the new Paris, as many travelers were quick to point out. In the words of Lady Sydney Morgan, visiting in 1816, "[T]he boulevards, forming a splendid belt round the narrow streets of Paris, are the girdle of Venus on a mortal form."[35] The city as a whole lacked any sense of plan or design, despite Napoleon's moves in that direction; each neighborhood was a separate enclave with its own distinctive character. To British visitors, accustomed to the broad streets and squares of London, this hodgepodge of old and new seemed unworthy of a great capital. Much of London had been rebuilt after the great fire of 1666, and massive construction in the first quarter of the nineteenth century had reshaped more of the West End, so the comparison wasn't quite fair, but even Théophile Gautier thought London compared favorably with Paris, describing it as "a capital in the sense of civilisation; all is great, splendid, disposed according to the last improvements. . . . Paris, in this respect is at least a hundred years behindhand, and, to a certain extent, must always be inferior to London." Ironically, at the very time Gautier wrote this pessimistic assessment, Louis-Napoleon, who came to power at the end of 1851, was laying plans for a reconstruction of Paris more ambitious than anything ever attempted in London. Under the direction of Baron Haussmann, Paris would be transformed in the 1850s.[36]

The Louvre itself was the biggest attraction for most postwar visitors. Originally a royal palace, by the late seventeenth century it housed most of the monarchy's enormous collection of art and sculpture built up over the previous two centuries. Under Louis XIV (who no longer lived at the Louvre but made Versailles his principal residence), the collections had been opened to the public—a policy discontinued by his successor, to much criticism. When the Revolution started, a plan was under way to create a national museum in the Louvre. The Revolutionary government appropriated the royal collections, as well as those of some government ministers, and opened the grand gallery of the Louvre as a museum in 1793. It closed within a few months, however, because the building itself was in serious need of repair. Napoleon then took up the idea of a national museum as one of his pet projects, requisitioning paintings from conquered territories and commissioning the artist Vivant Denon to create a museum in the Louvre to house these treasures of conquest as well as the best of the former royal collections. In this way Napoleon acquired more than five thousand works from Florence, Milan, Rome, Berlin, Potsdam, and Vienna, among other places. They included the Apollo Belvedere, the Venus de Medici, Raphael's *Trans-*

figuration, and Veronese's *Marriage at Cana.* Earlier, the Revolutionary government had appropriated a number of Rubens's paintings from Antwerp as well. The new museum opened on Bastille Day, 1801. In 1803, it was labeled the Musée Napoléon, a name that stuck.[37]

After Napoleon's defeat in 1815, most of the confiscated works were returned to their home cities. The exceptions included the *Marriage at Cana* (considered too cumbersome to move again) and several paintings from Florence by Giotto, Fra Angelico, and Cimabue, whose works were not much admired at the time. As a consequence, Florentine authorities did not press for their return.[38] Travelers fortunate enough to see the Musée Napoléon before its demise regretted the loss of the Italian masterpieces, but the original collection was magnificent in itself; the French kings had collected Italian Renaissance works (including several by Leonardo da Vinci, who spent his last years in France under the patronage of François I) as well as works by French, Dutch, Flemish, and German artists. Many tourists returned day after day, admiring in particular works by the painters who had helped define popular interest in picturesque landscape— Salvator Rosa, Claude Lorrain, Nicolas Poussin, and Gaspard Dughet—and works by the Italian Renaissance painters, especially Raphael, Michelangelo, Leonardo, Guido Reni, the Carracci, Correggio, and Titian.

The very idea of a public art museum open to all, free of charge, drew praise from visitors. Traditionally, works of art had been commissioned by churches, royal families, and other wealthy patrons, who often opened their private galleries only to visitors with the right sort of introduction. In transforming the Louvre into a museum, the French Revolutionary government broke with this tradition and created the first public art museum.[39] Napoleon extended this notion of art as a public trust, not only by reopening the Louvre but also by creating museums in some of the major cities under his rule, including Milan, Bologna, Venice, and several provincial cities in France. Louis Bonaparte, installed by his brother as king of Holland, established a museum in Amsterdam (later the Rijksmuseum), while King Joseph of Spain, another Bonaparte brother, created an art gallery in the Prado in Madrid.[40]

Most visitors to Paris found the social life of the city at least as interesting as its paintings and monuments. As Frances Trollope, professional traveler, caustic commentator, and mother of the novelist Anthony, remarked, sightseeing was fine for a few days, but one could become jaded quickly unless acquainted with French society.[41] For upper-class British travelers and social climbers (like Trollope, for example), this still meant presenting letters of introduction and spending evenings at Paris salons; in its outward forms, elite social life in Paris changed little after the Revolution. But the topics of conversation were likely to be quite different. Certain salons were frequented mainly by royalist sympathizers, others were republican, while still others eschewed politics for literary topics. Literary evenings were as likely to be devoted to discussing foreign writers— Shakespeare, Goethe, Schiller, Byron, and Scott were especially popular—as the French masters. A French translation of Cooper's *The Last of the Mohicans* won rave reviews, earning Cooper the label of "the American Sir Walter Scott." He and Scott, visiting Paris at the same time in the early 1820s, became the darlings of the literary salons. Even the Paris theaters, once devoted exclusively to French playwrights, added translations of British writers, notably Shakespeare, to their repertoires.[42] In part as a result of this interest in foreign literature, foreign visitors often found themselves the object of curious scrutiny, and one no longer had to be a member of the gentry or the nobility to gain entrance to a French salon.

But it was the informal social life of Paris that captivated visitors more than anything else. Parisians socialized in public more than at home, whether it was meeting friends in cafés, strolling on the Grands Boulevards or through pleasure gardens like the Jardin Mabille on the Champs Elysées, picnicking with their children in the public gardens, or attending the theater and opera. To British and American visitors, who socialized mainly in private—or, in the case of the British, at pleasure gardens like Vauxhall and Ranelagh, which by custom and the cost of their admission fees tended to stratify pleasure seekers according to class—partaking of Parisian society was at once exhilarating and unsettling. People of all social classes mingled in the shops and arcades of the Palais Royal, where gambling and prostitution flourished cheek by jowl with expensive boutiques, restaurants, and raucous entertainment, including circus performers and vaudeville acts. By the 1820s and '30s, the Palais Royal was known all over Europe as a center of decadent entertainment (so much so that the gambling rooms were closed down in the late 1830s).[43] The Grands Boulevards on the northern fringe of the city were a more respectable place to seek public entertainment. Laid out by Louis XIV on the site of the old city fortifications, the Boulevards formed the northern perimeter of Paris until the building boom of the 1820s and '30s began pushing its boundaries out to the northwest. Lined with cafés and shops as well as such curiosities as a Chinese bath, a Turkish café, and a "hindu pavilion," illuminated with gaslights at night, the Boulevards were, along with the Palais Royal, the liveliest part of Paris, where people of all social classes repaired in the evenings to promenade, take coffee and ices in the cafés, or watch the actors and musicians who were a regular part of the open-air entertainment.

Of all Paris's pleasures, the one that caused greatest comment was a relatively new one: dining in restaurants. The first restaurant was established in the mid-eighteenth century, serving simple meals billed as "restoratives" for the hungry—hence the name. But the idea didn't really catch on until the Revolution, when newly unemployed chefs from aristocratic households set up in business for themselves and the notion of people of all ranks mixing in public establishments became more generally acceptable. By Napoleon's time, Paris boasted dozens of restaurants, many of them located in and around the Palais Royal.[44] As much as British and American visitors enjoyed the cafés and promenades of Paris, the notion of dining in public struck many visitors as bizarre. (When staying in country inns, where a communal table d'hôte was the custom, British and American travelers often tried to have meals served privately, in their rooms.) Trollope remarked that it was the *public* nature of restaurant dining that made it seem so "utterly inconceivable to English feelings." For the British, privacy was a mark of "refinement" and social status. The wealthy entertained at home, at exclusive private clubs, or perhaps in a box at the opera. Only the lower classes found their entertainment in pubs. But the French actually seemed to prefer "living in public," as Trollope put it. "They are at home here," Emma Willard observed after a walk through the Tuileries gardens, while "we, of America, are at home by our own fire-sides." Much of the ambivalence about "living in public" stemmed from an exaggerated concern about protecting women. For a woman to appear in public, in a situation where one could not be certain who one's companions would be, bordered on impropriety in the eyes of upper-class British and Americans alike. It is no coincidence that the equivalent British institutions, coffee houses and public houses, were male preserves. No respectable woman would have dreamed of entering one. If one attempted to open a restaurant catering to women as well as men in London, it would quickly be taken over by a rowdy sort and would be utterly unfit for "ladies" within a week, Trollope thought. In Paris, by contrast, people of different classes mingled at the new restaurants with "deference and good breeding."[45]

Even so, British and American visitors quickly adopted the custom of dining out, although Cooper steadfastly refused to believe that the women he saw in restaurants were respectable members of society. "One feels at first as if it were a transgression," an American woman wrote, "but after a while this subsides into a feeling of agreeable abandon, unalloyed by any sense of naughtiness, and dinner at a restaurant becomes one of the natural events of a Paris day." Among other considerations, meals were cheap, and this generation of travelers was coming to appreciate French cuisine. Cooper, for one, enjoyed French cooking so much that he felt a bit guilty about taking such pleasure in something so mundane as one's daily bread; but then, he rationalized, "no one is the worse for a knowledge of what is agreeable to the palate." Even the smallest and rudest country inns were likely to produce a good meal, he discovered; "French cookery can even get the better of French dirt."[46]

In the late twentieth century, when Americans routinely breakfast on croissants and one can order "un sandwich" in any café in Paris, it is hard to imagine that early-nineteenth-century British and American travelers experienced culture shock on visiting Paris. But the differences were so profound that many Anglo-American travelers left Paris feeling deeply ambivalent about France and the French. On the most superficial level, Paris seemed to be a society given over to entertainment and sensuous pleasures, "an earthly Elysium," as

Bayard Taylor put it. Or as Harriet Beecher Stowe observed, "French life is different from any other. Elsewhere you do as the world pleases; here you do as you please yourself."[47] The hedonistic side of French life drew fire from many visitors, yet they couldn't help being captivated by it, by what Taylor characterized as the Parisians' "exuberant gaiety of spirit" and what seemed an almost innate sense of beauty, even among sometimes squalid conditions. Stowe remarked that "a poor family will give, cheerfully, a part of their bread money to buy a flower." Moreover, although the Parisians might seem frivolous, playful to a fault, too forward in their manners, and too open in their speech, even the most jaundiced visitors admitted that they were invariably charming, and never rude or offensive.[48]

For British visitors in the 1820s and '30s, of course, it was difficult to set aside a history of political enmity between Britain and France. The French Revolution and the Napoleonic Wars, only the most recent in a long series of conflicts with France, were still a recent memory. Cultural differences took on a political cast. It was not just that Britain and France were historically enemies but that the British and French had radically different views about revolution, monarchy, the proper form of government, religion, and the nature of a well-ordered society (with all due allowance for differences along the political spectrum in both countries, of course). Most British citizens viewed their own revolution of the mid-seventeenth century as a minor aberration supplanted by a revival of monarchy in a strengthened form—a mix of constitutionality and well-ordered stability superior to any system in the world. Revolution in France, in contrast, had produced only violence and instability. Subsequent political upheavals in the first half of the nineteenth century, beginning with the abdication of the king after a short-lived revolution in 1830 and ending with a coup d'état led by Napoleon's nephew Louis-Napoleon (the future Napoleon III), in 1851, only seemed to confirm the folly of violent revolution.

To the British, social stability and political stability were inseparable and depended on the maintenance of a clearly defined class structure characterized by specific canons of behavior and an understanding of one's "place" in the hierarchy—a system that was beginning to unravel by the 1820s in the face of dramatic economic change and pressure for political reform. Thus British travelers confronted the apparent easy mingling of social classes in Paris, quite literally a revolutionary concept to them, at precisely the time that they felt more constrained to reassert boundaries between social classes at home. Theirs was an imperfect view of French society, to be sure, and they were likely to exaggerate the mixing of social classes; but it was perceptions that mattered, and British visitors perceived that French society, in the wake of the Revolution, ignored those distinctions that helped maintain the social fabric. And yet they couldn't deny that the French pulled it off, without the sort of vulgar public behavior characteristic of lower-class British mobs, and that they all seemed to enjoy themselves immensely.

Many Americans were nearly as ambivalent about French culture as the British but for quite different reasons. They lacked the British class consciousness and abhorrence of revolution; on the contrary, most of them applauded the French Revolution and all subsequent efforts toward creating and re-creating republican government. Visitors in the early nineteenth century were still close enough to their own revolution to recall with gratitude the importance of French support in winning American independence (and to retain a touch of animosity toward the British, despite a common cultural heritage). Lafayette, leader of the French forces in the American Revolution, lived until 1834, becoming president of the short-lived republic established in the wake of the uprising in 1830. He often entertained American visitors to Paris, among them James Fenimore Cooper and Emma Willard, both of whom counted him as a good friend. Far from deploring French tendencies toward revolution and republicanism, Americans more often commented negatively on the ever-present police and military forces (throughout Europe as well as in Paris), which were to them ominous signs of arbitrary rule.

American criticism of French culture focused on religion and morals, not politics. Most American visitors were Protestants of evangelical leanings, accustomed to plain churches and simple services. They criticized the lavish ornamentation of many Catholic churches and the showiness of Catholic liturgy, as well as the French custom of devoting Sunday to amusement rather than churchgoing and quiet family gatherings. Criticism of Catholic worship extended itself to French society in general. For some Americans, Willard being a notable example, everything about Paris was too showy, too elaborate, too busy in comparison with what she and others perceived as the simplicity of American life. She contrasted the elegantly dressed crowds in Paris with the "real, enduring happiness [of] the faces of the throng, who issue from the door of a New-England church" and professed to prefer her work at home to the distractions of Parisian society because it gave her a sense of purpose that she found lacking among the Parisians.[49] And yet Willard loved the excitement of Paris, rubbing shoulders with the famous; she was presented to the queen, attended royal balls, and visited Lafayette's soirées regularly, all with obvious relish. Her ambivalence was shared by many Americans— going back to Abigail Adams, who had spent several months in Paris in 1784, constantly criticizing the French for being dirty and morally lax, always wishing herself back in New England at her simple home and humble fireside, all the while enjoying herself immensely amid the novelty of life in a foreign capital.

France beyond Paris held little charm for the postwar tourists, despite their generation's interest in landscape. Although Murray's guide to France extolled the beauties of Normandy, Brittany, and much of central and southwestern France, most travelers stuck to the traditional routes, rushing through France as quickly as possible to get to Switzerland and Italy. Those who traveled down the Rhone to the Mediterranean en route to Italy might linger briefly in Provence, at the Roman ruins and the sites associated with the Renaissance poet Petrarch, but otherwise they found the landscape bleak and uninteresting. Rural France, whether it was the arid hills of Provence or the vineyards of Burgundy, did not live up to early-nineteenth-century expectations of pastoral beauty. Accustomed to the highly cultivated fields and hedgerows and well-kept gardens of England, British travelers were bored by the unchanging quality of the French countryside and put off by its dirty and dilapidated villages. There were none of the "lovely and picturesque hamlets" of southern England, or "snug farm houses," or handsome "gentlemen's seats surrounded with parks and noble trees," no flower gardens or lawns or neatly trimmed hedges.[50]

Cooper realized that what made the French countryside uninteresting to Anglo-American eyes, besides the sameness of the terrain, was the poverty of rural France. No doubt there was poverty in England as well, he wrote, "but it is kept surprisingly out of the ordinary view." Even the famed French vineyards were a disappointment; Caroline St. Clair, the heroine of Charlotte Eaton's fictional travel account, *Continental Adventures,* declares that she imagined a vineyard as "the most beautiful and luxuriant object in the world," but found it instead merely "a dirty-looking field, planted with little low vines, like stunted currant bushes."[51]

Switzerland, on the other hand, gained enormously in popularity among postwar tourists. With its lakes, tidy villages, rolling hills and distant mountains, the area around Geneva fulfilled all the requirements of the picturesque, providing a welcome interlude between the mostly urban attractions of Paris and Italy. Cooper summed up the views of many when he wrote, "It was a great relief to be fairly rid of the monotony of French husbandry, and of the fatiguing plains, for a nature that in a great degree defied the labour of man" and houses which, "though still wanting in neatness, became picturesque and rural in their forms, ingredients in a landscape in which most of France is greatly deficient." Or, as Caroline St. Clair put it, "Going from France to Switzerland is like passing through purgatory to get to paradise."[52]

Geneva and environs were also rich in the literary associations prized by nineteenth-century travelers. Voltaire's home at Ferney and the villages made famous by Rousseau's novel *La Nouvelle Heloïse* continued to be popular attractions. Contemporary writers had their devotees as well, as travelers visited the thirteenth-century Castle of Chillon near Montreux on Lake Geneva, celebrated in Byron's poem *The Prisoner of Chillon;* the house where Shelley had lived in Geneva; and the little village of Coppet, birthplace of Madame de Staël, whose novel *Corinne, or Italy* (published in 1807) rivaled the works of Byron and Rousseau in popularity. Indeed, nineteenth-century travelers departed from their predecessors in the enthusiasm, bordering on hero worship, they displayed for sites associated with their favorite authors.[53] Like Wordsworth and Scott, writers like Rousseau, Byron, and the Renaissance Italian poets became cult figures among many travelers.

The taste for the picturesque that contributed so much to Switzerland's popularity created new interest in the Rhineland as well. The Rhine River between Mainz and Cologne, long popular with German tourists, offered all the requirements of picturesque beauty with a touch of the Gothic thrown in, as travelers floated slowly along the sinuous course of the river past countless ancient castles and ruins perched on wooded hilltops overlooking the water. By the end of the 1820s, steamships plied the river on regular schedules, making it easy and comfortable to add the Rhine to a Continental tour. For British tourists it became a popular route home from Italy and Switzerland.

ITALY CONTINUED TO be the premier destination for postwar grand tourists, as it had been for generations of travelers before them. Preparing to cross the Alps, Frances Trollope declared that she had never felt such a sense of anticipation in all her travels—which had included several visits to Paris as well as tours of Belgium, the Rhine, and the United States.[54] In the 1780s, Goethe had written that he felt all the cares of everyday life fall away as he crossed the Alps. Nearly forty years later, Cooper called Italy "the only region of the earth I truly love," saying that it "haunts my dreams and clings to my ribs," while the French writer Stendhal spent much of his adult life either living in Italy or scheming about ways to get there.[55]

Although history and art remained an important part of Italy's appeal, the sensual qualities of Mediterranean life that had so appealed to Boswell and Goethe became even more captivating to nineteenth-century visitors. There was the climate, of course, with its warm winters and brilliantly sunny days, a welcome contrast to the gray, cloudy skies and damp air of northern winters.[56] There were the splendid old cities, hardly touched by modernity, and the extraordinary beauty and variety of the landscape, with its heightened sense of light and color. Perhaps most appealing of all were the Italians themselves, who, like the French, seemed to value pleasure over work—they "appear disposed to make a *siesta* of life, and to enjoy the passing moment," Cooper thought—but without the superficiality and questionable moral values that many British and American critics professed to find in the French. The Italians seemed spontaneous and genuine, with a direct, unaffected manner that contrasted sharply with the rigid conventions of British society. Stendhal, captivated by "that aggregate of singular and ingrained preferences for love, for pleasure, for solitude, for plain speaking," thought the secret of happiness among the people of Milan (where he spent much of his time) was that they did most things because they wanted to, not out of a sense of duty, whereas among the British, it was precisely the opposite.[57]

Stendhal was unusual in that he lived in Italy over a period of several years, spoke the language well, and made a serious effort to assimilate himself into Italian society. The more typical early-nineteenth-century travelers, on the other hand, spent much of their time with other tourists, even more so than in the prewar years. Their view of Italian people and culture, as a consequence, was a highly idealized one shaped more by the vision of Italy depicted in the works of writers like Goethe and Byron than by concrete experience. One of the works they quoted most often, Madame de Staël's novel *Corinne,* provides probably the clearest statement of the qualities in Italian culture dear to foreign visitors. Driven from France in 1803 because Napoleon considered her writings subversive, de Staël spent several years in Italy, finding there much the same kind of personal and artistic freedom that so attracted Stendhal. Weaving what she saw as the essential qualities of the Italian character into a rather improbable tearjerker of a plot, she tried to convey the essence of "her" Italy to her readers.

The novel-cum-travelogue tells the story of a love affair between Corinne (modeled on the poet and priestess of Apollo in classical Greece), an Englishwoman who spent most of her life in Italy, and Oswald, an English aristocrat touring Italy in part to get over the traumatic death of his father. Oswald falls in love with Corinne practically at first sight, captivated by her artistic talent—this twenty-six-year-old paragon was renowned throughout Rome as a poet and improvisator who could also paint, sing, and act—her brilliant conversation, her open and sincere manners, and her unselfish devotion to her friends. Yet he is disturbed by hints of a dark past and a sense of obligation to his dead father, who, Oswald fears, would not have approved of Corinne, precisely because she shines in society rather than devoting herself to family and domestic matters. He is also puzzled by Corinne's apparent lack of concern with appearances and propriety: She travels freely with him and visits his house, alone, to care for him when he falls sick. When Oswald frets that she has "compromised" herself forever by her generous act, she has some trouble assuring him that such niceties are of little concern in Italy. Her explanation disappoints him, not because he disapproves of Italian morals but because, had her reputation indeed been compromised, it would be his "duty" to marry her, which would put an end to his agonizing indecision.[58]

Corinne—and Italy—represent art, love, unselfish devotion, and disdain for restrictive social conventions (not to mention an independent status for women, an important subtext in the novel); Oswald, and England, represent duty to family and an excessive concern for proper behavior. De Staël does not confine her gentle criticism to English customs, however—a French aristocrat traveling with Oswald is equally shocked at Corinne's easy manners, assuring Oswald that, in French society, appearances are everything.

Corinne was an enormous success as soon as it was published. Along with Byron's *Childe Harold's Pilgrimage* and Samuel Rogers's long poem *Italy* (first published in 1822, but best known in a lavish 1830 edition, illustrated with engravings by J.M.W. Turner), it helped create a romanticized image of Italy that shaped the expectations of thousands of travelers. Perhaps surprisingly, few seem to have been disappointed. Not that visitors to Italy were uncritical; they blasted the dirt, poverty, indolence, and ill effects of Catholicism in Italy as they did in France.[59] (American visitors, more than British, dwelt on the poverty they observed, contrasting it with the comfortable living standards of their own country, and were distressed throughout Italy, as in France, by the constant presence of the military.)[60]

But such comments were sporadic and muted. Even those who were initially negative came around quickly. During his first few days in Genoa, Charles Dickens observed that "the unusual smells, the unaccountable filth . . . the disorderly jumbling of dirty houses . . .

the disheartening dirt, discomfort, and decay; perfectly confounded me"; but Genoa "grows upon you," he admitted, and he soon came to love the unending variety of the city and "the Pink Jail"—his affectionate name for the ramshackle old house he and his family rented. Other travelers glossed over the inconveniences of Italian country inns, stressing instead their good points: the simple but well-prepared food and the kindness of the proprietors. One English-woman, for example, while noting the exceedingly "primitive" manners of the people she encountered crossing the Apennines, de-clared that "their morals [are] so pure, their affections so warm, and their language so artless and unrestrained, that they seemed as if just fresh from the hand of the Creator in the beginning of the world!"[61]

British travelers readily overlooked (or explained away) condi-tions in Italy similar to those they criticized in France partly be-cause of their highly idealized preconceptions, which romanticized even the poverty of rural villages. In addition, the vastly different positions of Italy and France in the European world order of the early nineteenth century influenced travelers' differing reactions to the two countries. Italy was valued for its past; in the present, it was viewed as a society in decline, a mere collection of minor principal-ities.[62] The Italians inspired sympathy as a people oppressed, whether by the Papacy, Austria, Sardinia, or one of several petty dukedoms. The French, on the other hand, were politically unstable revolution-aries whose government seesawed back and forth between monarchy and dictatorship. Travelers blamed the Italians' poverty and disin-clination to work on corrupt governments—which exercised arbi-trary rule and taxed their subjects excessively—and on the Catholic Church, which siphoned off money from the people to support an excessive number of priests and decorate already overly decorated churches. Given such poor examples and lack of incentive, visitors reasoned, the ordinary Italian could hardly be expected to better him-self.[63]

Some American visitors in the 1840s, notably Catherine Maria Sedgwick, Margaret Fuller, and Julia Ward Howe, became ac-quainted with Italian revolutionaries exiled to the United States and visited their families and friends while in Europe. Fuller married an

Italian partisan, Giovanni Angelo Ossoli, and became deeply involved in the movement for Italian independence; she became known
as "the Italian Corinne" (after the classical Corinne, not de Staël's
character) for her championing of the Italian cause.[64] Later in the
century, the movement for Italian independence and unification
would be taken up as a cause célèbre in England, and its leader,
Garibaldi, would become a popular hero.

The typical itinerary through Italy remained much as it had been
in the eighteenth century: Florence, Rome, and Naples were the favored destinations, and classical ruins and Renaissance art the main
attractions, although in Italy as in Switzerland, pilgrimages to sites
associated with favorite writers became increasingly popular. In
Genoa, for example, Byron's home remained a popular tourist attraction for decades.[65] On the whole, however, the cities of the north
merited only brief visits as travelers hastened to Florence. Cooper
described the Apennines as "the barrier of mountains that separates
the Upper from the Lower, the false from the true Italy"—and while
others were less dramatic in their comments, the notion that Italy
north of Florence was somehow secondary, less interesting, a place
to be gotten through on the way to the "real" Italy, was widespread.[66]

If Rome was the focus of the eighteenth-century grand tour, Florence became increasingly popular in the nineteenth century—especially with the British, who took to settling in for several weeks
during the winter, spending leisurely days visiting the art galleries
and their fellow tourists. Over time, Florence took on something of
the status of a winter resort, as visitors came to see the city more as
a pleasant escape than as a mecca for lovers of art. By the 1840s,
the annual British invasion had become so massive that Florence
supported an English church, newspaper, and reading room stocked
with London newspapers. The British also re-created their own style
of social life, from morning calls at each other's rented flats to horse
racing.[67] American visitors, far outnumbered by the British in the
early nineteenth century, gravitated to the tiny community of American artists, the most famous of whom were the sculptor Horatio
Greenough, who took up permanent residence in Florence in the
1820s (after some time in Rome), and Thomas Cole, one of the foun-

ders of the Hudson River school of landscape painting, who spent several years in Florence and Rome in the 1830s.[68]

The boundary between Tuscany and the Papal States proved almost as sharp a divide for travelers heading on to Rome as the Apennines did to the north. The landscape farther south seemed barren and uninteresting compared to Tuscany, and the people so poor that one might almost think them "a backward race," in Trollope's words. She and other travelers invariably blamed the Papal government, the most corrupt among all the Italian states, they believed, because it combined the evils of despotic rule with the evils of Catholicism. Even Rome itself could be disappointing at first. Rising from a flat plain, the city skyline was unprepossessing; it reminded Dickens of London, with its towers, steeples, expanse of roofs, and "one great dome." Within the city itself, squalid houses and narrow, dirty streets were bunched up cheek by jowl with magnificent public buildings, what William Hazlitt called "the contrast of pig-styes and palaces." In the older sections of the city, streets were so narrow and buildings so tall that little light penetrated the unpaved, muddy passageways, which never quite dried out after winter rains. St. Peter's, reputedly the most magnificent building in Rome, if not in all of Italy, appeared smaller than many visitors expected and rather unchurchlike in its architecture and decoration. Indeed, so many travelers expressed their disappointment in St. Peter's that Sedgwick felt obliged to write in one of her letters home, "We have been to St. Peter's, and are *not* disappointed. The great works of nature and art always surpassed my expectations."[69]

Ancient Rome, however, had not lost its power to impress, especially the Colosseum, "the ghost of old Rome," as Dickens called it. Here, Sedgwick wrote, "you first fully realize that you are in Rome— ancient Rome; that you are treading the ground Caesar, Cicero, and Brutus trod." ("A noble wreck in ruinous perfection" was the more irreverent judgment of another young American tourist.) What seemed to bother the critics was the encroachment of modern Rome on the ancient city. Hazlitt complained about the warehouses, restaurants, and shops in the old parts of the city, and about the "almost uninterrupted succession of narrow, vulgar-looking streets, where the smell of garlick prevails over the odour of antiquity." Modern Rome was not nearly so impressive as other modern cities, he thought; its setting unimpressive, its museums not so fine as the Louvre, St. Peter's not so grand as St. Paul's. It was the ancient city that was important, and the ancient city was being overwhelmed by modern expansion.[70]

Hostility toward the Catholic Church did not stop Protestant travelers from visiting the Vatican art collections and observing all the ceremonies during Christmas and Easter weeks—Dickens estimated that three fourths of the crowd at the Easter service he attended was British. Here, even more than in other parts of Italy, the contrast between the richly ornamented churches and the poverty of the people struck visitors, especially Americans, as a moral outrage. If the opportunity offered to witness the ceremony of a young novice taking the veil, they went to that too, clucking their tongues about the tragedy of a young woman renouncing the world before she was old enough to make a rational decision. (Sedgwick, however, was not surprised that "in a country where the alternative is, for the most part, between vice and vacuity, a woman should choose to give a religious colour to the latter.")[71]

There were, of course, other attractions: collections of painting and sculpture to rival those of Florence; the house where Claude Lorrain had lived (inhabited in the late 1820s by two American artists, John Vanderlyn and Horatio Greenough); the grave of the sixteenth-century poet Tasso; and a flourishing contemporary artists' colony, which attracted painters and sculptors from all over Europe as well as the United States. It was enough to keep people in Rome several weeks, aided by the pleasures of a social life that focused on other tourists, as in Florence. In Rome, foreign visitors tended to congregate in a single neighborhood, to the point that it became known as the "ghetto degli Inglesi"—"Inglesi" having become a general term for all foreign travelers.[72]

As travelers continued south to Naples, many observed that poverty appeared to increase the farther south they went—the land barely cultivated despite the favorable climate, the people barefoot and dressed in rags. "Begging stares the traveller in the face," Irving wrote. "He sees a perfect Canaan around him and the inhabitants starving in the midst of it." Throughout Italy, travelers were confronted with the contrast between the remnants of a great civilization and the corruption and poverty of the present—especially in Rome and Naples, where Irving saw "the works of former ages—magnificent in their ruins—reproaching the nation with its degeneracy."[73] Naples's major attraction for travelers was its spectacular seaside setting and seductive winter climate. It was a place to relax and savor the lovely surroundings before starting the long trip home, often by way of Venice and some of the northern Italian cities made famous by their associations with writers and artists.

In Ferrara, they visited the home of the Renaissance poet Ariosto, author of the famous epic *Orlando Furioso,* and chipped away fragments from the wall of the dungeon where Tasso had been imprisoned; in Arqua, near Padua, they visited the house where Petrarch had died, and observed, upon perusing the guest book, that Byron had been there too. Some made the pilgrimage to Dante's tomb in Ravenna. At Verona they visited Juliet's tomb and perhaps, like Dickens, reread Shakespeare's play.[74] In Venice they viewed the paintings of Titian, Tintoretto, and Veronese and toured, often with a kind of morbid fascination, the relics of the Inquisition: the Doge's palace with the narrow slits in its walls for depositing anonymous denunciations and the chamber where the infamous Council of Ten made its decisions, the Bridge of Sighs, and the dungeons. They admired the palaces along the Grand Canal and drank coffee in the evenings at the café Florian on the Piazza San Marco. But Venice, despite its charm, seemed to most travelers a decaying city, no longer the equal of Florence and Rome. "Indeed," Dickens remarked, "it seemed a very wreck found drifting on the sea."[75] Few visitors spent more than a week or two there before heading north to recross the Alps.

ALTHOUGH INCREASING numbers of travelers ventured beyond the well-worn routes by the middle of the nineteenth century, their numbers remained small compared with the legions of tourists in Paris, Florence, Rome, Switzerland, and the Rhineland. It was not yet fashionable to seek out little-traveled destinations, despite the occasional complaint about overcrowding, and for good reason: Travel in the remoter parts of Europe, not to mention places farther afield, remained slow, uncomfortable, and unpredictable until well into the nineteenth century. The Pyrenees might be as grand as the Alps, a point made by Mary Boddington, an Englishwoman who toured southwestern France and Spain in the 1820s, but roads throughout the region were poor at a time when one could travel through most of Switzerland in four-wheeled comfort, and the accommodations available were as primitive as the roads.[76] Moreover, for most early-nineteenth-century tourists, visiting the "right" places and socializing with their fellows were an important part of traveling. By the 1830s and '40s, the grand tour came to have not only a standard itinerary, but a standard schedule. British tourists making the complete circuit typically left early in the fall and spent several weeks in Paris and Switzerland, crossing the Alps no later than mid-October. After touring northern Italy, they spent November in Florence (the time of year when Sedgwick thought the city became "an English colony"), moved on to Rome in time for Christmas, and then continued south to pass the rest of the winter in Naples. Then it was back to Rome for Easter, on to Venice and the rest of northern Italy, and back across the Alps late in the spring, in time to spend part of the summer in Switzerland or on the Rhine.

These peregrinations took on the character of seasonal migrations, as everyone tended to move from one place to the next within a few days of one another. An innkeeper on the Rhine told William Thackeray early in the 1850s that his season always ended abruptly. One night he might have eighty or ninety guests and the next night ten. "We do as our neighbors do," Thackeray remarked. "Though we don't speak to each other much when we are out a-pleasuring, we take our holiday in common, and go back to our work in gangs." By the 1840s, the notion of wintering in Italy became fashionable with Americans as well, especially wealthy Bostonians seeking escape from cold winters. Far from being annoyed by the hordes of tourists in every town they visited, British travelers seemed to revel in it, spending much of their time calling on each other. They simply packed up their London social life and took it with them. "It would appear that they travel not so much for the purpose of studying the manners of other lands," the Countess of Blessington observed, "as for that of establishing and displaying their own."[77]

Such clannishness and predictable habits inevitably gave rise to criticism directed at British tourists. Outsiders remarked on the British tendency to stick together, ostentatiously criticizing anything that struck them as too "foreign." While living in Venice in the 1830s, the French writer George Sand remarked that the British seemed to travel as if insulated by "the British fluid," impervious to everything around them, concerned mainly with preserving their own comfort and decorum.[78] American travelers, not yet numerous enough to become the butt of jokes themselves, also liked to poke fun at the British. Washington Irving, for example, wrote a series of tales (published in 1824) about the mythical Mr. Popkins, a London alderman, and his family, who traveled about Italy in their comfortable carriage, "an epitome of England; a little morsel of the old island rolling about the world. Every thing about it compact, snug, finished, and fitting, . . . looking down from their heights with contempt on all the world around; profoundly ignorant of the country and the people, and devoutly certain that every thing not English must be wrong."[79]

As much as they liked to think of themselves as different, however, American travelers on the Continent were usually taken for British—naturally enough, since British travelers vastly outnumbered them and the United States was still little known among most Europeans. A Frenchman talking with Washington Irving couldn't quite place America, thinking it must be near Asia or Africa. Bayard Taylor, who traveled cheaply and therefore met more peasants and working-class people than most travelers, discovered that many of them "imagine we are a savage race, without intelligence and almost without law." Others thought the United States was part of Britain, as Sedgwick discovered when she tried to explain to an Italian that she was American, not English. "Ah—no," the man replied, "but English Americans—all the same." Later in the nineteenth century, when Americans were better known, Charles Dudley Warner found he had a choice between being a despised Englishman or a rich American—with the attendant risks of being overcharged.[80]

The British themselves took aim at their fellow tourists, usually for being loud and ill-mannered—in short, for giving their countrymen a bad name. While traveling along the Rhine, Trollope was embarrassed by a woman who ostentatiously refused to eat the food in a German inn, criticizing the table because it lacked salt spoons, and by a group of young men who rudely declined an invitation to join the table d'hôte, asserting that they never dined in public. Dickens was bemused by a family who seemed to be everywhere in Rome during Easter week, visiting the sights without seeming to absorb anything, talking incessantly. Blessington, Hazlitt, Murray, and many others deplored the national tendency to complain about everything that wasn't British, and urged their readers to leave their prejudices behind (advice that none of them entirely succeeded in adopting for themselves). "The first thing an Englishman does on going abroad is to find fault with what is French, because it is not English," Hazlitt observed. "If he is determined to confine all excellence to his own country, he had better stay at home."[81]

The British were infamous for their disrespectful behavior in Italian churches, viewing them solely as tourist attractions rather than places of worship. Several travelers observed thoughtless visitors munching sandwiches and even popping champagne corks during services. At one point during the 1820s, the pope felt compelled to issue an appeal against using St. Peter's as a fashionable promenade, and Stendhal claimed that the museum in Naples had to be closed before the customary British dinner hour because drunken tourists sometimes became so rowdy that they threatened to damage the statues.[82]

Apart from the champagne corks, none of these accusations was new in the 1820s and '30s—the eighteenth-century grand tourists had often been criticized for traveling in packs and absorbing little of what they saw—nor would they be the last to come in for such criticism. In future generations, similar charges would be leveled at Americans, Germans, Japanese—whatever group was perceived to be the richest and most numerous among foreign travelers at the time. What was different in the mid-nineteenth century, however, was the tone of some British travelers' criticism of their fellows. Critics often depicted rude tourists as people of less than the highest class, as Trollope did when she blamed the negative reputation of the British abroad entirely on a new breed of middle-class travelers— the people who "every year scramble abroad for a few weeks, instead of spending their money at Margate or Brighton."[83] Such men and women enjoyed calling attention to themselves, Trollope believed, unlike the "respectable class" of people, and so it wasn't surprising that foreigners equated the more obstreperous tourists with the British nation as a whole. Her elitism—interesting coming from one who was herself only middle-class—begs the question of the behavior of wealthy young gentlemen traveling abroad two and three generations earlier, but Trollope did make one astute observation in remarking that Britain was the only country in Europe prosperous enough to have a substantial population of tradesmen and professionals who could afford to travel abroad. As a result, she argued, Continental residents assumed that every Briton they encountered must be of high social standing. Indeed, it was just this point that most annoyed Trollope and others like her.

Middle-class travelers were criticized also because they were viewed as social climbers. Upwardly mobile families trying to pass themselves off as aristocracy, or perhaps make good matches for their daughters, became subjects for satirical fiction. Trollope herself wrote *The Robertses on Their Travels,* a cautionary tale about a family that comes to ruin after trying to rise above its station by moving to Paris, where they think the living is cheaper. Charlotte Eaton's *Continental Adventures,* in which the heroine goes from one potential love affair to the next, seeing a few sights along the way, features among its characters Miss Biddy Blossom, a middle-aged spinster who talks incessantly, snubs a member of the nobility, and then, upon learning his rank, proceeds to make a fool of herself by dogging his heels for the next several days. Thackeray's Mrs. Kicklebury, traveling up the Rhine with her family, several servants, and an immense quantity of luggage, talks constantly about making good matches for her daughters.[84]

Under the veneer of satire, such stories reflected the social changes in travel evident by the 1830s and 1840s. Anyone with enough money could take lodgings in Paris or Rome; on the roads in between, all stayed at the same inns, regardless of their personal wealth, for they had no choice. Some upper-middle-class families did in fact live on the Continent for extended periods as a way of living well at lower cost, and, in the more fluid social setting of a foreign capital, many sought to gain entry to families that would have been closed to them at home.[85] The British tried to re-create their society while abroad, class barriers and all, but it was impossible to succeed entirely. Nor was it possible to stem the tide of travelers to the Continent.

IN THE SECOND half of the nineteenth century, the construction of railroads cut travel time and costs so dramatically—far more than the improvements in roads and coach services of the late eighteenth and early nineteenth centuries—that any thought of limiting the grand tour, or any other form of travel for that matter, to a select few vanished forever. The first signs of this revolution were already apparent by the 1840s, when railroad construction in Britain, northern Europe, and the United States was well under way.

The first wholly steam-powered railroad, and the first to carry significant numbers of passengers, opened in 1830 between Liverpool and Manchester, cutting the travel time between those cities in half. Over the next decade, railroad lines connected London with Birmingham, Greenwich, Southampton, and Bristol. Expansion proceeded haphazardly in England, because railroads were built by private companies chartered by Parliament without any kind of centralized planning, in much the same fashion that turnpikes had been built earlier. By the mid-1840s, with a little over two thousand miles of track in use, there were over one hundred separate railway companies, most of them quite small; only eleven had more than fifty miles of track. During the late 1840s and early 1850s, however, many of these companies consolidated, and by mid-century a national railway network was in place, with seventy-five hundred miles connecting most of the major towns and cities in England.[86]

France at first followed a similar system, with rather less success. By 1837, nearly ten years after France's first railway line opened, only about one hundred miles of track were in use, all of it around Lyons or the mouth of the Rhone, all devoted mainly to carrying freight. When the first line from Paris began operations that summer, connecting the capital with the suburb of Saint-Germain-en-Laye just a few miles away, it created a sensation. More than 37,000 passengers rode the train in its first week, and almost 60,000 the following week. This was the first segment of a government-proposed network that would extend outward from Paris like the fingers of a hand, connecting the capital with Orléans, Tours, Marseilles, Rouen, and the Belgian frontier. In 1842, the government adopted a more elaborate scheme for a national railroad network; within a year, the first lines, Paris–Rouen and Paris–Orléans, were in operation. Further development proceeded slowly, however, hampered by a serious recession in 1846–47 and the revolution of 1848. Under the highly centralized and authoritarian government of Louis-Napoleon, who came to power in 1851, railroad construction proceeded more rapidly, and the many small railroad companies were consolidated into six, each controlling one major region of the country. Although the basic French rail network wasn't completed until about 1870, the routes most often traversed by tourists (notably Paris–Lyons–Marseilles) were completed by the mid-1850s.[87]

Belgium, Holland, and the German states also engaged in ambitious construction programs in the 1830s and 1840s. By the early 1850s, lines crossed Belgium from Antwerp to the French border and from Ostend to Germany; Amsterdam and Rotterdam were linked with Cologne, and Cologne with Hamburg, Berlin, Leipzig, Dresden, Nuremberg, Munich, Prague, and Vienna. Other lines ran south along the Rhine from Frankfurt to Freiburg and Stuttgart to Lake Constance. Farther south, on the other hand, railroad development lagged until the 1860s. The fragmented, decentralized governments of Switzerland and Italy made it extremely difficult to cooperate on such expensive and complex projects. Moreover, these were poor regions, without significant industry, and therefore lacking the incentives that pushed Britain, France, and Germany into railroad construction—the need to move freight more efficiently through mining and industrial districts. Difficult terrain in many parts of both countries only magnified the problems.[88]

Even so, the railroad network that covered much of northern and central Europe by mid-century simplified travel to a remarkable degree. The early trains were at least twice as fast as the best intercity coach services, and up to four times as fast in areas where roads were poor. Fares were somewhat lower than coach fares initially, a deliberate policy adopted by railroads to encourage passenger traffic. Later, as railroad lines expanded and passenger traffic increased, fares dropped still more. For the long-distance traveler, the railroads' speed in itself saved money by requiring fewer nights on the road. As a result, railroads gradually drove long-distance coaching services out of business. On the Liverpool–Manchester route, for example, twenty-nine coaches dropped to four within five months after a railroad opened between those cities.[89]

Early entrepreneurs, expecting the rails to be used more for carriage of goods than people, were surprised to find that passenger traffic accounted for half or more of their revenue from an early date, as the speed and economy of railroads encouraged many more people to travel. After a line opened in northern England between Newcastle and Carlisle in 1838, for example, the trains very quickly carried eleven times as many people as had traveled the route by coach. In Britain as a whole, passenger volume multiplied twentyfold between 1840 and 1870.[90]

The great bulk of this new traffic came from the middle and lower classes. Although the earliest British trains offered only two classes of service, on the assumption that poor people didn't travel, third-class cars soon became more common and were required by law on at least one train per day on every line after 1844. Continental trains provided at least two and sometimes three classes of service.[91] Although coach services had offered different levels of speed and comfort as well, with mail coaches and diligences, and inside and outside seats, the cost of even the cheapest form of coach transit had been beyond the means of many.

The very fact that railroads made it easier for people of lesser means to travel drew mixed reactions. There was much concern among wealthy Britons that railroads would make it too easy for people to move around and would therefore tend to weaken social distinctions. Many factory owners thought it was a waste of time for workers to travel even short distances from home. Evangelical Protestants and social conservatives pressured railroad companies not to run trains on Sundays, although the forces for moral order were soon outweighed by the railroads' concern for profit. Others applauded the possibilities for peaceful social integration. After the revolution of 1830 in France, some pro-republican forces advocated railroad expansion as a means of uniting people of all classes in peaceful industrial progress.[92] In Britain, some reform-minded politicians and industrialists espoused similar ideas, arguing that travel increased one's understanding of others and therefore promoted toleration and peace, although most railroad advocates emphasized the more practical benefits of occasional interludes in the country for urban workers. "Railways are everywhere contributing to the recreation and health of all classes, by removing them in the intervals of labour from the confinement of streets and lanes to the fresh air and verdure of the country," one writer announced in the mid-1840s. An 1845 report of the Board of Trade on the expansion of railroads argued that railroads benefited workers by helping maintain family ties through more frequent visits to relatives, making it easier to move to other areas in search of work, and "excursions for innocent and healthy recreation on holidays."[93]

The railroads' impact on the experience of travel also inspired a wide range of comment. There were those who delighted in the new technology, among them Karl Baedeker, who described to his father his first train trip (in 1838): "A bell indicates the start and the locomotive begins to groan and the wheels revolve first slowly and then faster and faster, and then faster and faster, and then the train flies with its twenty-three to thirty coaches. What fun traveling is now!" The English actress and writer Fanny Kemble, at age twenty-one, was one of the first people to ride the Liverpool–Manchester railroad in 1830. She marveled at the speed and smoothness of the train, and especially at "the little engine," which she described as a "snorting little animal, which I felt rather inclined to pat."[94]

Others disliked the faster pace. Just as many people in the twentieth century feel uncomfortable traveling by airplane because of a sense of disconnection from the land and a lack of control over their movements, so too some early-nineteenth-century travelers felt that railroads shattered the bond between travelers and their surroundings. "All travelling becomes dull in exact proportion to its rapidity," John Ruskin thought; the ideal pace, he believed, was "a quiet walk" of no more than ten or twelve miles a day.[95] Not only did the trains' speed make it more difficult to absorb and appreciate the

passing scenes, but the flattening of the land required for track construction produced a greater uniformity of terrain, as railroads, unlike the old carriage roads, cut through hills instead of moving over
or around them, a practical necessity that diminished the "picturesque" qualities of the landscape. Some people were also troubled
by the replacement of animals—a "natural" means of locomotion—
with mechanical engines which, with their smoke and noise, seemed
to intrude upon the landscape in an unnatural way. A Scottish gentleman, complaining in 1844 that the country between Edinburgh
and Inverness had become "an asylum of railway lunatics," claimed
that he could never again pass through any beautiful part of Scotland
"without being thankful that I have beheld it before it has been
breathed over by the angel of mechanical destruction."[96]

As train travel became commonplace, however, these early res-
ervations diminished in the face of the obvious advantages of speed
and cost, while travelers came to appreciate a different kind of scenic
experience: watching the landscape pass by them as if in a kind of
panorama, "an evanescent landscape whose rapid motion made it
possible to grasp the whole," in the words of a Parisian journalist.[97]
If anything, the long stretches of little-changing terrain that so bored
travelers in the 1820s and 1830s became more interesting when
viewed at the speed of twenty or thirty miles an hour. (One British
writer thought France was "so hideously ugly" that one should appreciate being able to get through it quickly.) Like Fanny Kemble,
travelers discovered that the smooth ride of the trains allowed them
to while away the less interesting stretches by reading or writing,
which also made it easier for British travelers to indulge their preference not to talk with strangers. Harriet Beecher Stowe was rather
distressed at the arrangement of small compartments on British
trains around mid-century because they made it difficult to meet people. But the British preferred it that way, she noted, because it helped
preserve privacy. "Things are so arranged here," she observed,
"that, if a man pleases, he can travel all through England with his
family, and keep the circle an unbroken unit, having just as little
communication with any thing outside of it as in his own house."[98]

Booksellers and publishers were quick to see an opportunity to
expand their markets, opening shops in railroad stations and pack-

aging books especially for travelers. Murray initiated a collection of "Literature for the Rail," followed shortly by Routledge with its "Railway Library," a collection of novels by popular contemporary writers like Cooper, Hawthorne, and Dumas. W. H. Smith, whose name is today attached to one of the largest bookstore chains in Britain, launched his business with a bookstall at Euston station in 1848 and soon obtained the franchise for the entire London and Northwestern System. Louis Hachette initiated a similar arrangement in France in 1852, expanding to sixty branches throughout the country within two years. He also published books especially designed for travelers, with a series called "Bibliotèque des Chemins de Fer" that included novels, children's books, and travel guides, as well as works on agriculture and industry.[99]

By mid-century, criticism of railroad travel focused not on the experience itself but on its inevitable effect: the vast increase in numbers of people traveling and the crowds that jammed popular tourist spots as a result. In the 1840s, shortened travel time and cheap fares lured people by the thousands to the popular seaside towns in England. Wealthier tourists responded by lamenting the ruination of their favorite stretches of seacoast and deserting them in favor of others not yet accessible by rail, thus encouraging a sort of class stratification among resorts. In what was perhaps the most dramatic example of this trend, the royal family abandoned Brighton after the London–Brighton railroad line opened in 1841. More distant places like the Lake District and Scotland increased in popularity among those who could afford the time required to get there.[100]

Eventually, of course, the railroads penetrated even the remote destinations. In 1844, a proposal to extend a railroad line from Kendal to Windermere, in the Lake District, drew heated opposition from Wordsworth, who lobbied his neighbors and wrote a series of letters to newspapers protesting the plan. Adopting a rather old-fashioned view of the purpose of railroads, he argued that the Lake District had no mining or industry, nor any major towns requiring rail transportation; its only resource was its natural beauty, which would be diminished by the expansion of railroads. Their only possible purpose, he wrote, would be to bring in tourists. It was a rather odd argument coming from one who had written a guidebook encouraging visitors to the Lake District, but Wordsworth had quite specific ideas about the kinds of people who should visit his beloved lakes and mountains. The appreciation of natural beauty was of fairly recent origin, he argued, and consequently it stood to reason that not everyone was equally capable of responding to nature. Indeed, he worried that visiting artisans and shopkeepers—the people most likely to take advantage of fast, cheap transportation to the Lakes—would expect "amusements" like horse racing and beer shops, thus inducing railway directors to provide such entertainment to drum up business. Better that the urban workers hone their powers of observation on Sunday afternoon walks closer to home. If they really wanted to visit the Lakes, they could walk the eight or nine miles from Kendal (then the terminus of the railroad) to Windermere, a more appropriate way to see the region, while those who wanted "noisy entertainment" should go to a puppet show or farce instead. In short, Wordsworth objected not to tourism per se, but to uninformed tourism.[101]

He was not alone in such attitudes. John Ruskin thought that ordinary folk encouraged to travel by the expansion of railroads had no idea what they were missing. He called them "poor modern slaves and simpletons, who let themselves be dragged like cattle . . . through the counties they imagine themselves visiting." Thirty years after the Kendal–Windermere Railway was completed, Ruskin deplored the "stupid herds of modern tourists . . . emptied, like coals from a sack, at Windermere and Keswick," arguing that further railroad expansion would turn the region into "a steam merry-go-round" with "taverns and skittle grounds round Grasmere."[102]

The Board of Trade, in its statement approving the proposed railway, criticized the elitism of such arguments for trying to restrict the use of a beautiful region to a select few, depriving "the artisan of the offered means of occasionally changing his narrow abode, his crowded streets, his wearisome task and unwholesome toil, for the fresh air, and the healthful holiday which sends him back to his work refreshed and invigorated." But there was no denying that the railroad brought many more people of just the type that Wordsworth and Ruskin criticized. By the beginning of the twentieth century, half a million people rode the trains to the Lake District each year, 90 percent of them on third-class tickets.[103]

As the possibility of mass travel began to take shape, well-to-do travelers, on the Continent as well as within Britain, tried to insulate themselves by booking first-class tickets and patronizing expensive hotels and resorts, as well as by seeking out more remote locations, where inaccessibility still guaranteed a certain measure of privacy and exclusivity. Tourism became organized increasingly along class lines, distinguished not only by money but also by time. Nostalgic travelers might choose the privacy and leisurely pace of travel by carriage, even in the railroad era, but only if they had unlimited time as well as the money to hire a carriage. Slower travel, oddly enough, became luxury travel (as it has in other situations, when travelers have preferred sailboats to steam, for example, or ships to airplanes). Resorts on the English coast, the Scottish Highlands, and even Paris might be overrun with ordinary folk, but the time required for a tour of Italy and beyond limited more distant regions to travelers of means, at least for a few more years.

CHAPTER 4

THE "FASHIONABLE
TOUR"

As Continental tours became commonplace among well-to-do Europeans in the first half of the nineteenth century, jaded travelers took to exploring lesser-known and more distant destinations. Usually that meant the fringes of Europe, or remote corners of France or Switzerland, or perhaps, for the very adventurous, the Middle East; but some struck out across the Atlantic, driven by curiosity about "that marvellous Anglo-Saxon offshoot of our little island," in the words of Charles Weld, an amateur scientist and writer who served as librarian to the Royal Society. Like most foreign visitors to North America in the nineteenth century, Weld, who toured the United States and Canada in 1854, was not a tourist in the usual sense of the word, for the New World had few of the attractions that lured visitors to the Continent. Instead, he was drawn by curiosity about the new nation. In particular, Weld wanted to see for himself how the country had changed since his older half brother Isaac had visited in the 1790s. Where Isaac had made his way by foot, horseback, and small boats, relying on Indian guides in wilderness areas and often camping out in the open, Charles traveled on trains and steamships, staying at comfortable hotels in cities and adequate if simple inns in rural areas. Isaac wrote as an explorer, describing a raw new nation to his European readers; Charles titled his book *A Vacation Tour* and offered practical suggestions to "those who may be disposed to exchange the hackneyed Continent for the boundless freedom and novelty of a tour in the New World."[1]

Charles Weld was just one of many Europeans who made the journey to North America by mid-century. (More than two hundred travel accounts by British visitors to the United States were published between 1816 and 1860.)[2] While he dutifully reported on the state of American cities, manufacturing, agriculture, government, social institutions, and the quaint habits of the natives, in the tradition of Alexis de Tocqueville and other early commentators on American society, Weld and other nineteenth-century visitors (especially in the late 1830s, '40s, and '50s, as the conditions of travel improved) also traveled for the fun of it. Niagara Falls, the Catskill Mountains, Lake Champlain, and the fashionable spa at Saratoga Springs were on their itineraries along with the Lowell cotton mills, the Massachusetts Asylum for the Blind, and the new and much-discussed prisons at Philadelphia and Auburn, New York.

Among Americans, who didn't have the hurdle of crossing the Atlantic to deter them, domestic pleasure travel boomed in the 1820s and '30s, for much the same reasons that substantial numbers of Americans traveled to Europe in those years: the return of peace after the War of 1812, the establishment of stable government, a degree of prosperity that gave a certain segment of the population the leisure and income to travel, and improvements in transportation. Entrepreneurs in the northeastern states began constructing turnpikes connecting major towns and cities even before the war ended and accelerated the process soon afterward. Travel on the nation's inland waterways expanded dramatically with the addition of steamships and, in the 1820s, with the construction of canals linking major rivers and lakes. By the early 1830s, the first railroads were under construction as well.

These internal improvements were necessary before travel over the formidable distances and often rugged terrain of the United

States could be seen as anything other than a challenge to be avoided. What encouraged Americans to make use of the new roads and waterways for pleasure travel, however, was the same kind of curiosity that drew Europeans, intensified by a newly developing pride in their country. America might lack the great cities, ancient monuments, art galleries, theaters, and opera houses of Europe, but it had beautiful scenery in abundance. For Americans, who shared Europeans' interest in nature and the picturesque, great natural monuments like Niagara Falls and scenic vistas like those along the Hudson River took the place of the man-made monuments that highlighted most European tours.[3]

AMERICANS WHO visited Europe in the years after 1815 helped popularize travel in their home country by comparing American scenery favorably with what they had seen in Europe. Both Washington Irving and James Fenimore Cooper, for example, traveled extensively in Europe, but were best known for the distinctly American settings of their enormously popular novels and stories—the Catskill Mountains, the Hudson River, and the Mohawk Valley west of Albany. Sunnyside, Irving's splendid Gothic mansion on the Hudson near Tarrytown, itself became a tourist attraction. In an essay comparing European and American scenery, Cooper noted several deficiencies in the American landscape—less meticulously cultivated farms than in Europe, no castles or fortified towns, more taverns than churches dominating village centers—but argued that America's lakes and rivers could hold their own with those of Europe, while the vast forests and uncluttered quality of the American landscape gave it a remarkable beauty when the viewer stood far enough away to "conceal the want of finish in the details." The American landscape might lack refinement, he concluded, but it had a "greater natural freedom" and "the freshness of a most promising youth."[4]

For many, the appeal of the American landscape was precisely this fresh, unpolished quality: wilderness tamed by civilization, but in a natural sort of way, with none of the artificiality of the long-settled, densely populated English landscape.[5] While writers like

Cooper and Irving, who had developed their tastes on European tours, often sounded defensive in comparing American and European scenery, younger writers were more likely to adopt a "see America first" line. The poet and editor Nathaniel Willis, for example, thought the American landscape superior to Europe's for the very reasons that Cooper was inclined to denigrate it. What Cooper called rough-hewn and unfinished, Willis praised as bold and grand in scale. "In comparison with the old countries of Europe," he wrote, "the vegetation is so wondrously lavish, the outlines and major features struck out with so bold a freshness, and the lakes and rivers so even in their fulness and flow, yet so vast and powerful, that he may well imagine it an Eden newly sprung from the ocean." The American landscape, he believed, matched in many respects the nation itself—its "Minerva-like birth, . . . its sudden rise to independence, wealth, and power," its continued economic and population growth. Picturesque scenes in Europe were rooted in the past, but the American landscape hinted at prospects for future growth. Instead of seeking out ruined castles and abbeys, ancient villages, and fields farmed by the same families for centuries, Americans (so Willis claimed) saw valleys of "virgin vegetation, untrodden and luxuriant," and imagined them dotted with villages, mills, canals, bridges, and railroads.[6] One might return to the same spot in Europe after a long absence and find it unaltered, while the rapid growth of American towns ensured a constantly changing landscape. Like Weld, Willis urged jaded travelers who had "exhausted the unchanging countries of Europe" to turn their attention to America.

Others believed that American travelers might skip Europe altogether. William Cullen Bryant, a poet and journalist who also wrote essays on travel, regretted American travelers' preference for Wales or Scotland over scenic American regions like the Hudson River Valley—"as worthy of a pilgrimage across the Atlantic as the Alps themselves," he claimed. His sentiments were echoed in a popular magazine, the *Atlantic Souvenir*, which proclaimed that Americans should not "leave this native land for enjoyment, when you can view the rugged wilderness of her mountains, [and] admire the beauty of her cultured plains." Comparing the Hudson favorably with the Rhine, or Lake George with Loch Katrine or Lake Como, became a standard feature of American travel writing. These early American travel writers appealed to an audience of Americans schooled in European cultural ideals but conscious of, indeed proud of, the distinctiveness of their own country. At a time when the United States' future as an independent nation was still far from assured, Americans' defensiveness about their landscape was part of a larger attempt to stake out an independent status culturally as well as politically.[7]

Although natural beauty was generally acknowledged to be the United States' greatest tourist attraction, the cities and institutions of the new nation drew visitors too, and became objects of favorable comparison with Europe. Travelers contrasted American prisons, mental institutions, schools for the blind and deaf, and textile mills (where young women lived and worked in apparently clean and healthy surroundings) with the dirty, decrepit, oppressive factories and poorhouses of Europe. They lauded Pennsylvania coal mines and the canals and steamboats on which they traveled as examples of American technical ingenuity, and hailed the nation's ports, though tiny by European standards, as exemplars of nascent commercial prosperity. Theodore Dwight, for example, who traveled widely in Europe and North America and admitted that he had once thought everything on the American side of the Atlantic beneath his attention, became a great partisan of American travel in the 1820s, urging his readers to study American institutions as well as its scenery. Dwight chided Americans for looking to Europe while many Europeans sought inspiration in America: "While we are reading of feudal castles," he wrote, "or recalling with misplaced enthusiasm our visits to foreign capitals or courts, they are asking admission into our printing-offices, or observing the apparatus and exercises of our colleges and schools." The young nation might not have the cities, castles, palaces, and monuments to compare with those of Europe, but its towns, manufacturing, trade, social institutions, and even some of its stately homes and public buildings, were remarkable considering "the infancy of our country," as one guidebook argued.[8]

For Americans, citizens of a nation only decades old, travel also helped define what it meant to be American. In choosing sites to visit, and publicizing them to subsequent generations, they identified what was important about their nation and their culture—nature, technology, progressive social policies—and helped enshrine these values by popularizing the monuments that represented them. Some commentators also saw travel as a unifying force (not insignificant in a nation forged out of a group of disparate, often quarrelsome, colonies). Dwight, for one, thought the expansion of roads, canals, and railroads fostered "brotherly love" by unifying the country physically and therefore making it easier for Americans to learn about and understand one another.

For Europeans, the United States was something like a miniature Europe dropped into a wilderness—a fascinating contrast between the familiar and the foreign. Weld thought it peculiar to step off a ship after a long voyage only to hear the people around him speaking English; long journeys usually meant landing in foreign countries and coping with incomprehensible languages and unusual customs. Despite the distance between the United States and Britain, and the two hundred years since the first colonies had been settled, there was much about American society that was comfortably familiar to British travelers, and yet there were also remarkable differences. Europeans almost invariably commented on the egalitarian spirit of Americans, observing, for example, that domestics in hotels and private homes didn't like being called "servants" and weren't always very eager to serve, but often seemed to be better educated and more refined than their European counterparts. At the same time, slavery, anathema to nearly all European visitors, made a mockery of the notion of a society of equals. Americans struck many Europeans as loud, boisterous, uncouth (the custom of chewing tobacco and spitting the juices in public places was especially shocking), always in a hurry, and passionately interested in making money. Even language could sound foreign to British ears, notwithstanding Weld's remarks, in the use of words as well as in accent.[9]

ON A PRACTICAL LEVEL, the increasing popularity of travel in North America owed much to improvements in transportation. Before the 1820s, travel conditions in the United States were notoriously bad. At a time when visitors to Europe traveled on well-maintained, often paved, roads in public coaches or private carriages, American roads were hardly better than wagon tracks, dusty or muddy depending on the season. Isaac Weld's light carriage sank up to its axles on a muddy stretch of the main road between Washington and Baltimore in 1796; later, as he was preparing to go on to Philadelphia, impassable roads delayed him several days in Baltimore, until a cold snap froze the road's surface. Conditions were so bad that even the public coaches halted service for over a week. The better thoroughfares, sometimes known as "corduroy roads," were paved with logs, forming a bumpy surface that kept passengers constantly jolting in their seats. No equivalent of the European posting system existed, and public coach services were limited, operating only between major cities when they were available at all. Inns were generally small and poorly supplied. Travelers counted themselves lucky to get a room to themselves and a decent meal. Traveling across New York State in 1804, Timothy Dwight (then president of Yale College) had to ride several miles and ford a river before he could find a tavern with enough food in its larder to provide his evening meal.[10]

The situation improved at the beginning of the nineteenth century with the construction of the first turnpikes. At the height of the turnpike-building era, in the early 1820s, a network of good roads covered most of southern New England, New York, and eastern Pennsylvania, while the longest of all the turnpikes, known as the National Road, ran from Cumberland, in western Maryland, into Ohio. By mid-century it extended to Illinois, and eventually became part of the cross-country national Route 40. Better roads permitted an expansion of intercity coach services, but even so, road travel remained slow—generally not more than six to eight miles per hour, even on the best routes.[11]

Travel by water, the cheapest way to cover long distances, became even more attractive as an alternative to bumpy stagecoach routes when steamboats were introduced and canals connected major waterways, making long-distance water travel feasible in many parts of the country. In striking contrast to its laggard progress in road construction, the United States was ahead of Europe in the development of inland water transportation. Robert Fulton's *Clermont*, launched on the Hudson in 1807, was the world's first steam-

powered ship. It was followed in 1809 by a steamship on the Dela-
ware River and in the winter of 1811–12 by the first steam passage
down the Ohio and Mississippi from Pittsburgh to New Orleans. By
the end of the 1820s, steamboats dominated river transportation and
had been introduced on the Great Lakes. (It look longer for steam
to replace sail on lake and ocean voyages because the early steamships could not carry enough fuel for long voyages; on river trips, it
was possible to pull ashore to take on fresh supplies of fuel. In addition, sailing ships operated more efficiently on large bodies of water
than on rivers, where narrow passages made it difficult for ships to
maneuver under less than ideal wind conditions.) Rival shipping
companies vied with each other to build larger, faster, and more
luxurious vessels, providing staterooms, baths, lavishly appointed
lounges, and dining rooms. Some even had bridal suites. Domingo
Sarmiento, a distinguished writer and educator from Argentina, traveling in 1847, described steamships as "colossal floating hotels . . .
with flat roofs and covered porches." Dickens thought the steamer
he took from New Haven to New York looked more like "a huge
floating bath" than a ship. Despite their ungainly architecture, the
fastest achieved speeds of twenty miles per hour.[12]

The practical advantages of river travel were much enhanced by
the construction of canals linking the major water routes, which began after the War of 1812 and peaked in the 1820s. By far the most
famous and the most frequently traveled was the Erie Canal joining
the Hudson River near Albany with Lake Erie, begun in 1818 and
completed in 1825. The Champlain Canal, opened in 1823, connected
the Hudson with the southern end of Lake Champlain. These two
canals made it possible to travel from New York City, up the Hudson, across New York State, and back via Lake Erie, the St.
Lawrence River, and Lake Champlain entirely by water. Others connected rivers to create water passages from the Erie Canal to Philadelphia and Baltimore, and from Lake Erie to the Ohio River.[13]

Travel by canal boat was much less comfortable than by river
steamer, however; the shallow, narrow canals permitted only small,
slow-moving craft, averaging two to five miles an hour, while the
locks on most canals could cause further delays. The journey along
the full length of the Erie Canal from Albany to Buffalo took about

a week. Although Theodore Dwight described canal travel as more comfortable than one might expect, most travelers disagreed. "With a very delightful party of one's own choosing, fine temperate weather, and strong breezes to chase the mosquitoes, this mode of travelling might be very agreeable," Frances Trollope observed, "but I can hardly imagine any motive of convenience powerful enough to induce me again to imprison myself in a canal boat under ordinary circumstances." (Trollope, who spent a great deal of her adult life traveling, toured the United States in the late 1820s with an extremely critical eye.) Passengers often complained about the cramped sleeping quarters (one room usually served as lounge and dining room by day and was converted into berths at night) and crowded decks; Dickens joked about having to duck every time the boat went under a bridge, which was only a slight exaggeration. Even the more serious Theodore Dwight cautioned his readers to keep heads and hands inside the windows of the boats. As for the overnight accommodations on board, what Dwight described as "mattresses" and "cots," Dickens likened to library shelves "with a sort of microscopic sheet and blanket."[14]

By the 1830s, railroads began to compete with turnpike and canal travel. As in Europe, the earliest railroads were short lines built to carry coal to the nearest canal or river. These were soon followed by freight and passenger lines organized and financed by entrepreneurs in Baltimore, Charleston, and Boston seeking to increase their export trade by tapping larger regions to the west. The Baltimore & Ohio completed its first stretch of track in 1830; lines originating in Charleston and Boston opened about a year later. From that point, expansion proceeded so rapidly that, by 1840, the United States had nearly twice as much track in operation as all the nations of Europe combined. Without a long history of entrenched business and political interests, lacking the political frontiers separating the various nations of Europe, motivated by vast distances—the United States east of the Mississippi is larger than all of continental Europe as far east as Germany and Austria—and aided by cheap land prices, it was easier for American businessmen to finance and build railroads. When a line from Charleston to the Savannah River was completed in 1833, it was, at 136 miles, the longest railroad line in the world under single management. Later that distinction went to the New York and Erie Railroad, completed in the late 1840s across the southern tier of counties in New York State. By mid-century, railroads covered much of the Northeast and had begun to make inroads west of the Appalachians.[15]

America's railroads, like those in Europe, were initially intended primarily to haul freight, but passenger traffic soon became one of the companies' most lucrative sources of income (about 30 to 40 percent of total revenues in the years before 1850), despite hazards that included flying sparks and frequent accidents caused by poor coupling mechanisms, faulty brakes, or excessive speed. Nor was rail travel especially comfortable in the early years. Passenger cars were long, boxy affairs with an aisle running down the middle and rows of hard, uncomfortable seats on either side. A single stove was provided for heat, ensuring that those close to it were too hot and those at the ends of the cars were too cold. (As early as the late 1830s, however, the first sleeping cars and the first approximation of "club cars," with comfortable chairs, were introduced on a few lines.) Many Europeans were unsettled by the single class of service on most trains—although separate cars were usually reserved for women, with or without escorts, to ensure their privacy. "The adage that travelling makes us acquainted with strange companions has more than usual force in the States," Weld noted, "where an honourable judge, a senator, or the President himself, may be seen seated next to a rough and unwashed mechanic." (Europeans were equally amazed at American women's freedom to travel, alone or with only another woman for a companion, without being molested or damaging their reputations.) Blacks also had separate cars, which were little more than freight cars with benches. Dickens described one as "a great, blundering, clumsy chest, such as Gulliver put out to sea in, from the kingdom of Brobdingnag."[16]

Just as there were those in Europe who regretted the speed and intrusion of the new trains, so too there were Americans who preferred the older style of travel. Theodore Dwight thought travelers missed much when they moved at the speed of trains and steamboats, preferring on occasion to revert to "a country stagecoach or a farmer's waggon, and feel delight in the rattling wheels and the healthful jolting motion of a stony hill . . . or set off on foot in company with some chosen fellow-traveller, to earn an appetite by a long walk before breakfast.'' Cooper complained that railroads destroyed the picturesque qualities of travel because tracks were built along the flattest, straightest possible terrain, whereas roads were more likely to follow the natural contours of the land. Irving waxed nostalgic for ''the good old times before steamboats and railroads had driven all poetry and romance out of travel.'' Bayard Taylor, on the other hand, disdained such thinking in an article praising the New York and Erie Railroad for its speed, comfort, and scenic route, remarking with satisfaction that ''the vulgar lament'' over the spread of steam transportation was heard less frequently as its advantages won converts. Oddly enough, Taylor's, Cooper's, and Irving's comments were all published at the same time, in a collection of essays titled *The Home Book of the Picturesque;* but Taylor was a much younger man, who had little experience of the earlier ways of travel.[17]

Ultimately the new technology won out, of course. Irving noted that a trip up the Hudson before the era of steam had taken as long as a voyage to Europe and cost almost as much; he seemed not to realize that those were precisely the reasons the older form of travel became obsolete. With every major technological advance in transportation, the time and cost of traveling dropped dramatically. At the beginning of the nineteenth century, for example, the journey from Boston to New York by stagecoach took three days and nights, with three overnight stops; improved roads helped reduce the time to two days with one overnight stop by the mid-1820s. Sailing boats required anywhere from two days to two weeks, depending on weather conditions, for the journey up the Hudson from New York to Albany, while the first steamboats took about fourteen hours. By the 1830s, that time was cut to ten hours and by the 1850s, to eight hours, while the cost dropped from $5–$7 in the early days of steam to about 50 cents. A longer, more complicated route, like that from Philadelphia to Quebec, required a series of steamboats and stagecoaches with several long stopovers in 1816—about five and a half days altogether. By mid-century, one could make the entire trip by rail in a little over a day, at less than half the cost of the earlier journey.[18]

The customs house in Boulogne, 1790s

Engraving by Thomas Rowlandson. Yale Center for British Art, Paul Mellon Collection

A crowded diligence, 1855

From Richard Doyle, The Foreign Tour of Messrs. Brown, Jones, and Robinson

Descending the Mont Cenis Pass in winter during the 1860s,
after the road was widened sufficiently to accommodate carriages
From Illustrated London News, *January 16, 1864*

A typical illustration from William Gilpin's book on the Lake District.
Note the small figures centered in the foreground, the tree juxtaposed
against the mountains, and the oval shape framing the drawing.
From Observations . . . on Mountains and Lakes of Cumberland and Westmorland.
The Bancroft Library, University of California, Berkeley

"Dr. Syntax Sketching the Lake," an illustration from
William Combe's satirical work *The Tour of Dr. Syntax
in Search of the Picturesque*
The Bancroft Library, University of California, Berkeley

Engraving of Loch Katrine by William H. Bartlett
From William Beattie, Scotland. *The Bancroft Library,
University of California, Berkeley*

View of the newly
constructed road over
the Simplon Pass
From Marianne Baillie, First
Impressions of a Tour upon
the Continent

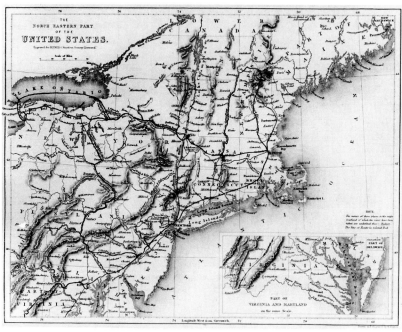

Map of the northeastern United States showing the
popular itinerary of early-nineteenth-century travelers
From Nathaniel Parker Willis, American Scenery

Niagara Falls from below Table Rock, one of the most popular vantage points among tourists
Engraving by William H. Bartlett in American Scenery

Railroad in upstate New York around 1840
Engraving by William H. Bartlett in American Scenery

The Catskill Mountain House
Engraving by William H. Bartlett in American Scenery

Thomas Cook, about 1848
The Travel Archive, Thomas Cook Ltd.

Cover of Cook's Scottish tourist handbook, 1858
The Travel Archive, Thomas Cook Ltd.

One of Cook's groups arriving at the Gare du Nord, Paris, 1861
The Travel Archive, Thomas Cook Ltd.

Jemima Morrell's party
in Switzerland
The Travel Archive, Thomas Cook Ltd.

An advertising poster for
Thomas Cook, 1903
The Travel Archive, Thomas Cook Ltd.

A view of the Promenade des Anglais at Nice, 1866
From Illustrated London News, *February 10, 1866*

On popular routes, across New York from Albany to Niagara Falls, for example, travelers had a choice of transportation by mid-century, including two major rail lines, the Erie Canal, or some combination of rail, canal, and perhaps a steamer on Lake Ontario for part of the way. Feeder railroad lines made it easy to combine routes and make side trips to points of interest. As a result, European travelers intending to "do" the United States in one grand tour were more likely to spend a few months on their travels rather than the year or more required by those rare eighteenth-century travelers, and Americans could reasonably make a vacation trip of a few weeks or less. Sarmiento surely exaggerated when he remarked about legions of newlyweds on trains and steamers, rushing to Saratoga, Niagara Falls, and dozens of cities, covering "a thousand leagues of countryside" in fifteen days; but certainly the notion of travel as a routine and pleasurable occupation was well established, especially in the Northeast, by the time of his visit in 1847.[19]

As travel became easier and more people took to the roads, services catering to travelers improved. Hotels, some quite large and luxurious, were built in the major cities and at the important tourist attractions like the spas at Saratoga Springs, New York, and White Sulphur Springs, Virginia. European visitors to Boston and New York were surprised at the size and opulence of hotels like the Revere in Boston and Astor House in New York (which boasted upwards of three hundred rooms, elegantly appointed public rooms, and hot-water plumbing), because such establishments were rare in Europe, where travelers typically rented lodgings in major cities. Some country hotels, notably the Catskill Mountain House, became destinations in themselves.[20]

Although Weld remarked that there was no "Murray" to direct the American traveler, there was no shortage of American-published guidebooks. Theodore Dwight's *Northern Traveller* was one of the first, predating even Murray's and Baedeker's earliest European guides. Originally published in 1825, it was initially a fairly straightforward guide to the popular circuit up the Hudson, across New York to Niagara Falls, and back via Canada. Subsequent editions added information on New England, the major East Coast cities, and the coal mining region of Pennsylvania. Like most guides in this period, Dwight's mapped out routes for his readers, specifying mileage between each town along the way, offered descriptions of important sights, and included brief listings of inns and hotels. A similar book, *The Traveller's Guide,* went through eight editions between 1822 and 1840, and was translated into French. An 1844 guide titled *The Picturesque Tourist* concentrated on scenic attractions from New England as far west as Chicago, and many other specialized guides focused on specific regions. Long, foldout panoramic maps of the Hudson River with accompanying descriptions were especially popular, as were guides to Niagara Falls. There was even a sort of reference work called *The Family Tourist,* billed as a compendium of descriptive information for those who couldn't afford to travel. Maps and atlases proliferated as well, for the armchair as well as the actual travelers. Sarmiento, convinced that Americans were possessed of a "mania for travel," was amused to note that nearly every American he met possessed a supply of them.[21]

THE MOST POPULAR destinations for travelers in the United States became established rather quickly as the "American grand tour"—or, as one of the early guidebooks labeled it, the "fashionable tour."[22] The heart of the tour was a loop from New York City up the Hudson to Albany, with stops in the Catskill Mountains and at Saratoga Springs and Ballston Spa, across upstate New York to Niagara Falls, and then back to the Hudson, perhaps by a slightly different route. New England was a popular destination as well, especially Boston and the Connecticut River Valley. Travelers with plenty of time might follow the Connecticut as far north as Vermont and then circle back through the White Mountains of New Hampshire, where the roads were rough and the accommodations rustic at best, but where the scenery was among the most admired in the Northeast. Those making the complete American tour added a loop through the mid-Atlantic states, from New York to Philadelphia, Baltimore, and Washington, perhaps with detours to the coalfields of eastern Pennsylvania, the Natural Bridge in Virginia's Shenandoah Valley, and Washington's home at Mount Vernon. Nathaniel Willis's book *Amer-*

ican Scenery included a map highlighting the major routes on this northeastern tour. (See page 4 of the first photographic insert.)

Foreign visitors, recognizing that an American tour was a once-in-a-lifetime affair, usually covered most of the area between Boston and Washington on the eastern seaboard and Niagara Falls in the West, while Americans were more likely to make separate, shorter tours, focusing on the scenic rather than the urban areas. Rugged conditions kept most travelers from venturing farther south or west, although foreign visitors were more likely to go beyond the standard tour, motivated by curiosity about slavery in the South and the conditions of life on the western frontier.[23]

The contours of the "American grand tour" were defined by what the traveling public wanted to see: primarily picturesque and sublime scenery, and secondarily the visual evidence of the United States' growth as a nation. American and European travelers shared a common cultural tradition that encouraged them to seek out particular kinds of landscape and describe them with a common vocabulary: the Hudson and Connecticut river valleys were prime examples of the picturesque, while the Catskill Mountains and Niagara Falls fulfilled the requirements of the sublime. Both European and American travelers also shared a common interest in observing American social and cultural institutions, as well as monuments to its political maturity and economic growth, although for rather different reasons; patriotic pride drove Americans to tour places like the Lowell mills, the prisons at Auburn and Philadelphia, the coal mines of eastern Pennsylvania, and government buildings in Washington, while Europeans were motivated by curiosity about the growth of a young nation—one that seemed, in the early nineteenth century, to be vastly different from the old civilizations of Europe.

The Hudson River Valley, perhaps more than any other American region, achieved the European ideal of picturesque beauty, uniting nature with history, literature, and art. Americans and Europeans alike invoked Washington Irving's stories as they sailed upriver, much as visitors toured Scotland with Sir Walter Scott's novels in hand or quoted Byron in Switzerland and Italy. The ancient castles of the Rhine were lacking, but the Hudson did have Revolutionary

War battlefields—the closest Americans could get to historic monuments—at Fishkill, West Point, Newburgh, Kingston, Stillwater, Schuylerville, and Bémis Heights. The English traveler Basil Hall was amused at Americans' preoccupation with scenes of their very recent history; but British visitors had their own associations with the Revolution, and many took care to describe the site where the British officer John André was executed after his conviction for spying against the Americans.[24]

Some travelers scoffed at the popular comparison between the Hudson and the Rhine—the American travel writer Charles Dudley Warner wrote, "Believe me, there is no resemblance; nor would there be if the Hudson were lined with castles, and Julius Caesar had crossed it every half-mile"—but the river's beauty in its own right was undeniable. Even the acerbic Frances Trollope, prepared to be disappointed by her experience, was enchanted. "Every mile shows some new and startling effect of the combination of rocks, trees, and water," she observed. "There is no interval of flat or insipid scenery" from one end of the river to another. Moreover, steaming up the Hudson had the virtue of being comfortable, fast, and inexpensive as early as the end of the eighteenth century, a time when travel through much of the country was still slow and cumbersome. By the 1820s, travelers could choose from a dozen or more steamboats following a standard itinerary with stops at the main points of interest. Harriet Martineau made the journey up the Hudson three times and remarked that she "should be tempted to ascend it three times a week during the summer" if she lived in New York.[25]

The Catskill Mountains, with their "rocky precipices," "primeval forests," and "savage glens rarely trodden excepting by the hunter" (to quote Washington Irving) were the highlight of a Hudson River tour. Every year, thousands of visitors disembarked at the little town of Catskill to make the twelve-mile excursion to Pine Orchard along a steep, winding road, "inspiring at times an unwelcome degree of terror." The journey took at least four hours, but those who made the effort were rewarded with a panoramic view of the Hudson over a thousand feet below: "more diversity of scenery than is to be found in any other part of the state, or perhaps in the United States," boasted one popular guidebook. Timothy Dwight described a prospect of "grandeur, gloom, and solitude"—a ravine enclosed by heavily forested mountains on both sides with a waterfall cascading from one of the highest points, producing clouds of mist and a series of rainbows. Apart from Niagara Falls, he considered it the grandest scene in nature.[26]

This excursion to Pine Orchard became so popular in the 1820s that the limited overnight accommodations available proved completely inadequate. However, as Basil Hall observed, "One of the enterprising companies, which abound in that country, soon found, in a money speculation, a remedy for this matter." (British travelers frequently remarked on the American propensity to invest in anything that might make money.) "Straightaway there rose up, like an exhalation, a splendid hotel, on the very brink of the precipice." In fact, the hotel's growth was not quite so instantaneous as Hall suggested, but remarkable just the same. The Catskill Mountain House, which opened as a small inn in 1823, added fifty rooms within two years and eventually expanded to accommodate five hundred guests, becoming one of the most famous American hotels of the nineteenth century. Situated to take full advantage of the stunning view below, the Mountain House offered its guests luxurious accommodations in the midst of sublime scenery. It combined the best of what American travel could offer—spectacular, untouched nature—with an unprecedented standard of comfort.[27]

Another popular detour from the Hudson River journey was a visit to the spas at Saratoga and Ballston, where Americans tried to reproduce something resembling the fashionable social life associated with European resorts like Bath. By the late eighteenth century, Saratoga and Ballston had already gained a reputation for the healthful properties of their mineral springs, along with several other sites, including Stafford Springs in Connecticut, Warm Springs and Yellow Springs in Pennsylvania, and White Sulphur Springs in Virginia.[28] Like their European counterparts, the American spas owed their popularity to a combination of belief in the curative power of mineral waters and the pleasures of the social life that developed among those "taking the cure." Accessible by rail from the early 1830s, Saratoga became the most fashionable spa in the North, boasting huge luxury hotels and a "season" of social events modeled on those of the European spas. Weld was astonished at the size of the United States Hotel, one of the largest hotels he had ever seen, and amused at the pretensions of young ladies in residence, who changed their dresses several times a day.[29]

Although the largest and most famous of the spa hotels, the United States was by mid-century only one of several huge establishments, some capable of accommodating as many as twelve hundred guests. One American visitor, disgusted by the whole scene, described Saratoga as "an immense wilderness of hotels—like stray cabbages in a potato patch." Another visitor joked that he managed to visit each of the region's spas (Ballston, Rockaway, and Lebanon as well as Saratoga) just a few days behind the fashionable set. Like the British in Italy, American socialites made the rounds of the spas in a specific order and at precise times. The same was true of what were known as "the Six" springs in Virginia.[30] The spas, like the Hudson River tour, were often the focus of a journey for American tourists. For those making the complete grand tour, however, the Hudson and Saratoga were mere warm-ups to the most popular American attraction of them all: Niagara Falls.

Discovered by Europeans in 1678 (by a French expedition headed by LaSalle), described and illustrated for the first time in Father Louis Hennepin's account of that expedition (published in 1697), Niagara lured travelers from a remarkably early period, when getting there meant a long journey by horseback or private carriage. Dozens of British soldiers visited the Falls in the years after the French and Indian War, en route to outposts in western New York or the Ohio Valley. Isaac Weld was among the first civilian travelers, in the 1790s, when the only sign of civilization was a tiny village "of about half a dozen straggling houses," and visitors had to seek hospitality at a nearby military fort—a situation little changed by the time Timothy Dwight visited in 1804. The region developed rapidly, however, after the opening of the Erie Canal in 1825. By the 1830s it was already a favorite choice for honeymooning couples, anticipating the post–Civil War period, when both the custom of the honeymoon and the choice of Niagara became firmly established among American newlyweds.[31]

Nothing in the American or European landscape evoked quite the same kind of emotional response from travelers—not even Mont Blanc, or the Simplon Pass, or the favorite haunts in the Scottish Highlands and England's Lake District. Visually, the Falls were breathtaking—two massive cascades nearly 180 feet high, they are the third largest in the world in terms of power and volume of water. For nineteenth-century travelers, however, experiencing Niagara Falls transcended the merely visual. Visitors heard the Falls long before seeing them. At closer range, they felt the earth tremble with the force of the water while the mist dampened their clothes and faces. With its grand scale and power, Niagara was the ultimate sublime experience, an opinion shared by visitors as diverse as Frances Trollope and Nathaniel Hawthorne. But it was also something more: For a generation accustomed to finding God manifest in nature, Niagara offered physical evidence of God's power. Charles Dickens spoke for many visitors when he wrote that he felt himself in the presence of God as he stood on Table Rock, a popular vantage point on the Canadian side of the Falls. Others described themselves as "pilgrims" to the "shrine" or "temple" of Niagara. For Americans, the Falls were also a symbol of national pride, a great natural monument rivaling any of the historical or cultural artifacts of the Old World.[32]

Nathaniel Hawthorne was still miles away when he began to listen for "the roar of the cataract, and trembled with a sensation like dread, as the moment drew nigh, when its voice of ages must roll." That first sight of the Falls inspired many visitors to pour out paragraphs of purple prose—"the awful rushing of the mighty waters," "the most sublime natural spectacle on which the eye of man ever dwelt," "Niagara was at once stamped upon my heart"—while others refused all attempt at description, saying that it was impossible to convey Niagara's grandeur in words. As Trollope (not usually at a loss for words) put it, "Any attempt to describe the sensations produced must lead direct to nonsense."[33]

Expectations ran so high that many visitors were disappointed at first, some because the flat, featureless landscape surrounding the Falls ("tedious," as one writer described it) paled by comparison with the picturesque, woodsy settings associated with waterfalls in Europe. More often, the reality simply couldn't live up to the overblown descriptions popular among travel writers. After two or three days, however, most tourists came to appreciate Niagara's sublimity. Hawthorne needed several visits "and much contemplation" to overcome his initial disappointment, but finally concluded that "Niagara is indeed a wonder of the world, and not the less wonderful, because time and thought must be employed in comprehending it." Margaret Fuller almost left the same day she arrived, but then returned at night to feel a divine presence.[34] Indeed, it took several days to appreciate Niagara fully, the more sensitive tourists agreed, dismissing with ill-disguised contempt those who spent only a few hours at the Falls before rushing on to the next destination. Hawthorne, for one, mocked the people walking around with their noses in their guidebooks, apparently seeing exactly what they had expected to see, leaving with no new ideas of their own.[35]

Most visitors first approached Niagara from the American side. After taking in the view from the top of the Falls, they could descend a wooden staircase to the base of the American Falls, a view that Willis claimed was the "most imposing scene" in nature. As early as the 1830s, ferryboats carried passengers across the river, allowing them to see the entire sweep of the two Falls from below (a scene that inspired Nathaniel Willis to quote Byron's lines from *Childe Harold's Pilgrimage* describing the Falls of Terni). Goat Island, which separates the two Falls, was accessible by a footbridge from the American side. On the Canadian side, Table Rock made an ideal viewing platform for the Horseshoe Falls. The intrepid could scramble down a staircase under Table Rock for a close-up view, and those who wanted to experience Niagara to the fullest hired a guide to take them behind the Falls—"behind the veil of the temple," as the English traveler Marianne Finch put it—to a point called Termination Rock.[36]

The tours behind the Horseshoe Falls were a popular concession run out of a modest building near Table Rock. Men and women alike donned canvas trousers, flannel shirts, and long oilcloth jackets and hats (which Lydia Sigourney compared to the rough clothing of pilgrims) to protect themselves from the mist, and then followed their guide through increasingly heavy spray into a cavelike area behind the Falls where they had a magnificent, close-up view of the sheet of water—like a "crystal wall," as Willis described it. Once safely back at Table Rock, the adventurers signed a book and received a certificate testifying to their achievement. Every person who ventured behind the Falls "has a very tolerable idea of the pains of drowning," Willis thought. "On the whole," he added, "this undertaking is rather pleasanter to remember than to achieve." For others, the feeling of connection between God and nature inspired by Niagara was intensified by the experience of being, in effect, surrounded by the Falls. Here one could not help but "meditate on the littleness of man" and the qualities of the God who controlled such power. For visitors like Marianne Finch, who "longed to precipitate myself into the Niagara; anything to *know* it—to *feel* its power," the walk to Termination Rock was the most moving experience of a visit to the Falls. "I emerged with a deeper feeling of awe than I ever experienced before," she wrote. "I was now content, Niagara was my own; I have *known* it, in its inner life, *felt* its unmeasurable power, and drunk deeply of its beauty, and henceforth (though I might never see it again), we were inseparably united." Less melodramatically, Sarmiento observed that "coming out of that watery inferno and seeing the sun and sky once again, one can say that he has fully experienced the sublime."[37]

Visitors less addicted to the sublime could partake of more conventional tourist attractions, including souvenir shops selling Indian crafts, a museum, and stunt performers, as well as the sociability offered by several hotels, some of them quite luxurious. (The Clifton House, on the Canadian side, was a favorite both for its standard of service and its panoramic view of both Falls.) In 1829 a stuntman named Sam Patch leaped from a hundred-foot tower at the base of the Falls, inspiring dozens of similar escapades. The site of his leap became a tourist destination in itself. In the 1860s, tightrope walkers crossing the river just below the Falls became a star attraction. The fad of going over the Falls in a barrel started toward the end of the nineteenth century and persisted well into the twentieth. Tales of people swept over the brink and of narrow escapes became a staple item in popular magazines and guidebooks.[38]

As early as the 1830s, many visitors complained that Niagara was becoming overcrowded and too commercial. Alexis de Tocqueville, in 1831, urged a friend to visit Niagara without delay. Otherwise, he wrote, "your Niagara will have been spoiled for you. . . . I don't give the Americans ten years to establish a saw or flour mill at the base of the cataract." Arguments raged between those who would build walkways and rustic temples on Goat Island and those who preferred it wild, and between those who hated the encroachment of hotels and shops and those who profited from them. Beginning in the 1830s, there was talk of harnessing Niagara's waterpower for industry. Disturbed by such talk as well as by the evident commercialization of the site, one British visitor in the mid-1830s predicted that the area around the Falls would be crowded with "grog-shops, humbug museums," and perhaps even cotton factories within twenty years.[39]

Such conflicts were indicative of Americans' contradictory attitudes about nature, both as something to appreciate in its wild state and as a resource to be developed. Many European visitors thought Americans cared little about nature in its unspoiled state; "improvement," among Americans, meant buildings, population growth, factories, and cultivation, Basil Hall observed. To Europeans, such "improvement" seemed hastily and carelessly undertaken, marked by indiscriminate timber cutting, wasteful methods of cultivation, and crudely built houses and fences. In reality, however, the question of nature versus development was one that had divided Americans, in part along class and education lines, from a very early point in the nineteenth century and perhaps even earlier. Timothy Dwight was as critical of Americans' rush to develop raw land as any British visitor, although he hoped, rather overoptimistically, that the proper balance between unspoiled nature and responsible cultivation would be achieved at some point in the future.[40] In the context of tourism, this contradictory set of attitudes bred the same sort of debates that divided people in other regions (including England's Lake District and the more popular spots in Switzerland) where natural beauty drew tourists who, by the very weight of their numbers, began to destroy the beauty and solitude that made these regions attractive in the first place.

In the case of Niagara, the arguments of those who would restrict or somehow control tourism had little impact until the end of the nineteenth century. A flood of books, articles, paintings, and engravings only encouraged more visitors. When Frederic Church, one of the most popular American painters of the mid-nineteenth century, exhibited his monumental painting of Niagara Falls in New York City in 1857, thousands of people paid 25 cents each to see it. It was also displayed to much fanfare at the Paris Exhibition of 1867. W. W. Corcoran purchased it in 1876 for $12,500, then the highest price ever paid for an American painting. By Church's time, hotels and commercial buildings lined the edge of the gorge on both the American and Canadian sides, and upwards of sixty thousand tourists visited Niagara each year. Another popular American painter, John Kensett, complained that he couldn't sketch at the Falls without drawing an audience of fifty people or more.[41]

Not until the 1870s did the number of tourists and the degree of commercialization of the Falls reach such proportions that New York State government officials took steps to restore its natural setting and scale back the commercial ventures. In 1879, the state commissioned Frederick Law Olmsted, designer of Central Park in New York City and a number of other parks, to prepare a proposal for the preservation of Niagara Falls. The eventual result was its designation as a state park in 1885.[42]

IF NATURE IN its myriad forms was the major attraction for travelers in the United States, the human landscape had its appeal as well, especially along the eastern seaboard from Boston to Washington. For foreign visitors in particular, touring American cities provided a glimpse into American society and politics, which seemed so remarkably different from what they were accustomed to in Europe. State-supported schools and independent churches (exactly the opposite of the situation in Europe), prisons and social welfare institutions designed along humane principles, and factories with what were, for the time, enlightened labor practices drew hundreds of curious visitors.

In Boston, then considered the cultural capital of the nation, European visitors were often surprised at the number and variety of churches, all of them supported merely by the contributions of their members. On his first day in Boston, Charles Dickens claimed to have received enough invitations to church services for "a score or two of grown-up families."[43] Boston's Unitarian church (a denomination unknown in Europe) and its renowned pastor, William Ellery Channing, drew an especially large number of visitors in the 1820s and 1830s. If the lack of state support for churches struck Europeans as curious, the fact that the state did support public education (in Massachusetts, although not everywhere) seemed equally remarkable, drawing praise from many reform-minded visitors. Sarmiento, a teacher by profession, went to Boston expressly for the purpose of meeting the noted educator Horace Mann and learning about the American system of education.

Boston's institutions housing the poor, the mentally ill, the disabled, and orphaned children were also popular tourist attractions. The best-known among them was the Perkins Institution and Massachusetts Asylum for the Blind, which drew visitors in the late 1830s and 1840s to observe Laura Bridgman, who had been rendered blind and deaf by scarlet fever at the age of two. Samuel Gridley Howe, one of Boston's most notable social reformers, had read about the girl and persuaded her parents to allow him to take her from her home in New Hampshire to Boston, where he hoped to teach her to read, write, and speak—a feat without precedent at the time. After months of effort, Howe succeeded, by fixing raised letters to common objects and devising a Morse-codelike system for "speaking." After visiting Boston in 1842, Dickens wrote a long, impassioned description of Bridgman that helped make her famous—and an object of curiosity for subsequent visitors.[44]

Visits to social institutions were popular elsewhere as well. Travelers en route to Niagara often stopped at Auburn, just west of Syracuse, where American-style prison reform was launched in 1819. Under the Auburn system, prisoners lived in solitary cells but worked in large common areas during the day, where they were forbidden to speak to their fellow inmates. The theory was to rehabilitate prisoners through useful, productive labor but prevent them from associating with other criminals, whose influence might undermine the beneficial effects of prison discipline. Travelers on the Hudson might also visit Sing Sing prison (near the town now called Ossining), which also employed the Auburn system. Prisons in Philadelphia and Pittsburgh (both established in the late 1820s) offered a different sort of arrangement, in which prisoners lived and worked separately, prohibited from all contact with other inmates. The two systems of prison discipline were hotly debated among social reformers in the 1820s and '30s.

Prison and asylum administrators encouraged visitors because they were proud of their institutions and recognized the value of publicity in raising money to maintain them. Guidebooks from the 1830s to the 1850s gave particulars about visiting them, much as they might explain the hours and charges for museums. For Americans, these institutions offered a demonstration of what an uncorrupt, republican government could accomplish; for Europeans, most of them quite unabashedly admiring, they were an example of a better way to fulfill public responsibilities to the unfortunate. For some Europeans (of whom Alexis de Tocqueville was the most famous), visiting social institutions was the major object of an American tour.[45]

In much the same spirit, tourists often made a side trip to the textile mills of Lowell, about twenty-five miles northwest of Boston. Here they found clean, well-ventilated mills and attractive boardinghouses where female workers, who constituted the great majority of the mill operatives, lived in homelike surroundings, strictly supervised by the older women in charge. More than anything else, they were impressed by the young women themselves, who appeared to be refined and well-educated, attended church every Sunday, and spent their spare time (after a twelve-hour day, or more, in the mills) reading books and publishing a literary magazine, *The Lowell Offering*. The contrast with the factories of Manchester and Birmingham could not have been more stark. Charles Weld, a bit skeptical about Lowell's reputation, visited several of the boardinghouses unannounced, discovering that the reality did indeed live up to the reputation. Among other things, he noted approvingly that the books borrowed from the town library were "of a healthy literary nature."[46]

A very different example of American industrialization drew tourists to the coalfields of eastern Pennsylvania, where river valleys and rolling hills provided a lovely backdrop for technological innovation.

It was perhaps the most beautiful industrial setting in the United States, although one soon destroyed as industry expanded. The Wyoming Valley, along the Susquehanna River around Wilkes-Barre, offered picturesque scenes worthy of "an admirer of Claude, or Poussin, or of Salvator," in the estimation of one English traveler, Charles Murray. If one considered the beauty of the Valley in combination with its potential for wealth, Murray thought, the Wyoming Valley was without parallel. Surely, he claimed, the valleys of the Susquehanna and Lackawanna rivers contained enough coal to supply all the cities of the world for one thousand years![47]

The most popular industrial site among tourists was a little town with the peculiar name of Mauch Chunk (now called Jim Thorpe) southeast of Wilkes-Barre, where coal mines operated by the Lehigh Coal and Navigation Co. were open to visitors soon after they began operation in the 1820s. Tourism soared in the late 1820s, after the company built a nine-mile, gravity-operated railroad (one of the first in the United States) from the hilltop mines to the Lehigh River at Mauch Chunk. Cars were loaded with coal and passengers at the top of the line, then rolled downhill to the river, providing tourists with a thrilling ride and unsurpassed views of the surrounding countryside. Expanded in subsequent years, the gravity railroad remained popular until late in the century, long after the construction of a tunnel and a far more sophisticated railroad system made it obsolete for carrying coal.[48]

After seeking out examples of American innovation and progressive social policies in their tour of the Northeast, travelers who continued south were confronted with what seemed to most Europeans (and many Americans as well) the one great blot on the American national experiment: slavery. Britain abolished slavery in its remaining colonies in 1833 after many years of reformist agitation, and so the persistence of the institution in the United States seemed, to British visitors, an anachronism as well as a moral outrage. Travelers typically blamed every negative feature they observed in the southern states—the lack of public schools, the poor roads, the low quality of services, the absence of industrial innovation of the sort they had seen in New England or Pennsylvania—on slavery. Even Baltimore, which had experienced extraordinary growth around the turn of the century, making it the third largest city in the nation by 1820, showed the ill effects.

The most popular tourist destination in the slaveholding South was, of course, Washington, a city of incongruities: Located in the midst of a region that struck many as a throwback to an older, more aristocratic way of life, it was a new capital, designed and built from scratch on an ambitious scale, intended to showcase the idealism of a new nation that billed itself as a model of republican government. In the early decades of the nineteenth century, however, it was only too obvious that the grand plan for Washington, conceived by the French architect Pierre L'Enfant, had overreached the capacities of a young republic. "It is sometimes called the City of Magnificent Distances, but it might with greater propriety be termed the City of Magnificent Intentions," Dickens wrote, a sentiment echoed by many American visitors as well. The Capitol and the White House were complete, as well as several of the grand thoroughfares; but most of the roads went nowhere, and such houses as had been built were shut up much of the year, whenever Congress was out of session. Even so, Frances Trollope thought the habit of ridiculing Washington's pretensions unfair. Only a small part of the plan had been realized, to be sure, but the completed portions were well done, in her opinion, offering all the charm of a European watering place.[49]

Washington did not, however, offer the kind of social life to be found in a European watering place—which could be a positive or negative feature, depending on one's point of view. Theodore Dwight told a story about a young Frenchman who left Washington out of boredom after a brief visit. "He missed the crowds and frivolities of Paris," Dwight remarked, piously noting that Americans were fortunate that their capital was not saddled with such Old World corruption—"in Europe, courts corrupt capitals, and capitals courts and kingdoms." Washington's attractions were, instead, the institutions of government. Tourists attended sessions of Congress and visited the White House, where Europeans were astonished to find no guards or any other sign of security. Indeed, it was often possible for visitors with the right credentials to have an audience with the president himself.[50]

*   *   *

FEW CASUAL TRAVELERS ventured south of Washington or west of the Appalachian Mountains. The reasons were quite simple: Roads were generally poor, railroads rare (even at mid-century), and accommodations for travelers sparse. The exceptions among nineteenth-century travelers were often foreigners interested in the growth of a young nation and its regional variations. Charles Weld, for example, curious about the developing cities of the West (then roughly defined as the region between the Appalachians and the Mississippi River), made a giant circuit from Niagara Falls to Chicago, south to Cincinnati, and finally back across Ohio and Virginia to Baltimore. Summer heat (grueling for Europeans, who were accustomed to a more temperate climate), jolting trains, and rude, tobacco-spitting passengers made the overnight train trips across Michigan to Chicago and between Chicago and Cincinnati an ordeal. Heading east, Weld had to put up with a long delay in Zanesville, Ohio, waiting for a change of trains; a twelve-hour stagecoach ride (covering just forty miles) west of Wheeling, where the railroad line was not yet completed; and a recklessly fast train ride through the mountains, ending in a derailment in western Maryland.[51]

Yet the major cities of the West often repaid the effort required to reach them. Weld was impressed by Cincinnati, with a population of over 100,000 and many of the commercial enterprises and cultural institutions of a major city, even though it was less than half a century old. He was pleasantly surprised to find accommodations at a large, comfortable hotel, when just three decades earlier (as he himself noted), a single rude tavern had been the only public accommodation. Chicago, seldom visited until the 1840s, was even more striking in its raw new construction, the obvious result of phenomenal growth. Founded in 1829, the city boasted a population of 75,000 by the time Weld arrived. "The oldest inhabitant *born* in the town . . . was only twenty-two years old in 1853," he wrote in amazement. Forty years earlier, the entire township could have been bought for $500; now it was worth millions, and the population had multiplied twenty times over in a decade.[52]

Charles Dickens, traveling a dozen years before Weld, also

praised Cincinnati, finding it "cheerful, thriving, and animated," with attractive houses and gardens, paved roads, and tile sidewalks. Continuing downriver to St. Louis, the Dickens family stopped overnight at Louisville, which proved to be a study in contrasts. They lodged at "a splendid hotel . . . as handsomely . . . as though we had been in Paris, rather than hundreds of miles beyond the Alleghenies"; but then, exploring the town the next morning, they shared the roads with dozens of pigs and passed the Magistrates Office—an unprepossessing little house where two or three men sat in the sunshine with nothing to do, "a perfect picture of Justice retired from business for want of customers." On the riverboat, Dickens encountered a leader of the Choctaw tribe on his way home after some weeks in Washington negotiating with the federal government on behalf of his tribe. The man gave Dickens his calling card, talked with him about the writings of Sir Walter Scott and James Fenimore Cooper, and expressed his deep interest in visiting England, while at the same time speaking with regret about his tribe's decline in population and their powerlessness in dealing with the American government.[53]

At St. Louis, Dickens wandered along the narrow streets of the old French Quarter and the wharves of the riverfront commercial district. Another day, eager to see the prairie, he and a group of male companions set off on an overnight jaunt, traveling by horse and carriage over muddy roads that slowed their progress to a mile or two an hour. (Dickens left his family behind, because such a journey was considered too arduous for women and children.) The prairie itself was a disappointment, "oppressive in its barren monotony," but the journey offered a fascinating glimpse at the American frontier. They stopped at an "inn" that was no more than a one-room log cabin run by a "swarthy young savage, in a shirt of cotton print like bed-furniture," and, in a village farther along, at a ramshackle "hotel" with a "low-roofed out-house, half-cowshed and half-kitchen," which served as a public dining room. Along the way they encountered a drunken farmer who claimed to be just biding his time before bringing his family from St. Louis, a party of German emigrants, and a self-styled phrenologist calling himself "Dr. Crocus."[54]

For travelers like Weld and Dickens, this curious mixture of the civilized and the primitive, the new and the relatively old and settled, was the most striking feature of touring America. With its cities that had grown from mere villages in a matter of two or three decades and its huge expanses of unsettled land, the United States offered a striking contrast to Europe. And yet there was much that mimicked Europe, as Americans followed familiar models in designing their cities and in creating their cultural institutions. For those following the American version of the "grand tour," the scenes were different, but travelers' interests and the vocabulary they used to describe their experiences followed closely the traditions of the Continental grand tour.

TWO

THE BUSINESS

OF

TRAVEL

CHAPTER 5

TRAVELING

WITH THE

MILLIONS

ALTHOUGH THE expansion of railroads throughout much of
northern Europe opened the possibility of leisure travel for people of modest means, significant obstacles continued to stand in their
way. Schedules and fares were complex because of the large number
of competing railway companies, low-cost accommodations were limited, and guidebooks for the budget traveler nonexistent. Perhaps
most significant, middle- and working-class people were unaccus-
tomed to the very idea of travel for pleasure. It took a new kind of
entrepreneur to persuade them that travel was both useful and agreeable, as well as within their reach.

The first of this new breed was, on the face of it, a rather unlikely
candidate for the task—a young temperance preacher from the Midlands region of England. Thomas Cook, a thirty-two-year-old cabinetmaker by trade, earned a modest living writing and distributing
temperance publications from his home in Harborough. While walking the fifteen miles to a temperance meeting in Leicester on a hot
summer day in 1841, he hit upon the idea of chartering a train to

135

carry the faithful to their next regional meeting. Train fares, even for short distances, were still high enough to give pause to the working-class people who dominated the membership of the Harborough Temperance Society and its sister organizations, so Cook persuaded officials of the Midland Counties Railway to offer reduced fares in exchange for his guarantee of a substantial number of passengers.

Although several working-class organizations had sponsored railway excursions for their members in recent years, the idea was still enough of a novelty to encourage a carnival atmosphere. Hundreds of curiosity seekers converged on the Leicester train station to watch as the 570 excursionists boarded third-class, open carriages. A brass band, arranged by Cook as part of the festivities, greeted the group at Loughborough. At one stroke, Cook managed to advance his cause by making it easier for temperance advocates to attend the meeting and turned the meeting itself into an occasion to remember. This excursion proved so popular that Cook kept himself busy over the next three summers organizing trips for Temperance Society members and Sunday school children throughout the region served by the Midland Counties Railway.[1]

His early successes encouraged Cook to move beyond his work with temperance and church groups. In the summer of 1845, he arranged an excursion to the seashore at Liverpool—a trip open to the general public, intended simply for pleasure, and sponsored under his own name rather than on behalf of an organization. It was a far more complicated undertaking than day trips to temperance meetings. The railroad fares alone required negotiations with four different companies; in addition, Cook researched hotel accommodations and restaurants (although participants made their own arrangements), planned side trips into Wales to visit Caernarvon and Mount Snowdon, and produced a guidebook called *A Handbook of the Trip to Liverpool,* detailing sights to be seen along the way. All 350 tickets had sold within a week of departure, and a few scalpers resold their tickets at higher prices. The obvious popularity of the Liverpool excursion induced Cook to run a second one two weeks later, with equal success. Climbing Mount Snowdon with his enthusiastic travelers, he decided an excursion to Scotland would be his next venture.[2]

It was a logical choice, given Scotland's continued popularity as a tourist destination, but one that brought a new level of complexity to Cook's work as a tour organizer. Because there was no through railway service between England and Scotland at the time, and the company that controlled the most direct steamer connections refused to negotiate special group fares, Cook worked out a complicated route involving a train to the west coast of England just north of Liverpool, a long ship passage to the Scottish coast, and then another train to Glasgow and on to Edinburgh. These convoluted arrangements proved no deterrent, however, as more than four hundred people signed up for the first tour in the summer of 1846. The prospect of such a large group of tourists descending upon Glasgow en masse was so novel that a crowd of gawking well-wishers met them at the train station. Later they were entertained with a parade and party at City Hall.[3]

Cook organized three more tours to Scotland in 1847, the last one made entirely by rail except for the crossings over the Tyne and Tweed rivers. Within another year, his arrangements were well established, drawing more than three thousand tourists annually. Meanwhile, he continued to develop excursions closer to home. Turning his powers of persuasion from railway and steamship officials to members of the nobility, he talked the Dukes of Rutland and Devonshire into opening the grounds surrounding their country homes, Belvoir Castle and Chatsworth, to his groups. But as Cook himself realized, his future as a travel organizer lay in planning longer tours. The continued expansion of railway service soon made short excursions inexpensive and ordinary; as a result they lost much of their appeal as vacation trips. In addition, railroad companies began introducing their own cheap fares, further diminishing the role for an organizer like Cook.[4]

In 1846, Cook's temperance publishing business failed, apparently the result of competition from other publishers, forcing him to declare bankrupcy and providing whatever further inducement he needed to transform his travel sideline into his primary business.[5] This shift from temperance to travel was entirely logical, however, if not entirely voluntary. Promoting travel for the working classes was as much a calling as a business for Cook, inspiring the same kind of moral fervor previously devoted to publishing temperance tracts. He believed that travel—whether linked to a specific purpose or designed simply for pleasure—broadened the mind and encouraged a thirst for knowledge, in the process breaking down barriers of class and nationality and promoting tolerance and Christian benevolence. He also argued for the positive benefits of fresh air and recreation. Such ideas were fairly widely shared in the mid-nineteenth century, but Cook went beyond standard wisdom to argue that everyone, rich and poor alike, had the *right* to travel, and that railways were the means to make this possible. "Railway travelling is travelling for the Millions," he wrote, adding that trains were a democratizing influence because they carried all kinds of people, "a mourning countess and a marriage party—a weeping widow and a laughing bride—a gray head and an infant of days," in the same conveyances, to the same places. Sights that had once been accessible only to the privileged could now be seen by nearly anyone, and in Cook's opinion, this was not only good for the working-class folk previously denied such pleasures, but also for society at large.[6]

Cook was unique in arguing for the positive benefits of working-class travel, and in the fact that he spoke from the workers' perspective. Schooled only to the age of ten, as an adolescent he had worked for a gardener and was then apprenticed to his uncle, a cabinetmaker, at about age fourteen. While still in his mid-teens, he joined the local Baptist church; soon after completing his apprenticeship, when he was about nineteen, he became an itinerant preacher. In his second year on the job, he traveled nearly 2,700 miles, most of them on foot. When the church began cutting back its missionary work because of limited funds, Cook set himself up as a cabinetmaker, but he continued to take an interest in church-related work. Perhaps because his early employers had been addicted to drink, he gravitated toward the temperance movement and in 1839 set up a small business in his home distributing tracts, pledge cards, and medals. He soon began writing the tracts as well, and in 1841 established the Midland Temperance Press in Leicester.[7]

Because of his background and his personal involvement with the people who patronized his excursions in the early years, Cook understood the aspirations of his clients and respected them as individuals. In particular, he recognized that they were just as curious about other parts of the world as those above them in the social hierarchy, and just as eager to travel, given the opportunity. This empathy with his clients—and the habit of traveling with them and listening to their opinions—would prove critical to his success, even as he expanded his business far beyond the limits of working-class excursions.

WHEN LONDON'S Great Exhibition opened at the Crystal Palace in the spring of 1851, the first of a series of world's fairs celebrating the achievements of industrial technology, Cook found the perfect opportunity to meld his moral beliefs about working-class travel with his career ambitions. These exhibitions, mounted regularly in cities throughout Europe, the United States, India, and Australia up to the Second World War, proved enormously popular, drawing people of all social ranks from substantial distances. As the first of these spectacles, however, the Crystal Palace Exhibition's potential attraction was untested. The promoters wanted to encourage attendance among lower-income people and provincial residents, but faced significant obstacles. The cost of admission, although modest, was a deterrent, especially for large families and out-of-towners, who had to pay for train fares and hotel accommodations. More significantly, anyone who lived more than a short distance outside London had to contend with competing railway lines and separate fares for each segment of the trip.

Cook's reputation for organizing low-cost excursions and his base in the industrial Midlands, an obvious source of visitors to the Exhibition, led Joseph Paxton, the designer of the Crystal Palace, and John Ellis, chairman of the Midland Railway, to approach him about arranging excursions to London. The idea appealed to Cook for practical as well as idealistic reasons. It would be a logical outgrowth of his business, with the potential to draw far more patrons than his day trips or Scottish excursions. He believed that working men and women, the people behind England's industrialization, had a special interest in seeing the Exhibition and should not be prevented by considerations of cost. "Now is the time for the working classes," he wrote in the midst of organizing his excursions; "the upper and middle classes have had the benefit of arrangements adapted to *their* circumstances, and the time for the millions has now arrived.'' The Exhibition, he thought, could exercise a "Harmonizing & Enobling Influence."[8]

In organizing the London excursions, his most ambitious undertaking to date, Cook expanded his established methods of operating and tested new ones. As usual, he worked with the Midland Railway, which gave him the exclusive right to organize tours on the southern section of their system. He searched out suitable accommodations in London, looking for boardinghouses that were inexpensive, clean, conveniently located, and whenever possible, "conducted on temperance principles." They ranged from large establishments like the "Mechanics Home" in the Pimlico district, which could accommodate one thousand people dormitory-style for 2 shillings a night, breakfast included, to rooms in private homes. One small boardinghouse near Regent's Park advertised a pew in the parish church and free entry to the botanic garden in Regent's Park, along with bed and breakfast. In addition to maintaining a list of accommodations, Cook set up an office at the Euston train station with an agent assigned to keep track of the availability of rooms each day. He also located omnibus routes that would take people from their boardinghouses to the Exhibition grounds. With these details arranged, Cook turned to promoting his tours, a task he had not bothered with much in the past. He launched a newspaper, *The Excursionist and Exhibition Advertiser,* devoted to articles about the Exhibition and details of his proposed excursions, including train schedules and advertisements for the various boardinghouses deemed acceptable by Cook. To help drum up business and solve the financial obstacles to a London trip, Cook and his son, John Mason, traveled throughout the Midlands setting up "Exhibition Clubs" among workingmen; members contributed a small sum each week until they had accumulated enough to pay for the trip.[9]

Part of Cook's task in marketing his excursions, besides convincing people that they could afford the trip, was persuading them that they really wanted to go. London was a long way from Leicester or Manchester, culturally as well as geographically. It was one thing to visit the seashore, but quite another to confront the metropolis. In his first issue of the *Excursionist,* he published an article titled "Why Should Working Men Visit the Exhibition?" urging workers to visit the Crystal Palace not merely for amusement, but as a means of improving their own skills by viewing the best examples of their trade from other parts of Britain and Europe. The Exhibition, in Cook's words, was "a great School of Science, of Art, of Industry, of Peace and Universal Brotherhood!"[10]

He noted approvingly that there would be no celebration of the anniversary of Waterloo on June 18, a fact he attributed to the "glorious Peace Demonstration at Hyde Park." The prospect of England and France joining forces in the Exhibition suggested that their traditional enmity might finally be ended and, with it, inappropriate "war demonstrations" like those customarily marking the victory at Waterloo. (Later Cook learned to his chagrin that he had been mistaken in believing that the usual celebration had been canceled.) He also pointed out how popular the Exhibition had proved in its first weeks, remarking that other sections of London seemed nearly deserted by comparison with the crowds at the Exhibition grounds. An added draw, for those of temperance leanings, would be the international temperance demonstration scheduled for August, at the height of the Exhibition season. For those who might prefer some other kind of entertainment, Cook ran articles in *The Excursionist* on the sights of London as well as points of interest along the way.[11]

Cook continued to work on ways to make the fair affordable to the working class. Articles in *The Excursionist* praised benevolent employers who provided lodging for their workers in company-owned buildings in London or helped finance trips by advancing wages or paying interest on savings deposited with the company. He argued for lower admission fees, suggesting special children's fees and single tickets good for four days, which would incidentally help keep the crowds to manageable size by giving people the freedom to come and go for a single price, without feeling that they had to see everything in a day or two. He also urged railroad companies to provide low excursion fares—an argument that backfired, since cheap fares would undercut his own business. Early in the season, the Great Northern Line began offering round-trip fares of 5 shillings, compared with the 15 shillings Cook had negotiated with the

Midland Railway. Cook had no alternative but to match the fares, covering the difference between what he charged his patrons and what he owed Midland out of his profit margin. (Competition from at least two other excursion agents cut into his business as well.) He attempted to make up the difference by generating even larger numbers, with some degree of success. One of his strategies was sending his seventeen-year-old son on a tour of Midlands towns, leading a band advertising the Exhibition.[12]

In the end, about 165,000 people visited the Exhibition on Cook's excursions, amounting to about 3 percent of the total number of visitors (and a much higher percentage of out-of-town visitors). Even so, Cook lost money on his London excursions. When the Exhibition had closed, he ceased running trips to London, turning his attention instead to expanding his country tours, adding trips to seaside resorts in Lancashire, Yorkshire, and along the southern coast. Cook didn't give up on industrial exhibitions, however. He organized tours to Ireland in connection with the Dublin Exhibition in 1853, and, in a move that would permanently change the character of his business, launched his first Continental tours to capitalize on the Paris Exhibition of 1855.[13]

When Cook began organizing his first Paris trips, he ran into resistance from Continental railway companies, which refused to negotiate special fares. The Brighton and Southeastern Railway Companies, which controlled trains to Dover, also proved uncooperative. As a result, he found the most advantageous route to be from Harwich to Hoek van Holland, then via rail to Antwerp, Brussels, and Paris with extensions for those who wished to visit the Rhine and parts of Germany. Cook offered assistance in making hotel arrangements—a plus for those who had never traveled abroad and couldn't speak French—and included advertisements for Paris hotels in *The Excursionist,* much as he had done in organizing his trips to London. Those willing to follow a fixed itinerary could join a tour escorted by Cook himself, thus taking all the uncertainty out of a foreign trip. Fifty people opted to join the "personally-conducted" tour (as Cook called it), which included Antwerp, Brussels, and the battlefield at Waterloo, "that interesting field of a feud now past and buried for ever (it is hoped)." Part of the group returned to England from Brussels, others went to Paris, while the majority followed Cook to Germany, sailing up the Rhine from Cologne to Mainz, then on to Frankfurt, Heidelberg, and Paris by train. A few continued to Switzerland on their own. A second tour later in the summer offered a wider choice of routes.[14]

Despite enthusiastic reviews from many participants, Cook lost money on these tours, but cleverly parlayed his problems into an advertisement for his second season, playing up the difficulties he and his groups had encountered with Continental railway companies, grasping hotelkeepers, money changers, and a bewildering array of currencies. "All these monetary perplexities caused continued annoyance to most of the Parties," he wrote. Not only the women, but even "shrewd commercial gentlemen" asked Cook to handle their bills for them. In short, readers of *The Excursionist* with designs on the Continent ought to seize the opportunity to travel with Cook. His prices would be a little higher this season, he admitted, and he had learned to demand a deposit at least a month in advance to secure places. But he offered a wider array of choices, with travelers free to diverge from the group at will. Evidently Cook didn't get a sufficiently large response to justify continuing the tours, however, because he made no effort to repeat them for the rest of the decade, preferring instead to concentrate on business closer to home, especially the Scottish excursions, now firmly established as the cornerstone of his business.

By the mid-1850s, more than four thousand people traveled to Scotland each summer under his auspices. About a quarter of them joined guided tours led by Cook himself, while the rest struck out on their own using tickets arranged by his company. The system he adopted for these independent excursions, which he labeled the "circular tour," consisted of a set of tickets for trains, steamers, and coaches covering a specified itinerary for a set price. Travelers could choose from several routes—in the mid-1850s Cook offered eight different options leaving from Edinburgh—combining more than one if they chose. Tickets were good for a fixed period of time (typically two weeks), but within that period travelers could decide for themselves when to proceed on each leg of the trip, and they could make changes along the way without forfeiting the cost of tickets already purchased. The system offered a considerable degree of flexibility without the complications of arranging for passage on each separate leg of the trip—a convenience in the Highlands, especially, where railroad service was still limited. One tour from Edinburgh, for example, included a train to Stirling, a coach to The Trossachs, a steamer on Loch Katrine, another steamer on Loch Lomond, a train from the foot of Loch Lomond to Bowling, and finally another steamer on the Clyde to Glasgow. For those who wanted the security of an accompanied tour, Cook published the complete itinerary that he planned to follow. Typically as many as five hundred tourists chose to travel with him each time.[15]

The spectacle of hordes of English tourists descending on Highland villages and peaceful lochs created a certain amount of skepticism and even ridicule among those accustomed to traveling more conventionally. Cook responded by continuing to argue for the social benefits of group travel as well as its economies. "There are some 'stuck up' people who affect to look down on 'cheap excursionists' as an inferior grade of tourists," he remarked, ". . . but our belief is that envy is at the bottom of such manifestations wherever they appear. Take a steam boat party of 100 passengers, 75 of them going under our arrangements and the other 25 in their own isolation; every one of the associated party may soon be identified by their courteous and joyous fraternization," in contrast to the "independent" tourists, who paid up to three times the cost "for the privilege of thus sitting solitary in a crowd of free elastic spirits." For Cook, the sociability of travel was part of the point. What he didn't realize was that, for wealthier travelers, privacy and the ability to maintain social boundaries were all-important. These travelers abhorred what they perceived as the noisy, gauche behavior typical of lower-class people moving beyond their station.

Cook's championing of social bonding and mutual assistance was especially important for single women, who under mid-nineteenth-century conventions would have been all but barred from traveling. From the beginning, a majority of Cook's patrons were women, either by themselves or with other female friends. One young woman, making her first trip to Scotland in 1855, remarked about the "pleasant and home-like" atmosphere of the excursion, "especially to ladies, of whom there was quite a majority; some in family parties of four, five, and six; others in twos or threes; and a few, having neither sister or friend to join them, had resolved to see Scotland alone rather than not see it at all." Such solo travelers need not be at all concerned, she wrote, because the group was friendly, yet not beyond the bounds of "respectful familiarity" and "anything in the shape of annoyance or ill behaviour was not known.... So tell all your anti-excursion folks, that their fears and fancies about this and that difficulty would all subside, if once brought into contact with our Leicester Excursion Manager."[16]

Other travelers, equally aware of the criticism leveled at excursionists, stressed the value of Cook's tours. A man making his second Scottish tour cheered, "Hurrah for the Excursion Trains, say I! They are a fine invention for men like myself, of small means and not much leisure.... He who can travel first-class express, with a valet to take his ticket and look after his carpet-bag, can afford to despise the humble mode of locomotion whose praises I sing: but these are the days of the million; and for my part, I am heartily thankful that the wants of the million are cared for, and that Bobson, Dickson, and Tomson (of course with Mistresses Bobson, Dickson, and Tomson), can o'erleap the bounds of their own narrow circle, rub off rust and prejudice by contact with others, and expand their souls and invigorate their bodies by an exploration of some of Nature's finest scenes." Few were aware, he thought, that one could actually travel from Cambridge (his hometown) to Edinburgh and back for a mere £1 14s. 6d.[17]

As far as the Scots were concerned, some praised the tourist boom, recognizing that it brought money into their economy. An Edinburgh publisher, writing in 1854, remarked that Cook's excursions "are really very curious ... for an attempt is made to gather up tourists from a number of tributary streams, then carry them in a body along a trunk-line of railway, and then distribute them over the north, to catch pleasure wherever it is to be found. Then, the pleasure being over, the wanderers are picked up from far and wide, they are brought back along the trunk line of railway, and they are distributed over the whole of the south, almost to their own doors." One could learn much from this system, he asserted, including the value of common railway gauges and the value of mass travel in reducing both railway fares and hotel charges. Finally, he pointed out, these tours "circulate money where money is not very abundant: when English pleasure-money gets to the heart of the Highlands, surely it will do some little good: surely it must give an impetus, even in a humble degree, to the spirit of commerce and traffic."[18]

THROUGHOUT THE 1850s, Cook continued to develop his business in other parts of the British Isles as well. Trips to Liverpool and Wales remained popular, and he added tours to several seaside resorts, the Lake District, the Isle of Man, and Ireland. By the end of the decade, Cook was receiving ever larger numbers of inquiries about tours to the Continent and other destinations farther afield. There were those who "would not be easy without a Trip to the Moon, if there were any possibility of such ascension," he remarked. But the financial losses of the 1855 tours and the threat of war on the Continent deterred him from expanding his business across the Channel until 1861, when a project dear to his heart pushed him to reconsider. The Working Men's Excursion to Paris originated in part to counter a proposal for a visit to Paris by an organization called the Rifle Volunteers. The prospect of a highly publicized visit to France by a military group met with considerable opposition as impolitic; instead, a group calling itself the London Committee of Working Men proposed an excursion of workers, who would tour Paris and "shake hands with the Parisian ouvriers, and assure them that, whatever may have been the case many years ago, this nation has now no other feeling towards France but that of good will, and that the British people have an earnest desire to live on terms of amity with neighbouring states." The committee itself was hardly a working-class group—its president was Joseph Paxton, designer of the Crystal Palace and a member of Parliament—but all the members, Cook noted, had risen from humble backgrounds. The excursion was intended to be a pleasure trip, but one with a moral purpose as well. This combination of travel for workers and promotion of peaceful relations between Britain and France coincided perfectly with Cook's own views, and he wrote to the organizers offering to help make arrangements for workers outside London to join the excursion.[19]

Escorting as many as five thousand Englishmen to Paris at a popular holiday period required special attention to lodgings, so Cook went to Paris some weeks ahead of time to inspect hotels and estimate the cost of living expenses for the excursionists. Despite a cool reception from some hotelkeepers, who were not enamored of the idea of a large working-class inundation, he put together a list of reasonably priced accommodations. For those who wanted to make all their arrangements in advance, Cook offered tickets for lodging at "good second class hotels" and meals at 5 to 6 shillings per day. "Our aim being to get practical information," Cook also decided while in Paris to try one of the city's well-known restaurants. He found the four courses, though a bit "spicy," much to his liking and reasonably priced, and noted with approval that those who did not care to drink the wine provided with the meal could have a dish of fruit instead: "More civil this than the tyranny of the English table laws which would compel a guest to pay for wine whether he drank it or not, and thus assist to make others drunk." Another evening he was just as happy to dine at his hotel, "where a good deal of 'plain English' in language and behaviour, as well as roast beef and Yorkshire pudding, were blended with French mixtures."[20]

The proposed trip generated considerable interest and many questions about who, exactly, was eligible for the "working men's excursion." Cook himself wished that the organizers had called it an International Excursion, because the label "working men" was vague and seemed to exclude people. Some criticized the proposed tour as "some great attempt at fraternization of English workmen with French *ouvriers*." In response, Cook urged women and men not generally thought of as "working class" to join in. As it turned out, about seventeen hundred people made the journey—many fewer than the three to five thousand Cook had predicted, but impressive nonetheless. Transportation arrangements went smoothly, including the transfer of nine hundred excursionists at a clip from Channel steamers to trains at Boulogne; and the visitors met a warm welcome in Paris, where city officials opened the Hôtel de Ville for a special tour. A French humor magazine poked fun at the English visitors, but, as Cook noted with some satisfaction, the hoteliers who had snubbed him on his reconnoitering trip later tried hard to gain the patronage of his clients.[21]

The Working Men's Excursion was a special undertaking for Cook, one he later described as a work "of love, minus profit." A similar expedition the following year was also a financial flop, in part because the London Exhibition of 1862 drew many of the people who might otherwise have visited France. Cook himself was heavily involved in organizing trips to the Exhibition, a business that proved more profitable than his French excursions. After his experience in 1851, he knew enough not to try to organize excursion trains himself, but rather to rely on the railway companies to cut fares as a way of increasing travel. Although he published advertisements from railway companies quoting fares and schedules, he put most of his energy into accommodating visitors once they reached London. Not content merely to scout hotels and assist in making arrangements, he hired a large, newly built tenement in the South Kensington district of London and converted it into a Visitors' Home providing bed, breakfast, and tea for 3 shillings per person. No alcohol was served, and smoking was limited to a single common room. The Visitors' Home proved so popular, with middle-class as well as working-class tourists, that Cook also engaged a group of smaller boardinghouses to provide lodging for those who could afford a somewhat higher standard of living. Trips to the Exhibition became a popular company-sponsored outing, with Cook catering especially to such groups. He was also proud of his international clientele. At one point during the summer he had a group of sixty-five Germans and another of forty Italians, in addition to his British guests. By the end of the season, Cook had accommodated about twenty thousand people.[22]

The following summer, Scottish railway companies put an abrupt end to Cook's popular tours in their country. For some years, Cook had operated under a system in which he paid the various rail and steamship companies a fixed rate per mile and then issued "circular tickets" allowing tourists to select the segments they wished to cover within a given itinerary. In 1863, however, the companies decided they could do better by issuing tickets directly to customers. Some of the companies apparently thought that Cook was favoring their competitors; railway officials also believed that the popularity of the large, escorted party was on the wane, that most travelers would be willing to pay somewhat higher fares in exchange for the privilege of greater choice and independence. Scotland was becoming sufficiently familiar (and, with the continued expansion of railroads, more readily accessible), so that fewer travelers felt the need of an escort. Cook continued to issue tickets as an agent for the railroads, but his days of conducting five hundred people at a clip, four times or more a summer, were over.[23]

Cook professed to understand the business motives behind the railway companies' decision, yet he was obviously hurt and angry that some sense of loyalty and gratitude for his years of service had not prevailed over purely financial considerations. Indeed, it seemed to him (probably correctly) that he had in effect put himself out of business by introducing English men and women to Scottish travel, enhancing the region's popularity and eventually making it so easy to travel there that his services were no longer needed. "We almost wish we could think with these gentlemen [the railway officials], and on personal as well as pecuniary grounds, resolve to give up all this anxiety, and toil, and risk, and quietly retire into some peaceful, noiseless occupation, away from the entreaties of friends and the cold influences of unappreciative finesse." But the comment was merely rhetorical. Cook was not about to retire early, and so he turned his attention once again to the Continent.[24]

He began by repeating his short, inexpensive excursions to Paris, arranging special trains and steamers from London to Paris with a stop in Rouen for what he boasted was the best fare ever offered. Moreover, those "delicate folk who do not like Excursion Trains (they are those who know the least about them)" might travel a few days later by regularly scheduled trains at the same price. The return trip could be made anytime over a period of ten days. Those who wished could be accommodated at one of two hotels in Paris, where Cook had reserved a block of rooms, while others were free to make their own arrangements. To assist them, Cook as usual published a list of accommodations he had inspected, with their prices and a brief description, noting those where English was spoken and where "plain English" food was served.

Concerned about potential resistance to foreign travel, Cook emphasized, as he had many times before, the importance of increasing knowledge and understanding between the two nations. One could learn much from the French, he argued, especially "in matters of taste and courtesy," and go home strengthened in one's own beliefs, especially those concerned with religion and observation of the Sabbath. Cook's disapproval of Parisian Sundays, celebrated as a day of merriment rather than rest, remained a persistent theme in all his commentary about France. The spectacle of people parading about parks and enjoying themselves in cafés bothered him, but even more disturbing to him was the fact that shops, cafés, and restaurants all remained open, forcing thousands of people to spend their Sundays working.[25]

The Paris excursions proved more successful this time around, encouraging Cook to try more ambitious itineraries. Searching for a substitute for his lucrative Scottish business, he set his sights on Switzerland, which had scenic similarities and posed challenges much like those he had faced in the early years of his Scottish tours: limited train service, rough terrain, and the need to combine train, coach, and steamer travel if one were to get beyond the major cities. If Cook could work out a system that would simplify the transportation problems and cut costs, he might reasonably expect to equal or even exceed his lost Scottish business.

During his spring trips to Paris, Cook met with railway officials who explained to him the various rail/steamer/coach links that were possible and promised special fares. Encouraged by these talks, he decided to make an exploratory trip through France and on to Switzerland late in June. Announcing his intentions in *The Excursionist,* he offered to take a small group with him.[26] The response far exceeded his expectations. About 140 tourists signed on for the trip to Paris, with about half that number continuing on to Switzerland on what would prove to be a whirlwind tour. Departing London at 6:00 A.M., the group arrived in Paris at 11:30 P.M., allowing an hour's stop for breakfast at Newhaven, five hours to tour Dieppe, and a mere fifteen minutes for refreshments at Rouen. (Serving supper to dozens of tourists in the space of fifteen minutes was no small feat. One member of the group remarked, " 'Jambon' sandwiches followed each other in about as rapid succession as balls do in firing, leaving one to infer that the commissary department had been subject to English justice.") They remained in Paris only long enough to catch a few hours' sleep, leaving for Geneva at 6:00 the following morning. Fortunately, the next day was Sunday, which Cook always tried to observe as a day of rest, so the group had a brief respite from trains and railway station food. In the evening they had their first opportunity for a leisurely dinner in the Continental style. The ten-course menu, remarked one, "reads like an index to a cookery book."[27] Some of the tourists were up by 5:30 Monday morning, despite pouring rain, to visit the confluence of the Rhone and Arve rivers.

At Geneva the group split up, some going to Chamonix with Cook and others heading east to the Swiss Alps. Among the Chamonix contingent was a high-spirited group of seven young men and women: Jemima Morrell, her brother William, and five friends. Calling themselves the Junior Alpine Club, they traveled with Cook's group as far as Chamonix, but then struck off on their own, determined to see as much of Switzerland as they could cram into the two weeks allotted to them. Their frenetic itinerary was typical of the new breed of traveler with just two or three weeks' vacation: days that began at 5:00 or 6:00 A.M. and ended late in the evening, hours spent on trains and in carriages, nearly every night in a different hotel. In their two weeks, the Morrell group crossed the Tête Noire Pass between Chamonix and Martigny, went up the Rhone Valley as far as Sion, visited the spa at Leuk, rode mules over the Gemmi Pass to Kandersteg, steamed across Lake Thun and Lake Brienz, toured Interlaken, visited the waterfalls at Lauterbrunnen and Giessbach, and climbed Mount Rigi. On one particularly grueling day near the end of their journey, the Morrells and friends traveled from Giessbach to Mount Rigi via three lake steamers and a diligence, with a four-hour break in Lucerne around midday, where they squeezed in a visit to the cathedral before lunch. ("It must be done," Jemima remarked.) Arriving at the base of Mount Rigi late in the afternoon, they proceeded to climb to the summit—a nine-mile hike that took four and a half hours, the last bit of it after dark. At 3:00 A.M. they were up again to view the sunrise in subfreezing temperatures with the other two hundred guests at the hotel.²⁸ By 7:00 they were ready to hike down the mountain and head back to Lucerne; "Time was despotic" was Jemima's comment.

Despite feeling rushed and often exhausted, the Morrells and their friends had no regrets. They approached the trip in a spirit of high adventure, prepared to be entertained with everything they saw, the people as well as the scenery. "I set off with an impression that we should find the annoyances of travelling considerable and that there would be some dangers," William wrote to his parents, but the opposite had proven true. "All has gone on as pleasantly as could be and as to the dangers they are very much overdone." He and his sister were enchanted by the unfamiliar, from the "minikin coffee pots only copious in supply to Lilliputians" and the "peculiar" tea to the multicourse dinners. They deliberately sought out the "foreign" hotels—that is, the ones that didn't make a practice of catering to British tourists. Not only were they cheaper, but "more novel," unlike those at Chamonix, which seemed altogether too much like being at home.²⁹

The Morrells' enthusiasm about their travels was widely shared among those who accompanied Cook on his Continental scouting trip. The response encouraged him to map out a full-scale tour for early August, which he boasted would be "one of the best excursions ever known on the Continent." Nearly eleven hundred people went as far as Paris (including a contingent from the "Glasgow Abstainers Union"), with more than three hundred continuing on to Switzerland. Some joined Cook on a conducted tour from Geneva to Mont Blanc and back via train, coach, mule, and lake steamer, while others took off on their own. Cook escorted another group in mid-September, finishing the season quite well pleased with his efforts. Clearly he had minor problems to work out; at times his groups had reached their day's destination only to find their hotel full, and the transit connections didn't all work smoothly, as Cook discovered when his group arrived at Lake Lucerne hours before the next steamer was scheduled to embark. (Rather than wait, he hired boats and had his group rowed across the lake.) Still, Cook finished the season with the basic elements of his French and Swiss tours in place.

The system was similar to the one he had worked out for his Scottish tours: The "Swiss Tourist Ticket," as he called it, provided transportation from Geneva to a variety of destinations of the traveler's choice, all for a fixed price, while the "Mt Blanc Circular Ticket" covered the excursion to Chamonix. Hotels and meals were charged separately, but in the course of the 1863 excursions, Cook had negotiated set fees at a series of hotels in Paris and Switzerland, so he could reassure his patrons in advance about what they would be expected to pay, an important consideration for those traveling on limited incomes. He also advised prospective tourists about passports (no legal requirement for France and Switzerland, but he encouraged those going as far as Switzerland to obtain one anyway), currency exchange, and language difficulties, which he generally minimized. In Paris he steered his patrons to hotels run by English-speaking proprietors who adopted a helpful attitude toward first-time visitors and catered to British tastes, while reminding them, "Our friends must remember that not Monsieur, but John Bull, will be the foreigner when we have landed on French soil." On the matter of food, Cook also adopted a middle ground, noting those hotels where British food was served but reminding tourists to be prepared for differences: "It is especially difficult to adapt a French dinner to a thoroughgoing roast-beef-and-pudding-eating Englishman. A little charity and allowance for taste and custom must be exercised at a French table d'hôte, or the best of French dinners would be by some disesteemed."[30]

The success of his first season in Switzerland convinced Cook to extend his offerings to include Italy. The following spring, he crossed the Channel to scout possibilities for Italian tours. Cook had in mind a much expanded version of his circular tour: across the Mont Cenis Pass to Turin, through the major cities of northern Italy, and then back to France via the coastal route from Genoa to Nice. The first part of this scheme worked out well. Crossing the Mont Cenis Pass by diligence was still an adventure despite recent improvements in the road, but Cook observed the early work on a tunnel (completed in 1871), which would eventually permit direct train service from Geneva to Turin. In Italy he concluded negotiations with railroad officials and found good hotels with English-speaking staffs. (He also noted with approval the signs of the struggle for Italian unification, evident in several cities along his route.)

The journey from Genoa to Nice was less successful. Two long days spent in a diligence riding over poor roads, with an overnight stop at an inn where the beds "had a very suspicious-looking appearance, suggestive of midnight intruders," were enough to persuade Cook to eliminate this segment of his proposed route until the railroad line, recently completed as far as Nice, was extended to Genoa. Instead, when he launched his Italian tours the following summer, Cook and his clients entered Italy via the St. Gotthard Pass and returned over Mont Cenis after touring the Italian Alps, Milan, Parma, Bologna, Florence, Pisa, Livorno, Genoa, and Turin. Cook also offered optional extensions from Milan to Venice and from Florence to Rome and Naples.[31]

Judging from an account written by one of the participants in the first season's tours, Cook's Italian groups maintained a pace rivaling that of Jemima Morrell and her friends in Switzerland. The journey over the St. Gotthard Pass, for example, began with a 5:00 A.M. departure from Lucerne in a driving rain. It continued with a brief stop at Flüelen to see Wilhelm Tell's chapel, followed by an all-day ride by diligence over the pass, stopping for dinner at Andermatt. The passengers arrived in Bellinzona, Italy, at 2:00 A.M., caught a few hours' sleep, and were up again at 7:00 to visit the local church before their 10:00 A.M. departure for Lugano. Despite its regimented quality, the tour took on something of a life of its own. In Milan the travelers met to decide whether they would take a side trip to Venice. They voted in favor and, true to form, did Venice in two days packed with sightseeing, arriving at 11:30 P.M. and rising early the next two days to fit in the Doge's Palace, the Rialto Bridge, a moonlight ride in a gondola, a stroll through the market, mass at St. Mark's Cathedral, coffee at the café Florian (very expensive, one traveler noted), and visits to the Armenian monastery (where Byron had studied the Armenian language) and to the Academy of Fine Arts. The next evening they were back in Milan, having left Venice at dawn and devoted three hours to touring Verona en route.

It seems to have been a cardinal principle of Cook's tours never to start on any journey later than 6:00 A.M. This particular group left Milan at 4:15 the next day, bound for Florence on a journey that rivaled the day spent crossing the St. Gotthard Pass. They "bolted dinner" at Bologna, getting back to the station just in time to catch their train; crossed the Apennines by diligence; waited an hour and a half for a new engine when the one hauling their train broke down; and finally arrived in Florence at 11:00 P.M. Like Venice, Florence rated two days of sightseeing, followed by yet another dawn departure, this time to Pisa and Livorno. Those who wanted to extend their tour to Naples and Rome traveled by sea from Livorno to Civitavecchia (an overnight trip of about twelve hours), where they transferred to a train for a two-hour ride to Rome on what Cook later described as a "roughly worked Railway" with miserable second-class carriages. After two and a half days in Rome, they continued on to Naples by train, spending just a day and a half—one day for an excursion to Pompeii and Mount Vesuvius and half a day for sightseeing in Naples itself. Then it was back to Livorno and Genoa by ship and across Mont Cenis to Geneva. The month-long tour finished up with back-to-back overnight journeys: Geneva to Paris followed by Paris to London.[32]

One of the keys to Cook's success was his care to build upon proven strategies in expanding his business; the Swiss tours had followed the Scottish model, and the Italian tours were an extension of the Swiss experience. When another international exhibition opened in Paris in 1867, he revived the methods he had used to attract tourists to earlier exhibitions in London and Paris, but on a much larger scale, expanding his Continental business substantially in the process. The 1867 Exhibition generated an enormous amount of advance publicity, which boded well for Cook's ambitions but also made preparations difficult, as the anticipation of huge crowds encouraged everyone in the travel business to hold out for high prices. Following the model he had worked out for the London fair in 1862, Cook intended to rent a large building in Paris and convert it into a boardinghouse for working-class visitors, but found that the only available spaces were run-down buildings in dubious locations, for which the owners nevertheless asked exorbitant rents. Most hotel proprietors, including many he had worked with for years, refused to make any advance arrangements, expecting that prices would rise as the Exhibition drew closer. Cook himself predicted that charges at the first-class hotels would jump 50 percent over current rates.

Eventually he negotiated terms at several moderately priced hotels and rented one large building, about twenty minutes' walk from the Exhibition grounds on the Champ de Mars, where he proposed to provide bed and breakfast for about half what even the most moderate hotels would charge. To make his clients feel at home, he installed a "thoroughly *English*" staff and offered afternoon tea in the English style, English newspapers, facilities for currency exchange, and assistance in posting letters. John Ripley, one of Cook's assistants (like his employer, a former temperance preacher), was in charge, available to help patrons organize sightseeing expeditions. Special arrangements could be made for workingmen's clubs. For wealthier visitors, Cook hired another house, newly constructed and beautifully furnished, where he could accommodate groups of ten to twelve in suites complete with "splendid" drawing rooms and individuals in rooms with access to a common drawing room and dining room.

The Paris Exhibition also found Cook reaching farther afield to encourage American tourists for the first time. He had made a trip to the United States in 1865 to explore the possibilities of organizing British-American tours, and his son, John Mason, who had officially joined the family business in 1865, led a small group on an American tour in 1866; but the distances and complications involved did not encourage them to pursue transatlantic excursions. As it turned out, persuading Americans to visit Europe proved much easier than getting the British to visit America. During the prosperous post–Civil War years, an estimated forty thousand Americans crossed the Atlantic annually. The 1867 fair was an especially popular attraction. Cook heard reports that ships of the Cunard Line were fully booked for May despite a substantial increase in fares. He worked hard to gain a share of the American business, even while cautioning his British clients to be wary about patronizing hotels popular with Americans, because the Americans were known for their free-spending habits and would be sure to drive up prices.

In November 1866, John Mason went back to New York in an

attempt to negotiate special steamship fares for American visitors to Europe. The companies initially agreed, but later reneged on their arrangements, seeing no reason to negotiate lower fares at a time of peak demand. Cook had to concentrate instead on encouraging Americans to patronize his hotel arrangements. In recognition of this potential new market, he called his two boardinghouses "Cook's English and American Exhibition Visitors' Home" and the "British and American First-Class Exhibition Boarding House." He also changed the name of his newspaper, the principal means of promoting his business, from *Cook's Excursionist and Tourist Advertiser* to *Cook's Excursionist — European and American Tourist Advertiser.* In 1873, he began publishing a separate American edition.[33]

As Cook's business grew and focused increasingly on Continental travel, the nature of his clientele also expanded far beyond the working-class men and women who had patronized his early excursions. The Paris arrangements provided clear evidence of this shift. Those attending the Exhibition under Cook's auspices could choose from three distinct categories of accommodation: a simple, inexpensive boardinghouse with heavy emphasis on "Englishness," where no liquor was served; rooms in moderately priced hotels at fixed rates, for those who could pay more for a greater degree of privacy and the privilege of taking wine with dinner, if they liked; and a luxurious boardinghouse run "in accordance with Parisian taste and custom." Cook continued to advertise his interest in cooperating with workingmen's excursion clubs and maintained an active business issuing tickets for short-distance excursions to seaside resorts and other popular destinations within Britain; he also continued to emphasize the modest cost of his tours in his efforts to attract new patrons. (A three-week tour to Paris and Switzerland should cost no more than £15 or £16, he observed, "a sum often spent at home, in fashion or folly, in a single night, leaving little for the disbursement but aching heads, wearied limbs, and restless *ennui.*") But by the mid-1860s Cook's focus had clearly shifted from making travel possible for the working class toward simplifying and packaging travel for a broad range of income groups.[34]

Tours within England and Scotland were patronized largely by tradesmen, clerks, and "mechanics" (i.e., artisans and other skilled workers); Continental excursions catered mostly to teachers and businessmen, although the Whitsuntide trips traditionally included "a good deal of the Cockney element." The early Italian trips, more expensive than most tours and therefore likely to attract an upper-middle-class clientele, included "clergymen, physicians, bankers, civil engineers, and merchants"—in short, the kind of people who could afford to take three or four weeks for a vacation (and had the kinds of jobs that permitted it), but did not have unlimited time and money. Cook catered especially to teachers and ministers, timing tours for periods in the summer when they were free to travel and directing notices in *The Excursionist* specifically to them.[35]

Single women, whether daughters of middle-class families or widows with a bit of money and the time to travel, continued to be prominent among Cook's tourists, partly because they were more likely than men to have time to travel. A newspaper writer observed of Cook, "Unprotected females confide in him; hypochondriacs tell him of their complaints; foolish travellers look to him to redeem their errors; . . . but the great conductor never flinches, and his eye is as bright and his smile as ready at the close of the most fatiguing trip as if he had never left home." From the outset, Cook's tours had attracted large numbers of women; by the mid-1860s, women were in the majority in most groups.[36]

Over the years, repeat business was common. An 1865 tour to Italy included five or six people who had been on one of Cook's previous trips to Switzerland or Italy; a Yorkshire man who had been part of his first tour to the Scottish Highlands, now accompanied by his wife; an elderly man from Cornwall, who had been the first to buy tickets for Switzerland last year; "one brave woman from Herts., who has been with us almost 'everywhere' for several years past"; and several men who had been on previous tours, in addition to a family of five from New Zealand and two sisters and a brother from Australia, all visiting Britain and bent on seeing some of the Continent before they returned home.[37]

WITH CONTINENTAL TOURS supplanting local excursions as the mainstay of his business, Cook found himself spending more time in London. In 1865 he moved his headquarters there, to a building he purchased on Fleet Street, while maintaining the Leicester office primarily for printing *The Excursionist* and his various other brochures and guides. The entire family was involved: John Mason managed the London office, while Cook's wife operated a temperance hotel on the upper floors (as she had in Leicester). John Mason had at first been reluctant to leave his job as a printer to join his father in the travel business, claiming that the two of them had not agreed on business matters in the past, but Cook insisted. The business had reached a point where he had to delegate if he was to expand further, and Cook felt he could hand over tasks to his son that he could not trust to anyone else. The partnership between father and son was never a comfortable one, however, as John Mason pushed the family firm toward becoming more businesslike and catering to wealthier clients, while Thomas never quite let go of his idealistic vision of travel as a way of uplifting the working class. By the end of the 1870s, the two men had broken irrevocably, leaving John Mason in charge of running the business, which, by then, had sixty offices throughout the world.[38]

Cook & Son, as the company continued to be known, added to its network of routes until it covered most of Holland, Belgium, France, Germany, Switzerland, Austria, and Italy. In 1869, the firm launched its first tours to the Middle East; in 1875 it introduced Scandinavian tours, including a "Midnight Sun Voyage" to the North Cape, noting that those people who had already covered all of France and Italy and found the popular destinations hopelessly overcrowded might do well to look farther north. Over the next decade, it added Spain, India, Australia, New Zealand, and the United States. Still, the great majority of Cooks' clients, like most British tourists of the nineteenth century, continued to choose Paris, Italy, Switzerland, and the Rhine as favorite destinations.[39]

Although the company continued to offer escorted tours, by the 1870s the great bulk of its clients traveled on circular tickets, mapping out their own routes within certain limitations. Even so, the specter of Cook's huge early tour groups dogged the firm for years, leading John Mason Cook to run articles in *The Excursionist* from time to time reminding potential customers of the distinction between escorted tours and circular tickets, and emphasizing that most Cooks' tourists traveled quite independently. Whatever the choice of route, tickets for each leg of the traveler's journey were bound in little booklets and enclosed in a leather or cloth case stamped with the label COOK'S TOURIST TICKETS. These ticket cases became so ubiquitous across the Continent that conductors often simply looked at the case itself without bothering to claim the ticket.

In 1868, Cooks introduced a similar arrangement for hotels. From the beginning, Thomas Cook had made hotel arrangements for those of his clients who requested assistance; beginning with the Italian tours, he had arranged to pay all hotel charges for a fixed sum for those individuals who didn't want to worry about their day-to-day charges. Hotel coupons, modeled on the circular tickets for transit, were the next logical step. Cook negotiated fixed fees with hotels in all the areas he served and then issued booklets of coupons, each one good for breakfast, dinner, or room. He printed the terms of the arrangement on the coupon booklet—breakfast, for example, was Continental style, with eggs or meat to be charged extra—and provided clients with a list of hotels participating in the system. By 1872, the list included 130 hotels; that number jumped to nearly 400 by 1876 and 500 in 1880.[40] In Thomas Cook's experience, dealing with hotel charges had always been one of the inexperienced traveler's greatest difficulties. Currency exchange was even worse, and by 1873 his son was well on the way to solving that problem too, by issuing what he called "circular notes"—the forerunner of the modern traveler's checks. Patrons paid Cook a given sum of money in exchange for notes issued in denominations of £5 and £10, which could then be cashed at hotels participating in the hotel coupon system.

Although it had required some effort to persuade hotel proprietors to accept the coupon arrangements, within a few months, much to Cook's annoyance, he discovered others imitating his system. At least one imitator, working through an agent in Paris, used Cook's name in soliciting cooperation from hotels and printed coupons that resembled Cook's very closely. Worse still was an article claiming that someone else had invented the coupon system in 1858. This kind of deliberate copying outraged him, but even legitimate competition was anathema to Cook, who threatened to stop patronizing hotels that allowed their names to appear on any other agent's list.[41]

It was a problem he could hardly expect to avoid, however, because the firm's success inevitably inspired imitators. An agency called Stangen was established in Breslau in 1863, the first of several German travel agencies. They were not a serious concern, since Cooks could not very easily tap the German market. American Express, although established in 1848, did not get into the travel business until early in the twentieth century, and thus posed no threat to Cooks' transatlantic business. (In 1902, the president of the company declared that there was no profit in the travel business and, even if there were, he would have no part of it. "I will not have gangs of trippers starting off in charabancs from in front of our offices the way they do from Cooks," he wrote.) But British agents were another matter. Cooks' first serious competitor, Henry Gaze, organized his first tour to Paris in 1844, long before Thomas Cook crossed the Channel. In the late 1850s, he launched excursions to Switzerland, accompanied by a guidebook titled *Switzerland and How to See It for Ten Guineas.* Thomas Cook denigrated Gaze's tours for using third-class hotels and "hard walking" at a cost little less than his own tours, although he did recommend Gaze's book to his own clients. (*Punch,* on the other hand, satirized the book in an article called "A Week in the Moon for a Pound.") The rivalry between Cook and Gaze became more serious when Gaze again got the jump on Cook in organizing tours to the Middle East and didn't hesitate to advertise the fact that he had been there first. The two firms also competed on tours to the Continental exhibitions. Several other travel agents established themselves in the 1870s and 1880s, among them Dean & Dawson (1871), John Frame (1881), Quentin Hogg (1886), and Sir Henry Lunn (1893).[42]

The Cooks reacted to competition as a kind of betrayal, much as Thomas had responded to the Scottish railroads' putting an end to his northern excursions. This was especially true when the issue involved someone trying to cash in on the family name or challenge the firm's originality. Despite the Cooks' overwhelming commercial success and the size and scope of their firm, in some ways they displayed a preindustrial attitude about business, one that emphasized loyalty and fair dealing over profit. Although his son built the company into the largest travel agency in the world, Thomas Cook never completely abandoned his origins as an artisan organizing excursions for the edification of the workingman and the promotion of peace and friendship among nations.

JUST AS THE Cooks' success generated competition, so it also brought criticism and even ridicule of their methods and clients. British travelers in general (especially those of less than upper-class status) were already targets of satire by the mid-nineteenth century, and Cooks' tourists were easy marks for those who regretted the demise of the good old days, when travel was the prerogative of the rich. In the early years of his business, Thomas Cook had often felt compelled to justify travel for the working class against the arguments of employers and others who considered travel for workers a waste of time and money. By the 1860s, one could no longer argue that working-class and middle-class people shouldn't travel. Clearly they did, and it would have been folly to suppose that they would cease doing so. Instead critics turned to ridicule, depicting group tourists as so many sheep racing mindlessly from one sight to another with little appreciation of what they saw. Cooks' tourists, the critics charged, were superficial, ignorant, and vulgar, failed to appreciate what they saw, wanted everything readily packaged so they wouldn't have to think about anything, and were suspicious of foreign food and foreign ways. Perhaps worst of all, they traveled in groups and therefore called attention to themselves. Upper-class men and women accustomed to visiting the Continent in the pre-Cook era resented the growing crowds and feared that they would be tarred by association with lower-class travelers.

One particularly vicious article appeared in *Blackwood's Magazine,* written under the pen name Cornelius O'Dowd, by Charles Lever, an Irish novelist and vice-consul at La Spezia. As a vice-consul Lever saw many tourists and obviously hated the new breed descending upon him (and perhaps also the increase in his workload). Lever's satire turned mostly on the need he felt to reassure Europeans around him that not all British people were like the tourist hordes; when "some platitude about English eccentricity" failed to convince his hearers, he claimed to have invented a story that the British government had devised a new system of dumping convicts. Lever's article was picked up by *The Pall Mall Gazette* with a favorable comment, while similar kinds of pieces appeared in *Punch* and other magazines. One article, commenting on Cook's proposal to organize school holiday tours for boys, remarked, "If they would only undertake to personally conduct a bridal party, their series of benefactions to the human race would be complete."[43]

Cook saw such criticism as a kind of social snobbery and responded by asserting the right of all to travel, decrying "Purse-proud younglings who affect to treat with disdain those who occupy a lower sphere than themselves, and then . . . think that places of rare interest should be excluded from the gaze of the common people, and be kept only for the interest of the 'select' of society. But it is too late in this day of progress to talk such exclusive nonsense; God's earth, with all its fulness and beauty, is for the people; and railroads and steamboats are the results of the common light of science, and are for the people also." When another critic, writing in the *Athenaeum,* made fun of Cook for organizing a tour to Rome that emphasized archaeology—implying that Cooks' tourists couldn't possibly understand archaeology, certainly not in the space of a few days—Cook replied, "The *Athenaeum* may sneer at Cook's Excursions and those who patronise them, yet these excursions have done more than all the articles in the *Athenaeum* . . . to familiarise the English people with continental life and manners as they really are, and thus assist in dispelling the international ignorance and prejudices to which we owe so many misunderstandings and disastrous wars."

Other writers defended Cook and the concept of inexpensive travel, using similar arguments. A profile in *All the Year Round,* a magazine edited by Charles Dickens, took the position that organizing travel for the working class "is a good thing, and ought to be encouraged. It is right that a hard-working man, labouring in one spot for fifty weeks in a year, should, in his fortnight's holiday, betake himself to some place as far away from and as different to his ordinary abode as lies within the reach of his purse, and this he is

only able to do by the aid of such providers as my excursion agent.''
Another supporter, reminding his readers that it had once been the
fashion to make fun of upper-class travelers—''Lord Foppington on
his travels; coarse Sir Stentor Stubble doing the grand tour . . . and
such like specimens of the stupidity and vulgarity of the British aristocracy let loose upon the continent''—criticized the hypocrisy of
attacking the new breed of traveler for his lack of sophistication,
when most wealthy travelers were no better. Most critics of Cooks'
tourists were not such masters of French and German, nor did he
believe that ''the veneration of some of them for either high art or
high nature is one whit more profound than that of an average
Cook's excursionist. It really is quite time to say a word in defence
of the Englishman of moderate means who likes to see a foreign city
or a foreign river, and yet cannot afford to travel express in a carriage
reserved, and with the courier to show all the sights. It does not
follow that every such being must necessarily be very vulgar or stupid.'' The Cooks themselves argued that it was better to encourage
people to travel and learn about other nations under the guidance of
a ''Conductor'' than restrict all contact with other nations to those
with the means to travel independently.[44]

The Cooks also felt compelled to defend themselves in more practical terms, by reminding the public that most of their clients traveled
independently and asserting that they were much the same as other
travelers. Cooks' tourists were accused of rushing from place to place
without enough time to see the places they visited. ''If this principle
were to be generally acted on,'' Thomas claimed, ''nine-tenths of the
visitors to the National Gallery and British Museum ought to stay
away.'' Moreover, he observed, in a dig at the mania for writing
travel books, Cooks' clients did not rush about a country and then
publish error-ridden books about them. ''They do not pretend to
master the topography, history, mode of government, social statistics,
and all the rest of it, of a large country in a single week, but they do
profess to have learnt a little from what they have seen, and to utilise
that knowledge, without sinking into pedantic men of learning, or
narrow-minded and superficial writers for literary journals.'' Although Thomas Cook defended the right of all classes of people to

travel, at the same time he asserted that his firm's clients were drawn from a better class of people than the critics implied.[45]

In some ways, however, the charges leveled at Cooks' tourists were justified. The few surviving travel diaries written by men and women who participated in the early tours, as well as articles written by Thomas Cook himself, make it clear that they did indeed rush from place to place, preoccupied with seeing as much as possible in a short time. Their travel accounts are superficial, mainly catalogues of places visited, which they tended to describe in comparison with familiar places closer to home. They talked mostly about what they could readily see—buildings, scenic vistas, faces of people—and the conditions of travel itself, especially the food and the endless train rides. Traveling rapidly and in groups, they seldom had contact with the people of the countries they visited, and seem to have formed little impression of life there.

Those who defended Cook argued that it was better to see Italy in three weeks than not at all. The more thoughtful critics of changes in the style of travel argued quite the opposite: that one needed time, knowledge, and mental preparation to be able to appreciate travel fully, especially travel to places of great scenic beauty. Wordsworth had opposed the construction of a railroad line to the Lake District because it would bring in people who could not fully appreciate the region's beauties in his terms. By implication, his argument was that no travel was preferable to imperfect travel, because the influx of ill-prepared visitors would spoil things for those who were capable of appreciating them. In the 1870s, John Ruskin made a similar argument about Switzerland, claiming, "All my dear mountain grounds and treasure-cities . . . are long ago destroyed by the European populace." The literary critic Leslie Stephen charged that tourists had no independent judgment, but went where they were told to go and admired what their guidebooks told them to admire. They could hardly do otherwise, he claimed, because an appreciation of art or natural beauty required lengthy study and a cast of mind foreign to the average Briton, who concerned himself with little other than work.[46]

Such critics were not out-and-out snobs, but their views could be sustained only in a society in which access to the monuments they held dear was limited to an educated elite—a society that was rapidly disappearing in the nineteenth century. "Steam is a great leveller, not only of roads, but of social rank," wrote Arthur Sketchley, the author of a series of humorous books about Cooks' tours. He recalled the experience of a friend who had spent three months traveling from London to Naples in 1815; in the 1860s, Sketchley made the journey in four days. A trip to the Continent, he remarked, had become "a mere everyday affair."[47]

Railroads and entrepreneurs like Cook, who packaged travel for people of moderate means, permanently changed the nature of travel. While many regretted the demise of an older, slower, more exclusive style of travel, others valued the opportunity to see places that had once seemed as inaccessible as the moon. In the words of Mrs. Brown, the Cockney globetrotter who was the principal character in Sketchley's stories, "I'm sure as Mr. Cook did ought to 'ave 'is statutes by law stuck about all over the world, as 'is a wonderful man."[48]

Writing in 1865, Thomas Cook described the time in which he lived as "the Age of Locomotion." Railroads, he wrote, "have unlocked the doors of districts hitherto barred against the masses of the people." British men and women who didn't travel seemed "as antiquated as dinosaurs." Inspired by idealistic motives, Cook and his family made a fortune by making it possible for the "masses" to travel. By the time the company celebrated its fiftieth anniversary in 1891, the Cook agency offered more than 30,000 series of tickets covering 1.8 million miles of railroads, rivers, and oceans. During the previous year, the company had sold nearly 3.3 million tickets, a figure that would rise to about 6 million by 1900.[49]

CHAPTER 6

TRAVELING

IN

STYLE

B Y T H E L A S T quarter of the nineteenth century, technology and commercial enterprise transformed European and American travel in ways that would have been unimaginable to the eighteenth-century grand tourist. Although Arthur Sketchley surely exaggerated when he remarked that a trip to the Continent had become a "mere everyday affair," such a journey was no longer a once-in-a-lifetime occasion limited to the very rich. An expanding network of railways, faster trains and steamships, newly constructed hotels, and the services of businessmen like Thomas Cook and his competitors speeded up travel and eliminated many of its frustrations and uncertainties. At the same time, a period of unprecedented peace and prosperity in Western Europe created a climate in which larger numbers of people could afford to travel.

As a result, travel became commonplace for a substantial segment of the upper- and upper-middle-class population. The author of a *Scribner's Magazine* article published in the summer of 1890 complained, only half jokingly, that he had lost all his social companions because everyone was off traveling—one family in Florida, another in Mexico, still others in Europe and Colorado. Another article, titled "How Shall We Spend Our Summer?" opened with the assumption that most of the magazine's readers would be contemplating a summer away from home, while noting that such a question would have been unheard of fifty years earlier. Travel articles, many of them offering practical advice, became a standard feature in several popular American magazines by the last quarter of the nineteenth century, while the first magazines devoted exclusively to travel appeared in Britain in the 1880s.[1]

The growing popularity of travel inevitably brought with it increased commercialization. Thomas Cook revolutionized tourism by catering to social groups that had never before had the opportunity to travel beyond their own local regions; in the second half of the nineteenth century, other entrepreneurs got into the business by catering to the rich, taking advantage of technological advances that made it possible to travel not simply faster, but far more comfortably than in years past. For wealthy Europeans, the expansion of travel among the middle class fostered efforts to separate themselves from undesirable "Cooks' tourists" and their ilk by traveling first-class, creating enclaves in popular destinations, and seeking out new, and often more distant and exotic, destinations. They helped create and sustain a market for luxury travel beginning in the last two decades of the nineteenth century.

THE END OF the Franco-Prussian War in 1871 marked the beginning of the longest period of peace and political stability in modern European history. One of the major consequences of the war was the unification of the German states under the rule of Otto von Bismarck, the Prussian chancellor. A year earlier, the unification of Italy (largely accomplished in 1860 when Sardinia brought most of the Italian principalities under its control) was finally completed with the inclusion of the Papal States. When Sardinia took control of Italy, it also ceded Savoy (the region around Chamonix and Nice) to France. With these changes, Western Europe assumed its modern form as a cluster of politically stable nation-states, linked by treaties and assumptions about balancing power and influence, which endured until the one remaining area of perpetually shifting rivalries—the Balkan states—propelled Europe into World War I.[2]

After a severe but relatively brief worldwide depression in 1873, western Europe entered the strongest, most sustained period of economic growth in its history. Despite occasional sharp downturns and declining agricultural prices, industrial output more than doubled from the mid-1870s to the mid-1890s. Wage rates rose by about 70 percent in Britain and even more dramatically in continental Europe and the United States between 1860 and the outbreak of World War I. Unlike earlier periods of economic expansion, when most of the benefit accrued to those at the upper end of the economic scale, the prosperity of the late nineteenth century brought higher income and shorter hours to the working class as well. Factory legislation gradually cut down working hours, while the number of holidays and the provision of paid vacations increased. In Britain, at least two weeks' paid vacation was standard for civil servants and workers in businesses like banks and insurance companies by the 1870s. Within another decade, the practice was spreading to factory workers as well.[3]

By the end of the 1870s, railroads linked most of the major towns and cities of Europe as far east as Warsaw and Vienna. Italy, long a laggard in railroad construction, embarked upon a serious program of expansion after 1860. Within a decade, trunk lines extended as far south as Naples, and several east-west links were completed as well. With the construction of a forty-eight-mile narrow-gauge railway over Mont Cenis in 1868, a tunnel through Mont Cenis in 1871, and a railroad line from Marseilles to the Italian frontier in 1870, it became possible to travel from the English Channel to Italy entirely by rail. (The invention of dynamite in 1867 helped speed up the construction of Alpine railways by making it practical to tunnel through rock.) Journeys that had once taken weeks were reduced to days. Traveling from Paris to Rome, for example, took about two days once railroad service was established over the entire length of the route. Add another ten to fifteen hours from London to Paris, depending on the route chosen, and British travelers could be in Italy in less than three days—a striking reduction from the two or three weeks of the prerailroad era.

Another decade brought the completion of several other Alpine tunnels, notably the St. Gotthard (in 1882), and the extension of Italy's railroad network to include most of its cities and larger towns. By the early 1880s, it was possible to travel throughout western Europe, the eastern half of the United States, and large parts of eastern Europe and western North America in a matter of hours, at fares that were affordable to large segments of the population. There seemed no limit to the demand for transportation under such circumstances; in 1882, for example, about 20 million people traveled by rail, nearly three quarters of them in Europe and most of the rest in the United States.[4]

The expansion of railroad travel had ramifications far beyond simply increasing the numbers of people on the move. Perhaps most strikingly, the many different companies involved were forced to standardize their times and cooperate on scheduling. Until well into the nineteenth century, localities followed their own time, based on the sun, and no one moved fast enough to notice discrepancies of a few minutes from one town to the next. Railroads, with their speed and demand for fixed schedules, gradually forced the adoption of standard time within broad regions. In Britain, some railroads began to observe London time (or, more precisely, Greenwich Mean Time) as early as 1840, although the practice wasn't adopted throughout the country until 1852 and was not officially enacted into law until 1880, when Parliament decreed that Greenwich time would be observed throughout Great Britain. French trains operated on Paris time, but as late as the 1890s, local time—a few minutes ahead or behind Paris time—continued in force for all other purposes; and Paris time was itself fifty-six minutes behind central European time.

The problem of standardizing times internationally was largely resolved when the International Meridian Conference voted in 1884 to establish Greenwich as the prime meridian (the point of zero longitude), although France did not finally accede to this plan until 1911. The United States adopted its present time zones in 1883. As in Europe, railroad companies took the initiative; Congress did not ratify their action until 1918. Beginning in the 1870s, railroad officials met annually at an International Time-Table Conference to coordinate and standardize schedules. (The term "timetable" itself was coined

by the London & Birmingham Railway in 1838, when it first began
issuing schedules of departures and arrivals.) Thomas Cook & Son
added the publication of timetables to its array of services, following
the example of George Bradshaw, a map printer and engraver, who
had first produced British timetables in 1839 and European schedules
in 1847. His volumes became the standard in Britain for 120 years,
and "Bradshaw" evolved into a noun synonymous with timetable.
Many railroad companies also extended their business interests beyond the mere provision of transportation. Thomas Cook's success
with his early excursion trains encouraged several British companies
to move into the excursion business, especially on the popular routes
to Scotland, and one French company set up its own travel agency
in the 1880s. Railroads also built many of the first large hotels in
Europe.[5]

Americans traveling to Europe benefited from improvements in
steamship design and competition among shipping lines, which began to speed up passage across the Atlantic and reduce fares as early
as the 1850s. Spurred by a contract from the British government to
operate a monthly mail service between Liverpool and Boston, the
Canadian shipowner Samuel Cunard launched the first regular transatlantic steamer service in 1840. By the late 1840s, Cunard had
added service to New York. He faced competition from two newly
established American companies, the Collins Line, founded in 1849
by a wealthy New England ship captain, Edward Knight Collins,
with the help of a mail contract from the U.S. government, and the
Inman Line, established in 1850 with service initially between Liverpool and Philadelphia. Over the course of the next decade, French
and German businessmen also entered the transatlantic passenger
business with the creation of the Hamburg-Amerika Line, North
German Lloyd, and the Compagnie Générale Transatlantique.

Cunard's motto, "Speed, Comfort and Safety," offered a fair indication of the basis for competition among the several steamship
companies. Although Cunard's flagship of the 1840s, the 1,200-ton
Britannia, was the largest and fastest steamer of its day, Collins's
ships soon gained a reputation for greater speed and comfort. Collins
had obtained his government subsidy in part on the condition that
he better Cunard's speed across the Atlantic, which averaged about

thirteen days westbound in the 1840s, compared with about twenty-two days for sailing packets. He succeeded when one of his first two ships, the *Atlantic* (at 2,856 tons, more than twice the size of the *Britannia*) set the transatlantic speed record with a passage from Liverpool to New York in just over ten and a half days. Collins's ships also offered comforts unheard of on earlier vessels, including more spacious public areas, a smoking room, steam heating, ice to preserve fresh produce, and even a barber shop—which caused more comment than anything else about the *Atlantic* when it docked for the first time in Liverpool.

The four Collins steamers—the *Atlantic, Pacific, Arctic,* and *Baltic*—remained the fastest ships on the Atlantic through the first half of the 1850s, reducing the minimum crossing time slightly, to about nine days westbound. This rivalry over speed was expensive, however, as each small increment required substantial additional outlays of fuel, and potentially dangerous. In an unofficial ''race'' between the *Pacific* and Cunard's *Persia* in January 1856, the former went down without a trace and the *Persia* had to be towed into New York after slamming into an iceberg, saved only by her steel hull. (The Collins ships were wooden-hulled.) Coming less than two years after the loss of the *Arctic* in a collision off Newfoundland, this disaster contributed to the loss of Collins's subsidy and other financial backing. In 1857, the company folded. Cunard, on the other hand, had an unrivaled safety record, with no fatal accidents in its first thirty-five years.

The Inman Line's major contribution to Atlantic passenger service was the introduction, early in the 1850s, of the screw propeller to replace the paddle wheel, which had powered all the early steamships. The innovation did not at first produce a marked increase in speed, but it allowed a more efficient use of space and proved considerably more economical to operate. Although paddle-wheel steamers continued in use on ocean liners through the 1860s, most new ships from the mid-1850s on employed the screw propeller. Over the next two decades, ship size and speed increased steadily. By the 1870s, 10,000-ton vessels typically crossed the Atlantic in about a week; by the 1890s, the size of the major transatlantic liners doubled again, while the time required to cross continued to drop, to as little as five days.[6]

Improvements in comfort came more slowly. The chief virtue of traveling by train in the 1850s and 1860s was speed; by making the trip faster, trains limited the hardships of travel. Until the 1870s, most European trains were unheated and few even had toilets, although French trains offered hot-water footstools to first-class passengers. Dining cars weren't introduced until the 1880s. Brief stops at stations were a mad rush to the toilets and the buffets, where the food got mixed reviews from guidebook writers. (Murray thought the French buffets a definite improvement over those in British railway stations.) Most writers advised travelers to come prepared with their own provisions.[7]

Passengers on the transatlantic steamers of the 1850s and 1860s had to put up with similar inconveniences. Only slightly faster than the best sailing ships, the early steamers were actually less comfortable because of their noisy operation and cramped quarters. Much of their space was, of necessity, given over to mechanical equipment and fuel. The steamers' main advantage was reliability—they were less subject to the vagaries of weather—a point that encouraged first the British and later the United States government to subsidize steamship lines with lucrative mail contracts. On the early Cunard liners, one large room served as both lounge and dining room, where passengers took their meals at a large common table covered with oilcloth. The food was monotonous (after the first day out, salt beef and fish replaced fresh), and the rough seas typical of North Atlantic crossings, especially in winter, could make it difficult simply to keep one's plate on the table. The less expensive accommodations were often berths made up by curtaining off benches lining the walls of this main room, while first-class cabins were tiny cubicles along corridors off the main cabin. Plumbing was primitive, with a minimal number of bathrooms serving all the passengers, and hot water nonexistent.

Charles Dickens, who made his journey to the United States on Cunard's *Britannia* in 1842, wrote comically of the contrast between artists' renderings of the ship's interiors, used for advertising purposes, and the reality of shipboard quarters. The snug little cabin with a sofa or two and plenty of room for steamer trunks turned out to be a "profoundly preposterous box" with a thin mattress on a shelf for a bed and two horsehair "slabs" in lieu of chairs. The steamer trunks, Dickens asserted, "would now no more be got in at the door, not to say stowed away, than a giraffe could be persuaded or forced into a flower-pot." The "saloon" or main lounge and dining room, far from being the imagined grand chamber at least the size of seven ordinary drawing rooms, was in fact a narrow, claustrophobic space "not unlike a gigantic hearse with windows in the sides," furnished with a single long, narrow table and, just above it, racks of glassware firmly secured in place—an unwelcome reminder of the prospects for rough weather ahead. Less than two days out, in fact, most of the passengers took to their cabins in agony as the ship pitched and rolled its way through what the crew liked to call "rather a heavy sea."[8]

Collins's ships had larger public rooms and central heating, but the staterooms were still quite small. The first screw-propeller ships only added to passengers' misery because of their noise and vibration. Not until the White Star Line entered the transatlantic market in 1870 were there significant improvements in passenger comfort. The new company's *Oceanic* was the first ship to place passenger cabins and public rooms in the center of the ship, where noise and vibration were lowest, rather than aft. Until the addition of stabilizers in the 1940s, little could be done about a ship's pitching and rolling in heavy seas, but moving the cabins to the quietest and most stable part of the ship certainly helped, giving the White Star Line a competitive advantage until other lines followed its example. As late as 1879, a travel writer urged readers contemplating an Atlantic passage to choose one of the modern ships with cabins amidships, and then take care to select a cabin well away from the engine. In addition to its quieter staterooms, the *Oceanic* featured skylights, bathrooms with running water, a smoking room for men, and a carpeted lounge for women. The lounge even had a piano, chained to the wall for safety. By the end of the 1870s, electric lighting was installed on the *Oceanic* as well.[9]

*   *   *

BEGINNING IN THE last two decades of the nineteenth century, as transportation networks spread to the limits of the European and North American continents and speeds approached their technological limits, a burgeoning travel industry began to compete increasingly on comfort and style. Men like Thomas Cook, John Murray, and Karl Baedeker had demonstrated as early as the 1840s and '50s that one could profit handsomely by making travel easier and cheaper. A later generation of entrepreneurs profited from making travel more comfortable. They found their clients among those who believed that travel had deteriorated because of its growing popularity; but in their own way, these new entrepreneurs were also in the business of making travel easier and more predictable, by guaranteeing a standard of comfort comparable to what their patrons were used to at home. Wealthy tourists in the late nineteenth century might ridicule the herd mentality of those who traveled on "Cook's tours," but they were not exactly trailblazers themselves, traveling on luxury trains or ships and staying in elegant hotels that insulated them from local customs, local food, unfamiliar languages—as well as low-budget tourists.

Three men stand out as especially important in developing luxury travel: the American railroad magnate George Pullman, who invented the concept of luxury train travel; his Belgian competitor, Georges Nagelmackers, who introduced Pullman's ideas to continental Europe and went him one better by inaugurating the first trains made up solely of luxury cars; and César Ritz, the Swiss hotel entrepreneur who refined hotelkeeping to a fine art, establishing a series of hotels that still bear his name. It is some small measure of their significance that Pullman's and Ritz's names, along with Cook's, have all entered the language in generic forms: the "Cook's tour," the "Pullman" car, "ritzy."

The first major efforts to improve the standard of comfort in rail travel came in the United States, where long distances and infrequent stops were more common than in Europe, especially after the completion of the transcontinental railroad line in 1869. Even as early as the 1850s, American trains had some significant advantages over European lines. Passenger cars were typically larger (a function of the wider track gauge used in the United States), better ventilated, and provided with oil lamps, stoves, and lavatories. By the early 1880s steam heating replaced the wood or coal stoves; electric lighting was added in the early 1890s. The open design typical of American cars, with its long center aisle, allowed passengers to move around, while the invention of the closed vestibule between cars, patented by Pullman in 1887, made it safe to roam the length of a train—no small matter for a bored passenger on a long journey. Europeans often found the lack of privacy on American trains troublesome, but the compartments typical of European railroad cars, each opening directly onto the track without any communication between them, could be stifling—and unpleasant if one were forced to share a compartment with strangers. The first sleeping cars were introduced on American trains in the late 1850s, but did not catch on until after the Civil War, when George Pullman gambled that passengers would pay not just for a bed, but for a level of comfort and service unprecedented on trains up to that time.[10]

Pullman, who started his career as a furniture salesman, conceived the notion of building sleeping cars after several long, tiresome journeys in the mid-1850s. He started in a small way, remodeling two cars with wood paneling and upholstered seats that folded into beds, and hiring a porter to cater to passengers' needs. Pullman began operating the cars in 1859 on trains running between Chicago and Bloomington, Illnois, collecting a fare supplement of 50 cents. This mode of operation became one of the most important features of Pullman's business. Rather than building cars and selling them to railroads, he operated the cars himself under contract with railroad companies. At about the same time, Webster Wagner began remodeling cars to be used as sleepers on the New York Central Line.[11]

By the end of the Civil War, Pullman had settled in Chicago and set about reviving his sleeping-car business. His career nearly ended before it began, however, when he chose to launch his new enterprise by building an enormous, luxurious sleeping car so large and cumbersome that it could not function. The Pioneer, as Pullman named it, featured walnut paneling, chandeliers, linen sheets, and marble washstands—a degree of luxury unprecedented on any railroad. It was also a foot wider and two and a half feet higher than any American railroad car then in service, which meant that it could not clear all bridges and tunnels along the tracks where it was proposed to run. Worse yet, it was so heavy that it simply wouldn't move when first tested. As a consequence, the Pioneer went into storage until Lincoln's assassination, when the state of Illnois asked that it be used to carry Lincoln's body from Chicago to Springfield for burial. Shortly afterward, Pullman offered the Pioneer to President Ulysses Grant for a journey from Detroit to his hometown of Galena, Ohio. In both cases, modifications had to be made to bridges and platforms along the route so the Pioneer could pass safely.

The publicity value for Pullman was incalculable. Thousands lined the tracks to watch both processions, and newspapers across the country published pictures of the amazing car, including its wood-paneled, splendidly appointed interior. Two years later, Pullman was well established, with forty-eight sleeping cars in operation on several railroad lines. These early sleepers (unlike the Pioneer) were fairly simple affairs, with a row of seats that folded down to form beds at night lining each side of a long central aisle. A wide, shelflike arrangement above the seats could be stowed against the ceiling during the day and lowered with ropes and pulleys to form an upper berth at night. Curtains separating each berth offered a minimal level of privacy, and a single sink at one end had to suffice for all of the car's occupants. Simple as they were in principle, even these early sleeping cars offered a sense of luxury, with their plush upholstery and wood paneling. Within a year after launching his first fleet of sleeping cars, Pullman began experimenting with "hotel" cars (a combination sleeping/dining car) as well. Meanwhile, Webster Wagner was back in business too, building sleeping cars for the Vanderbilt-owned New York Central Railroad. Several other railroads also experimented with sleeping cars, but Pullman, by remaining independent and contracting with many different companies to run his cars, had the edge over his rivals. Over time he bought out many of the smaller companies (including Wagner's, in 1899), and the name "Pullman car" became synonymous with "sleeping car."[12]

Luxury was in fact the key to Pullman's enormous success. From his earliest sleeping cars with their barely private berths, he expanded his operation to offer a range of accommodations, including sleeping cars with private rooms as well as open berths; wood-paneled "parlour" cars with carpeting, comfortable armchairs, a library, and sometimes even an organ; dining cars with extensive menus rivaling those of the best urban restaurants; and club cars where men could smoke and drink. By the late 1880s, all-Pullman-car trains operated on the major American long-distance routes, along with the more common trains combining Pullman and standard coach cars. These trains were the first to employ central heating by piping steam from the locomotive through all the cars. The porters assigned to each car, a hallmark of the Pullman operation from the beginning, provided a level of personal service unmatched anywhere except in the homes of the very rich. The company left nothing to chance in training its porters. A massive procedures manual gave step-by-step instructions for every possible contingency; the instructions for serving a bottle of beer, for example, included twelve steps, including the equipment to be placed on the serving tray, the method of chilling a glass (by pouring ice from one glass into another), the proper way of pouring beer to ensure just the right amount of foam, and finally, the correct placement of the bottle in front of the customer (with the label facing him).[13]

Although he got his start in the United States and continued to conduct most of his business there, Pullman's reputation spread across the Atlantic quickly. In 1872 the general manager of Britain's Midland Railway visited Pullman in Chicago and invited him to speak to the company's shareholders the following year. As a result of that meeting, the company granted Pullman a fifteen-year contract to run sleeping cars on its trains. This arrangement gave him the opening he needed to set up offices in London and Paris to begin negotiating contracts with other companies as well. His first sleeping car in England went into operation in 1874; shortly afterward he made his entry into the Continental market with cars running from the French Riviera and Mont Cenis into northern Italy.[14]

Within a decade Pullman dominated the British market, but he faced stiff competition on the Continent from Georges Nagelmackers, who had drawn inspiration from Pullman himself. The scion of a wealthy Belgian banking family, Nagelmackers visited the United States in 1868, dispatched by his parents in the hope that a change of scene would help him forget an unhappy love affair. The young man, fascinated by railroads, arranged to visit the officials of several American companies, including Pullman, who took him for a ride on the Pioneer, showed him the workshops where the cars were built, and talked with him at length about the company's business methods. Nagelmackers returned to Europe determined to launch a similar venture.

He faced more difficult problems than Pullman, however, for he had to negotiate not only with many rival railroad companies, but with several different governments as well. As with Pullman, war delayed his plans (in this case the Franco-Prussian War), but in 1872 he founded the Compagnie Internationale des Wagons-Lits. Nagelmackers obtained his first contracts, on trains running from Ostend to Cologne, Munich to Vienna, and other routes in Germany, partly through his father's friendship with the Belgian King Leopold. Despite the company's early success, Nagelmackers ran short of capital, and in 1873 he teamed up with an American living in London, William d'Alton Mann. Some years earlier, Mann had attempted to get started in the sleeping-car business in the United States but couldn't compete with Pullman, so he went to England where he started the Mann Boudoir Sleeping Car Company. Recognizing Europeans' distaste for the lack of privacy afforded by the standard Pullman sleeper, Mann adapted the European-style coach, with its separate compartments, to a sleeping car by developing compartments with two fold-down seats and two upper berths, accommodating four people at night. Each compartment had its own bathroom. Such an arrangement made it possible for a single family to reserve an entire compartment for its own use. This concern with privacy also kept dining cars from catching on in Europe, especially in England, until the end of the nineteenth century, as passengers continued to prefer carrying their own picnic hampers.[15]

The two men formed a joint venture, Mann's Railway Sleeping Carriage Company Ltd., which, despite its name and London base of operations, was run mainly by Nagelmackers. The venture expanded quickly, adding several contracts with French railways. In a gesture reminiscent of Pullman's offering the Pioneer to President Grant, Mann arranged for the Prince of Wales (later Edward VII) to use one of the company's cars when he traveled to Berlin and St. Petersburg for the wedding of his brother Prince Alfred to the daughter of Tsar Alexander II. The resulting publicity for the Mann/Nagelmackers company helped it gain a potentially lucrative contract on the Paris–Vienna line. But it was about this time that Pullman began operations in England, eventually overtaking his competitors in the British market, and Mann himself began to lose interest in the company, resigning as chairman in 1875. Nagelmackers bought out his partner shortly afterward, dissolved the company, and reestablished it in Belgium under its former name with King Leopold as the principal shareholder. The revived CIWL and Pullman's British operation became the two principal luxury-car companies in Europe, with Pullman in control of the British routes and Nagelmackers dominating in Germany and Austria. Each had its own distinctive style, Pullman with its deep brown cars and dark, polished-wood interiors and CIWL with royal blue cars and gilt lettering. They remained rivals in France and Italy, although the CIWL gradually came to dominate there as well.[16]

In their first years of operation, the sleeping-car companies attached their cars to trains running ordinary coaches as well, in a variety of different combinations. There were basic sleeping cars, dining cars (beginning in 1879), and "parlour" or "saloon" cars, including private cars for wealthy families. By the early 1880s, demand for berths in luxury cars was so great on the Paris–Vienna line that railways began running trains made up exclusively of sleeping and dining cars, which had the advantage of faster schedules by eliminating the need to stop for meals en route. In 1882, a much publicized run using only CIWL cars made the journey from Paris to Vienna in twenty-eight hours, three to four hours less than the normal time. It was the prototype for a more ambitious experiment: a luxury train service from Paris to Constantinople, which became famous as the *Orient Express*.[17]

The idea of a Paris–Constantinople rail service dated back a dozen years, when construction had begun on the first railroads linking Turkey with Europe. But the slow pace of railroad construction through the Balkan states and the persistence of international rivalries made it an elusive goal even in the 1880s. Neither the Russians nor the British favored easy rail access between central Europe and Constantinople—the Russians because they feared losing their influence in the Balkans and the British because a railroad line might take business away from British shipping interests. As a result, the planned Paris–Constantinople line initially extended only as far east as Giurgiu, a town on the Danube south of Bucharest.

Passengers on the maiden journey of the *Orient Express,* in June 1883, settled into the most luxurious train ever built. Its cars were like "rolling houses," as sumptuous as the most luxurious in Paris, according to Edmond About, a French journalist who was among the first passengers. Amenities included gold-embossed leather seats, teak- and mahogany-paneled walls, velvet curtains, Gobelin tapestries, engraved silverware, crystal goblets, silk sheets, steam heat, gas lighting, and running water. Moreover, the *Orient Express* traveled at great speed even on the sharpest curves, without jolting the passengers or upsetting the delicate crystal in the dining car. During a twenty-four-hour layover in Bucharest, passengers were treated to an excursion to Sinaia, a summer resort in the Carpathian Mountains popular with wealthy Romanians, where the Romanian royal family had just completed a new palace. All this luxury ended abruptly at Giurgiu, however. There, passengers boarded decrepit little boats for the crossing of the Danube, followed by a long, tedious rail journey through the depressingly impoverished Bulgarian countryside. The three-hundred-kilometer journey took seven hours, a striking contrast to the speed of the *Orient Express* north of the Danube. Not until 1888 was the CIWL able to run its own cars all the way to the Black Sea.[18]

Despite the enormous cost of the *Orient Express*—a round-trip ticket in the early years was about as much as the annual rent on a London town house—this first "train de luxe" became an instant success and encouraged the creation of other long-distance luxury trains.[19] Nagelmackers's second route was designed to capitalize on the British passion for Italy by providing through service from Calais to Rome via Paris and the French Riviera. He was nearly upstaged in this endeavor by Pullman, who, in concert with Thomas Cook, organized a special luxury train to travel from Calais to Rome via the Mont Cenis tunnel and Bologna, timed to coincide with the Italian Fine Arts Exhibition in Rome. Nagelmackers registered an official protest, because the route violated his exclusive contracts with two of the French railways involved; although he failed to stop the special train, Pullman was not permitted to run any more through trains from Calais to Rome. Because of Pullman's exclusive contracts in northern Italy, however, Nagelmackers had to operate his express trains along the Riviera instead of over the Alps. In the mid-1880s, he began buying out Pullman's contracts in Italy, eventually gaining a near-monopoly on Continental sleeping-car travel.

Nagelmackers launched his most ambitious project, the *Nord-Sud Express,* in 1884 after difficult negotiations with the Russian tsar. This train was to run from St. Petersburg to Liège, where it split, with some of the cars continuing to Brussels and Ostend (connecting with a special ship to Dover), while the rest traveled south to Paris, Madrid, and Lisbon. Politics and technology complicated the arrangements. Russia and Spain had different track gauges from the rest of Europe, requiring equipment to change the wheelbases on the cars; more serious was Bismarck's objection to the use of the Prussian State Railways to link France and Russia. His protests put an end to the *Nord-Sud Express* temporarily, and also resulted in the loss of the CIWL's contracts with the Prussian railroad. Nagelmackers countered by establishing service from St. Petersburg to Vienna via Warsaw, bypassing Germany. Eventually, in 1896, the German government was pressured into accepting the *Nord-Sud* service.

Meanwhile, Nagelmackers extended his trains de luxe on several other routes. By the 1890s, the CIWL was operating at least a dozen luxury expresses across much of Europe. Among the longest runs were those from Calais to Brindisi, connecting with British mail steamers to India, and from St. Petersburg to Nice and Cannes, catering to Russian nobility wintering on the Riviera. Pullman, meanwhile, launched luxury, Pullman-only trains in the United States, beginning in 1888 with the *Golden Gate Special* operating on the transcontinental route. In addition to the usual amenities of luxury trains—smoking cars, writing rooms, private parlors and separate sleeping compartments—it was one of the first trains to feature electric lights.[20]

PULLMAN HIMSELF called his sleeping cars "palace cars" to suggest that they offered luxury fit for royalty to anyone willing to pay for it. In a similar vein, a series of massive new hotels built between about 1870 and World War I imitated the grand scale and lavish appointments of royal palaces. Like the trains, these so-called "grand hotels" depended on a wealthy clientele who were willing to pay handsomely to live comfortably while abroad.

Until around the middle of the nineteenth century, hotels in the modern sense were rare in Europe. In cities, travelers generally stayed in boardinghouses or rented lodgings for longer stays; on the road, modest inns catered to their needs. But as the number of travelers increased and shorter trips became more common, making it less practical for most travelers to take lodgings in the cities they visited, the demand for hotel accommodations increased. At about the same time, technological advances like improved indoor plumbing and the invention of the elevator made it possible to build hotels on a larger scale, with a higher standard of comfort.

The earliest large European hotels had been built by railway companies adjacent to stations in London and provincial towns. The first, at Euston station, was completed in 1839. Others were built at major junctions and at Folkestone and Dover, embarkation points for the Continent, in the 1840s and '50s. Still larger hotels went up near other major London stations in the late 1850s and '60s—at Paddington (completed 1854), Victoria (1861), and Charing Cross (1864). Beginning in the 1850s and 1860s, hotels were built in several European cities along the lines of the railroad-owned hotels in Britain, among them the Amstel in Amsterdam (1867) and the Imperial in Vienna (1865). Claridge's, an old posting hotel dating from the late 1830s, expanded and upgraded its facilities to become one of London's most prestigious establishments by the 1860s.

Several hotels were constructed to accommodate the crowds anticipated for the great exhibitions: the Grand Hôtel du Louvre, built for the Paris Exhibition of 1855, the Langham (London, 1862), the Continental (Paris, 1878), and the Palais d'Orsay (Paris, 1900). The influx of American tourists in the decades following the Civil War provided further incentives to refurbish hotels and build new ones with more luxurious amenities. European travelers to the United States had long remarked on the size and comfort of many American hotels, and so it was not surprising that Americans traveling to Europe often found accommodations there lacking, notably for their paucity of private baths. Beginning in the 1870s, a number of hotels attempted to attract American visitors by adding bathrooms and services such as English-speaking concierges and omnibuses to meet arriving guests at railroad stations. One American visitor to London in 1880 remarked that there were at least six hotels that met American standards, where just a few years earlier none had existed. By the 1880s and 1890s, guidebooks could recommend several first-class hotels in any of the cities most commonly visited by travelers.[21]

In 1892, the CIWL built the Pera Palace, the first Western-style hotel in Istanbul, specifically to accommodate travelers on the *Orient Express*. Two years later, CIWL set up a subsidiary, the Compagnie Internationale des Grands Hôtels, which operated hotels in Nice, Monte Carlo, Lisbon, Ostend, and other cities. In one of its more ambitious projects, the company took over the palace of the Egyptian khedive at Gezira, near Cairo, and turned it into a luxury hotel. Similarly, in North America, the Canadian Pacific and several U.S. railroads built luxury hotels in the sparsely settled western regions of the continent in an effort to attract the wealthy patrons who were not likely to travel west unless they could be assured of comfortable accommodations when they got there. These new hotels differed from the older railway hotels in the addition of elegant dining rooms and larger, more lavishly appointed public rooms—in keeping with the sobriquets ''grand'' and ''palace'' that so often formed part of their names.[22]

The man who brought the grand hotel to its most elaborate form, whose very name became synonymous with luxury, came from a family of peasants. Born in 1850 in the tiny village of Niederwald in Switzerland's upper Rhone Valley, César Ritz displayed an ambition to move beyond his restricted surroundings at an early age. After schooling in Sion and a job as an apprentice wine waiter in nearby Brig, Ritz went to Paris to look for work during the 1867 Exhibition. For the next several years, he held a succession of jobs in Paris—notably at Voisin's, then the most fashionable restaurant in the city, and the Hotel Splendide, one of the most luxurious in Europe. From Paris he went on to a job in Vienna during the Exhibition of 1873, and then to Nice the following year, where he became restaurant manager at the Grand Hotel.

Early in his career, Ritz developed a knack for meeting and impressing influential people. In Nice he encountered the director of the Hotel Rigi-Kulm (the famous hotel at the top of Mount Rigi near Lucerne), who offered him a job the following summer. An incident toward the end of the season there illustrates the ingenuity and determination that helped make Ritz successful: The hotel got a last-minute call from Cook's office in Lucerne saying that a group of forty Americans on a luxury tour wanted to have lunch at the hotel. Unfortunately, it was a cold day and the central heating had broken down. Loath to lose the business, Ritz moved a large table from the cavernous main dining room into a smaller room decorated primarily in warm reds, wrapped heated bricks in cloths to create footwarmers, filled big copper pots (which normally held plants) with spirits that could be flamed for heat, and created a menu made up entirely of hot foods.[23]

After leaving the Rigi-Kulm because the hotel's owner wouldn't pay him enough, Ritz took a succession of jobs, moving back and forth every few months between winter and summer resorts. When the owner of the Grand Hotel National in Lucerne, then the most luxurious hotel in Switzerland, offered him the job as general manager in 1877, the hotel was in financial difficulties. By the end of his first season, Ritz had turned it around. He stayed at the National ten years (moving to Riviera hotels during the winters, when the National closed) with just one brief interlude, when he joined forces with one of his former employers in Paris to take over Les Roches Noires in Trouville, on the Normandy coast. The venture survived only one season, but it gave Ritz valuable experience in managing a hotel restaurant. The following winter, his first of several seasons at the Grand Hotel in Monte Carlo, he hired away a chef he had met in Normandy to upgrade the Grand Hotel's dining room.

Ritz's chef was so successful that another hotel hired him the following season. Ritz, in turn, hired his chef's teacher, Auguste Escoffier, initiating a lifetime partnership with the man who became Europe's most famous chef. Haute cuisine, at the time, meant elaborate, highly decorated dishes requiring hours to prepare; in fact, Carême, one of the best-known chefs of his time, had studied architecture as part of his training. Escoffier broke with that tradition, believing that "food should look like food." Though it may not seem so to anyone reading the French cookbooks of a generation or two ago, Escoffier revolutionized haute cuisine by simplifying it and emphasizing the nutritional as well as the aesthetic properties of food. More important than the dining room in ensuring the new hotel's success, however, was a visit from the Prince of Wales, whose position as arbiter of fashion in aristocratic society was guaranteed to bring more guests.[24]

For the next several years, Ritz and Escoffier worked summers in Lucerne and winters in Monte Carlo. Finally, in the winter of 1888, Ritz was able to buy the Hôtel du Provence in Cannes and a restaurant in Baden-Baden. The Prince of Wales, who had developed a great liking for Ritz, visited the Provence, once again helping to put Ritz on the social map. Another influential patron of the Grand Hotel in Monte Carlo, Rupert D'Oyly Carte, a principal investor in the Savoy Hotel then under construction in London, visited Ritz in Baden-Baden and tried to get him to move to London to become manager of the new hotel. Ritz refused, but agreed, at D'Oyly Carte's urging, to visit London for a few days to advise on the arrangements and lend his name to the hotel. Ritz had such a loyal following by this time (1889) that D'Oyly Carte thought even his temporary presence would help bring in wealthy patrons, and he was willing to pay Ritz enough money to make it worth his while to abandon his own operations for a few weeks. Even so, within six months of its opening, the Savoy was headed for financial failure. D'Oyly Carte again turned to Ritz, who finally agreed to take over the hotel's management, provided he had six months a year to run his own operations.

His first act was to hire Escoffier as chef. The Prince of Wales, still a fan, attended the opening of the restaurant under Escoffier's direction, which created a sensation because royalty, at the time, never dined in public. The Savoy dining room became so fashionable that it attracted high-class prostitutes, which Ritz feared would drive away other patrons, especially women. He solved the problem by decreeing that evening dress would be required at dinner and that no women would be admitted without escorts.[25]

Throughout his career, Ritz owed much of his accomplishment to a remarkable capacity for understanding what patrons wanted in a luxury hotel, an intuitive sense of taste, and an indefatigable attention to detail. He established the dining room as the hotel's social center, vastly improved the quality of hotel food, and emphasized cleanliness by installing more bathrooms and using paint and lightweight fabrics instead of wallpaper and the popular damask and brocade, which he considered dirt catchers. Like George Pullman, he was as much concerned with service as with the physical attributes of his hotels.

In the late 1890s, Ritz left the Savoy over a difference of opinion about management, taking Escoffier with him. Forming his own corporation, he opened the Ritz Hotel in Paris in 1898, the first hotel entirely planned and controlled by Ritz himself. The site was a row of buildings on the fashionable Place Vendôme, a beautifully designed square of nearly uniform facades conceived by Louis XIV and built between the 1680s and 1720s. Ritz hired a French architect, Charles Mewès, to transform the interiors into a modern hotel with every comfort and luxury while preserving the eighteenth-century facade. It was to be small by grand hotel standards, more like a well-appointed home than a commercial establishment. One of its most distinctive features was a private bath attached to every room, at a time when the hotel's chief competitor (the Hotel Bristol) had only one per floor. (Ritz remembered his first years in the hotel business, at the Splendide in Paris, when American guests complained about the lack of private baths.) A year later, Ritz opened the Carlton Hotel in London, the first in that city to have a bath for every bedroom.[26] These two hotels set the standard for the luxury hotels of the next generation.

Ritz was at the peak of his career when Queen Victoria died in 1901. The following spring, the Prince of Wales capped his long-standing patronage of Ritz establishments by selecting the Carlton for his post-coronation banquet. Ritz and his staff went through a frenzy of preparation, only to learn two days before the great event that the prince had been taken seriously ill with acute appendicitis. The coronation was postponed indefinitely. Ritz collapsed with an apparent nervous breakdown at this point (surely exacerbated by years of overwork) and never fully recovered, although he was only fifty-two. By this time, he had interests in an number of other hotels, including establishments in Rome, Frankfurt, Wiesbaden, Palermo, Monte Carlo, and Lucerne, while his company, the Ritz Development Corporation, planned still more. Among these were another hotel in London, the Ritz, which opened in 1906, and the company's first overseas venture, the Ritz-Carlton in New York (1907). Ritz's wife, Marie, took over the management of the company, while Ritz himself spent the rest of his life, until his death in 1918, in a sanatorium in Switzerland.[27]

Toward the end of his career, Ritz and his closest associates, Escoffier and Mewès, entered the luxury-ship business—an appropriate move, as ocean liners became more like floating hotels than simple modes of transport. With bigger and more stable ships, public spaces became larger and more lavishly decorated, culminating in the years before World War I with the Cunard Line's trio, the *Mauretania* (launched 1906), *Lusitania* (1906), and *Aquitania* (1914); the White Star Line's *Olympic* (1910) and *Titanic* (1912); the Compagnie Générale Transatlantique's *France* (1912) and *Paris* (1914); and the Hamburg-Amerika Line's *Amerika* (1903), *Imperator* (1912), and *Vaterland* (1914). The ill-fated *Titanic,* destroyed on its maiden voyage in April 1912, and the *Lusitania,* torpedoed by German U-boats in May 1915, have become the most famous, but the *Amerika* was generally thought to be the most fashionable at the time. With interiors designed by Mewès, it was the first luxury ship to be planned in a single, coherent style instead of the mishmash of designs borrowed from various eras that had characterized earlier ships. It was also the first to include an elevator.

The *Amerika*'s most distinctive feature (besides the elevator) was its restaurant, a space separate from the ship's main dining room, where first-class passengers paid a supplement to dine à la carte, at private tables, at any hour of the day. The Hamburg-Amerika Line's director, Albert Ballin—a man obsessed with detail and quality of service in much the same manner as Ritz or Pullman—hired Escoffier to plan the kitchen and Ritz to train the dining-room staff (although by the time the ship was actually launched, Ritz was no longer active). Ballin's goal was to reproduce the food and atmosphere of the Ritz-Carlton dining room on board ship. He spared no expense, even purchasing fine china and linens with the Ritz-Carlton crest and installing a greenhouse on deck to provide such amenities as fresh flowers, lettuce, strawberries, and mushrooms. The venture proved so successful that Ballin subsequently had the kitchen remodeled to double its size.

Mewès and Ballin continued their successful collaboration with the *Imperator,* a giant 52,000-ton ship with a capacity of four thousand passengers, and the *Vaterland.* (The *Amerika,* the *Olympic,* and the *Titanic* each accommodated around twenty-five hundred passengers.) Cunard tried to hire Mewès to design the *Lusitania* and *Mauretania,* but Ballin refused to modify his exclusive contract with the architect. For the third of the Cunard trio, the *Aquitania,* the company succeeded in negotiating a deal under which Mewès's English partner, Arthur Davis, would design the ship. The condition was that the two architects not consult each other. Even so, the *Aquitania* and the *Imperator* shared similar design features, as Mewès's influence put his stamp on ship design for some years to come.[28]

By the end of the nineteenth century, the rich could travel in a style of luxury unheard of thirty or forty years earlier. Across the Atlantic, along the most popular routes in Western Europe, and in all the major cities and resort areas, they could be assured of the highest standards of comfort and service. Off the beaten track, of course, it was a different story; there were still remote areas, especially in Italy, where travelers had to resort to diligences and vetturini and put up with inns reminiscent of eighteenth-century conditions. Remarking that "the popular idea of Cleanliness in Italy is behind the age," Baedeker still advised travelers visiting remote country inns around the turn of the century to sprinkle insect powder or camphor on bedding and clothes, close windows before turning on lights, and make use of mosquito curtains, face masks, and gloves. But along the favorite routes, well-to-do travelers could move from one first-class hotel to another, transported by trains with all the amenities of first-class hotels in more compact form.[29]

These new luxury trains, ships, and hotels homogenized travel, taking much of the "foreignness" out of it. Belgian-run CIWL luxury trains covered the Continent, providing the same food, the same linen sheets, the same impeccable service whether in Belgium, France, Italy, or Russia. The transatlantic liners of four nations offered the same appointments and service, differing only in matters of style and in the constantly escalating competition to see whose ships would be the biggest, fastest, and fanciest. The grand hotels in one city were very much like the grand hotels in another. As Baedeker noted, the dining rooms of first-class hotels in Italy served food that was a combination of French and Italian; French food set the standard for Continental cuisine, and under the influence of Escoffier and those he trained, his style of cooking became ubiquitous throughout Western Europe's finest restaurants and hotel dining rooms. Wealthy tourists may have looked down at those who didn't travel "independently," but they too exhibited a high degree of conformity in their preferred style of travel.

WITH THE CREATION of the packaged tour, the luxury train, the grand hotel, and the floating palaces, the very nature of travel changed in fundamental ways. Until about the middle of the nineteenth century, "travel" was more or less synonymous with "tour"—an extended journey to a series of places distant, and usually very different, from one's home. Although travel as recreation had long since eclipsed travel as education in the eighteenth-century sense, the notion that one traveled to broaden one's horizons, to see other kinds of places and meet different kinds of people, persisted well into the nineteenth century. By the 1880s, however, the speed and comfort of getting about encouraged traveling for its own sake. "These contemporary tramps of ours have long since passed the stage of learning anything," an American writer complained in

1888. "Their notion of travel is rest and repairs, and to have fun—good things in their way, but by this generation inordinately pursued." This writer also observed that many people seemed to travel to escape the pressures of work and daily life. An acquaintance who had been advised by his doctor to cease all work and go abroad responded by asking, why not quit work and stay at home? Fine, said the doctor, "if you can do it. What I want is to stop the work. The European part of it is nonessential."[30] The doctor's advice was a variation on an old theme—travel to recover one's health—except that, by the late nineteenth century, the notion of rest and relaxation as essential to counter the stresses of modern life (and the belief that one had to get away from home to relax completely) was already taking its place beside the older tradition of convalescing in a more hospitable climate. Such a notion would hardly have been possible in an era when stress and fatigue were more likely accompaniments to travel than pleasure or relaxation.

By making travel easy and comfortable, the luxury travel industry as well as packaged tours spelled the end of the European grand tour, although it persisted for a time among Americans, for both practical and cultural reasons. The time and cost required to get across the Atlantic encouraged Americans visiting Europe to make the most of their experience by spending several weeks or months abroad, covering as much ground as possible; and nineteenth-century Americans had much the same sense of isolation from the sources of Western civilization and culture that had propelled generations of British grand tourists across the Channel. Indeed, in many respects Americans began to supplant the British as the most prominent and visible group of tourists by the late nineteenth century, gaining a reputation as loud, self-important, boorish, and rich. Among Europeans, however, and Americans in their own country, shorter, more frequent journeys focusing on a single region became increasingly popular.

Middle-class travelers, who had limited time at their disposal, came to see the annual two- or three-week vacation almost as a right; this was the market that a growing army of travel agents set out to exploit. Wealthier travelers might still indulge their wanderlust with long stretches away from home, especially in winter, but instead of touring, they were more likely to settle in a single location, taking up residence in a grand hotel or renting a villa for the season. The very wealthy (or the very bored) might stay away from home for months at a time, moving from one fashionable resort to another as the seasons changed: Switzerland in the summer, the German spas like Baden-Baden or Wiesbaden in the spring, Italy or the Riviera in the winter, perhaps even Egypt or Algeria for the more adventurous. Some of these destinations had been popular for decades, but improved transportation and the construction of new hotels opened up new areas as destinations for wealthy travelers seeking diversion and a sunnier climate. Wherever they went, wealthy tourists re-created their own, familiar culture around them, much as the British travelers to Italy had in the first half of the nineteenth century.

One of the most striking examples of the changing style of travel among the rich was the growing popularity of southern France, especially the Riviera, which surpassed Italy as the most popular destination among British tourists in the 1870s. The region's appeal was much the same as Italy's—the warm, brilliantly sunny winter climate, the clear air (presumed to be healthful for invalids), the proximity of the sea. Perhaps more important, this region was still unspoiled, uncrowded, and ripe for development as an exclusive haven for the rich. Southern France may not have had the cultural treasures of Italy, but cultural treasures were no longer the point of travel for many people. The region did have beautiful scenery, a balmy winter climate, and, most important, privacy. Early visitors to towns like Nice, Cannes, and Menton on the Riviera and Biarritz and Pau in the southwest pretty much managed to keep them as winter havens for the rich until World War I.

The sort of mishaps Tobias Smollett endured on his journey to Nice in the 1760s were enough to deter all but the hardiest travelers in the eighteenth century, when the rough coastline road was barely passable for carriages and Barbary pirates were still a threat at sea. Politics also inhibited British visitors, as the Riviera east of Cannes and Antibes, long part of the Kingdom of Sardinia (an ally of Britain) was taken over by France in 1782. After Napoleon's fall, the region reverted to Sardinia, and small numbers of British tourists began visiting the area—enough so that in 1822, a group of British families who regularly wintered in Nice sponsored the construction of a small Anglican church. In the mid-1830s, the tiny fishing village of Cannes was "discovered" by Henry Brougham, recently retired as lord chancellor, while en route to Genoa. Much taken with the village and with everything he heard about its mild winter climate (not an insignificant issue, because he had an invalid daughter), he bought land and built a home for himself. Over the next several years, others followed Brougham's example, creating a substantial community of winter residents. They built their first English church in 1855. Despite a loyal following, however, the number of tourists on the Riviera remained modest until the late 1870s, when about 11,000 people visited annually; by the 1890s, the figure rose to 100,000 for Nice alone.[31]

Improved accessibility was the key to this rise in the Riviera's popularity. The railroad line east from Marseilles was completed as far as Cannes in 1863, Nice in 1864, Monaco in 1868, and the Italian border in 1870. The CIWL's through trains from Calais to the Riviera, which began operations in 1883, made it possible for British visitors to reach Cannes or Nice directly from Calais in a little over a day. A few years later, CIWL's luxury trains from St. Petersburg did the same for the Russian aristocrats who were another important segment of the Riviera's winter society.

The railroad's effect was immediate. In Cannes, for example, which had only a handful of hotels in the 1850s, the Grand Hotel—as big as the Louvre and always full, in the words of one visitor—went up within a year after the railroad was completed. Nice received two of its most distinguished visitors, Tsar Alexander II and his wife, a week after the railroad opened. Most dramatically, Monaco, a sleepy backwater until the early 1870s, was transformed into the gambling mecca of Europe. Early efforts to promote gambling, in the late 1850s, had failed because the site was accessible only by a single steep, narrow road. In 1862, however, the owners of successful casinos at Wiesbaden and Bad Homburg bought the concession for Monte Carlo's casino in anticipation of the railroad's completion. Their investment paid off, as more than forty hotels were built over the next thirty years, and Monte Carlo became the choice of the fast set among the Riviera's winter visitors.[32]

The Riviera's growing reputation as a health resort also contributed to its popularity. Several books, beginning in the 1860s, touted the beneficial effects of the warm climate for consumptives and other invalids. Among the most widely read was Dr. James Henry Bennett's *Winter and Spring on the Shores of the Mediterranean,* first published in 1860 and reissued several times through the 1870s. A German translation appeared in 1863 and an American edition in 1870. A similar book by another physician, Alexander Brown, became a best-seller upon its publication in 1872. Bennett, himself suffering from tuberculosis, went to Menton, a small village east of Nice, in 1859, expecting to die there. Instead he recovered sufficiently to resume his London practice in the summers and work in Menton during the winters. In the spring, he often traveled to other popular winter vacation spots to assess their value for recovering invalids, but found nothing to compete seriously with the Riviera. The popular destinations in Italy, he maintained, were either too cold (like Pisa), too foggy (Florence), or too dirty (Naples). Nor could the more exotic destinations like Algeria or Spain pass muster—Algeria because it was too damp and the coast of Spain because its limited accommodations were unsuitable for invalids.[33] But ultimately it was fashion more than health that made this strip of coastline the most popular winter destination in Europe. The Prince of Wales's first visit to Cannes in 1872 probably did almost as much as the railroad to boost tourism. He returned regularly, and Queen Victoria herself came occasionally during the 1880s and '90s, as did King Leopold of Belgium and several other heads of state.[34]

As tourism expanded on the Riviera, each town took on a slightly different character. British visitors favored Nice and Cannes. The former was known for a lively social life; tourists generally stayed in hotels and socialized in a more public manner than in Cannes, where it was more common to rent villas for the season and socialize privately. (Probably for that reason, Cannes was also popular with the German and Russian nobility.) Each town had separate British quarters by the 1880s, several Anglican churches (as well as a Scottish Presbyterian church), many shops selling British goods, an English newspaper, and a yachting society. Cannes had a cricket club and a golf club as well. Among the dozens of hotels were several with

names hinting at their predominantly British clientele—the d'Angle-
terre, Victoria, Grande Bretagne, des Anglais, and the Iles Britan-
niques—and many more advertising their "English sanitary
arrangements." (There was also a Hotel St. Petersbourg in Nice.)
Perhaps to avoid the British and other foreigners, French visitors
(ironically probably the smallest group of tourists) gravitated to Hy-
ères, west of Cannes. Menton, best known as a retreat for invalids,
was also popular with clergymen—the Baptist revivalist Charles
Spurgeon wintered there through the 1880s—and had a reputation
as a rather dull place until the late 1880s, when its proximity to
Monte Carlo began to attract the gambling set. The ill and the religious subsequently transferred their patronage to San Remo, a few
miles southeast on the Italian Riviera.[35]

Although southwestern France, notably Pau and the coastal
towns of Biarritz and Royan, enjoyed a considerable following by
the end of the nineteenth century—Pau had a large British winter
colony, and Biarritz was popularized by the patronage of the French
royal family of the Second Empire—the Riviera remained unsurpassed as a winter playground for the rich until World War I.[36] (In
the 1920s, American visitors, among whom F. Scott Fitzgerald was
the most famous, began touting the Riviera as a summer resort; its
primary season today is summer rather than winter.) Much of the
Riviera's popularity, besides the undoubted advantages of climate
and scenic beauty, stemmed from its exclusivity. The region's inaccessibility kept tourists away until the mid-nineteenth century and
therefore allowed the early visitors to shape these former fishing villages in their own way, to become exclusive havens for the well-to-
do of Europe from London to St. Petersburg. Other areas equally
well suited in terms of climate to appeal to northern Europeans in
search of winter sunshine were either much more crowded (like Italy)
or more remote (like Greece and Spain).[37] Oddly enough, in the 1880s
Egypt emerged as a winter rival to the Riviera among the fashionable set—but that is an altogether different story, to be taken up in
a later chapter.

CHAPTER 7

THE "PLAYGROUND
OF EUROPE"

IN THE PREFACE to his revised guide to Switzerland, published
in 1879, John Murray noted that two new types of visitors had
become commonplace in that country since the publication of his first
guide in 1838: "mountaineers" and "tourists." He made no pretense
of advising the first group, those men (and a few women) whose idea
of a summer vacation was scaling ice- and snow-covered peaks, preferably those as yet unclimbed; and the "tourists"—"persons more
or less incapable . . . of taking care of themselves while abroad"—he
held in ill-disguised contempt.[1] Murray's constituency would remain
the upper-middle-class traveler who could afford the six weeks to
three months he considered necessary to see Switzerland properly.

The tendency of travelers to segregate themselves according to
their interests and the size of their traveling budgets was nowhere
more evident by the late nineteenth century than in Switzerland and
the adjacent Alpine regions. If the French Riviera was the prime
example of a remote area rapidly transformed into a tourist mecca
for the rich, Switzerland—aptly labeled "the playground of Europe"

by literary critic and amateur mountaineer Leslie Stephen—was quite the opposite: a region long favored by travelers, where tourism grew steadily by appealing to a broad range of visitors, from solitary adventurers like Wordsworth and genteel families summering on the lakes, to Cook's groups, to mountaineers and winter-sports enthusiasts. During the second half of the nineteenth century, Switzerland became a kind of microcosm of leisure travel, with a little something for everyone—actively promoted by the Swiss themselves, who were among the first to see tourism as an economic boon to an impoverished country.[2]

Although Alpine tourism dates back to the early eighteenth century, the number of visitors to Switzerland and environs grew slowly over the next several decades, partly because mountain scenery remained an acquired taste until early in the nineteenth century, and partly because the region remained quite primitive and inaccessible, even after railroads extended across much of Western Europe. Difficult as it is for the modern traveler to believe after shopping in Geneva or riding trains and buses to tiny mountain villages, until the mid-nineteenth century, Switzerland (apart from the major cities) was a poor country, isolated by its geography and dependent mainly on localized subsistence agriculture. Most Alpine villages declined in population during the eighteenth and early nineteenth centuries, as young men sought employment in the cities or outside the country.[3]

Improvements in transportation networks proceeded slowly. Before 1855, there was only one short railroad line in the entire country: a fifteen-mile link between Zurich and Baden, which opened in 1847 but did not generate enough traffic to sustain itself for more than a few years. Mountain terrain posed a serious obstacle, but railroad construction lagged even across the relatively gentle landscape of the north, mainly because of the country's highly decentralized government. Along with investor conservatism and disputes over how to finance and control any sort of transportation infrastructure, the absence of any kind of central government made building major roads and railroads a cumbersome process.[4]

This situation changed significantly after the Swiss civil war of 1848, when the various cantons agreed to a federal constitution providing for a central authority to handle foreign policy. Over the next decade, the federal government also improved the nation's transit and banking systems as part of its effort to strengthen its position within Europe. Among the new government's first acts were establishing a uniform system of measurement and surveying the distances between major towns. In 1850, a uniform currency was adopted, matching that of France. A nationwide system of posting came in 1852; the government also sponsored publication of a directory of public conveyances. Most significantly, in 1849 the government commissioned two Englishmen to prepare a plan for a network of railways. They proposed six main lines through the principal valleys, connected by steamboat services on the large lakes. By 1860, the basic components of this network were in place, and railroad mileage, which nearly doubled in the 1870s, continued to rise steadily until World War I. The 1870s also saw the beginning of efforts to build funicular and cog railways in the high mountain regions, as well as the first tunnels through major Alpine passes.[5]

EVEN BEFORE THE railroad era, Alpine tourism expanded steadily, if modestly. There are no statistics on numbers of tourists before the late nineteenth century, but the sales of guidebooks offer some indication of the region's growing popularity. Murray's *Hand-Book for Travellers in Switzerland,* first published in 1838, went through seven editions by 1857, selling about 26,000 copies, while Baedeker's three editions of his guide, published between 1844 and 1857, sold 13,000. By 1880, an estimated one million tourists visited Switzerland annually; the rate of growth between the 1880s and World War I continued to increase dramatically, as ridership on the railroads jumped fivefold during that period.[6]

Before about 1830, most Alpine tourists came from Germany and Switzerland itself, with a sprinkling from Britain. In later decades, the number of British visitors rose so sharply that they vastly outnumbered travelers from central Europe—in part because the British had more money and therefore tended to drive up prices until they were the only people who could afford to travel in certain areas. (The French writer Alexandre Dumas, visiting Switzerland in the early 1830s, remarked that tourism was "the third English invention to overturn the world, with humor and the steam engine.") After the Civil War, Americans also began to visit Switzerland in significant numbers; by the 1880s, they made up about a fifth of the total number of tourists, contributing to the image of Switzerland as an English-speaking preserve in the summer months. The estimated four thousand French who visited Switzerland in 1865 were but a fraction of the number of English and Americans.[7]

Swiss entrepreneurs actively encouraged tourism by building hotels and studying the tastes of foreign visitors. As early as 1838, Murray observed that Swiss inns maintained high standards, except in the remote southern regions, and accommodated British visitors by serving the table d'hôte dinner at their preferred hour of 4:00 or 5:00 P.M. Some of the larger innkeepers even built chapels for English church services. In the 1840s, a group of hotel proprietors organized an association to establish uniform rates throughout the country. This association disintegrated within a few years, although its schedule of charges remained a fixture in subsequent editions of Murray's handbooks. Hotelkeepers formed a more permanent organization, the Société Suisse des Hôteliers, in 1882. By that time, there were nearly 1,700 hotels in operation, rising to almost 3,600 by 1912.[8]

A talent for organization and for making their guests comfortable proved a double-edged sword for the Swiss, however, as innkeepers developed a reputation for overcharging their guests. Murray regretted the transformation of the simple, virtuous peasant into the calculating businessman—a characterization that hardened into a stereotype over the years. Amelia Edwards, a popular journalist and pulp novelist traveling in a remote part of the Italian Alps in the 1880s, lamented that an increase in tourism would eventually force part-time village innkeepers out of business, and then "extortionate speculators, probably Swiss," would move in and take over. And in the 1920s, a British journalist quipped, "The Swiss are inspired hotelkeepers. Some centuries since, when the stranger strayed into one of their valleys, their simple forefathers would kill him and share out the little money he might have about him. Now they know better. They keep him alive and writing cheques."[9]

*   *   *

WITH INCREASED TOURISM, predictably enough, came complaints that the Alps were becoming too crowded. Such complaints were hardly new—Gibbon had declared Switzerland overcrowded in the 1780s—but by the 1860s and '70s, they were more frequent and more strident, and directed primarily at lower-middle-class tourists. In the Alps as elsewhere, wealthier travelers responded to the influx of tour groups by seeking out enclaves where they could associate exclusively with their own kind. As early as the 1830s, wealthy British visitors congregated in the most expensive hotels in Interlaken and Lucerne; the grand hotels built in the last third of the nineteenth century, of which Ritz's Grand Hotel National was the best known, became self-contained resorts where the rich could count on setting themselves apart.

Swiss businessmen were well aware of the need to attract wealthy travelers if they wanted to retain this lucrative part of their tourist trade. The hotel Burgenstock in Lucerne responded to a decline in tourism during the depression of the early 1870s by turning itself into a luxury establishment resembling a private mansion, complete with paintings, gardens, greenhouses, and tennis courts. By 1900, the Tourist Association of Thun openly urged its members to work harder at attracting upper-class visitors. The association's directors believed that continued expansion of tour groups was inevitable, but "the essential interest of the resort nevertheless demands that the high class public, which stays for long periods and expends a small fortune on its vacations, be retained. Ways must be found to compensate people of quality for having to suffer the presence of the disgusting masses."[10]

One of the ways adopted by a few clever entrepreneurs was creating new luxury establishments in remote parts of the country. Perhaps the most notable example was St. Moritz in southeastern Switzerland, until the 1850s a sleepy little village lacking a single hotel. Within forty years, enterprising local businessmen transformed it into one of the most fashionable resorts in the Alps. Not that St. Moritz was altogether unknown before the mid-nineteenth century. Situated on a hill above a mineral spring renowned for its healthful properties, the village had attracted a small but loyal following as far back as the seventeenth century. Most of the early visitors came from northern Italy by way of a fairly easy route over the Maloja Pass south of St. Moritz. Until the completion of a carriage road over the Julier Pass in 1826, however, access from the north and west was difficult and expensive; the journey from Zurich, the nearest major Swiss city, took two or three days by wagon.

With the completion of a good road over the San Bernardino Pass in 1819, even the very limited tourist trade in St. Moritz declined, as Italians found that regions farther west were now easier to reach and offered better accommodations. Realizing that St. Moritz would have to provide more creature comforts for visitors if its tourist trade was to revive, a small group of local businessmen formed a company in 1832 to improve the amenities around the mineral springs. They also persuaded the village council to offer free land and lumber to anyone who would build a hotel there. Even so, it was twenty years before a hotel was built. When finally completed, the large, elegantly furnished new establishment, known as the Kurhaus, was an immediate success.[11]

Three years later, a local entrepreneur named Johannes Badrutt bought the Kulm, a small pension in the village uphill from the springs, and transformed it into a luxury establishment. He added running water and the region's first indoor toilets, furnished the rooms with antique furniture and paintings, hired a good chef, and engaged an orchestra to play during meals. (Much later, after witnessing a demonstration of electricity at the Paris World's Fair of 1878, he had a generator built to provide electric lights.) Recognizing that he couldn't compete with the Kurhaus for the patronage of visitors who came to St. Moritz for the waters, Badrutt set out to attract those in search of a new setting for their mountain holidays, lobbying the village council to maintain local footpaths and organizing climbing clubs and a mountain guides' association.[12]

Both the Kurhaus and the Kulm expanded several times during the 1860s and '70s, and thirteen new luxury hotels were built, as well as many smaller establishments. Taken together, village hostelries provided close to three thousand beds by the 1880s, up from a mere eighty in 1850. This kind of growth was possible only as St. Moritz began to attract visitors from greater distances, a shift aided by the extension of the railroad as far as Chur, about forty miles to the north, and by the introduction of regular carriage service from there to St. Moritz. By the 1870s, about 70 percent of visitors to St. Moritz were British, with the rest divided more or less equally between Italians and Germans.[13]

Becoming accessible to the world, yet not *too* accessible, allowed St. Moritz hotelkeepers to adopt a deliberate policy of catering to wealthy visitors who came for the season with their families, servants, and dozens of steamer trunks. An American travel writer described the village as a place where one might meet "representatives . . . from all parts of the world. . . . You may see an English earl chatting with some Germanfrau; a handsome Italian officer flirting with a belle from California; some Russian polyglot making himself agreeable to a charming Frenchwoman; statesmen exchanging confidences as they walk . . . princes and princesses from Rome, Naples, and Milan; and, most charming of all perhaps, some graceful and accomplished Venetian countess, looking as if she ought to have lived when there was a Titian to hand down her likeness to after ages."

Because St. Moritz's growth was compressed into a relatively short time, the town fathers, in their efforts to keep their village exclusive, could exercise a high degree of control over its development. (In this respect, it was similar to villages like Cannes and Menton on the French Riviera.) In Lucerne and Thun, long popular with travelers, hotelkeepers had to work to differentiate themselves; in St. Moritz, the entire village set itself apart—and, incidentally, increased prices steadily despite minimal inflation during the late nineteenth century.[14]

BY THE 1860S AND '70S, a new breed of traveler emerged, one who genuinely wanted to get away from it all—including people of whatever class. Often highly educated professionals with enough private income to allow a certain degree of independence, these travelers placed a high value on scenic beauty and on travel as a means of escape, however temporary, from the pressures of an increasingly complex world.

One of the more colorful examples of the type was the sharp-tongued and adventurous Amelia Edwards. A veteran of several trips to the Continent, disgusted with both the tourist hordes and the inn-keepers and merchants who profited from them, in 1872 Edwards and her frequent traveling companion (a woman identified only as L) decided to bypass Switzerland in favor of a tour of the seldom-visited Dolomites in northeastern Italy. Until railroad lines extended to the edges of Italy's Alpine region in the late 1860s, pleasure travelers rarely visited the Dolomites, and even then travel within the region remained primitive.[15]

Notwithstanding her preference for out-of-the-way locations, Edwards observed certain proprieties, traveling with a maid and a male escort, an old friend whom she referred to as her "courier." Both were to be obstacles in planning the Dolomite trip (as was her insistence on a sidesaddle, no easy thing to procure in this remote region). The maid was "delicate." More seriously, the male escort was, in Edwards's words, "a gentleman of refined and expensive tastes, who abhorred what is generally understood by 'roughing it,' despised primitive simplicity, and exacted that his employers should strictly limit their love of the picturesque to districts abundantly intersected by railways and well furnished with first-class hotels." To shield herself from his objections, Edwards planned the trip secretly and presented her gentleman friend with a fait accompli.[16]

Having dragooned the gentleman into accompanying them and put aside doubts about their maid's stamina, Edwards and L traveled to a point forty miles north of Venice by train and then hired a carriage to take them another fifty miles or so north to Cortina. There they found a "tolerable" inn, with good if simple food; but after two days of such rustic accommodation Edwards's gentleman friend quit, unable to face the prospect of several more weeks of the same. (Perhaps it was the "rough" barbera from Piedmont and the poor-quality kirsch—the only alternatives to thin local wine or beer, according to Edwards—that made him pack his bags.) Beyond Cortina conditions deteriorated further. The party traveled mainly by horse and mule, hiring a carriage only for those rare stretches suitable for wheeled transit. On one steep slope, they all had to get out and help the carriage driver push their vehicle uphill. A little farther along, they encountered construction workers who were astonished to see people actually trying to use the as yet unfinished road. "You must be Inglese!'' the men exclaimed.[17] Rough roads, filthy inns, and meals of eggs and coarse cheese notwithstanding, Edwards maintained that traveling in the Dolomites more than repaid the effort, freeing one "from hackneyed sights, from overcrowded hotels, from the dreary routine of table d'hôtes, from the flood of Cook's tourists."[18]

Other travelers found quiet retreats within Switzerland itself simply by getting off the main tourist circuit, which still, even in the late nineteenth century, focused primarily on Geneva, Chamonix, and the lakes and mountains around Lucerne and Interlaken. The basic itineraries recommended by Murray and Baedeker changed little over several decades; as a result, the independent traveler didn't have to go too far from the beaten track to find refuge from what Leslie Stephen snidely referred to as "Cockney travelers." "There are innumerable valleys which have not yet bowed the knee to Baal, in the shape of Mr. Cook and his tourists," Stephen remarked, "and within a few hours of one of the most frequented routes in Europe there are retired valleys where Swiss peasants . . . will refuse money in exchange for their hospitality."[19]

At the beginning of the twentieth century, Edith Wharton could still gloat over the hundreds of tourists who crossed the Splügen pass from Switzerland into Italy "in a cloud of diligence dust" while she relaxed in a village just off the main road. "From the vantage of the solitary meadows above the village one may watch the throngs descending on Thusis or Chiavenna with something of the satisfaction that mediaeval schoolmen believed to be the portion of angels looking down upon the damned," she wrote.[20] Jane Freshfield, an Englishwoman who visited Switzerland with her family nearly every summer during the 1850s and '60s, favored Mürren, just south of Lauterbrunnen, and Engelberg, only a few miles from Lucerne and Meiringen, in addition to more remote areas near St. Moritz and south of the Rhone Valley along the border between Switzerland and Italy. She blamed Murray's guide for channeling travelers along the same well-worn routes, and especially for discouraging women from undertaking any excursion considered the least bit strenuous.

To get to these unspoiled spots, however, one had to plan carefully, hire a local guide, and be willing to ride a horse or mule, walk, and put up with substandard accommodations. A sense of humor helped too—as, for example, when the Freshfields traced a peculiar odor permeating their rustic village inn to the previous day's hunting ventures of another guest, who had shot a wolf and skinned it in the hallway near their rooms. The incident "had at least the charm of novelty," Freshfield remarked.[21]

TRAVELERS LIKE the Freshfields spent as much time on foot as they did in carriages, and were not intimidated by high mountain terrain, even when it meant roping up and carrying ice axes for safety. Their style of travel bordered on serious mountain climbing, a sport that gained increasing popularity in the Alps beginning in the 1850s. (Freshfield's son became a fairly well-known climber in later years.) Although only a small proportion of Alpine visitors took to the slopes in such a serious way, climbing contributed to the expansion of mountain vacations and helped promote tourism in previously little-traveled regions.

As far back as the late eighteenth century, the popularity of Chamonix demonstrated the potential links between mountain climbing and tourism. Horace-Bénédict de Saussure's offer of a prize to the first person who scaled Mont Blanc created so much publicity that tourism in Chamonix soared among travelers who were beginning to seek out mountain scenery. Its fame and easy accessibility from Geneva made it the favorite Alpine destination until well into the nineteenth century. Few of the early visitors actually attempted to scale Mont Blanc or the neighboring peaks, however, contenting themslves with guided walks up the lower slopes or along the Mer de Glace. Serious climbing remained a localized sport, as Swiss, French, German, and Austrian men tackled peaks in their native regions.[22] This situation changed dramatically around the middle of the nineteenth century, however, when more British tourists visited the Alps and discovered the challenge of climbing. As with so many other forms of travel, once the British discovered climbing, they quickly took it over.

The first Briton to take a serious interest in climbing was, like Saussure, motivated by science rather than sport. J. D. Forbes, a

professor at Edinburgh University with a particular interest in gla-
ciers, began exploring the high Alps in the late 1830s. He made the
fourth recorded ascent of the Jungfrau in 1841 and the first of the
Stockhorn, also in the Bernese Oberland. Forbes's 1844 book, *Travels
Through the Alps,* though heavy on scientific analysis, helped spark
British interest in Alpine climbing. Significantly, it was reissued in
1855, stripped of most of its scientific content and retitled *A Tour of
Mont Blanc and Monte Rosa.*[23]

The man who did more than anyone else to popularize mountain
climbing with the British was not a scientist or even an especially
serious climber, but a flamboyant entertainer named Albert Smith.
A physician-turned-journalist, Smith packed lecture halls all over
London in the late 1840s with his talk on Mont Blanc, illustrated
with three-foot-high paintings fitted to a mechanism that allowed
him to roll the pictures in sequence, creating a moving panorama.
Such "entertainments" were extremely popular in the era before film
and television, with travel themes among the most prominent. After
the success of his Mont Blanc show, Smith created an even more
elaborate panorama simulating a tour of the Middle East. At about
the same time, Londoners could see an exhibition displaying Fré-
mont's route to Oregon, a diorama of the India Overland Mail, and
a hippopotamus displayed by the viceroy of Egypt.

After the successful run of his Middle Eastern show, in the summer of 1851, Smith and three friends decided to fulfill an old dream
by climbing Mont Blanc. That they succeeded is evidence of how
routine the climb had become. Aged thirty-five and out of shape,
Smith went up the mountain with his friends, sixteen guides, and a
supply of provisions that included fifty fowls and one hundred bottles
of wine. (In the six seasons after Smith climbed Mont Blanc, there
were sixty-four successful ascents of the mountain, all but four by
British groups.) Shortly after returning to London, Smith put together another, much more elaborate Mont Blanc show, with paintings by one of his traveling companions and a script featuring several
characters—all played by Smith himself. The show opened at London's Egyptian Hall in 1852 to packed audiences, attracting nearly
200,000 people, including Queen Victoria, in the first season. After
more than two thousand performances over five seasons, Smith's

show finally closed, not because its popularity was diminishing but because he was tired of it. For diversion he went on a trip to China.[24]

One of Smith's contemporaries, a lawyer named Alfred Wills, is usually credited with establishing mountain climbing as a sport among the British. Wills first gained fame for his ascent of the Wetterhorn from Grindelwald in 1854. His was not the first ascent—at least two local men had climbed the mountain earlier—but, like Saussure's ascent of Mont Blanc, his was the climb that garnered publicity. He too wrote a popular book, *Wanderings Among the High Alps*, published in 1858, which along with Smith's second show and the reissue of Forbes's book helped promote mountaineering and mountain travel in general during the middle years of the century. John Murray criticized mountain climbing as merely a fad, reminding his readers of its dangers and declaring that those who persisted in this new sport were "of a diseased mind"; but the trend continued. In the ten years after Wills's ascent of the Wetterhorn, most of the major peaks in the Swiss and French Alps were climbed for the first time, usually by British mountaineers.[25]

The Britons who took up mountain climbing were primarily middle-class professionals, many of them educated at Oxford and Cambridge, where sports and the competitive spirit were an essential part of their education and manliness was associated with endurance and courage. Climbing offered both sport and danger, as well as competition against the forces of nature (especially appealing for those who did not excel at team sports—with mountain climbing, it was individual strength and determination that counted). The public school and university experience also encouraged these men to be joiners, so it was no surprise that a group of them banded together in 1857 to form the Alpine Club. Conceived by two men, William Matthews and T. S. Kennedy, the club enrolled nearly three hundred charter members, most of them Oxford- or Cambridge-educated professionals; over a third were lawyers or clergymen. Among the members were several notable intellectuals, including John Ruskin (who spent more time writing about mountains than climbing them), Matthew Arnold, and Leslie Stephen, who served as club president from 1865 to 1868.[26]

The club's stated purpose was to increase knowledge about

mountains through literature, science, and art, as well as to promote climbing as sport and fellowship among mountaineers. Given the intellectual bent of the members, it was to be expected that one of their first projects would be a journal, *Peaks, Passes, and Glaciers,* devoted to accounts of climbs and scientific and historical essays. (It was renamed the *Alpine Journal* in 1863, and has been published continuously under that name ever since.) The first president, John Ball, wrote a series of specialized guides to the Alps, which provided much more detailed information and advice than either Murray or Baedeker. In the two decades after the club's creation, mountaineers in several other Western European countries formed similar groups. The Austrian Alpine Club was first, in 1862, followed by Switzerland (1863), Germany (1869), and France (1874).[27]

Membership in the Alpine Club remained exclusive. Prospective joiners had to fulfill a technical qualification and be approved by a vote of the membership. No votes from 10 percent of the members were enough to kill an application. The club was, of course, all male, and indeed, mountaineering was an overwhelmingly male sport, although there were a number of notable female mountaineers. Women formed their own club, the Ladies' Alpine Club, in 1907. Many of the early female mountaineers were introduced to the sport by fathers or brothers, notably Lucy Walker, who started climbing in 1858 and scaled ninety-eight peaks over the next twenty-one years, always with a male member of her family. An American climber, Marguerite Brevoort, introduced her nephew, W.A.B. Coolidge, to the sport; he would become one of the best-known mountaineers of the last decades of the nineteenth century. Two sisters, Anna and Ellen Pigeon, climbed together. Mrs. Stephen Winkworth made the first recorded ascent of the Jungfrau by a woman in 1863, on an expedition with her husband. After spending the night in a cave partway up, they rose at 1:00 A.M. and climbed seven and a half hours to the summit— "not bad walking for a lady," as Mrs. Winkworth put it.[28]

Female mountaineers, including the first woman to reach the summit of Mont Blanc, often had to fight criticism from those who thought climbing was no sport for a lady, however. When Henriette d'Angeville announced her intention of climbing Mont Blanc, her friends denounced the adventure as dangerous and unfeminine. Undaunted, she made the climb in 1838 with an entourage of six guides, six porters, and provisions enough to rival Albert Smith, including two legs of mutton, two ox tongues, twenty-four fowls, eighteen bottles of good wine, one cask of vin ordinaire, one bottle of brandy, three pounds of sugar, and a supply of chocolate and French plums. An Englishwoman, Elizabeth Burnaby LeBlond, also launched her climbing career on Mont Blanc after visiting Chamonix in 1881 to recuperate from tuberculosis. She climbed with only her guides for companionship, to the consternation of her aunt, who urged LeBlond's mother to persuade her daughter to stop climbing. "She is scandalising all London," the aunt wrote, "and looks like a Red Indian." LeBlond, who went on to a distinguished climbing career, settling eventually in St. Moritz and scaling peaks as far afield as northern Scandinavia, became the first president of the Ladies' Alpine Club.[29]

What to wear was a problem for the female mountaineers. D'Angeville, who continued to climb mountains until she was sixty-nine, wore flannel-lined tweed knickers and jacket, woollen stockings, heavy nailed boots, and a fur-lined cape. Together with her fur-lined bonnet, straw hat, velvet mask, veil, and green glasses—all for protection from the sun—she must have been quite a sight. By the 1860s and '70s, however, most women (including d'Angeville) wore skirts, in conformity to prevailing notions of feminine propriety. Mrs. H. W. Cole recommended a lightweight wool dress with rings sewn into the seams of the skirt and a cord strung through them; on difficult mountain paths, one could readily draw up the skirt several inches above the ground. A riding shirt made of waterproof cloth, to protect the dress from dirt and rain, a broad-brimmed hat, and strong boots with hobnailed soles completed her outfit. "One looks with perfect horror at such heavy boots" at home, she wrote, but on mountain trails they were essential. Cole admitted that dresses were "inconvenient," but never hinted that ladies might properly adopt any other sort of costume. Some women wore riding breeches under their skirts, removing the skirts once they had passed the last villages on their routes.[30]

In keeping with the competitive spirit that was so much a part of their motivation, serious climbers were mainly interested in "firsts"—the initial ascents of what were known as "virgin peaks." But the climbers' influence extended far beyond their own small circle. For every man and woman who climbed Mont Blanc, thousands more got a taste of mountaineering from hiking the lower slopes there and in other regions.

Toward the end of the nineteenth century, technology and entrepreneurship made it possible for even the relatively sedentary traveler to experience the high Alps at close range, with the construction of funicular and cog railways. The first of these, opened in 1871, took passengers to the summit of the ever-popular Mount Rigi. By the end of the century, forty-five more such railways were built, making it possible for anyone with the price of train fare to stand on a mountaintop, among them the Wengernalp near Grindelwald, Mount Pilatus near Lucerne, and the Gornergrat, with its spectacular views of the Matterhorn and Monte Rosa. In the late 1890s, work began on the most ambitious mountain railway of all, the 5.4-mile line from Kleine Scheidegg, above Grindelwald, to a point just below the summit of the Jungfrau. The first segment of the route opened in 1898; it took twelve more years to complete the line to the last station at Jungfraujoch. At 11,333 feet, it is still the highest-altitude railway station in Europe.[31]

The link between mountaineering and tourism was most obvious in the growth of Zermatt, south of the Rhone Valley near the Italian border. Located at the end of a narrow valley several miles south of the main road through the Rhone Valley, the village remained largely isolated as late as mid-century. Although there was a good road up the Rhone Valley, Zermatt and its neighboring villages south of the Rhone were accessible only by a rough cart track, parts of it so narrow that it was passable only on foot or mule. As late as the early 1870s, the American writer Charles Dudley Warner described the region around Zermatt as "the wildest and most savage part of Switzerland." Not until the late 1870s was it included on the standard itineraries of popular guidebooks.[32]

Until the late 1830s, Zermatt's only accommodation for visitors had been a few rooms in a local physician's home; in his first season as a part-time innkeeper, he had twelve guests. In the 1840s, two brothers, Joseph and Alexander Seiler, started a six-bed hotel in a rented house and then built a second, slightly larger hotel. Mrs. Cole, a guest there in 1850, found the place reasonably comfortable despite dirty floors, rustic furnishings, and boring food (always mutton, though cooked in different ways). Despite the lack of amenities, she and other hardy travelers in search of solitude (including the Freshfield family) began to favor the region for its pristine mountain scenery and the many possibilities for challenging, but largely nontechnical hikes. On Cole's first visit, tourists were such a novelty that she found it difficult to hire horses and guides, but by the late 1850s, lodgings and other tourist services had improved markedly.[33]

Over the course of three trips to the area, Cole made a complete circuit of Monte Rosa, a massive, 15,000-foot peak south of Zermatt on the Italian border. It was a route that could be covered quite comfortably over the major roads, but repaid the traveler willing to tackle more rugged tracks around the base of the mountain itself with even more spectacular views. Although Cole's recommended route required travel by mule and on foot, she dismissed the difficulties mentioned by some previous writers as exaggerated. (Like Freshfield, Cole had no use for male writers who designated challenging routes as off limits for "ladies.") Another favorite hike, for both Cole and the Freshfields, skirted the base of the Matterhorn from Breuil, a village on the Italian side of the mountain, to Zermatt. Starting from Zermatt itself, the hike up the Gornergrat offered 360-degree views taking in both Monte Rosa and the Matterhorn. At 10,272 feet and a 5,000-foot elevation gain, it was a serious climb, but one that could be accomplished without special equipment. Peering through telescopes at climbers on Monte Rosa was part of the entertainment for those who made it to the summit. The cog railway completed in 1898 turned this into a popular day trip with tourists of all descriptions.[34]

Beginning in the late 1850s, the Matterhorn itself drew increasing numbers of visitors to Zermatt and environs. Distinctive in its shape, set off from the surrounding peaks, the 14,692-foot peak dominates its region much as Mont Blanc does the area around Chamonix. In striking contrast to Mont Blanc, however, the Matterhorn was considered all but unclimbable. One has only to look at the mountain to understand why: Even at relatively short range, its surfaces at higher elevations appear almost perfectly smooth, rising at an angle so steep as to defy anyone to scale them, especially from the Swiss side. Guides often refused even to consider leading parties on the Matterhorn, and local lore perpetuated superstitions about a ruined city on the summit, inhabited by angry spirits who would take vengeance on anyone who approached too closely.[35] By 1860, the Matterhorn was one of the last remaining unconquered peaks in Switzerland—an irresistible challenge to mountaineers running out of possibilities for "firsts."

Local mountain guides were the first to attempt the Matterhorn, unsuccessfully, in 1858 and 1859, followed the next summer by two equally unsuccessful British teams. In 1861, serious competition began between two of England's most notable climbers. John Tyndall, veteran of many expeditions and the first man to scale the Weisshorn (along with the Matterhorn, one of the last major Swiss peaks to be conquered), tackled the Matterhorn from the Italian side, generally considered to be the most feasible route to the summit. Challenging him was Edward Whymper, a less experienced climber and one who did not fit the usual Alpine Club mold. The son of a printer and engraver, Whymper left school at the age of fourteen to be apprenticed in his father's business. He made his first trip to the Continent in 1860, when a prominent London publisher commissioned him to prepare a set of illustrations for a book on the Alps. That tour inspired him to take up mountain climbing and, more precisely, to attempt the two major Alpine peaks not yet climbed: the Weisshorn and the Matterhorn. When he made his second trip to the Alps, in 1861, and learned that Tyndall had just successfully climbed the Weisshorn, Whymper immediately turned his attention to the Matterhorn. For him, the appeal of climbing lay not in the beauty of the mountains—in fact, he thought the Matterhorn misshapen—but in the challenge of achieving something that no one had accomplished before. In this respect Whymper was like many other British mountaineers, but he was an extreme case, both in his lack of aesthetic appreciation of mountains and in his obsession with being first. When Whymper arrived at Breuil in August 1861, he was distressed to find Tyndall there ahead of him, although relieved to learn that his rival had not yet attempted the climb.[36]

Both Whymper and Tyndall failed in their attempts on the mountain that summer and for several summers afterward, although they became celebrities among other tourists just the same. Part of the two men's rivalry turned on the issue of the best route up the mountain. In the summer of 1865, on his seventh attempt, Whymper decided to start from Zermatt instead of Breuil and go up the east face, which most experts considered unclimbable. In fact, as Whymper discovered, the upper face—which looked nearly perpendicular from below—was only about a 40-degree slope, and the weather was usually more consistent than on the Italian side. Still, Whymper was forced to turned back once again, but he saw enough to persuade him that this was the route of choice.[37]

Later that summer he tried again, with three guides and three other Englishmen, whom he had met by chance at his hotel in Zermatt. While making their preparations, the group learned of an Italian party setting out from Breuil, so it became a race for the top. This time Whymper made it, but as he finally approached the summit, he worried that he would find the Italians there ahead of him. It gave him the greatest pleasure to peer down into Italy and see them struggling far below him. But Whymper's triumph ended in tragedy. Heading down from the summit, on an icy stretch of the upper face, one of the less experienced climbers slipped. All seven men were roped together, using three ropes; the middle rope broke, sending four men to their deaths. Only Whymper and two of his guides survived.[38]

A formal inquiry at Zermatt exonerated all members of the party. Back in England, however, the tragedy was blown up into a major news story and became the subject of a string of dime novels and melodramatic plays. The more lurid of these suggested that someone had cut the rope deliberately. Serious news coverage attacked mountaineering as a dangerous and self-indulgent sport. *The Times,* observing that men in dangerous jobs were at least doing something useful while occasionally risking their lives, suggested that "in the few short moments a member of the Alpine Club has to survey his life when he finds himself slipping, he has but a sorry account to give of himself. What is he doing there, and what right has he to throw away the gift of life and ten thousand golden opportunities in an emulation which he only shares with skylarks, apes, cats, and squirrels?"[39]

Nonetheless, the Matterhorn tragedy scarcely dampened enthusiasm for mountain climbing. The subsequent history of the mountain was much like that of Mont Blanc after Saussure—climbing it became fairly common, although never entirely routine. Among those who followed Whymper were Lucy Walker, who became the first woman on the summit in 1871, and Marguerite Brevoort, the first woman to traverse the mountain, a few years later.[40] The publicity generated by the Matterhorn tragedy was in the long run good for tourism in Zermatt, where the Seiler family, proprietors of the sole village hotel in 1850, expanded their holdings to the point that they averaged about four thousand guests a season by the late 1860s— despite the poor roads that remained the only means of access to the village.

Mountaineering became fashionable throughout Switzerland, even among those who had no intention of climbing "anything higher than the top of a diligence," to quote Charles Dudley Warner. Mountain-climbing gear was especially popular among British tourists, he claimed, who were easily spotted with their veils and green glasses, alpenstocks and spiked shoes, even though not one in a hundred got close enough to the ice and snowfields to make good use of their outfits.[41]

BY THE LAST quarter of the nineteenth century, tourism had become a mainstay of the Swiss economy, yet climate seemed to place finite limits on further growth, for the "season" was confined to the summer months. The enterprising Johannes Badrutt of St. Moritz was one of the first to demonstrate the lucrative potential of extending the tourist season into winter. He began at the end of the summer of 1864, when four of his English guests expressed the usual end-of-vacation reluctance to go home. Badrutt invited them to return in the winter as his guests, assuring them that Alpine winters were much warmer and sunnier than they might believe. He thought that tourists who enjoyed Switzerland in the summer had only to be exposed to its beauty in the winter to become hooked, and correctly so, as the four Englishmen became regular winter visitors. By the mid-1870s, the winter season was well established in St. Moritz and beginning to catch on in other areas too. Davos, for example, which had become a haven for tubercular patients in the late 1850s after a local doctor demonstrated the restorative qualities of dry mountain air, extended its season as it became obvious that the sunny and relatively mild winters were just as curative as the summers.[42]

After Johannes Badrutt, the man who probably did most to promote the Alps in winter was a British travel agent, Henry Lunn. Like Thomas Cook, Lunn launched his career in travel as an outgrowth of his religious interests. A wealthy businessman and evangelical Christian who had trouble reconciling his wealth with his principles, in 1881 Lunn began training for the Methodist ministry. A year working as a missionary in India persuaded him that differences among Christian denominations were trivial compared with those separating all Christians from other faiths. Returning to England with the goal of working toward Christian unification, Lunn started a journal devoted to the cause and, in the winter of 1892, organized a Conference on the Reunion of Christendom in Grindelwald. While the conference may have fallen short of its lofty goals, as an outing it was a great success. Commenting on the pleasure of traveling "with those of kindred tastes," several of the participants asked Lunn to organize a similar trip to Rome the following Easter. He expected 50 or 60 to join the group, but had 440 instead, at a price that undercut even Cook's cheapest tours. A year later, he launched cruises to Egypt and the Holy Land. By focusing on religious and educational tours—his Italian and Middle Eastern tours featured lectures by experts in history and archaeology—Lunn avoided head-to-head competition with Cook while rationalizing what became a highly successful business as an extension of his missionary training.[43]

Lunn had one of the same problems Cook experienced: overcoming resistance to traveling in large groups. He had skirted this problem in his first years of operation by catering specifically to church groups, who enjoyed traveling together because they could avoid "a certain element whose devotion to cards and spirits would not have made them pleasant travelling companions."[44] In later years he simply extended this principle by organizing different kinds of groups. In 1902 he sent a letter to Harrow and Eton graduates proposing winter trips to a little-known village called Adelboden, a few miles southwest of Interlaken. The notion of visiting Switzerland in winter had gained popularity by this time, but was focused on a few of the better-known resorts. Lunn capitalized on his clientele's desire for exclusivity by limiting his group to graduates of these prestigious schools and taking them to an "undiscovered" place. At that time, the hotels in Adelboden closed for the winter, but Lunn persuaded one proprietor to open exclusively for his group—an arrangement that obviously would have been impossible anywhere in Switzerland in the summer. His clients had the run of the hotel and the village, surrounded only by people of their own class background.

Over 400 people joined Lunn's groups that winter, rising to about 650 the following season. Lunn had to negotiate with other hotels in Adelboden to accommodate the demand, and in subsequent years, as his patronage increased to about 5,000 annually, he extended his tours to other towns as well, including Kandersteg, Klosters, Mürren, and Wengen—mostly all places that had not yet developed a winter clientele. He kept his groups exclusive by organizing the Public Schools Alpine Sports Club, with membership limited to graduates of public schools. Lunn later organized a similar group, the Hellenic Travellers Club, for schoolteachers interested in summer cruises to Greece.[45]

Describing the appeal of the Swiss tours, Lunn quoted one of the club members who compared Switzerland in winter to what it had once been in the summer: "In the olden days . . . one of the great charms was the character of the people by whom they were surrounded and the companionships which they made year by year. But a great change came. The old comradeship of the hotels was rendered impossible, . . . the old places which were known began to be buried under the mountains of hotels which almost dwarfed the mountains of nature that surrounded the places, and the old familiar comfort of our Alpine summer disappeared." Or, as Lunn's son later explained it, "The problem of travelling Lunn without appearing to travel Lunn had been solved, and for some years my father was extremely successful in enticing back to Switzerland in the winter those whom he had driven out of Switzerland in the summer."[46]

The very idea of a winter season depended on the growing popularity of active sports. Badrutt had helped promote winter in St. Moritz by persuading the village elders to maintain areas for skating and curling and by putting up the capital for a sled run himself. Mountaineers, not surprisingly, quickly embraced the possibilities for expanding their favorite sport. Although winter mountaineering was not altogether new—a Swiss science teacher named Franz Joseph Hugi climbed several peaks in the 1830s, and a British climber, T. S. Kennedy, reached 11,000 feet on the Matterhorn in 1862—it did not become widespread until the 1870s. The notion of climbing Alpine peaks in winter offered, in effect, a whole new series of "firsts." Among the notable feats were Coolidge and Brevoort's ascent of both the Wetterhorn and the Jungfrau in the winter of 1874. In the 1880s, Elizabeth Burnaby LeBlond made a specialty of winter mountaineering, tackling Mont Blanc, Monte Rosa, and the Matterhorn, among others; in 1883, she published *The High Alps in Winter,* the first book devoted entirely to winter mountaineering.[47]

Most significant for Switzerland's future as a winter resort, by the 1890s the new sport of Alpine skiing was finding favor among a few adventurous visitors. Eventually it would transform the winter season into at least the equal of the summer. Although skiing dates back to ancient times in Scandinavia, where it was a basic means of getting around in winter, and there is some record of Nordic skiing in Austria as early as the seventeenth century, it never really caught on in the Alps, probably because Nordic-style skis, with their flimsy bindings, were unsuitable for Alpine terrain. Skis with front and rear bindings were developed around 1850, but were not widely used until the end of the century.[48]

The pioneers in promoting Alpine skiing included a German, Wilhelm Paulcke, who learned to ski from his Norwegian tutor and subsequently introduced the sport to Davos in the mid-1880s, and a Swiss, Christopher Islein, who accomplished the first long-distance ski tour in 1893 and founded the Swiss Ski Association a year later. In 1894, Arthur Conan Doyle, the popular author of the Sherlock

Holmes stories, skied from Arosa to Davos (about fifteen miles) and then published an article about the experience, which did a great deal to publicize the sport in Britain. Other Britons introduced skiing to Grindelwald in the early 1890s and to St. Moritz around the turn of the century. Henry Lunn was among the most active promoters, launching one of the first Alpine skiing competitions in 1911. His son Arnold first tried skiing in Chamonix in 1898 and subsequently became a great advocate of the sport.[49]

Although skiing would not become the winter sport of choice and the winter season would not rival the summer season in Switzerland until after World War I, the potential was apparent by the turn of the century. In the 1890s, yet another group of village entrepreneurs bent on attracting tourists to their region focused specifically on the attractions of the winter season. Although situated roughly halfway between Geneva and Interlaken, the village of Gstaad remained isolated until the end of the nineteenth century because of its location in a nearly inaccessible valley off the main roads. Looking at a map without regard for topography, one would see that the shortest distance between the eastern end of Lake Geneva and Interlaken would pass close to Gstaad; but in reality, nineteenth-century travelers along this popular route had to detour northeast to Bern to avoid impassable mountains. Until the 1870s, Gstaad did not even have regular postal service. Attempts by local businessmen to construct a railroad to Thun failed twice for lack of funds. Not until 1905 was a railroad opened across this region.

By then, local entrepreneurs were primed to act. Having rebuilt their village after a disastrous fire in 1898, they directed their energy toward attracting tourists. Although only thirty-nine hotel beds were available when the railroad opened, within a year local businessmen tripled the number, formed the Société de Développement pour Gstaad et les Environs, and began to advertise in British newspapers. From the beginning, the Gstaad businessmen focused on attracting a winter clientele by establishing a ski club, developing bobsled and luge runs, and publishing brochures on the attractions of Gstaad in winter. It proved to be a successful strategy, and the number of hotels rose steadily, to nearly twelve hundred beds by 1914. (There were enough English visitors by 1911 to begin construction of an English church.) Less than a decade after the town fathers launched their first efforts to promote the village, Gstaad was well established as a popular Alpine winter resort.[50]

By the first decade of the twentieth century, Switzerland was indeed the "playground of Europe," even more than it had been in Leslie Stephen's time. In the two decades before World War I, tourism more than doubled (as measured by investment of capital and number of hotel rooms occupied per year), transforming the Swiss economy.[51] Although skiing would eventually overshadow everything else, around the turn of the century individual towns and villages in Switzerland were very much identified with particular activities and styles of travel: Zermatt for mountaineers, Interlaken for wealthy families who liked to mix society and scenery on their summer vacations, St. Moritz for a quieter and more exclusive version of the same, Gstaad for winter sports. The very success of the Alpine tourist industry, however, created a continuing tension between the need to improve accessibility and the quality of tourist accommodations and the need to preserve the beauty, simplicity, and peacefulness that attracted tourists in the first place. The town fathers of St. Moritz, for example, found that a railroad terminus twenty miles from their village was an essential precondition of expanding tourism, but a line directly into their village threatened its exclusivity. As early as the late 1870s, an American travel writer found St. Moritz too crowded and recommended seeking out smaller villages in the region instead.[52]

Amelia Edwards, driven to the Dolomites in search of some unspoiled scenery, found even there signs of encroaching tourism, encountering rude British travelers and construction workers already accustomed to identifying tourists as inevitably British. Switzerland, of course, was not the only place confronting the dilemma between developing its natural resources and spoiling them; travelers to the English Lake District and Niagara Falls, to mention just two favorite destinations, had faced the same kind of problems much earlier. For travelers with enough time and money, the solution was to seek out new possibilities for their journeys, often farther away and therefore—for a time—unsullied by the general run of tourists.

THREE

BEYOND EUROPE

CHAPTER 8

THE GRAND TOUR

MOVES EAST

S OON AFTER finishing her book on the Dolomites, Amelia Edwards and her traveling companion decided to escape a dreary
English autumn by spending a few weeks in central and southern
France, only to encounter weather more like London than Provence.
After nearly a month of unrelenting rain, the pair headed for Marseilles, where they boarded a steamer for Egypt. By the end of November they were in Cairo, settled into a first-class hotel and
planning a trip up the Nile to enjoy the winter sunshine and explore
the ancient monuments of the Nile Valley.

As usual, Edwards chose to travel in a relatively unknown place,
where she would be unlikely to encounter hordes of British tourists.
Central and southern France (apart from the Riviera between
Cannes and Nice) filled the bill; Egypt did so even more. Although
still considered remote and exotic, Egypt and the coastal regions of
the Middle East were relatively easy to reach from Western Europe
by the second half of the nineteenth century. Regular steamship services operated from England and the major Mediterranean ports;

comfortable hotels in Alexandria, Cairo, Jerusalem, Beirut, and Constantinople catered to foreign tourists; guide services of all sorts, ranging from boat trips on the Nile to desert treks in Palestine, were well established in the major urban centers; Murray's and Baedeker's guides, as well as a host of works by earlier travelers, advised the tourist about what to see and how to go about it.

For those who had the time and money—a tour of Egypt required two or three months, depending on how far up the Nile one chose to go, and the journey to Palestine would add at least another month—a visit to the Middle East offered an unusual travel experience with little sacrifice of comfort. Indeed, there was some danger, by the time Edwards visited Egypt in 1873, that it would soon go the way of the Swiss resorts she shunned. The Prince of Wales had chosen to convalesce in Egypt the previous winter, thus greatly increasing its social cachet, and Thomas Cook and Henry Gaze had launched tours to Egypt and Palestine in the late 1860s. Edwards noted that between two and three hundred people dined on any given day at Shepheard's, the oldest and most famous of Cairo's luxury hotels. About half of them, by her estimate, were government officials in transit to or from India or Europeans spending the winter in Cairo; the rest were short-term visitors, in Cairo for a few days before going up the Nile.[1]

THE FASHION FOR "Eastern" travel and the relative ease with which it could be accomplished were of fairly recent origin when Edwards made her trip. Although pilgrims had visited Jerusalem for centuries and the major European powers had maintained trading agreements with the Ottoman Empire since the sixteenth century, European contacts with the Middle East were confined largely to the coastal ports. From the end of the Crusades to the beginning of the nineteenth century, fewer than two dozen Europeans traveled more than a hundred miles inland.[2] The rulers of the Ottoman Empire, which controlled nearly all of the Middle East except Persia, discouraged contact with Europeans apart from specifically negotiated trade and diplomatic agreements. Official disapproval combined with Muslim hostility to Christian and Jewish outsiders made travel in the Middle East risky, and certainly beyond the reach of the casual tourist.

This situation changed at the end of the eighteenth century, in the aftermath of Napoleon's invasion of Egypt. By 1798, Napoleon had subdued Switzerland and Italy in his bid to dominate Europe. British officials feared that his next move would be across the Channel, but instead he decided to attack Britain indirectly, as well as further his colonial ambitions, by invading Egypt. In May 1798, French forces landed at Abukir Bay near Alexandria and quickly overpowered the inferior weapons of the Egyptian army. Napoleon then marched on to Cairo, where he easily defeated the remains of the Egyptian forces at the Battle of the Pyramids.

Napoleon chose Egypt as the next target of his imperial ambition because it was strategically important to Britain as the bridge between the Mediterranean and the Red Sea—and therefore between Europe and India. A base in Egypt would be a way of threatening Britain's power without actually attacking Britain. In addition, Egypt's distance from Constantinople and relatively weak ties to the Ottoman government made it an easy target. Moreover, Napoleon had long been fascinated by the Middle East, especially Egypt, and imagined himself a modern-day Alexander liberating the seat of a glorious ancient civilization from its corrupt modern rulers. Like many of the travelers who would come after him, he was captivated by the very foreignness of Egypt. Installed in Cairo, he slept in a tent and adopted Arab dress. "In Egypt I found myself freed from the obstacles of an irksome civilization," he wrote. "The time I spent in Egypt was the most beautiful in my life because it was the most ideal." Paradoxically, he also envisioned himself bringing European civilization to Egypt and, eventually, to all of Asia: "I saw myself founding a religion, marching into Asia, riding an elephant, a turban on my head and in my hand a new Koran that I would have composed to suit my needs."[3]

As a first step in effecting his exalted ambitions, Napoleon took with him to Egypt a small army of scientists, engineers, artists, and historians to map the region and undertake a detailed survey of its antiquities. Nicknamed "the donkeys" by the army men, this Scientific and Artistic Commission, as it was officially known, spent more than a year exploring and documenting the ancient culture of Lower Egypt. Vivant Denon, the commission's chief artist (and director of the Louvre), made the first accurate sketches of the temples at Karnak and Luxor; others excavated temples and collected artifacts to send home to France. The most important single discovery was a large tablet covered with inscriptions, found by a soldier near the Nile Delta town of Rosetta. When the inscriptions on the Rosetta Stone were finally deciphered two decades later, they provided the first important key to understanding the ancient Egyptian system of writing.

Napoleon's Middle Eastern ambitions were short-lived. He was correct in his assumption that a blow struck at Egypt would be a blow struck at Britain, and the British government quickly negotiated an alliance with the Ottoman Empire to drive out the French. In August, the British fleet under Horatio Nelson attacked and defeated the French navy off Alexandria. A land attack was planned for the following summer, but meanwhile Napoleon led his army north into Palestine, defeating garrisons at El Arish, Gaza, and Jaffa. The small contingent of scientists with him spread out over the countryside to continue their surveying and mapping. Meanwhile, Napoleon continued north to Acre, where his troops encountered heavy resistance. A British fleet offshore intercepted heavy artillery and siege equipment sent from Egypt, while plague broke out around Jaffa. Still Napoleon persisted, launching near-suicidal missions in an attempt to breach the walls at Acre. Finally, with his army reduced to little more than half its original strength, he ordered a retreat to Egypt, recalling his far-flung scientists with some difficulty. The commodore of the British fleet, Sidney Smith, landed a small force and marched to Jerusalem, becoming the first foreign Christian to enter that city since the Crusades. A few weeks later, in August 1799, Napoleon fled to France, leaving his army and his scientists in Egypt, where they remained for another two years.

When they returned to France, members of the Scientific Commission began the task of publishing their findings. Denon recorded his own impressions in *Voyages dans la Basse et la Haute Égypte*, in 1802; translated into English and German soon after, it became a best-seller. The official publication of the commission itself took on the same monumental proportions as the research in the field: *Description de l'Égypte* ran to twenty-three lavishly illustrated volumes, each one meter square, appearing between 1809 and 1828. Providing the first detailed account of Egyptian civilization to a European audience, these volumes helped launch a new generation of scholarship on the Middle East.[4]

The early exploration of Palestine and Syria proceeded much more haphazardly, the work of a series of explorer/adventurers. Among the first was a prominent geographer, Cambridge don, and world traveler, Edward Daniel Clarke. Traveling to Palestine aboard a British supply ship in 1801, in just under three weeks he produced the most complete archaeological report then available on the region. Unable to find anything resembling an ancient tomb at the Church of the Holy Sepulcher (supposedly the site of Christ's burial), Clarke abandoned the traditional pilgrimage route through Jerusalem and environs in favor of an independent search for ancient sites. Although his claim to have found the site of Mount Zion was later proved false, he established an important precedent in employing modern methods of scholarship to explore ancient sites shrouded in centuries of myth.[5]

After Napoleon's defeat, British scientists and explorers established the Palestine Association in 1804. The association's first mission failed when the two men commissioned to explore and map the region were forced to leave prematurely after the pasha of Acre (who had led the defense against Napoleon) died and fighting broke out over his succession, making travel unsafe throughout the region. A second expedition, headed by Johann Burckhardt, a young Swiss scholar and student of Edward Clarke's, was charged with seeking out possible new trade routes into Africa from the north. Burckhardt never fulfilled his specific task, but in the course of five years in the Middle East (1812–17), he explored much of Syria, Palestine, the western Arabian Peninsula, and the Nile Valley. Fluent in Arabic and disguised as an Indian Muslim merchant, Burckhardt discovered the ruins at Petra, south of the Dead Sea, and the great temples at Abu Simbel just above the second cataract on the Nile. Most remarkably, he traveled with a caravan making the annual pilgrimage to Mecca, becoming the first European to enter the Muslim holy cities of Medina and Mecca.[6]

Among the people Burckhardt met on his travels was an adventurer of a different sort: Lady Hester Stanhope, favorite niece of William Pitt, who had left England in 1810 to visit Spain with her brother, a maid, and her physician, Charles Meryon. From Spain she went on to Malta, where she fell in love with a wealthy Scottish man eleven years her junior. They traveled together for more than two years, going first to Athens (where Stanhope met and took a dislike to Byron, and he to her), Constantinople, and Cairo, where she created a stir as the first Englishwoman to visit Egypt. By this time, Stanhope was fluent in Arabic and had adopted the dress of Turkish men. (After losing all her clothes in a shipwreck en route to Alexandria, she adopted Eastern dress as more practical than European, and men's in preference to women's because she refused to wear a veil.) A chance meeting with Burckhardt in Nazareth inspired Stanhope to try some serious exploration herself; against all advice, she traveled to Damascus, then considered a dangerous place for Christians to visit, where she organized an expedition to the ruins of Palmyra, an ancient Roman city about seventy miles to the east, which had up to that time been visited by only a handful of Europeans. Her adventures in Syria confirmed Stanhope's love of the Middle East and its people, and she decided to make her home there permanently. In Britain she would have been confined to the restricted life of a genteel woman, made worse by her spinster status and her relatively modest income. In the Middle East, she commanded respect for her imposing appearance—she stood six feet tall, dressed flamboyantly, and rode well—and her courage. After living some time on the Syrian coast, she leased an estate in the mountains of southern Lebanon, where she became increasingly reclusive. Although Stanhope wrote no books about her adventures, by the 1830s she was a legendary figure, a tourist attraction herself until her death in 1839.[7]

In the 1820s, the serious study of the ancient Middle East—both Egypt and the Holy Land—expanded enormously. Probably the best known (and most notorious) of these explorers was Giovanni Battista

Belzoni, a veteran traveler and sometime entertainer who left his native Padua in 1798, traveled for several years, and ended up working as a music-hall entertainer in London. Dubbed the Patagonian Samson because of his enormous size and strength, Belzoni's most popular stunt was the Human Pyramid, in which he wore an iron frame large enough to hold ten to twelve people. Tiring of the music-hall routine, in 1815 Belzoni and his wife went to Constantinople. During a stop at Malta, they met an agent of the Egyptian government who was looking for European engineers. Belzoni, who had once studied hydraulics, agreed to sign on. In Egypt he came to the attention of the newly appointed British consul general, Henry Salt, who was interested in collecting antiquities for the British Museum. Salt commissioned Belzoni to remove a huge granite bust from Thebes, a task he accomplished successfully over the objections of local residents. Belzoni then continued to travel up the Nile, excavating and drawing at several sites. Among his achievements were opening the temple of Rameses II at Abu Simbel, discovering the entrance to the second pyramid at Giza, and unearthing several tombs in the Valley of the Kings. Back in London, he wrote a book about his discoveries (published by John Murray in 1820) and put together an exhibition of his casts and drawings, which opened to great fanfare at the Egyptian Hall in May 1821. That same year, French scholars created a sensation when they decoded the Rosetta Stone, thanks largely to the work of Jean-François Champollion, who corrected and completed the work done by earlier scholars.[8]

John Gardner Wilkinson continued Belzoni's work in a much more systematic way. He went to Egypt in 1821 and spent twelve years producing the first systematic survey of all major archaeological sites and the first chronology of Egyptian dynasties. His *Manners and Customs of the Ancient Egyptians,* published in 1827, established the modern science of Egyptology and served as a guide for travelers. A substantially revised edition, published by John Murray in 1843 under the title *Modern Egypt and Thebes,* condensed the scholarly content and added more practical information for travelers. In 1858 the text, with minor revisions, was issued as Murray's *Hand-Book for Travellers in Egypt.*[9]

Following in Wilkinson's footsteps, Edward Lane went to Egypt in 1825 to study Arabic and stayed on to study the country. He lived in Egypt nearly four years and returned again in the 1830s to complete a systematic survey of contemporary Egyptian life. Critical of the *Description de l'Égypte* as too general and "careless" and of Burckhardt's book for being "merely a collection of proverbial English wisdom," Lane lived among Egyptian peasants, adopting their dress, eating their food, even passing himself off as a Muslim. His book, *Manners and Customs of the Modern Egyptians,* published in 1836, was the companion to Wilkinson in most travelers' luggage; like Wilkinson, Lane had a major influence on subsequent scholarship on Egypt.[10]

After the abortive mission of the Palestine Association and the rambling adventures of Johann Burckhardt, serious study of ancient Palestine and Syria was revived in the late 1830s by men interested in proving the truth of the Bible. Edward Robinson, a young American scholar who published a translation of the *Iliad* and then decided to turn his linguistic and philological talents to biblical studies, traveled to the Middle East in 1837 accompanied by an American missionary, Eli Smith. Starting in Cairo, they retraced the route of the ancient Israelites across Sinai and then went on to Jerusalem, Samaria, Galilee, and Beirut. Like Edward Clarke, Robinson concluded that the famed site of the Holy Sepulcher was nothing more than "pious superstition," and turned his attention to a comprehensive examination of Jerusalem and rural Palestine. Employing modern scholarly methods, including comparing modern Arabic names of villages with biblical names in a search for linguistic similarities, Robinson was able to identify many biblical sites. In 1841 he and Smith published a book describing their discoveries, which brought them recognition throughout the United States and Europe and earned Robinson the distinction of becoming the first American to be awarded the gold medal of the Royal Geographical Society.[11]

A series of writers, artists, and adventurers helped popularize these more scholarly works and inspire the sort of curiosity that encouraged travel to the region. Among the first of the more imaginative travelers was the Frenchman François-René de Chateaubriand, who undertook what he called a pilgrimage to Palestine and Egypt in 1804—a journey that might best be characterized as one of personal rather than geographical exploration. Inspired by the work of Napoleon's commission, Chateaubriand did nothing to add to it but did introduce some persistent themes among Middle Eastern travelers, most notably the idea that the region's present inhabitants had degenerated markedly from ancient civilizations and that Europeans had a responsibility to teach Arabs about liberty and the glories of their own past. (He was also one of the first of a long line of travelers to inscribe his name at the base of the Pyramids.)[12] Other French writers, among them Alphonse de Lamartine, Gérard de Nerval, and Gustave Flaubert, continued this style of travel as romantic self-exploration with journeys to the Middle East in the 1830s and '40s.

Artists also found inspiration in the Middle East during these years, in the process adding substantially to the pictorial record produced by Napoleon's commission. Among the most influential was the Scottish painter David Roberts, who visited Egypt and Palestine in the late 1830s seeking accurate backgrounds and models for paintings of biblical scenes. His book, *Views in the Holy Land, Syria, Idumea, Arabia, Egypt, and Nubia,* provided the first comprehensive pictorial record covering the entire Middle East. William Bartlett's book of engravings, *The Nile Boat,* published in 1850 and reprinted many times, was at least as influential if artistically less significant. He later produced two other books on the Middle East, one on Jerusalem and another on the Sinai.[13]

Then there were those rare early travelers who went to the Middle East purely for the sake of adventure and amusement. Among them was Alexander Kinglake, a young Englishman who toured the Middle East from Constantinople to Cairo in 1835, traveling in much the same spirit as had inspired earlier generations of young men to make the grand tour of Europe. He assured readers of *Eothen,* the account of his journey, that they would find in its pages no geographical discoveries, no "antiquarian research," no biblical discussions, scientific illustrations, statistics, or political analysis, but merely the truthful account of his travels as they happened. (Kinglake's adventures included an audience with Hester Stanhope, by then permanently settled in the hills above Beirut with her retinue of Arab servants.) Despite its apparently modest pretensions, Kinglake's book became a classic of travel literature—one of those that subsequent travelers were most likely to read before embarking on their own journeys.[14]

These early visitors to the Middle East, varied as they were, exemplified certain types of travelers who multiplied in subsequent decades: romanticists seeking personal fulfillment like Chateaubriand and Flaubert, adventurers like Burckhardt and Stanhope, scholars and classifiers like Wilkinson, Lane, and Robinson. Through their writings they helped promote interest in the Middle East and helped shape travelers' expectations about what they would find when they got there. Their works were augmented by classics like Herodotus's *History* and *A Thousand and One Nights* (made widely available to readers of English in a translation by Edward Lane); imaginative literature by writers like Sir Walter Scott, Victor Hugo, and Goethe, who never went to the Middle East but were inspired by their own reading to set poems or stories there, usually in highly romanticized settings; and by artists like Eugène Delacroix and Jean-Auguste-Dominique Ingres, who took scenes from the Middle East or episodes from the history of the region as subjects for paintings. As Victor Hugo put it in the preface to his *Les Orientales* (published in 1829), "In the age of Louis XIV everyone was a Hellenist. Now they are all Orientalists. Never have so many intellects explored at one time this great abyss of Asia. . . . The East, either as image or idea, has become a sort of general occupation of the mind as much as of the imagination."[15]

BY THE LATE 1830s, a settled political climate in the Middle East and improved transportation made it more practical for the casual traveler to go there. Regular steamship services made the journey from Marseilles or Brindisi to Alexandria in four to eight days, and from Southampton in about two weeks. Or one could sail down the Danube from Vienna to Constantinople.[16] Until the end of the nineteenth century, however, travelers had to allow several extra days in transit because of the possibility of quarantine for bubonic plague. In the early decades of the century, plague was a very real threat; Lady Hester Stanhope spent months on the Syrian coast to avoid an epidemic raging in the interior of the country, Burckhardt was in

Cairo during an epidemic, and Alexander Kinglake encountered cases of plague in both Constantinople and Cairo. By mid-century, epidemics were rare, but it was still common to quarantine ships returning from southeastern Europe, the Middle East, Africa, and Asia.[17]

By the 1840s a fairly standard route for Middle Eastern tours (often called "the grand tour," of course, by guidebook writers) had evolved. The typical traveler started in Alexandria in late fall or early winter, moving on quickly to Cairo and the Nile. Those making the complete tour would continue to Palestine and Syria, either by sea from Alexandria to Jaffa or overland by camel from Cairo across the Sinai desert and then north to Gaza and Jerusalem. After the completion of the Suez Canal in 1869, this portion of the journey became simpler, as most travelers took a train to Suez and then a ship through the canal to Port Said and on to Jaffa. The typical tour of Palestine and Syria covered, at a minimum, Jerusalem and environs (including Bethlehem, Jericho, the Jordan River, and the Dead Sea), followed by a journey north from Jerusalem to Nablus, Nazareth, and the Sea of Galilee, usually ending at Beirut. A few ventured farther north and east, to Damascus and perhaps Palmyra, but this region remained difficult to reach and potentially risky. One might then return home directly from Beirut or via Smyrna, on the coast of Turkey, Constantinople, and Athens.

A Middle Eastern tour required elaborate preparations, especially for those going up the Nile or traveling in the desert. Wilkinson listed four pages of recommended items, including an iron bedstead, horsehair mattresses, sheets and towels, blankets, washtub, camp stool, drawing table, dishes and silverware, candlesticks and candles, gun and ammunition, mosquito netting, wine, brandy, paper, pencils and pens, a saddle and bridle, thermometer, barometer, an umbrella lined with a dark color to provide shade from the sun, and an iron rat trap for the boat. Tents, if needed, could be made in Cairo, and most provisions obtained there. For those "who wish to be entirely protected at night from intruders," he recommended a contraption consisting of two sheets sewn together at bottom and sides with mosquito netting attached to the top. A flexible cane fit into loops in the top of the netting to hold it open above the head; the open end of the netting, above the cane framework, was closed with a drawstring, which was then hung on a nail to keep the netting from collapsing back on one's face. The total effect was like a close-fitting sleeping bag with a small tent suspended over the head. To conclude the traveler's preparations, Wilkinson advised taking along a library of about twenty-five books, most of them weighty tomes on Egyptian history and archaeology, including Herodotus, Ptolemy, Strabo, Pliny, Champollion's *Phonetic System of Hieroglyphics,* Mengin's *Égypte sous Mohammed Aly,* the works of Denon, Lane, and Burckhardt, as well as Wilkinson's *Customs and Manners of the Ancient Egyptians* and a good map. This list, he assured his readers, included only "the most useful works." Later in the century, as the number of travelers increased, it became easier to obtain travel gear in Cairo; Baedeker's 1885 edition advised travelers to pack only clothing and toilet articles; everything else could be obtained in "modern" shops in Egypt.[18]

Given the time and complications of a Middle Eastern journey, it is perhaps remarkable that so many Europeans and Americans accomplished it. A bibliography of books written by travelers to the Middle East in the nineteenth century, now among the holdings of a research library in Athens, includes 1,044 titles. Many of these were written by explorers or adventurers rather than tourists, and some were largely confined to Greece rather than the Middle East itself, but even so, the numbers offer testimony to the increasing popularity of travel to the area. Lucie Duff-Gordon, who lived in Egypt for seven years during the 1860s, estimated that 70 to 120 boats made the journey upriver each winter, compared with 5 or 6 in the 1830s. By the late 1880s, after steamer services on the Nile and travel agents' packaged tours were well established, over five thousand people a year registered at Thomas Cook's offices in Cairo.[19]

Most travelers to the Middle East seem to have been upper-middle-class rather than truly wealthy. They included young men in that state of limbo between education and career, making a different sort of grand tour, like Kinglake and Flaubert. There were young women in a similarly unsettled state, like Florence Nightingale, who sailed up the Nile with two friends in 1849–50, six years before she found her vocation nursing troops in the Crimean War; and older, unattached women as well, often veteran travelers like Amelia Edwards, Harriet Martineau, and Ida Pfeiffer, an Austrian woman of modest means, who, unlike most women, traveled alone and second class. There were couples and families with adolescent or older children. Edwards estimated that 90 percent of the guests at her hotel in Cairo were British or American and most of the rest German, with a handful of Belgian and French. At Luxor, anchored among two or three dozen boats, she remarked that, of any given twenty-five boats, twelve would be English, nine American, two German, one Belgian, and one French. (This was in 1873; before the late 1860s, the proportion of Americans would have been much smaller.)

Others remarked on the diversity of travelers: Charles Dudley Warner, an American writer traveling in the early 1880s, found among his shipmates en route to Alexandria a German baron and his wife, a "difficult" Italian woman, two clergymen from Australia on an around-the-world tour, and two eccentric Americans. Edwards remarked that her fellow tourists in Cairo included "invalids in search of health; artists in search of subjects; sportsmen keen upon crocodiles; statesmen out for a holiday; special correspondents alert for gossip; collectors on the scent of papyri and mummies; men of science with only scientific ends in view; and the usual surplus of idlers who travel for the mere love of travel, or the satisfaction of a purposeless curiosity."[20]

DISEMBARKING AT ALEXANDRIA—for most travelers the first stop on their tour of the Middle East—could be a rude, noisy, often disturbing reminder that this journey would be markedly different from the usual European holiday. From the moment the ship dropped anchor in Alexandria's harbor until one was settled in a hotel, chaos reigned, or so it seemed to the average Western traveler. Dozens of boats surrounded the ship as men climbed aboard, crowding around the passengers, "shouting at us in all the broken languages of three continents," urging travelers in loud voices to follow them, sometimes seizing luggage without waiting for a reply. "I know no din to be compared to it but that of a frog concert in a Carolina swamp," Harriet Martineau remarked. To Florence Nightingale, the "gesticulating, kicking, and dancing" crowd appeared to be "an intermediate race . . . between the monkey and the man, the ugliest, most slavish countenances." Charles Leland, an American traveling in the 1870s, called the scene upon arriving at Alexandria "the eighth plague of Egypt."[21]

Those who tried to cope with the crowd by asking for the representative of their hotel generally found that every man within earshot claimed that role. Others literally fought off the crowds with sticks, "purely from the strength of their philosophical conviction that this is the only way to deal with Arabs," as Martineau put it. Once onshore, the onslaught started again as men with donkeys ("the cabs of Egypt," Wilkinson called them) demanded the privilege of taking travelers and their luggage through customs and on to their hotels, clamoring loudly for "bakshish"—bribes, in the eyes of Western travelers. Wilkinson urged his readers never to pay donkey drivers more than one piaster (about four cents), no matter how much they complained; excessive generosity only made the demands louder and the prices higher for subsequent travelers.[22]

Whether they landed first at Alexandria, Constantinople, or one of the Levantine ports, travelers' first reactions to "the East" were never neutral. As much as these men and women had read about Egypt and the Middle East, as much as they had imagined what they would find, nothing could quite prepare them for the reality of Alexandria or Constantinople. "In one moment the Orient flashes upon the bewildered traveler; and though he may travel far and see stranger sights, and penetrate the hollow shell of Eastern mystery, he never will see again at once such a complete contrast to all his previous experience," Warner explained. "One strange, unfamiliar form takes the place of another so rapidly that there is no time to fix an impression, and everything is so *bizarre* that the new-comer has no points of comparison." Nightingale thought she had landed in the midst of the Arabian Nights, starting with sunrise over Alexandria as her ship approached the harbor—the colors brilliant but "so transparent and pure that one really believes one's self looking into a heaven beyond"—and continuing with visits to gardens filled with tropical flowers and a lunch of bananas, dates, and oranges. Crowds, noise, brilliant colors—whether sky, flowers, or people's clothing—

above all, the sheer number of images competing for attention were what dominated visitors' first impressions. Warner wanted everything to slow down, so he could absorb what he termed "a revolving kaleidoscope" of "bewildering figures and colors."[23]

Once past those first impressions, however, visitors were often disappointed. The skyline of Constantinople, with its domed buildings so unlike those of Western European cities, gave way to a maze of narrow, crowded, dirty streets and alleys, while Alexandria was an odd blend of East and West. By mid-century, a substantial group of European traders and consular officials had taken up residence, living in a part of the city designed along Western lines and including within it most of the hotels catering to travelers. Martineau looked out her hotel window the morning after arriving in Alexandria and saw "nothing peculiarly African"—until a string of camels happened along. The so-called "Frank Square" boasted large houses, but "would be considered shabby and ugly any where else." ("Frank" was the generic term for Europeans in the Middle East.) Once first impressions wore off, Alexandria was a little too European for people who had come to Egypt for an exotic adventure, without compensating by offering the kinds of luxuries they had come to expect in Europe. One American traveler described the city as "half Oriental, half European . . . in the lowest style of architecture of both." Many thought Alexandria was not the "real" Egypt, by which they meant ancient Egypt, and few stayed more than a day or two before moving on to Cairo.[24]

Their journey took two or three days via boat until a railroad was completed in 1855. The river steamers, which offered few amenities and were often crowded, made up in local color what they lacked in comfort. Nightingale described sitting up all night "nine to the square yard," in a boat filled with people of every nationality, including hordes of screaming, flea-ridden children. She did not complain, however, for this was more of the exotic East: "The screams are Egyptian, Greek, Italian, and Turkish screams; and the fleas, &c are Circassian, Chinese, and Coptic fleas." "I would not have missed that night for the world," she concluded; "it was the most amusing time I ever passed, and the most picturesque."[25]

Larger than Alexandria and much less touched by European influence, Cairo seemed more authentically "Eastern" and therefore more enticing to European travelers—"the queen of Arabian cities," Martineau called it. Though sometimes troubled by the crowds, the noise, the dirt, and the evidence of poverty all around them, visitors for the most part relished "the spectacle of the streets." As Warner noted, everything happened there: eating, sleeping, praying, working, selling goods, all boisterously crowded together in passageways so narrow and twisted that two loaded donkeys sometimes had trouble passing each other. "It seems one booth and Bartholomew Fair—a grand masquerade of mortality," Herman Melville wrote in 1857, a sentiment echoed by Warner two decades later. Edwards remarked on individual scenes, each worthy of a picture: "Every shop-front, every street-corner, every turbaned group is a ready-made picture. The old Turk who sets up his cake-stall in the sculptured recess of a Moorish doorway; the donkey-boy with his gaily caparisoned ass, waiting for customers; the beggar asleep on the steps of the mosque; the veiled woman filling her water-jar at the public fountain—they all look as if they had been put there expressly to be painted."[26]

The more sensitive recognized that what they saw was but the veneer of Cairo society—Warner thought of the street life as a "mask" hiding the real life of the city—but for most, Cairo was "the real Arabian Nights," as Lucie Duff-Gordon put it. To enjoy Cairo to its fullest, Martineau suggested, one had to forget one was in Egypt—forget the poverty that lay below the surface, forget the ancient culture that might give one serious thoughts—and "surrender himself to the most wonderful and romantic dream that can ever meet his waking senses."[27] Here she and others found that same quality that many earlier travelers had sought in Italy: a less restricted, more sensuous way of life, one less constrained by schedules and social obligations. Richard Burton characterized it as the Arabic sense of *kayf,* a word loosely meaning pleasure but really untranslatable, in Burton's estimation.

A few visitors threw themselves with abandon into what they imagined to be Eastern-style hedonism. Gustave Flaubert, for example, visiting Cairo in 1849–50, spent much of his time there going from one prostitute to the next. A handful went so far as to settle permanently in the Middle East, including a friend of William

Thackeray, who visited Egypt in 1844. Thackeray (who received free passage to the Middle East on one of the new Peninsula and Orient Company steamers in exchange for an agreement to write a book about his experiences) couldn't quite understand his friend's decision. "Cairo is magnificently picturesque," he remarked; "it is fine to have palm-trees in your gardens, and ride about on a camel," but how could one give up London? He finally decided it was "an indulgence of laziness such as Europeans, Englishmen at least, don't know how to enjoy"—that same sense of pleasure and indulgence that later attracted Flaubert and Burton. Most Westerners were quite content with a brief escape, "a short season of transport," as Martineau put it.[28]

By the 1880s, there were enough wide streets in the newer sections of Cairo to get around by carriage, but much of the city could be seen only on foot or donkey; and indeed, riding a donkey was part of the picturesque experience, "cheap and exhilarating," Warner thought. For visitors with limited time, Wilkinson mapped out a six-day sightseeing program that called for three days in the city itself, touring mosques, palaces, royal tombs, bazaars, and public buildings, and three daylong excursions outside Cairo, including the ruins at Heliopolis and the pyramids at Giza. It was an ambitious program; most tourists seem to have contented themselves with a portion of it. As Warner put it, just being in Cairo in the winter was lovely, sitting on the hotel terrace or enjoying the gardens. It was easy to put off sightseeing for another day, especially since one could always be certain of good weather.[29]

To foreigners, the manifestations of "Eastern" culture and Islamic religion were endlessly fascinating. Some of Cairo's mosques were open to non-Muslims, especially in later years as Western tourists became more commonplace. Visitors admired them for their simplicity of design—"no one has said a tenth part enough of the beauty of Arab architecture" was Lucie Duff-Gordon's judgment—and the quiet, peaceful atmosphere of prayer within, a remarkable contrast to the noisy turbulence of Cairo's streets. "Nothing charmed me so much about them as the spectacle of the houseless poor, who find a refuge there," Martineau wrote. "We are accustomed to say that there is no respect of persons, and that all men are equal, within the walls of our churches: but I never felt this so strongly in any Christian places of worship as in this Mohammedan one, with its air of freedom, peace, and welcome to all the faithful." For Protestants, especially those of an evangelical bent, the simplicity of the mosques, the piety of the average Muslim, the prohibition of alcohol, and the absence of a priestly hierarchy encouraged a certain admiration for the fundamental moral values of Islam.[30]

Visitors to Cairo also encountered the indigenous Coptic Christian community and, in many cases, visited their churches. While a few felt some affinity for their fellow Christians (often those who felt most hostile toward Muslims), most were if anything more negative about Copts than they were about Muslims. (Martineau pronounced the church she visited "disgusting.") Some were put off by the ritualistic nature of Coptic religious practice, but the more compelling reason for hostility toward Arab Christians seems to have been that they appeared more Arab than Christian. Their churches were just as dirty and bug-infested as many other buildings in Cairo, and the Christians themselves seemed ignorant and greedy. Duff-Gordon, who met dozens of travelers during her residence in Egypt, argued that the key distinction for Europeans encountering Eastern culture was not between Christian and Muslim, but between "East" and "West," Western civilization having been shaped by the legacy from Greece and Rome, which obviously had nothing to do with Christianity. Thus it was no surprise to her that European travelers were critical of the Copts.[31]

Those travelers who had the opportunity to visit private homes did so, discovering that Arab family life contrasted sharply with the open, boisterous quality of Cairo's streets. Houses faced courtyards; women were closely veiled, if they went out at all. Baedeker cautioned his readers never to ask an Arab man about his wife or other female relatives, for it was considered a great breach of etiquette; nor should men look too closely at women they might encounter in public. Visitors to Arab homes were entertained with great hospitality and ceremony, but only by the male members of the family. Female travelers had an advantage, however. They could partake of their host's hospitality because their foreign (and non-Muslim) status set them apart from native women; but they might also be invited into the harem. Such opportunities, when granted, were probably the most popular and talked-about feature of a visit to Cairo or other Middle Eastern cities, for nothing excited Westerners' curiosity or indignation more than the Muslim treatment of women. Here too, as Duff-Gordon pointed out, the issue was more one of East/West than of Muslim/Christian, as many non-Muslim women in the Middle East also wore the veil and lived in seclusion.[32]

The harem, in its general sense, referred to that part of a home where women and children spent their time, separated from the public rooms where visitors were received. In the wealthiest families, the sort Westerners were most likely to visit, servants handled the domestic work as well as most errands outside the home, leaving the women of the family to spend most of their time in enforced idleness. Several points about harems disturbed the Western women who visited them: the practice of polygamy and slavery (some of the women in wealthy harems were slave concubines), the restrictions on women's movements, their idleness, and the presence of eunuchs (usually black slaves) as guards. Underlying these criticisms was a perceived image of the harem as scene of sexual dalliance, a view that often remained unspoken but was evident in much of the Orientalist painting and literature produced in the middle decades of the nineteenth century. To the artists who created these paintings, the harem was part of the mystique of the East; to Western women of conventional morals, it was an outrage.[33]

Until the 1880s, when the city itself became fashionable as a winter resort, Cairo remained simply an introduction to Egypt. It was ancient Egypt, not the modern nation, that drew Europeans and Americans; and although one could get a taste of the ancient civilization by riding out to the pyramids at Giza, the *raison d'être* of an Egyptian tour was the journey up the Nile. The standard itinerary included, at a minimum, sailing upriver to Aswan, stopping at Thebes, Karnak, Luxor, and the Valley of the Kings. Those with sufficient time and money might continue as far as the second cataract and the great temple at Abu Simbel.

Nile-bound travelers had to hire their own boats and crews until the late 1850s, when passenger steamers were introduced as far as Aswan. By the mid-1860s, steamer services operated regularly and a railroad was completed as far as Minyah, about 150 miles south of Cairo, but even then, those who could afford it preferred to travel in the flat-bottomed, bargelike sailing boat known as a *dahabeah*. A trip to the first cataract required at least two months by dahabeah, compared with three weeks by steamer, and cost at least twice as much; but, as Amelia Edwards put it, "The choice between Dahabeeyah and steamer is like the choice between travelling with post-horses and travelling by rail. The one is expensive, leisurely, and delightful; the other is cheap, swift, and comfortless. Those who are content to snatch but a glimpse of the Nile will doubtless prefer the steamer."[34]

Preparing for the Nile journey started with hiring a dragoman. (The term is a corruption of the Arabic *tariuman,* meaning "interpreter.") These men were a cosmopolitan lot, many of them Greek, Turkish, Maltese, and Coptic as well as Arab Muslims. Most spoke English, French, and Italian. The dragoman generally handled all arrangements for the journey, including hiring the boat and crew, buying provisions, and supervising preparations for departure. Baedeker cautioned his readers about being cheated by dragomans, but nearly all travelers seemed quite devoted to their men, often engaging the same men to organize their journeys across the desert to Palestine and Syria. Martineau went so far as to remark that "some of us might look very small in our vocations, in comparison with our dragomen."[35]

Selecting and outfitting a dahabeah could be a formidable task for those who preferred not to hire a dragoman. Anywhere from one hundred to three hundred boats were usually anchored on the river near Cairo at the beginning of the winter season. Edwards's experience was fairly typical. She spent three or four hours each day for more than a week inspecting boats, a task worse than house-hunting, she declared. All appeared more or less alike, varying mainly in size and degree of cleanliness. Their captains also struck her as indistinguishable, "for to a person who has been only a few days in Egypt, one black or copper-coloured man is exactly like every other black or copper-coloured man." All of them had letters of recommendation from former patrons, but even the letters resembled each other. Edwards thought the men probably passed the same batch of papers

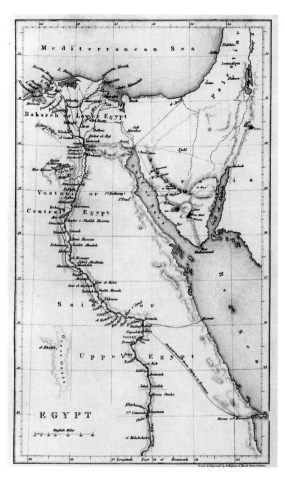

Map of the Nile
From William H. Bartlett,
The Nile Boat

A dahabeah on the Nile around mid-century
Engraving by William H. Bartlett from The Nile Boat

One of Cook's groups in Palestine
The Travel Archive, Thomas Cook Ltd.

A dragoman in the 1890s
The Travel Archive, Thomas Cook Ltd.

Climbing the Great Pyramid, 1903
The Travel Archive, Thomas Cook Ltd.

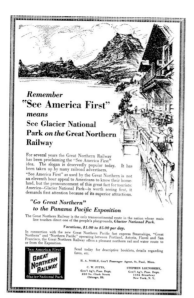

Advertisement for the
Great Northern Railway
From Travel, *February 1915*

Advertisement for the
Santa Fe Railroad
From Travel, *December 1908*

Advertising poster for
the Santa Fe Railroad
The Huntington Library

Cover of an advertising brochure
for the Union Pacific Railroad
*The Bancroft Library, University of
California, Berkeley*

Visitors wading in the hot springs at Yellowstone
Yellowstone National Park Museum

Tourists at a Wylie camp
Yellowstone National Park Museum

Leidig's Hotel, one of the first in the Yosemite Valley, about 1870
Yosemite National Park Research Library

Sightseeing in Yosemite: A stagecoach
drives the length of a downed giant Sequoia.
Yosemite National Park Research Library

One of Cook's early automobile tours, en route
from Paris to Versailles, 1905
The Travel Archive, Thomas Cook Ltd.

On the Lincoln Highway in Iowa
From Travel, *March 1915*

Camping along the Lincoln Highway in Wyoming
From Travel, *March 1915*

Postcard from the Panama-Pacific Exposition,
San Francisco, 1915
The California Historical Society.
Exposition Publishing Company, Publishers

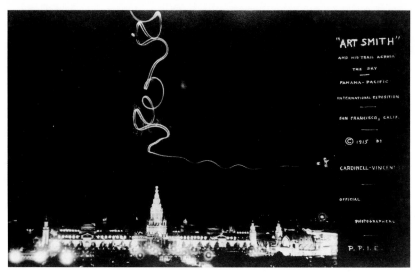

Postcard from the Panama-Pacific Exposition, San Francisco,
showing one of Art Smith's night exhibition flights.
The building at the bottom is the Tower of Jewels.
The California Historical Society, Cardinell-Vincent Co., Photographers

A crowd watching one of Art Smith's
exhibition flights at the Panama-Pacific Exposition
The California Historical Society

around among themselves. The asking prices varied wildly, though all were at least double what was reasonable in her estimation.[36]

Wilkinson urged travelers to sink their rented boats to rid them of rats, and then have all rooms washed and painted. In addition to taking an iron rattrap on board, he recommended obtaining an ichneumon fly (a type of insect that eats other insects). By the time his 1858 edition appeared, Wilkinson could report that such drastic steps were no longer necessary, as most dahabeahs were by that time employed exclusively in the tourist trade and were kept clean. (In early years, the boats were often used to haul cargo at other seasons of the year.) Provisions and whatever utensils the travelers had not brought with them had to be purchased and taken aboard. These were often elaborate, for European travelers gave up their "civilized" habits with difficulty; many dressed for dinner and expected to dine and drink well, with fine dishes and crystal. (Not all observed such formalities, however; John Lloyd Stephens, an American traveling in 1836, reveled in "not shaving for two months, washing . . . shirts in the Nile, and wearing them without being ironed.") Crew members were expected to be responsible for their own provisions, but Wilkinson cautioned his readers that, when "ladies" were part of the party, "the boatmen should be supplied with drawers, and an order given that they never go into the water without them." Duff-Gordon was amused by the practice: "My crew have all sported new white drawers in honour of the Sitti Ingleezee's supposed modesty—of course compensation will be expected."[37]

Once under way, travelers proceeded upstream as quickly as possible to take maximum advantage of the winds, which were typically more reliable during the early part of the winter, stopping on the way back to explore the ancient sites. Just above Aswan, nearly six hundred miles from Cairo, boats had to be towed through the first cataract, an adventure resembling river rafting in reverse. With extra hands hired from nearby villages, crewmen began the process by tying ropes at intervals along the sides of the boat. Some of the men then stood on rocks protruding from the rapids while others remained in the boat and tossed ropes to the first group, who then jumped from one rock to the next, pulling the boat forward. Farther upstream, where the rapids were spaced more widely apart, the men swam from one rock to the next, fastening the ropes around each one. The boat's crew then hauled on the ropes to pull the boat forward.

Passing the cataracts was one of the most exciting experiences of the trip—better, in its way, than the most spectacular ruins, as travelers glimpsed a different side of the native people in the extraordinary strength and agility of the men guiding the boats. "Here the poor Arab is in his element, and, instead of the sensual, debased creature you see him in his idle moments, he seems the god of the winds and the whirlpool," Nightingale wrote. The experience was, for her, "as grand an epic poem as any I ever read in Homer or Milton." Martineau described the sight as "the perfection of savage faculty. . . . The quickness of movement and apprehension, the strength and suppleness of frame, and the power of experience in all concerned this day contrasted strangely with images of the bookworm and the professional man at home, who can scarcely use their own limbs and senses." She contrasted the civilized European, "whose prerogative lies wholly in the world of ideas," with the "savage" Arab, "where the dominion was wholly over the power of outward nature."[38]

Sailing upstream into Nubia, travelers became increasingly aware of the differences between lower and upper Egypt. More rugged, barren terrain contrasted with the fertile floodplains of the lower Nile. Nightingale described the landscape as a desert version of the view toward Mont Blanc: "If you can imagine the largest glaciers you every saw, the Mer de Glace at Chamounix, with all the avalanches golden sand, and all the ridge purple granite, not one blade of green anywhere . . . that is Nubia." Martineau preferred a comparison with the less settled regions of the United States, remarking that "the Mississippi is wild: and the Indian grounds of Wisconsin, with their wigwam camps, are wild: but their wildness is only that of primitive Nature. This is fantastic,—impish. It is the wildness of Prospero's island." The people were "wild" too, "especially the boys, who were naked and excessively noisy. I did not dislike their behaviour," Martineau remarked, "though they had to be flogged out of the path, like a herd of pigs."[39]

The Nubians were darker-skinned and quite different from the

Arabs in both physical features and dress. Less accustomed to contact with foreigners, they were also more polite and more dignified. To Europeans brought up on notions of the virtue and innocence of primitive peoples, the Nubians—unlike urban Arabs who had been corrupted by too much contact with "civilization"—were yet one more representation of the noble savage. Martineau was especially taken with the natural grace of one young boy sitting on a boulder: "I longed to petrify him, and take him home, an ebony statue, for the instruction of sculptors. . . . An attitude of such perfect grace must be natural: but not, I supposed in our climate, or to any one who has sat on chairs."[40]

To some travelers, the Nubians' faces resembled images carved on temple walls; others described their features and clothing as having a kind of timeless quality—"the antiquity of Egypt stamped upon individuals," as Herman Melville put it. Such associations strengthened travelers' sense that they were observing two Egypts: the ancient civilization, equivalent to Greece and Rome in its art and culture, and an impoverished, backward country that was no more than a shell of its former greatness. As Nightingale explained it, "Egypt" meant the ancient civilization of the Nile; Cairo and its environs were not Egyptian but "Arabian." She even went so far as to suggest that the present residents of the country essentially counted for nothing: "Egypt to an European is all but uninhabited," she wrote. "The present race no more disturbs this impression than would a race of lizards, scrambling over the broken monuments of such a star. You would not call *them* inhabitants, no more do you these."[41]

About 175 miles past the first cataract, travelers reached Abu Simbel, one of the greatest of the ruins of upper Egypt. Edwards stayed there nearly six weeks, engaging in some amateur archaeology, a popular pastime with tourists at a time when professional archaeology was still in its infancy and even the best-known sites were not fully excavated and documented. She set her boat crew to work cleaning up the face of one of the Colossi, which had been disfigured when an earlier explorer made a plaster cast, leaving bits of plaster adhering to the surface when he removed the cast (to be added later to the collections of the British Museum). The men improvised scaffolding from spars and oars, scraped off the plaster, and used coffee to stain the exposed parts to match the surrounding stone. Edwards laughed at the spectacle of her men hauling pots of coffee up the makeshift scaffolding, but in fact she was outraged at the damage done to the ancient monuments by unthinking visitors, who appropriated artifacts as souvenirs—a habit encouraged by the native residents, who themselves sold whatever they could scavenge to tourists, collectors, and museum agents. As it became more difficult to collect genuine objects, enterprising Egyptians manufactured fakes.[42]

From the second cataract at Wadi Halfa, travelers turned back to begin their leisurely progress down the Nile. One of the most impressive stops along the way was the island of Philae, with its temple of Isis and kiosk built by the emperor Trajan. Although Nightingale thought Abu Simbel the grandest of the Egyptian sites, she found Philae more compelling because of its spiritual quality. She spent much of her time sitting in the tomb of Isis, meditating on the similarities between the myths associated with Isis and the New Testament, half expecting a vision of Christ. Duff-Gordon, less fervent in her religious convictions, nevertheless also felt a "supernatural" quality at Philae, rather like the feelings she experienced gazing at the best landscapes of Claude Lorrain. Nightingale's vigil in Isis's tomb was not uncommon. Some travelers even slept in the tombs when the weather was especially hot. And Duff-Gordon, after her first winter cruising up the Nile, lived in a house that had been constructed in 1815 on top of one of the temples at Thebes by the first British consul stationed there.[43]

Thebes, the next major stop after Philae, was the center of the richest group of antiquities, including the famous temples at Karnak and Luxor and the tombs and palaces of the Valley of the Kings. Where Philae was like a perfectly formed jewel, contained on its own tiny island, Thebes's enormous temples were scattered over a broad area. No pictures or written descriptions could prepare one for the grandeur of these monuments, Martineau remarked, in a sentiment shared by other travelers. Appleton thought the temples at Luxor and Karnak "the scene of man's highest achievement in religious architecture," more impressive even than St. Peter's in Rome or the

Parthenon; Martineau found them more affecting than anything else in her experience. These monuments were already ancient when Herodotus visited them, she observed; here he seemed "a modern brother-traveller." More irreverently, Warner remarked that the antiquity of the Egyptian ruins made one jaded about anything less than four thousand years old—"we have come to have a singular contempt for anything so modern as the work of the Greeks, or Romans."[44]

Predictably, with its vast ruins and its location about halfway between Cairo and the second cataract, Thebes became a popular gathering place for travelers, especially during the Christmas holidays. By the 1840s, five or six dahabeahs typically would be anchored there during the height of the season, a number that would more than triple over the next four decades, giving Thebes the look of "a fashionable watering-place," as Warner put it. The dahabeahs all sported the national flags of their occupants, a custom so ingrained by mid-century that guidebooks included information about where to have the flags made.[45]

At Thebes all the usual social rituals reasserted themselves. After a day of sightseeing, travelers spent their evenings dining and paying social calls—a custom that seemed absurd to some despite its popularity. "It is very hard to be all day by the deathbed of the greatest of your race, and to come home and talk about quails or London," Nightingale remarked. But as it became easier to travel in Egypt, the Nile attracted many who were more interested in the warm winter climate, or shooting alligators, or just the novelty of it all than in ancient history. For them, the society of the dahabeahs took on a life of its own, with tourists competing to see who could put on the most elaborate dinner. Sportsmen shot pigeons, antagonizing local residents who depended on the birds for food. (Duff-Gordon once had to intercede to stop the carnage; by the time she had established residence at Thebes, the number of tourists with guns posed a serious threat to the townspeople.) Europeans on the Nile re-created their own little social hierarchy. As Edwards explained, "The people in dahabeeyahs despise Cook's tourists; those who are bound for the Second Cataract look down with lofty compassion upon those whose ambition extends only to the First; and travellers who engage their boat by the month hold their heads a trifle higher than those who contract for the trip."[46]

Warner might rhapsodize over the freedom from clocks and schedules on the Nile, and John Stephens about the pleasures of wearing unironed shirts and not shaving, but most retained the social conventions, carrying with them fine wines, good china and crystal, and observing the niceties of dressing for dinner. About the proper Englishman on the Nile, Appleton wrote sarcastically that "he must carry England in little with him wherever he goes. He cannot escape. England expects every man to do his duty, and that duty consists in this:—To split his hair up behind with a couple of brushes; to have by him his india-rubber bath-tub, even though the Nile flow at his foot; to believe in 'Murray' and the 'English Book of Common Prayer' as sufficient gospel for the Hawadji everywhere; to carry the feelings, habits, and prejudices of the temperate zone to the equator, and to consider the natives of the countries he passes through as merely 'foreigners.' "[47]

In contrast to Europe or the United States, in Egypt travelers and residents remained almost entirely separate. Egyptians did not travel as "tourists," in the manner that Europeans did, although they did in fact travel—most significantly for religious purposes. To make the pilgrimage to Mecca at least once was the goal of every devout Muslim, and in the nineteenth century thousands gathered in Cairo every spring to begin the journey, an impressive sight witnessed by a number of European and American travelers. But to travel in the seemingly purposeless manner of Westerners was utterly unaccountable to the Egyptians. When Duff-Gordon met a wealthy Indian man sailing up the Nile in 1866, it was the first time she could recall seeing an Asian or Middle Easterner traveling for pleasure.[48]

If the travelers' primary focus was ancient Egypt, they did not completely ignore the modern nation. Many took an interest in Egyptian politics, which they judged through the lens of Western liberal ideas about human rights and representative government. Floating hundreds of miles up and down and Nile, past dozens of villages, they could not help but observe the extreme poverty and the effects of the pasha's forced-labor policies. As Appleton explained, "Amid all the comfort and independence of our boat life, we are sometimes startlingly reminded of the heavy hand of tyranny which weighs upon Egypt behind its smiling azure.'' Egyptians would do anything to avoid contact with the government, even mutilating children so they would be unfit for military duty. Early travelers remarked on the number of men killed (estimates ranged up to twenty thousand) building the Mamudieh Canal (completed in 1820), one of the public works that the pasha, Muhammad Ali, undertook to improve his status among Europeans. Martineau was not sanguine about the prospects for a railroad from Cairo to Suez or a canal through the Isthmus of Suez, rumored to be among Muhammad Ali's next ambitions. As valuable as they would be for European commercial interests, such monumental works were a mockery alongside the poverty of the Egyptian people.[49]

Muhammad Ali did not live to achieve such ambitions. He died in 1848 and was succeeded by his nephew Abbas, who was murdered by two of his slaves in 1854. Muhammad Ali's son Said ruled until 1863, followed by Said's nephew Ismail, who masterminded the construction of the Suez Canal, which opened in 1869. In the 1860s, travelers often remarked on the large groups of men being force-marched along shore or carried downstream in barges, bound for labor on the canal. The men, who were paid only a token wage and had to provide their own food, died in huge numbers, victims of heat, exhaustion, and malnutrition. Forced labor was hardly new to rural Egyptians, but the scale increased in the 1860s because of the enormous demands of the canal project. As a result, tensions in the countryside increased, directed both at the pasha and at the French government, which managed the construction of the canal. Eventually, political unrest in Egypt would lead to Britain's taking over control of the country in 1882, a move supported by many who claimed that the Egyptian people lived under tyranny and were incapable of governing themselves. In Egypt, wrote Appleton, ''we have entered that East where a king has always been a despot. . . . Everywhere it is some Ramses, some conqueror, some satrap above, and the millions of unconsidered people below. By all with whom I have talked here of giving to the fellah more freedom, I have always been told that it was impossible—that he could not bear liberty, and would abuse it.''[50] This line of reasoning helped justify the British takeover: The people, debased caretakers of a glorious ancient culture, would be better off under the protection of the British Empire.

AFTER RETURNING TO CAIRO, travelers making the complete "grand tour" of the Middle East turned toward Jerusalem. Trading boats for camels and a leisurely life on the river for the rigors of desert travel, they put the monumental remains of the pharaohs behind them to seek out antiquity in a different form, less grand but even more significant to most nineteenth-century Western travelers. This was "holy ground," as Murray's guide put it. "Every footfall is upon soil trodden by patriarch and prophet; every view the eye rests on was seen by Abraham, Isaac, and Jacob, by Samuel, David, and Solomon."[51]

Travelers from Egypt to Palestine either went by ship from Alexandria to Jaffa, where they hired a dragoman and pack animals for the two-day journey to Jerusalem, or made the trip entirely by land across the desert from Cairo. Until the 1840s, the desert route was the usual choice because the ships ran on erratic schedules and were small and cramped. Once regular steamship service was introduced, the sea route became the less arduous way, requiring only three or four days compared with two weeks by land. However, some travelers still preferred to follow the track of the Israelites from Egypt to Canaan or simply wanted to experience the desert.[52] Construction of a railroad from Cairo to Suez in the late 1850s made this route more practical; and with the completion of the Suez Canal in 1869, travelers could sail through the canal to Port Said on the Mediterranean coast, a new town constructed in the 1860s in anticipation of the shipping that would be generated by the canal. From there ships departed regularly for Jaffa. Although railroad lines were constructed between Suez and Port Said and between Jaffa and Jerusalem, as late as 1894, Baedeker's guide advised travelers that the railroad was still not fully functional.[53]

Palestine and Syria presented the most primitive conditions that nineteenth-century tourists were likely to encounter. The lack of roads left travelers no choice but to ride horses or camels, or walk.[54] Guides were essential for all but the most adventuresome, and most travelers chose to carry camping gear and provisions. Accommodations for travelers in the desert, where they existed at all, fell far below European and American standards of comfort.[55]

Camping in the desert was an elaborate affair, with huge tents, carpets, tables and chairs for dining, and a small army of animals and men for carrying gear and tending to the wants of their employers. "They call *this* camping out!" was Mark Twain's reaction to desert travel in the Holy Land. After seeing one frivolous item after another emerge from his dragoman's stores, Twain remarked that one of his companions "has gone out now to inquire if the dragoman has brought a piano along." Another American traveler, William Prime, required between ten and fifteen men to manage his expedition. Upon arriving at Jaffa, he had his tents (specially made for him in Cairo) set up outside the city walls, furnishing them with Persian carpets, iron bedsteads, tables and chairs, all before a curious audience of the local residents, "eyeing us as if they had never seen white men before." As a final touch, he ran up an American flag. That evening Prime and his traveling companions dressed for dinner "with as much care as our limited wardrobes would permit" and sat down to a table set with china and crystal, still with their local audience looking on.[56]

Travelers on the overland route from Suez to Jerusalem also needed Bedouin guides, both to chart the course and to offer protection against possible attack. In certain parts of Palestine and Syria, local guides were also advised. By the mid-nineteenth century, the threat of random violence against travelers was minor (and probably much less than most travelers imagined it to be), but Bedouin who lived in areas commonly traversed by foreigners had established a custom of guiding tourists through their territories, guaranteeing their safety, for a fee. It was a lucrative business, and one that they jealously guarded. Hence the importance of contracting with the appropriate tribe for each region; if men from one group attempted to conduct a party through land controlled by another, they faced the danger of attack as interlopers. All arrangements could be made in Cairo with representatives of the tribes—so organized had the business of guiding tourists become by the 1850s. Guidebooks also advised travelers to carry a revolver conspicuously, especially if venturing out alone from camp. "The robbers of Syria are generally amateurs," Murray's guide noted, "who take up the profession when opportunity offers." They usually would not attack an armed party, and in any case, "by cool self-possession and a determined manner one can generally owerawe them."[57]

Such language was typical of guidebooks' advice on dealing with Arabs, whether they were strangers encountered en route or one's own dragoman and servants. One needed to be polite but firm, always in charge, never too familiar. Above all, one ought never to show fear and never be overly generous lest the dragoman take advantage. Such advice was perfectly in line with British opinions about their nation's superiority and their view of the Arabs as child-like; indeed, the advice about controlling servants in the desert was similar to what might be offered for managing wayward children. William Prime offered a good example of how not to behave: He yelled for his servants when he wanted them (while insisting that they keep quiet because he couldn't stand their noise), and "ordered" animals to be brought for his inspection. In Jaffa he flailed at men crowding around him with his whip in an effort to drive them off; in Jerusalem he fired shots into the kitchen of the house he had rented when the staff refused to be quiet. Most travelers, however, seem to have managed well with their dragoman and servants, and some even developed quite affectionate relations, if limited to the clearly defined roles of master and servant.[58]

However they got there, Jerusalem was the most important destination for nineteenth-century travelers to Palestine. Many thought of their journey to the Middle East as a pilgrimage, and even those who didn't usually had enough religious conviction to approach the biblical city with a sense of anticipation and awe. First impressions of Jerusalem were often negative, however, just as in Alexandria or Constantinople, because reality did not match imagination. Elsewhere in the Middle East, expectations were shaped by the romanticized fantasies of the Arabian Nights; in Palestine they were shaped by the Bible. In both cases, the sense of being let down was similar.

The streets of Jerusalem were narrow, dirty, and crowded with impoverished people clamoring for bakshish, like those of other Middle Eastern cities but without the splendor of Cairo or the European-style amenities provided by luxury hotels there and in Alexandria. Moreover, Jerusalem was small in scale. Mark Twain claimed that he could walk all the way around it in an hour. Nor did the landscape outside the city help, for it was barren and dry, far from the "land of milk and honey" of the Bible. Many shared Mark Twain's view of Palestine as "a howling wilderness instead of a garden." One of the women in his group remarked, "I would rather remember 'that sweet story of old' as I learned it in my childhood than encumber it with any of the unlovely associations of modern Palestine."[59]

Twain blamed earlier travel writers for painting an unrealistically rosy picture. "The wild enthusiasm of Palestine sight-seers is to be found only in the books they write, I think—not in their actual experience," he wrote. He was especially hard on William Prime, whose *Tent Life in the Holy Land*, published in 1857, was widely read in the United States. Prime loved everything about Palestine as much as he despised his Arab servants. His description of Jerusalem was purple prose at its worst: "I wept when I saw Jerusalem, I wept when I lay in the starlight at Bethlehem, I wept on the blessed shores of Galilee." (Prime "went through Palestine and irrigated it from one end to the other," quipped Twain. "How his horse ever kept his health, being exposed to these periodical showers all the time, is a wonder.")[60]

Guidebooks were much more temperate, cautioning readers that "a journey to Palestine and Syria cannot be looked upon as an ordinary pleasure-trip." Baedeker's second English edition (published in 1894), perhaps influenced by reports of returning travelers, stated explicitly that the initial experience of modern Jerusalem could be disappointing: "It would seem, at first, as though little were left of the ancient city of Zion and Moriah, the far-famed capital of the Jewish empire." Only by patient searching, informed by plenty of advance preparation, could one get past "the modern crust of rubbish and rottenness, which shrouds the sacred places from view.... The longer and the oftener he sojourns in Jerusalem, the greater will be the interest with which its ruins will inspire him, though he will be obliged to confess that the degraded aspect of the modern city, and its material and moral decline, form but a melancholy termination to the stupendous scenes once enacted here."[61]

Unlike the other major Middle Eastern cities, Jerusalem had substantial Christian and Jewish populations. Travelers reacted to the
Arab Christians as they had to the Copts in Egypt—as more Arab
than Christian. Worse was the spectacle of the various European
Christian denominations that had appointed themselves protectors of
the sacred places. Beginning in the sixteenth century, France and
Russia had claimed this right; the various regional sects, including
Copts, Armenians, Syriacs, and Abyssinians, also wanted to exercise
some control over the local shrines. The Ottoman Empire attempted
to mediate among these competing groups by such schemes as divid-
ing the Church of the Holy Sepulcher (built on what was supposedly
the site of Christ's crucifixion and burial) among them. In Bethlehem,
both the Eastern Orthodox and Roman Catholic churches had been
allowed to build a church at the supposed scene of the Nativity, each
with right of passage to the sacred grotto belowground. The spectacle
of Christians fighting among themselves over sacred sites (further
complicated by the arrival of Protestant missionaries in the 1820s)
was disturbing, to say the least. "The contempt, with which the
orthodox Jews and Mohammedans look down on the Christians is
only too well deserved" was Baedeker's comment.[62]

The Church of the Holy Sepulcher was the most important and
controversial monument in Jerusalem. Guidebooks strove for a tone
of careful neutrality, suggesting that locating biblical sites with ab-
solute precision was less important than the knowledge that sacred
events had taken place in the general vicinity. Travelers' opinions
depended on their own preconceptions and degree of religious piety.
Devout pilgrims were prepared to take every shrine at face value.
Others were more skeptical, like Harriet Martineau, who called the
Church of the Holy Sepulcher "the pretended sepulchre," and cat-
alogued all the reasons that the site couldn't possibly be Christ's
tomb. The very spectacle of the church, with its lavish ornamentation
and separate chapels set aside for the competing Christian churches,
led her to compare it to a "heathen temple, but without its grace,"
a "puppet-show" compared with the temples of Egypt. "The only
thing to be done in such places as this church is to put aside entirely
the Christianity with which one is familiar, and look at what is before
one's eyes as one would look upon the ceremonies of the Joss-house

in China, or the exhibitions of Medicine-Mystery at the Falls of the Mississippi.'' When she observed a fellow Englishwoman prostrate herself and kiss the ground at the supposed site of the crucifixion, Martineau couldn't bear to watch. "It was painful to see numbers of English persons joining the Romish processions," one man remarked. An American clergyman thought the claims made for the church were intended solely to extract money from the gullible. Mark Twain derided its "claptrap side-shows and unseemly humbuggery of every kind," but was moved nonetheless by the very thought of standing at the place where Christ was crucified. (In fact, the Church of the Holy Sepulcher was about the only monument in Palestine or Syria that impressed him.) Ida Pfeiffer, on the other hand, a Roman Catholic, went again and again to the church and on one occasion spent the night there, a common practice among devout pilgrims.[63]

Guidebooks recommended a minimum of a week to do justice to Jerusalem's holy sites. Mark Twain grew heartily sick of it all, declaring that there were far too many things to see: "No single foot of ground in all Jerusalem or within its neighborhood seems to be without a stirring and important history of its own. . . . We visited David's tomb, but we felt no enthusiasm in the knowledge that David had a tomb. I think we felt a resentment toward him for having a tomb at all. If he hadn't had one we need not have gone there." Touring Palestine, a place "no larger than an ordinary county in the United States," was exhausting, Twain complained; "it wears a man out to have to read up a hundred pages of history every two or three miles—for verily the celebrated locations of Palestine occur that close together."[64]

Several of the important biblical sites were within a day or two's ride from Jerusalem. The most popular were, of course, Bethlehem, an easy day trip, and the route encompassing Jericho, the Jordan River, and the Dead Sea, usually a three-day excursion. Most travelers then headed north to view the scenes of Jesus' childhood, touring Nazareth and Tiberias, on the Sea of Galilee. More varied in terrain and more extensively cultivated than southern Palestine, this area was more attractive to Western sensibilities. Martineau thought Nazareth the most beautiful part of Palestine. Others, however, saw only poverty, dirt, and Muslim hostility toward Christians. As one

British visitor put it, "The site of Nazareth is exquisite; the city itself dirty in the extreme." Mark Twain described Nazareth as nothing but "dirt and rags and squalor; vermin, hunger and wretchedness; savage costumes, savage weapons and looks of hate," with rude mud huts, "ragged" children, "dilapidated" men, "scurvy" women, "hungry dogs and cadaverous cats." Visiting the grotto of the Annunciation, he had trouble reconciling the biblical scene with the little stone grotto before him. "Imagination labors best in distant fields," he remarked. "I doubt if any man can stand in this Grotto of the Annunciation and people with the phantom images of his mind its too tangible walls of stone."[65]

Touring Palestine gave travelers who had not crossed the Sinai from Egypt their first sustained exposure to the desert Arabs. Their reactions were heavily colored by stereotypes reinforced by guidebooks and the writings of earlier travelers, producing a mélange of divergent images: romantic, exotic Orientals; primitive, ignorant people inferior to Europeans; noble Arabs, characterized by a belief in honor, family, and hospitality; rapacious, thieving, violent Arabs; Muslim fanatics. Murray's guide offered a fairly typical opinion: "Hard fare and desert life are not calculated to pamper the passions; but, even independent of this, there is a principle of honor in the breast of the wild 'son of the desert' which we seek for in vain beneath the silken robe of the citizen." The Bedouin had a strong sense of family and tribal loyalty, returning to the same lands generation after generation; they were less likely to keep their women in seclusion, and although they might prey on strangers, they did not steal from members of their own tribe, and their hospitality was legendary. The influence of Islam also seemed stronger in the towns, whose inhabitants guidebooks characterized as "fanatical" and "turbulent," while religion seemed to sit more lightly on the nomadic Bedouin.[66]

Closer contact with the Bedouin, however, tarnished the positive image. Over time, they came to be perceived—like urban Arabs—as ragged, impoverished, often prematurely aged, with children who appeared ill and malnourished and animals that looked little better. As Mark Twain put it, admittedly in extreme fashion, the Bedouin he saw riding their "old crowbait horses" bore little resemblance to the " 'wild, free dons of the desert, speeding over the plain like the wind, on their beautiful Arabian mares' we had read so much about and longed so much to see! . . . I wonder if it was to this kind of scallawags the angels brought tidings that a Saviour was born? It rather staggers me to believe it."[67]

WITH THE COMPLETION of the Suez Canal in 1869, travel to the Middle East changed dramatically. Designed by the French engineer Ferdinand de Lesseps and financed through a combination of Egyptian and European capital, the canal linked the Mediterranean and the Red Sea, thus opening a continuous sea route from Europe to Asia. The Egyptian government staged a lavish series of events to celebrate its opening, inviting distinguished guests from all over Europe. Ismail Pasha built the Gezirah Palace in Cairo to house visiting royalty, who included the Empress Eugénie of France and the Prince and Princess of Wales. Among the other notable guests was Thomas Cook, who attended the festivities with a party of sixty tourists.[68]

Publicity generated by the canal focused attention on the Middle East in a way that nothing before had. Over the next decade, a tour of the Middle East was transformed from an adventure requiring time, money, and ingenuity in abundance to a fairly straightforward vacation trip—if still an expensive and time-consuming one. By the 1880s, Egypt became a popular winter resort for wealthy Britons tired of Italy or France, while packaged tours of Palestine and Syria made it far easier to visit biblical shrines.

As usual, Thomas Cook led the way. For some time, the idea of promoting travel to Palestine had appealed to the elder Cook's piety, while the potential profits of the business appealed to his son, who wanted to expand their business by attracting a wealthier clientele. After an exploratory trip in the fall of 1868, the Cooks organized a three-and-a-half-month tour covering Cairo, the Nile, Palestine, Syria, Smyrna, Constantinople, and Athens, followed by a second tour coinciding with the Suez Canal ceremonies in the fall of 1869. Building on existing ticket arrangements for trains through Europe, the Cooks offered a seven-day passage from London to Alexandria at what they boasted was the cheapest possible price—under £20 first-class.

The tour got off to a rocky start when the group of about thirty, attempting to disembark at Alexandria, was mobbed by aggressive would-be guides who commandeered their luggage and nearly managed to dump it all in the sea. Cairo lived up to its billing, however, as "most wonderfully Oriental," in the words of one young woman. For their journey up the Nile, on steamboats chartered from the Egyptian government, they had the added attraction of following in the wake of Edward, Prince of Wales, and his entourage.[69]

After the Nile excursion, the group went by sea to Beirut, where the Cooks had hired a dragoman with a full complement of men, animals, and equipment: a large tent for cooking and an even bigger one for dining, which could accommodate all twenty-five people at once; iron bedsteads, wool mattresses, linens and carpets; seventy horses and mules; and thirty muleteers and servants. The tents were lined with a dark blue fabric trimmed in red—"very smart," according to a young woman in the group, with mattresses, bolsters, and red-striped blankets for each bed and carpets underfoot. "We thought ourselves in clover," she remarked. The dining tent was equally "smart," in dark blue and crimson. After sightseeing in Jerusalem the Cooks' group followed the customary route through Palestine, to Bethlehem, Jericho and the Dead Sea, Nazareth, Galilee, and then north to Damascus and Beirut.[70]

On this tour, the Cooks set in motion what would become the two key features of their Middle Eastern packages: steamer trips up the Nile and luxury camping in the Holy Land. Beginning in the spring of 1870, they arranged annual tours of varying lengths, including a hundred-day version that encompassed Cairo, the Nile, and the Holy Land, and a seventy-day trip that excluded the Nile journey. Although shorter than the traditional grand tour of the Middle East, Cooks' excursions were still time-consuming and not much less expensive than traveling independently; their main selling point was convenience. Using strategies reminiscent of Thomas Cook's early efforts to encourage English men and women to travel to the Continent, they played on people's nervousness about traveling in a region where they knew nothing of the language or customs, exaggerating the difficulties of dealing with "haughty, imperious dragomans" and the complications of Eastern currency, stressing the peace of mind that came with having someone else make the arrangements.[71]

At the same time, the Cooks dismissed fears about the dangers of desert travel as overstated. They repeatedly emphasized the good health of their travelers and ridiculed the idea that women couldn't stand up to the rigors of desert travel. "I only wish the theorists who hold this opinion had been there to see," Thomas Cook wrote after his first Palestine tour. "During the past thirty years I have seen a good deal of lady travellers, and I never yet saw a difficulty which gentlemen could overcome to which ladies would succumb." The food, much of it shipped from England, was good; the bugs not nearly so bothersome as readers of travel books were led to believe. (One almost gets the impression that the Cooks willed the bugs to stay away.) The steamers on the Nile might not be so convenient, private, or picturesque as the dahabeahs, but they more than made up for such shortcomings with their greater size, comfort, and speed; the Cooks were not among those who enjoyed drifting slowly past little-changing scenery. (Charles Dudley Warner disagreed, as he noted with some disgust when one of Cook's steamers went "thundering down stream, filling the air with smoke and frightening the geese, who fly before it in vast clouds.") As for any concern about traveling in groups—the point for which Cooks' tourists in Europe were so often ridiculed—in the Middle East one had no choice. Whether the group included ten people or twenty-five (the maximum size for Cooks' tours in Palestine) made little difference.[72]

The Cooks' Middle Eastern tours increased steadily in popularity. By the early 1870s, when Thomas Cook turned them over to his son, they were the most significant part of the business. During the next decade, the Cooks negotiated contracts with individual dragomans to work exclusively for them, and had new tents and equipment made especially for their tours. (In 1874, a group of Egyptian dragomans wrote to the London *Times* protesting that Cook and other travel agents were monopolizing Egyptian tourism, forcing them out of business.) To avoid the sort of problems that had proved so disconcerting to their first Egyptian tourists, they employed their own agents to meet ships at Alexandria and other ports. (One young man traveling in 1874, describing the scene upon arrival at Alexandria, remarked upon his relief at having "two fine, tall Arabs with, round their necks, 'Cook's Men' " come to his rescue.)[73]

In 1873 the firm established offices at Shepheard's Hotel in Cairo and in Jaffa. More significantly, they took control of the steamers on the Nile when the viceroy of Egypt appointed John Mason Cook sole agent for passenger traffic on government-owned steamers in 1870; five years later, Cook received permission to set up his own passenger steamer service. In 1880, the government gave the Cook company the right to manage all passenger steamers on the Nile. Toward the end of the decade, the company took over the mail steamers as well, first buying steamers from the Egyptian government and then, dissatisfied with their quality, having new boats constructed. The mail steamers offered passengers with limited time a quick tour up the Nile, requiring about two weeks instead of three. For a more leisurely tour, the Cooks would arrange dahabeahs. To exercise closer control over that branch of their business, they began building their own small fleet, including one steam-powered dahabeah. By the 1890s, the Cooks were operating six tourist steamers, four mail steamers, five old-fashioned paddle steamers, two steam dahabeahs, five steam launches, and fifteen dahabeahs on the Nile. Two dragomans, one lecturing in English and the other in French, led the shore excursions; they even told the travelers exactly how much bakshish to pay. As a result of their near monopoly, the Cooks became so influential that many Egyptians developed an exaggerated sense of their importance. The residents of Aswan erected an inscription to John Mason, which described him as "king of Upper and Lower Egypt"; some Egyptians actually thought he was King of England.[74]

During the 1880–81 and 1881–82 seasons, John Mason Cook claimed that three fourths of all tourists in Palestine used his company's arrangements; by the end of the century, about twelve thousand people had traveled in the Holy Land on Cooks' tours. In the late 1880s, five to six thousand tourists a year passed through the Cook office in Cairo. A writer in *Blackwood's Magazine* described Cooks' control over Egyptian travel: "Cook's representative is the first person you meet in Egypt, and you go on meeting him. He sees you in; he sees you through; he sees you out. You see the back of a native turban, long blue gown, red girdle, bare brown legs; 'How truly oriental!' you say. Then he turns round, and you see 'Cook's Porter' emblazoned across his breast.... Cook carries you, like a nursing father, from one end of Egypt to the other.''[75]

Even the very wealthy began to make their travel arrangements through Cook. When the Prince of Wales sent his two sons to Palestine in 1882, Cook planned their tour. In 1884, the British government commissioned the company to transport troops up the Nile to the Sudan and, some months later, to organize the relief party sent to rescue General Charles Gordon, trapped in Khartoum after trying unsuccessfully to put down a native revolt. The Pilgrimage Committee of France commissioned Cook to arrange a tour for a thousand French pilgrims, mostly "old Catholic nobility"—unusual clients for a man who started his career taking working-class men and women to evangelical Protestant temperance meetings. And when Kaiser Wilhelm of Germany decided to make an official pilgrimage to Jerusalem in 1898, he chose Cook to plan it, much to the amusement of the British press, which referred to the kaiser as "Cook's Crusader.''[76]

By end of the nineteenth century, Egypt had become a popular winter resort. Several luxury hotels constructed in Cairo in the late 1860s and '70s supplemented the famous Shepheard's, which was rebuilt in more modern style in 1890. In 1887 Cook opened a luxury hotel in Luxor. Conceived originally as a convenience for passengers going up the Nile—there were no good hotels anywhere on the Nile above Cairo—the Cooks soon discovered a new market among invalids and others who wanted to spend the winter in Egypt's warm, dry climate. The Luxor Hotel proved so successful that they built a second hotel nearby, staffing both with a resident physician and chaplain. Later they added a third, at Aswan. As a result, one could winter on the Nile without hiring a boat.[77]

With the beginning of luxury train service on the Cairo–Aswan line, launched by the CIWL in 1898, travelers could reach the Nile resorts speedily and comfortably without going on the river at all. The CIWL trains featured sleeping cars and a dining car cooled to about 77°F. by air blown over three hundred pounds of ice. A double roof on all cars and slats over the windows helped keep the other cars comfortable. The CIWL increasingly became Cooks' chief competition in the Egyptian travel business, adding Nile steamers and luxury hotels to its holdings; in the 1890s, the company bought the Gezirah Palace, converting it into a luxury hotel, and soon thereafter took over Shepheard's.[78]

By 1898, one of Cooks' promotional brochures claimed, "Egypt has . . . become the favourite winter residence," going so far as to label Cairo "no more than a winter suburb of London." A bit of hyperbole, to be sure, but evidence of a widespread sentiment that travel to the "East" was no longer a formidable undertaking. "A winter at Cairo is nothing now," observed Thackeray around mid-century, while the American minister Edward Everett Hale could write in 1882 that "such is the ease of travel now, that it is safe to take for granted, in any considerable assembly, that someone is present who has walked in the streets of Jerusalem."[79]

CHAPTER 9

AROUND

THE

WORLD

U NTIL THE LATTER part of the nineteenth century, few people traveling for pleasure ventured beyond the boundaries of
Europe, the Middle East, and the eastern third of the United States.
The experiences of one who did—Ida Pfeiffer, who followed her adventures in the Middle East with an around-the-world tour in 1846—
illustrate the reasons why: Once beyond the limits of regularly
scheduled steam-powered transportation and tourist accommodations, travel required abundant time and ingenuity, along with a willingness to cope with the unexpected and the unpleasant. Pfeiffer
spent two and a half years on her tour, crossing the Atlantic to Brazil,
then sailing around Cape Horn to Valparaiso and across the Pacific
to the coast of China, a thirty-nine-day voyage broken only by a few
days at Tahiti. She traveled in Chinese junks to Canton and Hong
Kong, and in British steamers to Singapore, Ceylon, and Calcutta;
sailed a thousand miles up the Ganges to Benares and then made her
way overland by horse cart and camel to Bombay. There she took passage in a small steamer bound for Iraq, one of only two Europeans on

board, and finished off her journey by attaching herself to a series of caravans traveling across Iraq, Persia, and southern Russia.

By herself or with companions encountered along the way, she tramped through Brazilian jungles, took lodgings in a one-room shack with a carpenter and his family in Tahiti, put up with jeers and taunts while walking through the streets of Canton, slept on the deck of a crowded, dirty ship for nearly three weeks between Bombay and Iraq, and was detained by suspicious customs officials at the Russian border. After crossing the Atlantic, she had to negotiate every leg of her trip on the spot, staying mostly with local families or camping, eating whatever kind of food the region produced. The entire journey took two and a half years. Only in major port cities with established trade connections could the traveler expect anything resembling the kind of transportation and accommodations that were becoming standard across Europe and the United States.[1]

By the late 1860s and 1870s, this situation began to change. Completion of the Suez Canal inaugurated direct steamship service between Europe and Asia. The opening of Japan to foreign trade in the late 1850s provided the impetus for similar services across the Pacific; monthly crossings between San Francisco and Yokohama began in 1867, while the British P&O line extended its India–Singapore–Hong Kong route to Japan at about the same time. With the completion of the first transcontinental railroad across the United States in 1869, it was possible to travel around the world by way of regularly scheduled steam-powered transit.

In an era that revered technology, the very possibilities offered by modern transportation encouraged an interest in world travel, if only of the armchair variety. Writing in the fall of 1869, a Sacramento newspaper publisher noted with enthusiasm, "Now that the Pacific Railroad is complete, few of our readers are aware that a journey around the world can be made in eighty days."[2] Three years later Jules Verne published his famous novel *Around the World in Eighty Days,* in which Phileas Fogg undertakes his improbable journey, inspired by an article in a London newspaper calculating that the latest advances in transportation made it possible to circle the globe in eighty days. The story opens with Fogg and a group of his acquaintances, fellow members of London's Reform Club, debating whether such a journey could actually be accomplished. It might be possible in theory, argues one man, but the reality—with delayed trains, bad weather at sea, missed connections, and any number of other mishaps—would be quite another matter. Nonsense, says Fogg, a man of rigidly regulated habits who never ventures beyond his home and club and never deviates from his daily routine. With proper planning, the trip could be completed on schedule. So certain is he that he bets half his fortune that he can make the journey in eighty days. His wager accepted, Fogg and his French servant, Passepartout, depart that very evening, taking with them only a small valise with the barest essentials of clothing and £20,000 in cash.

Passepartout, who has been employed by Fogg for a mere twenty-four hours, having accepted the job precisely because Fogg is a homebody of boringly regular habits, is mystified. Why does such a man suddenly decide to travel, and on a seemingly lunatic mission at that? Clearly it is not to *see* the world, as becomes obvious along the route. At Suez, Fogg leaves the ship only long enough to have his passport stamped. On board ship, he plays whist, apparently his only passion in life, with scarcely a nod to what goes on around him. In Bombay, Passepartout goes sightseeing and manages to get himself in trouble for entering a Hindu temple without removing his shoes, but Fogg spends his time with train schedules, calculating the pair's next move. Soon, however, Fogg discovers the limitations of planning and schedules. Several hours out of Bombay, the train suddenly stops. Despite his careful planning, Fogg has failed to discover that a fifty-mile stretch of the route is still incomplete. Passengers are left to themselves to find alternative means of transit to Allahabad, where the railroad resumes. Better-informed passengers have already commandeered all the readily available local transportation, leaving Fogg to improvise. He tries to hire an elephant, but the owner isn't interested, until Fogg offers to buy the animal at a price so exorbitant the man cannot resist.

From that point, the adventures and misadventures begin. Tramping through a forest on their elephant, the party chances upon a *sati* (widow burning) in preparation. In a daring and highly improbable stunt, Passepartout rescues the young woman from her funeral pyre and the group continues on its way, now with the addition of Mrs. Aouda, a beautiful, well-educated, English-speaking, remarkably European-looking Indian woman. The rescue has cost them two days' time, but no matter; they had made it to India faster than planned, so are still on schedule. In Calcutta, an overzealous Scotland Yard inspector named Fix catches up with them, convinced because of a similarity in description that Fogg is a bank robber on the lam. Fix manages to get Passepartout arrested for his indiscretions in Bombay, but Fogg posts bail in time for them to make the steamer to Hong Kong. Bad weather delays their arrival, but by good fortune the steamer bound for Yokohama is also delayed, giving them plenty of time to make the connection—until Fix, still tailing Fogg, takes Passepartout to an opium den and has him drugged. With his servant out of commission, Fogg doesn't learn until too late that the Yokohama steamer has moved up its departure by a few hours. Undaunted, he hires a small craft to take him to Shanghai, where he can pick up the Yokohama–San Francisco steamer at its point of origin. Accompanied by Mrs. Aouda (who has decided to accompany Fogg back to Europe) and Fix (still in the guise of a fellow tourist coincidentally following the same route), the group weathers a typhoon and finally makes its rendezvous with the San Francisco steamer only by the stratagem of running up a distress flag at the mouth of the Shanghai River just as the steamer is about to pass them.

Meanwhile, Passepartout, still in a state of stupor as the effects of the opium wear off, manages to get himself on board the Yokohama steamer and lands in Japan with neither money nor traveling companions. Ever ingenious, he joins an acrobatic troupe, hoping to earn enough money for his passage across the Pacific. Spotting Fogg in the back of the theater, Passepartout rushes toward him, collapsing a human pyramid in the process, and the trio are reunited just in time to catch the steamer for San Francisco. The success of the journey seems assured now, for the rest of their itinerary employs regularly scheduled, steam-driven transportation: the Pacific mail steamer, the transcontinental railroad across the United States, one of the many transatlantic passenger steamers, and finally a train from Liverpool to London.

But they fail to reckon with the hazards of the American West. In a wonderful parody of American travel accounts, Verne subjects his characters to a herd of buffalo crossing the train tracks (three hours' delay); a shaky bridge over a deep gorge (potentially a long detour until a speed-happy engineer decides to race the train across the bridge at full throttle, hoping it will land on the other side before the bridge collapses); a Mormon preaching to his captive audience (no delay, but a bit of aggravation); and a near-duel between Fogg and an uncouth San Franciscan, averted only by the final disaster, an Indian raid. Passepartout saves the day by employing his acrobatic skills once again, crawling along the underside of the train to detach the locomotive and stop the train. Conveniently, the cars come to a halt near Fort Kearny, where soldiers drive the Indians away. But Passepartout and two other passengers are missing and presumed captured. If Fogg attempts to rescue his servant, he will almost certainly be delayed long enough to lose his bet, and will risk his life in the bargain. Mrs. Aouda, who understands what is at stake, despairs; but the unflappable Fogg hesitates not a moment before recruiting a band of soldiers to join him in the rescue effort. They succeed, but a full day is lost and it will be many more hours before the next train passes through, whereupon Fogg hires a man with a fantastic contraption: a flatbed car fitted with wheels and a sail. Taking advantage of the prairie winds, their guide sails the party (with Fix still trailing along) to Omaha, where trains for New York depart regularly.

Despite such heroic efforts, the travelers yet again miss their connection by a hairsbreadth. Arriving in New York, they discover that the Liverpool steamer has just sailed, so Fogg once more hires his own craft. They reach Liverpool with just enough time to get to London within the deadline, when Fix, back on English soil and therefore within his jurisdiction, delivers the coup de grace by arresting Fogg for bank robbery. By the time Fix discovers his mistake (the real robber having been arrested a few days before), Fogg's only alternative is to hire a special train. Even that stratagem isn't quite good enough, and he arrives in London five minutes too late. It would appear to be a bittersweet ending: Fogg has lost his fortune but gained happiness, as Mrs. Aouda confesses her love for him and the two decide to marry. And then comes the final twist. Dispatched to find a minister to perform the wedding, Passepartout rushes back to announce that it is in fact a day earlier than they had thought. Despite his obsession with time and schedules, Fogg has failed to realize that he gained a day by traveling east to west. Racing to the Reform Club in the nick of time, he wins his bet and the lady too.

Around the World in Eighty Days was an instant success and remains one of the most enduring works of travel literature. Part of its contemporary appeal was Verne's clever blurring of fact and fiction. The very idea of traveling around the world in a matter of weeks seemed fantastic, yet it was in fact technically possible; the trains and steamers Fogg took on his travels all existed, and the times specified for each leg of the journey were accurate. The places he visited (or, more accurately, passed through en route to the next destination) were described in dozens of travel accounts. In the hands of Verne, a master storyteller, the odd assortment of characters and their preposterous adventures were captivating enough to make readers suspend disbelief, and to win new generations of readers even after circling the world in eighty days ceased to be a remarkable notion.

Nearly twenty years after Verne published his novel, Phileas Fogg's adventures inspired a real-life imitator: a petite, twenty-two-year-old journalist named Elizabeth Cochrane, who wrote under the pen name Nellie Bly. Ambitious and remarkably precocious, with a number of important articles to her credit—on divorce, working conditions for women in Pittsburgh's steel mills, political unrest in Mexico, and mistreatment of inmates at the insane asylum on Blackwell's Island—she was looking for an idea for her next big story when she decided, in the fall of 1889, to see how fast she could travel around the world. Bly persuaded the editors of the New York *World* to sponsor her journey and set herself a goal of circling the globe in seventy-five days. A fan of Verne's novel, she modeled her tour on Fogg's, with one significant exception: After crossing the English Channel, she detoured to Amiens to visit Jules Verne and his wife.

Bly also made it a point of principle to take only regularly scheduled transportation—no hired elephants or leaky coastal steamers—although she did fudge matters a bit, cadging a ride on a mail train from Southampton to London and hiring a special train from San Francisco.[3]

"A veritable feminine Phineas Fogg," the *World* called her (spelling Fogg's name wrong throughout its coverage of the tour), milking the connection between Bly and Fogg for all it was worth. Judging from the newspaper coverage, many of the *World*'s readers were as skeptical as Fogg's cronies, even though improvements in transportation made such a journey feasible. Bly's tour, like Fogg's, was mainly a blur of trains and steamships, with scarcely a moment to see anything along the way. She had her share of near-misses and delays. A longer than normal passage across the Atlantic cost her a connection at Southampton, a difficulty solved when the *World*'s London correspondent arranged for her to travel on the mail train instead. Then she had to race to catch the train at Dover, spent five days waiting for a ship at Ceylon, hit a monsoon en route to Hong Kong, and endured more delays waiting for ships at Hong Kong and Yokohama. Arriving in San Francisco, she faced the prospect of a two-week quarantine aboard ship because of a smallpox scare, while on the final leg of her journey, a blizzard blocked the main railroad line, forcing her to hire a special train running on a different route (in a maneuver reminiscent of her fictional hero). Despite it all, she beat her own goal, arriving in New York after just seventy-two days.[4]

The *World*'s editors did their best to sustain interest in Bly's journey, sponsoring a contest to guess how long it would take, playing up her meeting with the Vernes, and printing letters cabled back from various points along the way. When letters didn't arrive—Bly managed to send only a handful during her time in transit—the *World* kept up the barrage of coverage by printing articles about what she must be seeing along her route and quotes from articles about Bly appearing in other newspapers. In fact, Bly's own articles were pretty bland stuff. As she herself pointed out, she spent most of her time at sea, with the result that she had little to say about her experiences. For the reporters who covered her journey, however, none of this mattered. The important thing was the feat itself, that it had been accomplished by an American (and a woman), and entirely by methods of transportation available to anyone. "What a wonderful achievement of modern travel," one writer gushed. Another, comparing Bly's accomplishment with Henry Stanley's search for David Livingstone, praised her for demonstrating "the vast possibilities of social and commercial intercommunication between the peoples of the earth" and for setting an example for American womanhood.[5] Fascination with technology and speed, chauvinistic pro-Americanism, vicarious adventurism, and the achievement of making a journey that had seemed possible only in fantasy kept Nellie Bly's name in the headlines.

FOR MOST PEOPLE, following Nellie Bly's adventures in the newspapers was as close as they would come to traveling around the world, but for a growing number of wealthy travelers, around-the-world tours developed a certain cachet.

Not surprisingly, Thomas Cook recognized the possibilities for world travel on a large scale, and set about mapping itineraries and packaging tickets that would make it relatively painless. Just a few months before Jules Verne launched Phileas Fogg on his fictional tour, Cook set out on the real thing, following much the same itinerary in reverse. (It has been suggested that Cook may have provided the inspiration for Verne's novel; his tour was advertised widely in the spring of 1872, while Verne wrote and published his novel in a matter of months toward the end of the year.)[6] Cook's account of his travels, published serially in *The Times,* drew fewer readers than Verne's best-seller and is now long forgotten. But for the would-be Phileas Foggs, Cook's tour, with its goal of mapping out the most practical itinerary for well-heeled but not terribly adventuresome tourists, helped make their travels possible. If Fogg's adventures proved that schedules aren't flawless but enough money will buy most anything, Cook set out to prove that one could in fact make the journey around the world on a schedule, albeit a somewhat more extended one. He shared some traits with his fictional counterpart;

both had enormous faith in the power of technology to overcome all obstacles, and both were obsessed with time and schedules.

In the spring of 1872, Cook proposed his first personally conducted tour around the world. He chose a west-to-east route; across the Atlantic and the United States, with stops at favorite American tourist attractions, including Niagara Falls, Chicago, Salt Lake City, and San Francisco; across the Pacific to Yokohama, followed by a tour of the major Japanese cities; then on to Shanghai, Hong Kong, Singapore, Penang, Ceylon, Madras, and Calcutta. At Calcutta, Cook and his group left the ship for their first extended overland tour, via rail to Benares, Agra, Kanpur (Cawnpore), Lucknow, Delhi, Allahabad, and Bombay, where they boarded another ship for the voyage to Egypt, their last major stop before returning to England via steamer across the Mediterranean and rail through Europe. Although the entire tour took 222 days, it followed Cook's typical pattern of cramming as much as possible into the time available—a mere twenty-four hours in Shanghai, two days in Singapore, three in Ceylon. The most luxurious stretch of the journey, in terms of time, was the month devoted to India, where the group spent several days visiting Protestant missionaries in addition to taking in popular sights like the Taj Mahal and the temples of Benares.[7]

Though far more leisurely than the fictional Fogg's tour, Cook's journey was also much more prosaic. Other than the occasional need to adjust a schedule and make small modifications in the itinerary, the real 1872 tour went off without a hitch. The success of this first effort encouraged Cook to make the around-the-world journey an annual event. Subsequent tours followed his original itinerary, adding a few days in places he had skipped over too quickly the first time around and providing flexibility for members of the group to expand or contract the American and European segments of the journey. Cook also launched a program of rail and steamer tickets as well as optional side trips that could be packaged in various ways for those who wanted to travel on their own. Following the model that had served so well in Europe and the Middle East, by the mid-1870s the company had developed a complete program that made travel around the world predictable and relatively uncomplicated. In

1894, one of Cooks' clients broke Nellie Bly's record by completing his world circuit in sixty-five days—although most of Cooks' tourists followed a much more leisurely pace.[8]

Over the next several decades, the route charted in fiction by Fogg and in reality by Cook and Bly became the standard itinerary for world travelers, for rather obvious reasons: Their route followed the easiest transportation lines, which in turn followed the course of Western influence in the Middle East and Asia. Most travelers hopped from one outpost of the British Empire to the next, with the American-dominated Japanese ports (and, for the more adventurous, French Indochina) thrown in. They took British steamers from Egypt to Bombay, where they could choose between crossing India by rail—the line between Bombay and Calcutta was completed in 1870, the first long-distance railway in Asia—or continuing around the subcontinent by steamer and on to Singapore and Hong Kong. Both British and American ships operated between Hong Kong and Yokohama, where travelers booked passage in American carriers across the Pacific to San Francisco.

Deviating from this standard route was difficult for anyone on a schedule. The Pacific Mail Steamship Company, which operated ships between San Francisco, Yokohama, and Hong Kong, initiated direct service between California, New Zealand, and Australia in 1875, but discontinued it ten years later when the U.S. government canceled its mail contract with the company; passenger traffic alone was not enough to sustain the route. Throughout most of the nineteenth century, those who wanted to visit Australia and New Zealand from the United States had to go by steamer to Honolulu and then take their chances on whatever ship might happen to be sailing onward across the Pacific.

In the 1890s, when Mark Twain made an around-the-world lecture tour, service between North America and Australia still remained unpredictable. He and his family booked passage on a ship sailing from Victoria, British Columbia, to Sydney via Honolulu, where additional passengers were scheduled to board for the voyage to Australia. They were forced to delay their plans, however, because of a cholera epidemic in the Hawaiian Islands. Honolulu-bound passengers could disembark, but no one was permitted to board; otherwise the ship would have been forced into quarantine at Sydney. Twain was disappointed because he had visited the islands nearly three decades earlier and looked forward to seeing them again, but his inconvenience was nothing compared to that of the people left stranded in Honolulu, who might wait weeks for the next Australia-bound ship. "It is easy to make plans in this world," Twain observed; "even a cat can do it; and when one is out in those remote oceans it is noticeable that a cat's plans and a man's are worth about the same." To avoid this sort of problem, Thomas Cook & Son advised its customers to arrange Australia and New Zealand as a side trip from Ceylon aboard one of the regularly scheduled British P&O steamers, although that routing, while it had the advantage of reliability, added weeks to a standard around-the-world itinerary.[9]

Crossing the Asian continent by land was all but impossible until the Trans-Siberian railroad was completed in 1904. Even brief excursions into China beyond the ports of Shanghai and Canton were hard to arrange. (One of the few who managed was William H. Seward, secretary of state under Presidents Lincoln and Johnson, who visited Peking in 1871.) Pre–World War I globetrotters saw most of the world from the deck of a ship, filled out a bit with brief excursions in and around the major port cities.

By the end of the nineteenth century, tours of Japan and India became increasingly popular as journeys on their own. Cook, in particular, put a great deal of energy into developing tours to India; but for the European who wanted to go as far as Japan, or the American who wanted to visit India, it was just about as easy to go home by circling the globe as to retrace one's steps.[10]

WITH LIMITED EXCEPTIONS, Japan was closed to all foreign contact from the early seventeenth century to the middle of the nineteenth, as successive generations of rulers feared that outside influences would threaten the cohesiveness of Japanese culture and encourage revolt. Beginning in the 1840s, the United States and the major European powers began pressuring Japan's rulers to permit trade and diplomatic relations, culminating in 1854 when Commodore Matthew Perry sailed his squadron into Edo (now Tokyo) Bay, demanding trading privileges for the United States. The result was an agreement allowing American ships to obtain provisions at the remote ports of Shimoda, on the east coast south of Edo, and Hakodate, in the far north on the island of Hokkaido, with the promise of diplomatic relations later. British officials concluded a similar agreement later that year. In 1856, the first American consul was posted to Japan; two years later, he concluded a treaty that would expand trade to include the ports of Nagasaki and Kanagawa in 1859, Niigata in 1860, and Kobe in 1863. Foreigners would be permitted in Edo in 1862 and in Osaka in 1863. Under the terms of this treaty and similar agreements worked out with the major European powers, foreigners could conduct trade, establish commercial and residential buildings in certain areas, and live under their own laws.[11]

Opposition to foreigners remained widespread in Japan throughout the 1860s, however, erupting in occasional violence—two Russians were killed in Yokohama in 1859, a Dutch ship captain and the secretary to the American consul in 1860, and a British official in 1862, among other incidents. Resentment against Japan's ruling elite for its role in admitting foreigners to the country contributed to the bloodless revolution of 1868, which restored the emperor, long a mere figurehead, to power. The Meiji Restoration did nothing to stop the growth of foreign influence, however. Ports scheduled to open in the early 1860s, including Osaka, Kobe, Niigata, and Edo, were finally opened after years of government foot-dragging, and foreign visitors were permitted in Kyoto, Japan's ancient capital and seat of the imperial family, for the first time.[12]

Under Japanese law, foreign visitors were limited to treaty ports and a few other major cities and their immediate environs. Travel beyond these limits required government approval, as well as some ingenuity in making travel arrangements and a willingness to accept accommodation in simple local inns and eat native food. As a consequence, few Western visitors to Japan saw anything of the country beyond the treaty ports, leaving them with a rather skewed impression of the country, one that emphasized commerce and modernization over the persistence of traditional culture.

The standard itinerary started in Yokohama, took in Tokyo and perhaps Nikko (about one hundred miles north of Yokohama), then continued to Kobe, Osaka, and Kyoto, and concluded with a cruise across the Inland Sea from Kobe to Nagasaki. Even this limited tour, traveling mainly by sea and over Japan's few railroads, offered remarkable contrasts. Yokohama was a sleepy little fishing village until the late 1860s, when government officials selected it as one of the treaty ports in place of Kanagawa, hoping that its more remote location, off the main road between Tokyo and Kyoto, would limit foreign influence in the region. Instead, within a few years Yokohama became the busiest of the treaty ports and the first port of call for nearly all transpacific steamers. Because its growth stemmed almost entirely from foreign trade, the town came to seem more Western than Japanese, with its busy commercial district and substantial foreign residential quarter where Western-style architecture predominated. "It is hard to realize that we are in the land of the Mikado, so homelike do the houses appear," observed a member of one of Cook's tours. Western-style hotels went up quickly, turning Yokohama into a comfortable base of operations for visitors who wanted a taste of the exotic without giving up familiar comforts. One of them, naturally, was called the Grand Hotel. A visitor in the early 1880s described a meal in its dining room: "Fish, entrees, and joint were presented in due sequences, as though I were sitting in the Grand Hotel at Paris; while grouped on dishes were tins of Crosse & Blackwell's potted meat, and Keiller's Dundee marmalade and jam." After dinner, one could retire to a reading room stocked with newspapers from London, Paris, and New York.[13]

Just a few miles north of Yokohama, Tokyo was a city of well over a million people, where the presence of foreign businessmen and diplomats could have only minimal impact. Completion of a railroad between Yokohama and Tokyo in 1872 made it an easy day's excursion. Another popular day trip took visitors to Kamakura, capital of Japan in the thirteenth century and site of the Daibutsu, a giant bronze Buddha that stood over fifty feet high. Visits to Mount Fuji and to Nikko, famous for the tombs of the Tokugawa shoguns and for its beautiful setting in the foothills surrounded by forests and spectacular views of mountain peaks, gave travelers a taste of traditional Japanese life, as they had to travel by *kuruma* (also known as jinrikisha), the two-wheeled, human-drawn cart that was the ubiquitous form of transportation in Japan, staying overnight en route at local teahouses.[14]

Kobe, Osaka, and Kyoto, clustered about three hundred miles south of Yokohama and Tokyo, formed the second major focus of the typical tour. Travelers could reach Kobe and Osaka by sea or follow the highway known as the Tokaido between Tokyo and Kyoto. One of the country's few roads suitable for carriage travel, and noted for its scenic beauty, the Tokaido was familiar to many Western travelers through a series of prints made in the 1830s by the artist Ando Hiroshige, whose works were popular in Europe and the United States. By the 1880s, one could arrange to travel the length of the Tokaido by kuruma through a company that also maintained hotels at regular intervals along the route.[15]

Osaka's port was not ideal for large ships, so nearby Kobe became the major foreign port in the region and the base of operations for most tourists. Like Yokohama, Kobe quickly took on the trappings of a Western city. Rudyard Kipling, visiting in 1889, hated the "wide, naked streets between houses of sham stucco, with Corinthian pillars of wood, wooden verandahs and piazzas . . . keeping guard over raw green saplings miscalled shade trees." Indeed, he thought, "Kobe is hideously American in externals. Even I, who have only seen pictures of America, recognized at once that it was Portland, Maine." But Kipling enjoyed the misnamed "Oriental Hotel," with its French coffee—one of several luxury hotels catering to foreign visitors—and the local "Club," where tourists could fraternize with resident foreigners and join in a game of cricket, baseball, or lawn tennis.[16]

Kobe's appeal lay mostly in its convenience as a jumping-off point for excursions to Kyoto. An ancient city of great beauty, home to the imperial family, Kyoto combined a spectacular setting, innumerable temples and other historic sites, and a lively cultural life, ranging from theater to sumo wrestling. Some visitors labeled it the Paris of Japan, but in fact Kyoto was the closest most visitors would come to seeing traditional Japanese culture. Osaka, by contrast, was just another big city—flat and dull in appearance, too big and commercial to be charming, too thoroughly Japanese (despite its status as a treaty port) to be comfortable for Western tourists.[17]

Travelers curious about Japan beyond the capitals and treaty ports had to contend with difficult conditions, but were rewarded with lovely scenery and glimpses of a country still little known to outsiders. After obtaining a special passport from the Japanese government, visitors traveled by kuruma (or on foot in the more remote areas, with packhorses or porters carrying their luggage), and stayed in local inns. Murray's *Handbook for Japan* (first published in 1884) advised carrying all provisions and bedding, as well as specially made clothing. Loose, flannel pajama-style garments were best for walking, worn with Japanese sandals (ideal for fording streams), socks, and gaiters. The sandals had to be made to order—ready-made versions were not available in sizes large enough to fit European and American feet—and in quantity, as each pair would last only a day or two. Because laundry facilities were unavailable in the more remote regions, travelers were advised to send changes of clothing to several points along their route.[18]

The local inns varied widely in quality. Even the best seemed spartan and lacking in privacy to Western travelers; movable partitions made of wood and rice paper separated the rooms but did nothing to dampen sound, while furniture consisted solely of flea-ridden mats and futons spread along the floor. (Murray's guide noted that most inns frequented by foreigners could provide tables and chairs upon request.) Foreigners were objects of great curiosity in outlying areas, and Western visitors often complained of prying eyes spying on them through tears in the paper or gaps in the partitions. A young American traveler, C. D. Irwin, was amused at the curious stares and the servants popping into his "room" unbidden, but Isabella Bird, an experienced traveler who avoided standard itineraries, came close to turning back after two nights in noisy inns north of Nikko. Murray's guide advised travelers to carry insect powder and oiled paper to place between the mats and bedding, noting that camphor and carbolic acid would also be useful against "offensive odours" at "inferior" inns, while a portable filter would guard against contaminated water. Eventually, Japanese entrepreneurs built traditional-style inns with enough Western amenities to please tourists, who found native authenticity charming when leavened with the luxuries they had come to expect while traveling. "The Japanese hotels are very picturesque, and are constructed of European materials in Japanese style, the combination being most satisfactory," observed one tourist in the 1890s.[19]

Japanese food could be pleasing and even artful, if rarely tasty or filling, when served in the home of a merchant or government official in Yokohama or Tokyo, but out in the countryside, few Westerners could cope with a diet of rice and raw fish. Murray's guide recommended carrying easily portable provisions like dried meat, sausage, Chicago corned beef, tinned milk, biscuits, jam, cheese, bacon, tea, and sugar, which could be supplemented by fresh fish, fowl, and eggs available in the larger towns. Candlesticks, silverware, tumblers, a corkscrew, and a can opener would also come in handy. Isabella Bird left Tokyo armed with a traveling bed, folding chair, India-rubber bath, air pillow, sheets and blankets, candles, and plenty of food, but still found the going difficult. North of Nikko, she encountered scrawny packhorses, rocky, muddy trails, and impoverished people with tattered clothing, who seemed prematurely aged. Food was hard to come by, and everything seemed dirty. "Truly this is a new Japan to me," she wrote, "of which no books have given me any idea, and it is not fairyland."[20]

But "fairyland" was what Japan looked like to most tourists who stuck to the well-traveled sights. Not only were the Japanese people small by American and European standards, but everything about the country seemed small-scale and designed with exquisite delicacy. Describing a dinner in a Japanese home, a British traveler, E. A. Gordon, commented, "We feel as if we were in the nursery, playing at a make-believe dinner-party. Instead of breakable plates and dishes, lacquer trays, or boxes, of many forms are used; and the porcelain cups hold just three birdlike sips of tea or *sake*. Everything looks so pretty, so dainty, ranged in a circle on the floor.... When we rise we fear to stand up, lest we should smash the fairylike arrangement." The houses seemed like "doll-houses," the railroads narrow gauge, the roads narrow, and two-wheeled, human-powered jinrikishas substituted for bigger, clumsier carriages. "We cannot get over the idea that we are in a toy-land," Irwin wrote.[21]

Although many visitors found Japanese homes too spare and open for their tastes, they admired the simplicity of design, the high quality of workmanship, and especially the use of these simple spaces as a backdrop for displaying a few well-chosen works of art. Japanese prints and ceramics, among the earliest Asian exports to the United States and Europe, were widely admired, so visitors to Japan were likely to be familiar with the elements of Japanese style, and many purchased prints and other objects to take home. (Irwin observed that, while the Japanese made quantities of "bric-a-brac" and "curios" for foreigners "to load up their houses with, and dust and forget about," they were much too tasteful to clutter their own homes with it, preferring a more elegant, spare style.)[22] The Japanese love of beauty extended to the countryside as well; visitors noted with approval the carefully cultivated landscape, "all homelike, live-able, and pretty," according to Bird, "the country of an industrious people."[23]

The quiet, dignified demeanor of the Japanese people seemed to match their surroundings. They lived peacefully, despite a high population density, worked hard, and placed great value on family ties. In what must have been the highest compliment from an English-woman, Gordon remarked that there was "absolutely *no vulgarity* about these people." Children were as quiet and well-behaved as their elders—perhaps too much so, thought Isabella Bird, who characterized Japanese children as miniature adults, wearing pared-down versions of adult clothing and mingling freely in adult gatherings. A crying baby was a rare sight in Japan.[24]

The only jarring note to Western sensibilities was the Japanese custom of public baths, where both sexes mingled with no apparent concern about nudity. Some concluded from this that the Japanese had no concern for "decency" and that their women were "de-based" by such practices, noting also that it was the "common people" who frequented the public baths. The well-to-do were more likely to have their own baths at home. One English traveler was astonished to find Japanese men, women, and children rushing naked from their homes to stare at him as he passed by. Others, however, interpreted this lack of concern about nudity as evidence of "primitive" simplicity. Such sentiments were rare, however, and became less common toward the end of the nineteenth century, when the Japanese government banned mixed bathing in public.[25]

In fact, the Japanese people were quite remarkably Westernized, at least in the major cities and trading centers, by the time travel to Japan became popular; indeed, Japan appealed to American and European travelers precisely because it offered a taste of the "exotic East" in a setting that shared enough cultural similarities with Western societies to make tourists feel comfortable. Japan's rapid modernization in the 1870s and 1880s owed much to internal conditions, including substantial economic growth and the creation of a centralized government bureaucracy, which provided fertile ground for the adoption of Western-developed technology. In addition, Japanese officials made serious efforts to learn about the West, sending a delegation to travel abroad and observe foreign customs, permitting a limited number of students to study abroad, and introducing Western art and architecture to the curriculum of certain schools. As a consequence, Western tourists visiting Japan in the 1870s and later observed a rapidly growing, modernizing country and met people eager to learn more about the West, thus confirming the visitors' own sense of cultural superiority even while they marveled at the beauty and uniqueness of Japan.[26]

The contrast between traditional and modern could still be jarring, however, and many travelers expressed a decided preference for what they called the "real Japan." They objected especially to the hastily built foreign districts of the treaty ports, especially Yokohama; the Western-style government buildings in Tokyo and the increasing popularity of Western dress among the urban elite also drew adverse comment. "We thought it a piece of barbarism to discard the easy, graceful kimona for the stiff, ill-fitting European costume," Katherine Baxter remarked in 1895. "With all our superior civilization, we cannot teach them anything about dress, and why, with all the world to choose from, they should choose ours is inscrutable."[27] Railroads might be an improvement on jinrikishas, but trading a kimono for a Western suit was pointless.

The extent to which this blend of traditional and modern made Japan a popular destination becomes obvious in comparing travelers' reactions to China, typically the next stop on a round-the-world tour. The usual route took travelers to Hong Kong, where they could easily arrange an excursion to Canton. Some went also to Shanghai on their way to Hong Kong. Shanghai and Canton were major sea ports, but neither had taken on the trappings of Western culture and technology in anything like the manner of the Japanese ports. Both cities (apart from Shanghai's foreign residential quarter) appeared to be huge mazes of flimsy, wood-frame buildings jammed together along narrow streets no more than six or eight feet wide, accessible only on foot. The overwhelming impression was one of crowds, noise, dirt, and smells. The streets of Shanghai are "offensive and disgusting," Seward remarked. Irwin thought Canton an "enormous pig pen," with "an omnipresent, indescribable, *oriental smell,* proceeding, I suppose, from opium, bad tobacco, unwashed bodies, . . . and want of sewerage." Nearly every visitor made negative comparisons with Japan. The dirt, in particular, overwhelmed visitors to Shanghai and Canton after the impeccable neatness and cleanliness of Japan—the "utter difference between the filth of the Chinese junks and the spotless purity of the Japanese," as Gordon put it.[28]

The Chinese people struck Westerners as noisy, with loud, unpleasant voices, "like a hive of bees when swarming"; moreover, they remained far more hostile to foreigners than the Japanese. The Chinese, wrote Anna D'Almeida, an Englishwoman traveling in the early 1860s, "are surly, impertinent, independent, self-sufficient, in their manner towards foreigners," while the Japanese "have an innate politeness which is exceedingly pleasing, and address strangers in a respectful manner but rarely witnessed on the other side of the water." Irwin thought the Chinese "a conceited, self-satisfied people," who held the Japanese in contempt because they so readily adopted Western customs. Most offensive to American and European visitors, the Chinese obviously cared nothing for Western culture, looking down on European and American visitors, secure in their belief in their own superiority. As Seward put it, "All [Chinese] ways manifest a spirit of self-assertion and independence, if not a contemptuous one."[29]

*   *   *

VASTLY DIFFERENT from Japan in its landscape, climate, languages, and culture, India also had a much more complicated history of interaction with the West. French, British, Dutch, and Danish merchants established trading centers at several locations along the Indian coast during the seventeenth century. In contrast to Japan, the size and decentralized nature of the Indian subcontinent, which was in no sense a single "nation" like Japan, offered a more hospitable climate for foreign traders.

By the end of the seventeenth century, the British East India Company had well-established operations at Surat, north of Bombay on the west coast; Madras, on the southeastern coast; and Calcutta in the northeast, while French merchants maintained their major base at Pondicherry, south of Madras. For the most part, European merchants enjoyed the support of the leaders of the Mughal Empire in north India as well as the various regional rulers of the central and southern states. But by the middle of the eighteenth century, the political situation throughout India had become increasingly unstable, leading foreign companies to move toward gaining political control over the country. The British East India Company, which held a monopoly on British trade with India, defeated local rulers in the region around Calcutta and established a company-managed state with the backing of the British government in 1757. Over the next half century, the British gradually increased their influence. The decades-old rivalry with France in southern India came to a head as part of the broader British-French conflict during the late eighteenth and early nineteenth centuries with the result that the British forced the French out of India and unified the country under British rule in 1818. By the middle of the nineteenth century, Britain controlled the entire region encompassed by what are today the nations of India, Pakistan, Bangladesh, and Myanmar (Burma) and had begun to expand the scope of its rule to intervene in Indian affairs, encouraging Christian missionaries and legislating against traditional practices like *sati*.

In the second half of the nineteenth century British military and civil service officers and their families comprised the majority of foreign travelers on the subcontinent. Murray published guides to the various regions of India beginning in 1859 (the first of his handbooks to cover any Asian region) primarily to serve this group; the advice meted out made travel in India sound a great deal more like a mission of exploration than a pleasure trip. By the 1870s, however, India was attracting an increasing number of tourists, while significant progress on an extensive network of railways—built by the British to increase military and administrative efficiency—as well as construction of hotels in the major cities made travel across the subcontinent much less of an ordeal. The first major rail line across India, between Bombay and Calcutta, opened in 1870. Within three decades, the subcontinent boasted the most extensive rail network in Asia: forty thousand miles of track extending from Lahore in the north to Madras in the south. Good hotels were established in Agra, Delhi, and Calcutta beginning in the 1850s. The Great Eastern Hotel in Calcutta and the Great Western in Bombay, both opened around 1860, qualified as grand hotels by European standards.[30]

By the time Murray published the first comprehensive handbook for travel in India in 1891, its author could write that "a trip to India is no longer a formidable journey or one that requires very special preparation. The Englishman who undertakes it merely passes from one portion of the British Empire to another." English was widely spoken, even among servants, and it was no longer necessary to have special clothes made or carry tents and massive quantities of provisions. Even so, traveling in India was not likely to please those who expected a high standard of luxury and comfort. Cook compared Indian railways favorably to American trains, but others complained of slow schedules, dirty cars, long lines at ticket windows, and station platforms mobbed with Indians.[31]

Apart from the few first-class establishments in major cities, most hotels were barely acceptable by Western standards. C. D. Irwin complained that Indian hotel proprietors failed to understand the importance of providing fresh towels every day or seeing that napkins were distributed at each meal to the same people who had used them at previous meals. Many hotels were designed with bedrooms opening off a large central area that served as both parlor and dining room, offering minimal privacy to guests. Irwin and his traveling companions resorted to hanging makeshift curtains over their doors in Delhi, which had plain glass without any sort of covering.[32] Outside the major towns, travelers relied on what were known as "dak bungalows," cottages with bedrooms and cooking facilities built by the British at regular intervals along well-traveled routes. Even as late as the 1920s, travelers were advised to carry their own bedding, for it was not provided on trains or in any but the best hotels. Many also hired servants to handle tickets and baggage at railway stations and provide the kinds of services in hotels that one might, in Europe or the United States, expect from hotel staffs.

Travel to India was considerably simplified when Thomas Cook & Son expanded its activities on the subcontinent. India had been part of its annual round-the-world itinerary since Cook's first world tour in 1872, but in the 1880s the firm added an extensive program of tours between Britain and India and within India itself. Oddly enough, the impetus came from the Italian government, which, in 1880, offered Cook a commission on all passengers booked on steamers from Brindisi to India in hopes of encouraging more people to travel to India via the overland route through Italy, instead of taking steamers directly from Britain. This opportunity encouraged Cook to seek support from the British government to establish services in India, which he readily obtained, and to undertake a scouting trip to India in 1881, where he negotiated with Indian government and railway officials and arranged to open an office in Bombay. His plan was to encourage tourism in both directions, catering to Britons interested in the Empire as well as to wealthy Indians who wanted to visit Europe, and to organize itineraries within India for both British and Indian tourists. In a throwback to his early days, there were even attempts to organize low-cost, short-distance excursions for middle-class Indians. (The first took one hundred people on a four-day, 120-mile jaunt between Bombay and Poona.)[33]

By organizing annual escorted tours, arranging circular tickets for those who preferred to travel independently, and putting out a series of brochures and articles in the *Excursionist* advising potential travelers about when to travel (November through March, to avoid searing heat and monsoons) and what to expect (the trains were comfortable, and English widely spoken), Cook presented Indian travel as only slightly more complex than visiting France or Italy. The only serious problem, Cook admitted, was the sorry state of Indian hotels, "which need very considerable improvements to meet the tastes and requirements of British and American travellers," but, with typical optimism, he believed that the situation would improve with the expansion of tourism.[34]

In another typical move, when an international exposition was planned for Calcutta in 1883, Cook obtained a license from the Indian government to serve as sole agent for tours to the fair. The firm also opened an office in Calcutta that year. In 1885 they arranged tours to the Colonial and Indian Exhibition in London for thousands of people, ranging from British workers to Indian maharajahs. This was but a warm-up for the much more elaborate arrangements made two years later, when the British government contracted with Cook to transport British officials and Indian princes to each other's countries as part of Queen Victoria's Golden Jubilee celebration. After the official ceremonies, several of the maharajahs went on European tours—a complex business to organize, for they traveled with dozens (in some cases hundreds) of retainers and enormous quantities of baggage. (One maharajah included ten elephants and thirty-three tame tigers in his entourage.) The business proved lucrative, leading Cook to establish an Indian Princes Department in the 1890s.[35]

The firm also catered to Indians of more modest means. In 1885, the Indian government, seeking to curb abuses in the business of transporting Muslims making the annual pilgrimage to Mecca, contracted with Cook to organize passage from Bombay, the main departure point, to Jidda. One of the most unusual of the firm's business ventures, it lasted only a few years because of the complexities of organizing the massive annual exodus and competition from Indian entrepreneurs. Cooks' Indian business continued to focus on British travelers; by 1888, when the firm opened a new, larger office in Bombay, it was offering an extensive program of tours throughout the subcontinent. A brochure issued in 1914 advertising tours to India, Burma, and Ceylon boasted that "the picturesque Empire of the Moguls may now be visited as comfortably as the Continent of Europe."[36]

Whether arriving from the east, perhaps as a stop on an around-the-world tour, or from the west, the most common route from Britain, most visitors to India bracketed their tours with stops in Calcutta and Bombay, the two major seaports. As tourists invariably noted, India was a study in contrasts, and no place more so than Calcutta. The capital of British India until 1912 (when the capital was moved to Delhi), Calcutta combined splendid buildings and broad, tree-shaded streets with some of the most wretched slums in the country. In the European districts, British residents lived in magnificent houses with armies of servants and socialized with each other at their clubs or along the fashionable promenades. Wealthy Indians had their own separate neighborhoods with equally lavish homes, while most of the population lived in squalid mud huts with barely enough food to eat. For some, this contrast provided evidence of the superiority of Western "civilization" over Asian "barbarism." "One may walk broad streets with palatial buildings, European stores, and Christian churches on either hand, and suddenly, by deflecting from the main avenue, may find himself face to face with all the abominable arts and idolatries of heathenism," observed one American. Others, seeking the romantic East, were disappointed that Calcutta, although beautiful, seemed too familiar.[37]

At the other end of the journey, Bombay also appeared to be a modern, highly Europeanized city, although very different from Calcutta. Having developed as a major port only after the opening of the Suez Canal, Bombay owed its growth almost entirely to commerce rather than to the government bureaucracy that dominated the European community in Calcutta. No amount of modernization could strip the city of a certain exotic appeal, however, at least not for tourists who arrived with fixed expectations of "the Orient." Mark Twain, for example, who started his tour of India in Bombay, was not disappointed. The city was for him "a bewitching place, a bewildering place, an enchanting place," like something out of the Arabian Nights, with its luxuriant foliage and its "picturesque natives of both sexes" dressed in brilliant colors.[38]

The typical itinerary across India was quite similar to the one Ida Pfeiffer had followed, taking in Benares, Allahabad, Kanpur, Lucknow, Agra, and Delhi. Benares drew tourists as the holy city of the Hindus—"It is to the Hindu what Mecca is to the Muhammadan, or Jerusalem to the Jew," Irwin observed—and Agra as the site of the Taj Mahal, the most famous monument built by the Muslim rulers who had controlled northern India from the sixteenth through the late eighteenth centuries. (Mark Twain described Benares more irreverently as "just a big church, a religious hive, whose every cell is a temple, a shrine, or a mosque . . . a sort of Army and Navy Stores, theologically stocked.")[39]

The chief attraction of the other cities along the route, especially for the British, was their association with the Mutiny of 1857. The uprising began near Delhi when Indian troops, angered by changes in military policy that appeared to threaten their religious principles, revolted against their British officers and restored the former Mughal emperor. Their actions touched off similar outbreaks in other parts of northern India, especially in the region around Lucknow. The British administration, caught by surprise, was ill prepared to quash the rebellion, which dragged on for nearly a year with heavy casualties on both sides. For decades afterward, visitors to Delhi, Lucknow, and Kanpur toured the sites associated with the violence, among them the burned-out remains of the Residency at Lucknow, where European citizens and their Indian servants held out for months until relief troops arrived, and the cemetery and gardens at Kanpur, commemorating the deaths of four hundred British residents killed while attempting to escape the city by boat. The events of the Mutiny were particularly horrifying to the British because they appeared to be sudden, unprovoked acts of vicious hatred, in which civilians, including women and children, were killed simply because they were British. Blind to the simmering tensions fostered by decades of British rule, most British citizens perceived the Mutiny as a case of senseless, unjustified violence. For tourists in India, American as well as British, the Mutiny was still fresh in the collective memory even as late as the early twentieth century, dominating their perceptions of the country. Even the often cynical and irreverent Mark Twain was deeply moved by his experiences visiting Kanpur and Lucknow, and recounted the events of the Mutiny at some length, emphasizing the bravery of the British men and women who resisted the uprising. Crushing the Mutiny, he believed, was the "greatest chapter" in British military history.[40]

What sparked the most comment among visitors to India, however—even more than the Mutiny and the political issues surrounding it—was the Hindu religion. Unlike Japan, where Buddhist shrines were major attractions but religious faith seemed to exercise little hold over the people, in India Hinduism was a constant presence. Travelers observed devout Indians bathing in the sacred waters of the Ganges at Benares, encountered mendicant holy men, witnessed religious festivals, and came away from it all confused and sometimes hostile to what seemed to many an elaborate form of paganism. With its multiple gods and goddesses and its varied traditions, Hinduism was a difficult faith to understand for people rooted in a monotheistic religion based on the authority of a single written text. ("India has 2,000,000 gods and worships them all," quipped Mark Twain.) That some of the deities were envisioned as animals (like Hanuman, the monkey god, and Ganesh, the elephant) and others were overtly evil or violent (like Kali, the warlike goddess) did not help. "They even venerate the most preposterous stories detailed in the traditions of their bards," fumed one Englishman, unable to comprehend that the two great ancient Indian epics, the *Ramayana* and the *Mahabharata,* had deep religious significance as well as entertainment value for Indians.[41]

Thomas Cook, who spent much of his time in India visiting Christian missionaries, predictably castigated Hinduism as "idolatrous filth and obscenity, combining bull, peacock, monkey, and other nameless objects of worship." In Benares, he wrote, "there are said to be 5,000 Hindoo temples and shrines in the city; but one in a thousand, with the bulls and monkeys, were quite as many as we cared to see." Another visitor thought Hinduism the embodiment of "ignorance and fanaticism." Belief in reincarnation and the apparently passive acceptance of caste distinctions led some visitors to assume that Hindus had no incentive to lead moral lives, while their lively, colorful religious festivals reinforced the notion that this was an immoral "religion." Holi, a boisterous holiday featuring processions, street dancing, bonfires, and a tradition of throwing orange powder on one's fellow celebrants, seemed especially bizarre. "It is the most indecent of all the Hindu festivals and about the most popular," observed Robert Palmer, an Englishman traveling around the turn of the century. "I could hear the processions from my rooms, singing songs to Shiva, whose taste is certainly not Puritan. They also fling red paint over each other, and produce a disgusting mess." Christian women couldn't venture forth during the festival, he claimed, because "the whole Hindu population adopts for the time being the ethics of Lot's fellow-citizens." In contrast, Palmer applauded the evident devotion of pilgrims in Benares. They "really meant business," he remarked. "It was all a jumble, but a reverent jumble."[42]

If it was a short step for people like Palmer and Cook to seize upon every story they heard about loose morals and attribute it to the "idolatry" and "heathenism" of the Hindu faith, others, like Sidney and Beatrice Webb, romanticized Hindus as "spiritual" and otherworldly, even while feeling troubled by the moral implications of a faith that seemed to emphasize ritual observance over individual action as the path to salvation. Several travelers took an interest in two Hindu reform movements that emphasized a unified concept of "god," attacking the worship of images representing the multiple Hindu gods and the more extreme manifestations of caste while promoting reason and education. The Brahmo Samaj (Divine Society), founded in 1828 by Ram Mohan Roy, a Bengali intellectual well versed in the teachings of Christianity, Islam, and Buddhism as well as Hinduism, aimed to "purify" the faith by going back to first principles and incorporating certain features of Western thought. Although it resembled the Brahmo Samaj in its social concerns, the Arya Samaj (Society of Aryans), established in 1875, rejected all Western influences, arguing for a return to the earliest Hindu texts as the authentic word of God. Because these movements deemphasized the plurality of deities and rejected such traditional practices as rigid adherence to caste, early marriage, and the near-ostracization of widows, Westerners applauded them, even though the members of the Arya Samaj, in their insistence on returning to ancient Indian ideals, also rejected the concept of British rule.[43]

Travelers linked Hinduism and caste, viewing caste as a rigid social system in which everyone was assigned a specific place in the social and occupational hierarchy. In fact, caste was never so immutable as British officials and other Western observers believed, but the notion of a fixed social system fit well with what they saw as passive, otherworldly qualities in the Hindu religion. It also enabled some observers to pronounce Indians unfit for democracy—and, by implication, for self-rule. Few travelers questioned the British rule of India. If they thought about it at all, they accepted it as another example of a superior civilization ruling an inferior one. Seward found it remarkable that a nation as populous as India was ruled by the much smaller Britain, but then observed that this was often the case, for "weak and ignorant tribes and nations are generally found dependent on stronger and more enlightened ones."[44]

Between Delhi and Bombay, travelers passed through states controlled by Indian princes with only the most general oversight by the British. The Webbs, whose tour of India in 1912 was devoted primarily to observing the country's political and social systems, thought them well managed. They were especially impressed by the efforts of the woman who ruled Bhopal to educate women and modify the strict rules of *parda* (purdah), the seclusion of women. In both Bhopal and Gwalior, a small state south of Agra, paved streets and spacious houses stood in marked contrast to the urban slums of British India, "all telling of the Indians in possession of their own country, making for a civilised India 'without the English.'" Of course, they added, the Indian officials running these states had been educated in Britain or recruited from the ranks of the British-controlled administration in India; but there was no indication of any inherent corruption among them, nor any evidence of the conflict between Hindu and Muslim that was so common in the British-controlled regions. Other Westerners were more critical of the princely states, despite evidence that they were well governed, pointing to the persistence of traditional customs and a reluctance to adopt "modern" ways.[45]

It was the exceptional traveler who ventured any criticism of the Western presence in Asia—as Ida Pfeiffer did, remarking that missionaries and government officials lived far more lavishly in India than they would have at home—or recognized that Asian cultures had been producing highly sophisticated art forms for centuries—as the Webbs did after viewing the Taj Mahal and other monuments at Agra. Everyone who visited Agra stood in wonder before the Taj Mahal, but few observed as they did that "250 years ago, these peo-

ple were capable of conceiving and executing work of quality unsurpassed by anything of any race in the world."[46]

THE AUTHOR OF Murray's guide to India may have exaggerated
when he wrote that traveling in India was easy because it was simply
a matter of going from one part of the British Empire to another,
but in fact, tourists who ventured beyond the boundaries of Europe
and the United States before World War I confined themselves
mainly to those places where Western influence, if not outright rule,
provided some measure of familiarity and comfort. Travelers en
route from Japan and coastal China to India, for example, typically
stopped at Singapore, center of British influence in southeast Asia.
A remarkably diverse city, with substantial Malay, Chinese, and European populations, Singapore evoked conflicting reactions. Like
Calcutta, it had a large European district with elegant houses, imposing public buildings, lovely gardens, and luxury hotels—the famous Raffles opened in 1877—which impressed visitors as beautiful
but rather ordinary. The older sections of the city were more suitably
exotic but also crowded and dirty.[47]

Most tourists also stopped briefly at Point de Galle on the southern coast of Ceylon. For nineteenth-century travelers, Ceylon was
the stuff of legend, often thought to be the original Garden of Eden
and by others the land of Ophir, where King Solomon kept his gold
and jewels. As a practical matter, because of its location off the
southern tip of India, Ceylon became a transit point for ships headed
to and from Calcutta, Bombay, Hong Kong, and Australia. Taking
advantage of its accessibility and tropical beauty, enterprising businessmen built luxury hotels with all the amenities of European resorts, where sea-weary travelers could relax for a few days, spending
languid hours touring cinnamon groves and gardens brilliant in their
displays of bougainvillea, hibiscus, gardenias, and every other imaginable kind of tropical flower. It was "utterly Oriental; also utterly
tropical," in the words of Mark Twain, who added that "to one's
unreasoning spiritual sense the two things belong together." Ceylon
met all the requirements of a tropical paradise: luxuriant foliage, a
gentle climate ("that swoon in the air," as Twain put it), a certain

air of mystery, exotic natives in their brilliantly colored "costumes."
Indeed, the Sinhalese people could well have been the perfect noble
savages, dark-skinned but tall with European-style features. Irwin
remarked that they would look exactly like "us" if not for their skin
color and the men's habit of wearing their hair long, while another
visitor thought them "among the comeliest and handsomest of man-
kind . . . harmonizing quite exquisitely with the tropical-hued foliage,
birds, and butterflies."[48]

Fewer tourists visited French Indochina, but those who did encountered another version of European rule grafted onto an ancient
Asian civilization. Visitors to Saigon invariably remarked about how
much it resembled a French city; Seward thought the European settlement there differed from others he had seen only in being French
rather than British. Somerset Maugham remarked that Saigon has
"all the air of a little provincial town in the South of France," with
its wide streets, its tree-lined quay along the river, its opera house,
and its "large, dirty, and pretentious" hotel where French merchants
and bureaucrats gathered for their aperitifs each afternoon "and for
a moment forget that they are not in France."

Tourists were much less likely to visit Bangkok, capital of the
independent kingdom of Siam, which did not have a large European
population or extensive trade ties with Europe. As late as the mid-
1920s, the European population numbered only about one thousand
(at a time when Saigon, one of the smaller colonial capitals, had a
European population four times that size). In 1930, Maugham left
Bangkok on a dirty, decrepit little steamer infested with cockroaches,
which he shared with a small set of eccentric travel companions,
including two French merchants, a French government official and
his wife, a Belgian army officer, an Italian tenor, and an American
circus proprietor.[49]

By the 1890s Cooks' around-the-world itineraries included Australia and New Zealand; in 1894, the firm offered its first tour to
South Africa, another outpost of the Empire. But most of Asia, Africa, and Latin America remained terra incognita to pleasure travelers, despite enormous public interest in the exploration of these
regions—Africa in particular—and an increasing number of articles

in popular magazines about travel to remote, relatively inaccessible corners of the world.[50]

This situation began to change somewhat in the first decade of the twentieth century with the completion of the trans-Siberian railroad, as well as other lines in China, Manchuria, and Korea. In 1899, Cooks arranged for a small group to travel on the partially completed trans-Siberian railroad from St. Petersburg to Vladivostok. In 1909— a year after making travel history by conducting the first group of Japanese tourists on a trip around the world—the firm launched tours following what it called "the new way around the world," across the Pacific to Japan, Korea, the Philippines, and China. After stops in Hong Kong, Canton, and Shanghai, the tour went by steamer up the Yangtze River to Hankow and then by train to Peking (Beijing) and Harbin, where they boarded the trans-Siberian railroad to Moscow. Cook & Son (by this time maintaining offices in Hong Kong and Yokohama) also promoted separate tours to East Asia, starting and ending in San Francisco. For the well-traveled looking for new diversions, for "picturesque novelty and variety of interest," nothing could equal China and Japan, Cooks claimed, for "the romance and charm of travel among primitive, little-known peoples, the wonderful remains of barbaric splendours of the historic past, and present scenes and modes of life full of striking contrasts."[51]

CHAPTER 10

SELLING

THE

AMERICAN WEST

Wᴴᴇɴ Rᴜᴅʏᴀʀᴅ Kɪᴘʟɪɴɢ, the British writer who spent
most of his life in India, decided to return to England for a
visit in 1889, he chose to travel east, to Burma, Singapore, China,
Japan, and the United States, instead of taking the more usual route
west via steamer across the Indian Ocean and the Mediterranean.
Feeling compelled to explain why he chose the longer and less commonly traveled route, with tongue in cheek Kipling described an
encounter with a British tourist in India, who "discussed India with
the unbridled arrogance of five weeks on a Cook's ticket. He was
from England and had dropped his manners in the Suez Canal."
The tourist and his ilk felt free to analyze India on the basis of
superficial acquaintance, contradicting the judgments of those who
had lived there for years. It was time to turn the tables, Kipling
joked, "to avenge India upon nothing less than three-quarters of the
world," by becoming one of the hated "globe-trotters" himself,
"with a helmet and deck-shoes," making uninformed pronounce-

ments as he traveled "toward the rising sun till I reached the heart of the world and once more smelt London asphalt."[1]

Armed with his own set of Cook's tickets, Kipling visited the Asian ports that made up the typical round-the-world itinerary, crossed the Pacific, and embarked upon a leisurely tour across the United States. He was astonished by San Francisco—"a mad city," he wrote, "inhabited for the most part by perfectly insane people whose women are of a remarkable beauty"—where the rough-and-tumble informality of a frontier outpost jostled uneasily with the social pretensions of a growing metropolis. In the one-thousand-room Palace Hotel, reputed to be one of the largest and most luxurious in the United States, an indifferent desk clerk picked his teeth and men dressed in frock coats and top hats spat tobacco juice in the vast and elegantly appointed reception room. A single letter of introduction yielded several dinner invitations and a temporary membership in the elite Bohemian Club. Kipling marveled at the spectacle of well-dressed men and women strolling along streets lined with expensive shops while "talking something that was not very different from English," at the cramped, dingy dwellings in Chinatown, at the steep, sandy hills and the cable cars that seemed to move vertically as easily as horizontally.[2]

From San Francisco, Kipling traveled by train north to Portland (where he indulged his passion for fishing), Seattle, Vancouver, and Victoria before doubling back via ship to Tacoma, terminus of the Northern Pacific Railroad. He chose the Northern Pacific line, which passed through Idaho, Montana, North Dakota, Minnesota, and Wisconsin en route to Chicago because it offered easier access to Yellowstone than the more direct Central Pacific/Union Pacific route. Established as the first national park in 1869 and heavily promoted as a tourist attraction by the Northern Pacific Railroad, Yellowstone, with its remarkable mix of mountains and geysers, had become one of the West's most popular destinations.

Guidebook writers called Yellowstone "Wonderland," but as Kipling noted, "wonderland" started long before the train came within striking distance of the park. His journey opened with the conductor shoving a man who refused to pay his fare through one

of the train's plate-glass windows and continued with the easy ca-
maraderie of people thrown together on a long trip. Crossing the
deserts of eastern Washington and Idaho—a region more desolate
than anything he had seen in India, Kipling thought—passengers
traded stories, mostly about the exploits of gunfighters in the Old
West, told with a mixture of admiration and nostalgia. Kipling reacted to this taste of American folklore with horror. These were not
war stories, he explained to his readers, nor cases of self-defense, but
drunken brawls, pure and simple. He found the Americans' comments about Indians, another staple of western storytelling, equally
appalling. Occasionally the train would stop at a station where a few
Indians had gathered—usually impoverished, pathetic-looking crea-
tures wrapped in ragged blankets. Invariably these encounters elic-
ited comments about the "heathen" and opinions favoring their
extermination as soon as possible. Even more offensive to Kipling
were those who asked him how long he thought it would be before
the British managed to eliminate the Indians from India.[3]

The Yellowstone excursion got off to an inauspicious start. A spur
line carried Yellowstone-bound passengers from the main Northern
Pacific line south to a small town near the park boundary, where
they boarded stagecoaches for Mammoth Hot Springs, one of the
park's major attractions. Once on the stagecoach, Kipling found himself in the midst of a loud, boisterous crowd, described by the driver
as one of "Rayment's tourist parties." "Rayment" referred to Raymond & Whitcomb, the Boston-based travel agency that dominated
the business of organized western tours. Kipling did his best to dis-
sociate himself from what he considered a vulgar crowd. "I do not
know Mister Rayment," he told the stage driver. "I belong to T.
Cook and Son." The Raymond group, in Kipling's estimation, did
not speak well for the quality of American travelers. "A brake-load
of Cook's Continental tourists trapezing through Paris . . . are angels
of light compared to the Rayment trippers," he wrote. "It is not the
ghastly vulgarity, the oozing, rampant Bessemer-steel self-sufficiency
and ignorance of the men that revolts me, so much as the display of
these same qualities in the women-folk." The next day, Kipling
shared a carriage with a couple from Chicago who viewed every

geyser and bubbling pool as a sign of hell. But if the company was often bizarre, the wonders of Yellowstone did not disappoint; and, in the time-honored tradition of travel writers, Kipling remarked that the scenery defied description—hence his refuge in telling tales about his fellow tourists, among them the well-read and charming young woman from New Hampshire who might have been a character from one of Henry James's novels and the stuffed-shirt Englishman traveling with his valet, who announced to Kipling that one couldn't be too careful about talking to strangers in these parts.[4]

Rather than continuing east on the Northern Pacific, Kipling traveled south to Salt Lake City and then through Colorado to pick up the Union Pacific line across the heart of the country. The narrow-gauge railroad from Livingston, Montana, to Salt Lake was a low point of the journey. "The run between Delhi and Ahmedabad on a May day would have been bliss compared to this torture," he wrote after enduring the dry, dusty desert landscape while listening to the conductor tell more stories of the Old West, this time about Indian atrocities. In Salt Lake City, Kipling found himself alternately fascinated by the residents' enterprise in building a prosperous, garden-like city out of the desert and appalled by their unorthodox religious beliefs. The Mormon women appeared tired and unattractive to him (a common reaction), their tastes in both dress and home decoration several decades out of date. Only one impressed him: a spirited Englishwoman who voiced her resentment at seeing her adopted city and its residents turned into a tourist attraction.[5]

After a detour through Colorado's spectacular landscape, Kipling boarded the Union Pacific at Cheyenne for the long, dull journey across the plains to Omaha, terminus for the UP's transcontinental line, and then on to Chicago and across the eastern third of the country, where the most memorable event of his journey was not gazing at Niagara Falls or sailing up the Hudson, neither of which rated so much as a mention in his book, but a visit to Elmira, New York—home of Mark Twain, one of Kipling's heroes.

Mark Twain's own round-the-world journey was nearly a decade in the future when he and Kipling met, but already he had a reputation as a globetrotter. After publishing a collection of sketches

drawn from his years in California, Twain had established his reputation with *The Innocents Abroad,* about his tour of Europe and
the Middle East; for his third book, *Roughing It,* he once again drew
upon his experiences as a traveler.[6] Like his earlier book, *Roughing
It* was a loosely fictionalized account, in this case of his journey
across the United States from Missouri to Nevada in 1861 in company with his brother Orion, who was about to take up a post as
secretary to the governor of the Nevada Territory. Kipling (whose
admiration for Twain's travel writing is obvious in his own attempts
to imitate it) and Twain covered much the same ground in the western United States, but with some remarkable differences that demonstrated how much travel there had changed in less than two
decades.

Twain and his brother rode in stagecoaches operated by the Overland Mail Company, the fastest form of transportation across the
western states in the prerailroad era. Charged primarily with carrying the mails, these coaches also accommodated a few passengers,
but with little attention to comfort. They operated around the clock,
stopping every ten to fifteen miles to change horses, a task that could
be accomplished in four minutes or less, and taking on a new driver
every fifty to one hundred miles. The stations were simple adobe
huts with sod roofs—"the first time we had ever seen a man's front
yard on top of his house," Twain quipped—dirt floors, holes cut in
the sod for windows, and minimal furniture. Every other post was
equipped to serve simple meals, but the quality of the food was dis-
mal. Stale bread, rancid bacon, and a beverage so revolting Twain
couldn't bring himself to drink it made a typical breakfast. Always
the emphasis was on speed, getting coach, horses, and passengers on
their way in the least possible time. At night, passengers rolled up in
blankets and slept as best they could while the coach jolted along
rough dirt roads. In this fashion, the mail coaches covered the distance between the Mississippi River and San Francisco in fifteen to
eighteen days, an impressive performance compared with the weeks
it took western settlers in wagon trains to cover the same distance.[7]
Once the transcontinental railroad was completed, however, the
same journey took just four days. As Twain himself noted, by the

time *Roughing It* was published in 1872, the style of travel he described was nearly obsolete.

PERHAPS NO OTHER event in modern history made quite such a sudden, dramatic difference in the speed and comfort of travel as did the transcontinental railroad, completed in May 1869 when the Union Pacific and Central Pacific joined their lines at Promontory, Utah. The railroad itself was not enough to draw travelers west, however, despite popular interest in the region. Crossing the United States cost as much as crossing the Atlantic in the 1870s, and touring the Far West, a journey most nineteenth-century Americans were likely to make only once, required the same investment of time that one might devote to a European tour.[8] In addition, the West offered few of the amenities that wealthy travelers took for granted. Readers may have enjoyed stories about "roughing it," but they were less eager to try it for themselves, except perhaps for a little taste of camp life, preferably in a scenic spot. From the beginning, railroad companies realized the importance of providing comfortable accommodations en route—Pullman Palace cars were standard—but once passengers were off the train, luxuries ended. First-class hotels were nonexistent. Many of the most interesting sights could be reached only by stagecoach or horseback. And there was little in the way of printed advice.

By the end of the 1870s, however, this situation changed dramatically as a host of entrepreneurs began to develop, package, and promote the West. Selling the West to tourists was only part of a massive effort to promote the western half of the United States—one that involved local newspapers and chambers of commerce, land speculators and government officials, as well as railroads in a campaign to encourage investment and settlement in the western states—but it proved to be a critical means of building awareness of the West in the population centers of the East. It was also a remarkable example of how scenic beauty, popular attitudes, transportation improvements, and clever promotion came together to transform a sparsely settled frontier into a mecca for tourists. Led by the railroad companies and aided by a host of independent entrepreneurs and self-appointed boosters, western promoters built luxury hotels, produced guidebooks, and organized package tours. Their success was obvious from the numbers. Nearly 30,000 people traveled from Omaha to San Francisco in 1871, rising to 75,000 by 1875 and about 100,000 by the end of the century.[9]

Western travel promoters seized upon the region's spectacular scenery as their primary strategy in persuading Americans to travel west. Samuel Bowles, a Massachusetts newspaper editor who toured the West twice in the 1860s, led the way in claiming that western scenery was at least the equal of Europe's. Soon after his second trip, Bowles wrote a book titled *The Switzerland of America,* a label that stuck and was endlessly repeated. The Colorado Rockies were "first cousins to the Alps," he wrote, and the view from Gray's Peak one of the three or four natural wonders of the world (Niagara Falls being one of the others). "No Swiss mountain view carries such majestic sweep of distance, such sublime combination of height and breadth and depth; such uplifting into the presence of God; such dwarfing of the moral sense, such welcome to the immortal thought." It seemed remarkable to Bowles that this region, all but inaccessible and unknown twenty years earlier, was now only a two-week journey from the East Coast. "When the Pacific Railroad is done," he predicted, "our Switzerland will be at our very doors."[10] Bowles followed *Switzerland* with several other books, repackaging the same basic material in slightly different ways, always mixing descriptive information and travel advice with a heavy dose of patriotism. His message was quite simple: The American West offered scenery even more magnificent than the best Europe had to offer; Americans owed it to themselves and their country to see it; and with the completion of the railroad, they no longer had any excuse for crossing the Atlantic in preference to crossing the Great Plains.[11]

In some respects, Bowles and the other western promoters were following the example of early-nineteenth-century writers like Cooper and Irving, who had found in the eastern American landscape scenery to match that of Europe; but the earlier writers' arguments had been mainly rhetorical as few Americans had actually visited Europe before the middle of the nineteenth century. By the 1870s, however, European travel had become increasingly common, and late-nineteenth-century travel writers who juxtaposed American and European scenery did so in a far more literal way. Seeking to persuade Americans to see their own country, they could think of no better way to accomplish this aim than to compare America to Europe. Facile comparisons became a staple among travel writers. If Colorado was the American Switzerland, then California was the American Italy; Pikes Peak was as impressive as Mont Blanc; Monterey was as beautiful as Naples. Bowles, whose enthusiasm often got the better of his accuracy, claimed for California glaciers larger than any in Switzerland, volcanic eruptions that had changed the face of the continent, a hundred mountains over 13,000 feet high, and a waterfall fifteen times higher than Niagara.[12]

Other writers, not content to let description of western wonders speak for itself, took Americans to task for traveling to Europe when their own country offered attractions at least as spectacular. Charles Nordhoff, author of one of the most popular guidebooks to California, observed, "There have been Americans who saw Rome before they saw Niagara; and for one who has visited the Yosemite, a hundred will tell you about the Alps, and a thousand about Paris. Now, I have no objection to Europe; but I would like to induce Americans, when they contemplate a journey for health, pleasure, or instruction, or all three, to think also of their own country, and particularly of California"—which, as he went on to argue, offered the brilliant skies and balmy climate of the tropics without the "enervating atmosphere," disease, "semi-barbarous habits of the people," or the "lawless state of society" found in many tropical countries. Yet another writer claimed that a journey to California was far more satisfying than one to Europe (although no less expensive, he admitted) because it was more beautiful and less foreign. In California, one could enjoy spectacular landscapes without having to cope with unfamiliar customs and languages.[13]

Recognizing the potential value of visual images in advertising a landscape that was all but unknown to most Americans, officials of the Union Pacific and Central Pacific companies took advantage of the relatively new medium of photography to publicize their soon-to-be-completed transcontinental line. In 1868, the companies hired two men to document the construction of the railroad and the scenery along its route: the photographer Andrew Joseph Russell and Ferdinand V. Hayden, head of the U.S. Geological Survey and explorer of the Yellowstone region, whose task was to write a text about the Rocky Mountain region to accompany Russell's photographs. The resulting book, *Sun Pictures of Rocky Mountain Scenery,* was organized in the form of a journey on the railroad from Cheyenne to Salt Lake City. A broader selection of Russell's photographs, covering the entire Union Pacific route, was published both as a series of stereographs (an early type of transparency, viewed with a simple handheld device) and as a book titled *The Great West Illustrated.*[14]

Shortly after the transcontinental line opened, the Union and Central Pacific lines organized a trip from Omaha to San Francisco for passenger and freight agents from several U.S. and Canadian railroads, and then sponsored publication of a book written by one of them. Providing free passes to writers, artists, and photographers, as well as to representatives from the travel industry, was a common strategy. Some years after passenger traffic was well established, the UP created a "literary bureau" to prepare promotional books and pamphlets, an innovation that was widely copied. Eventually all the major railroads created passenger departments, which produced reams of promotional literature, ranging from timetables and brief descriptions of particular routes to detailed guidebooks.[15]

Promoting the West by praising its scenic beauty had one major drawback, however—the hundreds of miles of flat, treeless plains between the Missouri River and the "American Switzerland." While some writers urged travelers to stop off for a day or two in the great American heartland to familiarize themselves with a region that was important for its agricultural production, the notion of sightseeing in Nebraska never caught on. Instead, passengers remained cocooned in their comfortably appointed Pullman cars, emerging only to take meals and stretch their legs at station stops, until they reached the Rockies. The middle section of the country became little more than an obstacle to be crossed, much as one endured the Atlantic passage to get to Europe. Early transcontinental passengers were quick to draw the analogy of a European voyage. The stations at Chicago or Omaha became the quay, the plains were the equivalent of the sea, the rolling motion of the train was like the roll of a ship.[16]

With its long days spent confined to a train, transcontinental rail travel inspired a new kind of guidebook, one that provided a blow-by-blow description of what passengers could expect to see from the train, supplemented by background information about the towns and regions through which they passed. The Union Pacific/Central Pacific line was barely completed when the first of these guides appeared: *The Great Transcontinental Railway Guide,* written and published by George A. Crofutt, a Denver businessman and former newspaper editor. Originally from Connecticut, Crofutt followed the gold rush to Pikes Peak in 1860 and eventually established himself in the long-haul freight business. He was among those in the crowd at Promontory, Utah, when the final spike was driven to complete the transcontinental railroad, a moment he later recalled as one of the most thrilling in his life. Even before then, Crofutt had conceived his plan for a guide to the sights along the railroad line. Joining forces with H. Wallace Atwell, a San Francisco newspaperman better known as "Bill Dadd, the Scribe," he began work on his guide as soon as the tracks were completed. By the end of 1869, their book was available for sale in bookstores, newsstands, railway stations, and on the trains themselves. It was an instant success. New editions appeared twice annually throughout the 1870s, selling over 350,000 copies during the course of the decade. Crofutt also claimed credit for coining the term "transcontinental."[17]

Crofutt had many imitators, with at least twenty-five other guides published during the 1870s. Some were outright copies, while others were produced by established companies extending their business into new markets, including *Appleton's Hand-Book of American Travel: Western Tour,* part of Appleton's series of American travel guidebooks, and Rand McNally's *Western Railway Guide.* Crofutt's most serious competition came from *The Pacific Tourist: Williams' Illustrated Trans-Continental Guide to Travel,* compiled by Henry T. Williams in 1876 and reissued in many editions through the end of the century. Williams's book, although following a format similar

to Crofutt's, was more comprehensive and included many more illustrations.[18]

In addition, the UP's publicity department issued its own guides,
including a pamphlet titled *Scenes from the Car Windows on the
World's Pictorial Line,* which quite literally assumed that passengers
would be doing their sightseeing from their train compartments, and
a series of more comprehensive books, informative rather than
overtly promotional in tone, about the various states through which
the railroad passed. In later years, other transcontinental lines followed suit, issuing promotional brochures like the Great Northern's
From the Car Windows, the Southern Pacific's *Wayside Notes,* and
the Santa Fe's *New Guide to the Pacific Coast: Santa Fe Route* and
US West, a narrative description of a tour along the Santa Fe's route.
Like the UP's guides to western states, *US West* attempted to appear
objective despite its railroad sponsorship, opening with a disclaimer:
"This book is wholly devoted to a description of Western scenes,
and nothing in the nature of a railroad advertisement has been admitted." Nevertheless, the author notes, readers inspired to visit the
scenes described in the book are "respectfully requested" to consult
a representative of the Santa Fe line.[19]

In the early years of transcontinental rail travel, promoting the
railroad by touting the scenic beauty of the West had a second drawback in addition to the long stretches of barren territory: The Union
Pacific/Central Pacific line passed north of the "American Switzerland," crossing Wyoming instead. Not until it reached the Sierra
Nevada were travelers treated to the kind of breathtaking mountain
scenery that could be called an American version of the Alps. Not
surprisingly, regional railroad companies and local businessmen were
quick to see the potential for developing spur lines to the most
sought-after scenic spots as well as comfortable accommodations to
lure wealthy travelers accustomed to the luxury resorts of Europe
and the eastern United States.

Within a year after the UP/CP line opened, the Denver Pacific
Railroad completed a link from Cheyenne to Denver. At about the
same time, William Jackson Palmer, a Civil War general turned businessman, established the Denver & Rio Grande Railway with the
intention of building a line from Denver to El Paso, possibly contin-

uing into Mexico. In 1871, when tracks were laid as far as Colorado Springs, a newly planned town near Pikes Peak, Palmer formed the Colorado Springs Company to promote the region as a luxury resort. In addition to capitalizing on the area's spectacular scenery, he sought to entice visitors by advertising the state's healthy climate and playing to Americans' interest in European culture. He brought physicians to Colorado to testify to the value of its clear, dry mountain air for invalids; one even proclaimed the climate superior to Davos, the Swiss resort that had made its reputation as a refuge for consumptives. Recognizing Americans' fascination with British culture, Palmer took to describing Colorado Springs as "little London." He landscaped the town with trees and English-style gardens, laid out sites for "villas," and encouraged an English style of architecture in the early homes. In an effort to add a note of authenticity, he cultivated prominent Britons as investors and visitors, and hired an Englishman to edit the town paper, which emphasized gossip about Europe's royal families over local and national news. Palmer also purchased land around the mineral springs at nearby Manitou and opened a luxury hotel there in 1872. Eight years after Palmer began his project, *The Pacific Tourist* called it the "Saratoga of the Far West," noting that the resort boasted several elegant hotels and a year-round population of five thousand. Not all travelers agreed; one observed that "one thinks of S. as a city of magnificent hotels and splendid elm-shaded sts. of M— as a city of small catch-penny shops—and donkeys. Manitou and mules!"[20]

In California—along with Colorado the primary attraction of the transcontinental journey—businessmen seeking to promote tourism looked to the area south of San Francisco, where claims for California as the "Italy of America" might actually be sustained. (Complaints about summer fog in San Francisco were a familiar refrain among travel writers.) In the mid-1870s, the Southern Pacific Railroad began constructing a line from Oakland to San Jose and on through the Central Valley to Los Angeles. The SP then formed a subsidiary company, the Pacific Improvement Company, which bought thousands of acres on the Monterey Peninsula with the intention of building a luxury resort, to be accessible via a spur rail line from San Jose to the coast. The Del Monte Hotel, completed in

1881, quickly became the premier watering place in the Far West, rivaling even the most luxurious of the Colorado establishments.[21]

Travel agents did their part in promoting western travel by packaging rail tickets, hotel accommodations, and excursions to scenic areas—many of them still accessible only by stagecoach or horseback. Thomas Cook & Son, fresh from a highly successful showing at the Centennial Exposition in Philadelphia, offered a conducted tour to California in 1876, the first of an annual series.[22] Cook & Son encountered stiff competition, however, from the Boston-based travel agency Raymond & Whitcomb. Founded in 1879, R&W offered its first western tour in 1881, a forty-four-day journey across the continent following what was by then the standard western itinerary: Chicago, Omaha, Cheyenne, a detour through Colorado, back to Cheyenne and west to Ogden, Utah, another detour south to Salt Lake City, and finally on to San Francisco and Monterey. Overnight stops were planned in Chicago, Denver, Manitou, and Salt Lake City to break up the long journey and allow time for sightseeing, including a carriage ride to the Garden of the Gods near Manitou and an optional twelve-mile horseback ride to the summit of Pikes Peak. In Colorado, tourists would visit Royal Gorge, Pueblo, and Canon City, and ride on the narrow-gauge railroad to the gold mines at Black Hawk and Central City—"one of the most remarkable and picturesque railway routes in the world." A single price of $400 covered all transportation, hotels, meals, and excursions. Train tickets were valid for ninety days, so travelers could extend their stay on the West Coast if they chose, taking optional side trips to Yosemite, the Sonoma County geysers, Santa Cruz, Los Angeles, and Lake Tahoe, perhaps detouring through Oregon on the way home.

As with Cooks, R&W's main selling point was relieving the traveler of any responsibility for planning an itinerary or arranging for transportation and hotels. In the words of the company's brochure, one could now see the West with "the same ease and elegant comfort that have served to render our Eastern tours free from all the cares, responsibilities and annoyances of ordinary travel." Arrangements were first-class, and a guide accompanied the party, allowing "ladies" to travel on their own. To ensure added privacy on the train, R&W booked its clients two to a section instead of the usual four;

each section on a Pullman Palace car had two upper and two lower berths, so this arrangement not only guaranteed more space, but meant that a couple traveling together would not have to share a section with strangers. R&W emphasized its first-class arrangements, proclaiming that the company always tried to bring together "tourists of a refined and cultivated class, and to make up our parties of persons of congenial tastes." Recognizing the preponderance of devout churchgoers among its clientele, R&W also made a point of noting that the tour would stop in Manitou and Salt Lake City on Sundays, allowing tourists to observe the Sabbath in appropriately inspiring settings.[23]

BEGINNING IN THE 1880s, expansion of railroad lines broadened the possibilities for tourists' itineraries and generated stiff competition for their business, first with the proliferation of regional lines in Colorado and later with the completion of new transcontinental routes. Two regional lines operating primarily in Colorado, the Denver & Rio Grande and the Colorado Midland Railway, capitalized on the popularity of Rocky Mountain scenery by establishing new routes that made it easier to reach areas previously accessible only by stagecoach. Among the first of the new routes was the Denver & Rio Grande's line between Denver and Salt Lake City, completed in 1883. While not the most direct route between the two cities, it featured some of the most spectacular scenery in the Rockies and eliminated the need to double back to Cheyenne after touring Colorado. Proclaiming itself a "transcontinental railroad," the Denver & Rio Grande published a series of pamphlets urging travelers to "cross the continent via the scenic route," providing point-by-point descriptions of the sights along the way.[24]

In 1886 the Colorado Midland opened a line between Colorado Springs and Leadville covering some of the same territory as the D&RG but with a standard-gauge track. To compete effectively, the D&RG, which ran mostly narrow-gauge trains, was forced to widen its tracks. By the early 1890s, the D&RG's expanded network offered a thousand-mile circular tour from Colorado Springs as far south as Santa Fe, west to Durango, and north to Denver. "Around the Circle" tickets good for sixty days allowed passengers unlimited stop-overs at sights along the route, with stagecoach connections available to scenic attractions off the railroad line. The passenger departments of both railroads churned out dozens of posters and pamphlets describing the attractions en route, some with print runs of 250,000 to 500,000 copies.[25]

Beginning in the mid-1880s, completion of new transcontinental railroad lines offered broader choices of itinerary. The Northern Pacific line between St. Paul and Tacoma was the first of the alternatives to be completed, in 1883, followed by the Canadian Pacific from Montreal to Vancouver (1885); the Atchison, Topeka & Santa Fe between eastern Kansas and San Diego (1886); the Southern Pacific between New Orleans and Portland (1887); and the Great Northern from Minneapolis to Seattle (1893).[26] Each new line attempted to lure passengers by promoting the scenic beauty of its particular slice of the continent and developing tourist accommodations at major attractions.

As the second transcontinental line to be completed, the Northern Pacific faced formidable competition from the well-established Union Pacific/Central Pacific. In an effort to overtake its rival, the NP launched a massive campaign to promote Yellowstone National Park, the most famous scenic attraction along its route. The railroad and its founder, Jay Cooke, had a hand in the development of Yellowstone from the beginning. After a group of Montana prospectors discovered the Grand Canyon of the Yellowstone and the Lower Geyser Basin in 1869 while searching for gold, a government-sponsored expedition was mounted to explore the region more fully, under the leadership of Henry D. Washburn. Among its members was Nathaniel Langford, whose job was to publicize the group's discoveries. Jay Cooke hired Langford to undertake a speaking tour of the eastern states at the conclusion of the expedition, promoting Yellowstone as part of a publicity campaign for the railroad. In addition, Langford published a series of articles in *Scribner's Monthly*, illustrated with woodcuts by the noted landscape painter Thomas Moran (who produced the images from Langford's verbal descriptions). After hearing one of Langford's lectures, Ferdinand V. Hayden decided to petition Congress for funds to mount an expedition of his own. Moran went with him, at Cooke's suggestion, to produce a pictorial record. (He painted one of his most famous works, *The Grand Canyon of the Yellowstone,* shortly after he returned.) The NP then conceived the idea of creating a national park in the Yellowstone region—an idea that Hayden proposed to Congress. The result was the creation of the United States' first national park in 1872.[27]

When the NP declared bankruptcy during the panic of 1873, plans to extend the line and promote tourism in the new national park were shelved until early in 1883, when the Yellowstone National Park Improvement Company was established as a subsidiary of the railroad with the mandate to develop tourist services in the park. By this time the railroad line was nearly complete across Montana, with a branch line from Livingston to Cinnebar, near the park's northern entrance. The company's first projects included building a hotel at Mammoth Hot Springs and contracting with a local company to provide stagecoach service from the nearest railroad station to Mammoth. To help draw visitors, the company organized a tour of the park for speculators and reporters, including correspondents from *The New York Times,* New York *World, New York Tribune,* London *Telegraph, Le Figaro,* and Munich's *Algemeine Zeitung.* Among the participants was Thomas Cook's twenty-one-year-old grandson, Frank. Henry Villard, then president of the Northern Pacific, organized his own tour, while the company's marketing got an unexpected boost from President Chester Arthur, who visited Yellowstone on a hunting trip.[28]

Over the next three years, the Yellowstone Improvement Company established what amounted to a monopoly of tourist arrangements in the park, acquiring long-term leases from the Department of the Interior for land at the most significant potential tourist sites—Mammoth Hot Springs, the Upper and Lower Geysers, Yellowstone Lake, and the Grand Canyon of the Yellowstone—as well as the right to build a loop road connecting them. The company opened its first hotel, a garish Queen Anne affair painted green with a red roof, at Mammoth Hot Springs in 1883, and set up tent hotels as temporary accommodations at three other sites. In the next few years, more permanent hotels were added and roads within the park developed to the point that visitors could make a five-day loop trip, spending each night in a different hotel, with all transportation and accommodations arranged by the Yellowstone Improvement Company.[29]

To promote Yellowstone—and, of course, the NP railroad as the way to get there—the railroad launched a publicity campaign designed to capitalize on the park's distinctive and unusual features. Yellowstone, in the words of one promotional brochure, was "unique among the great scenic districts of the world because it has all the attractions of the others and, in addition, the most wonderful natural phenomena known to scientists or geologists." The company's publicists came up with the label "Wonderland," launching their campaign with a brochure called *Alice's Adventures in the New Wonderland* written in the form of a long letter from "Alice" to her friend "Edith" about her experiences in this real-life "land of wonders," a place *"literally crowded* with natural curiosities of the most wonderful character." Yellowstone Lake was even more beautiful than Lakes Como and Maggiore; the Grand Canyon of the Yellowstone was the "most sublime spectacle I ever gazed upon"; her two days in the park were more memorable than visits to the Pyramids, Jerusalem, Venice, Rome, and even Niagara Falls. The authors of this bit of hyperbole did not neglect to have Alice remark on the "enlightened policy" that set aside Yellowstone as a national park and conclude her letter with a postscript advocating the benefits of traveling on the Northern Pacific Railroad—"by far the best route" because of the opportunities it afforded travelers to see the "magnificent scenery" of Puget Sound and the Columbia River.[30] The Wonderland label remained a trademark of NP publicity, touted in such publications as *The Northern Pacific Railroad: The Wonderland Route to the Pacific Coast* and a one hundred-page book titled *Six Thousand Miles Through Wonderland,* which became an annual publication.[31]

Raymond & Whitcomb helped boost Yellowstone tourism by including the park in their tours. By the 1890s, about ten thousand people were visiting the park annually. Around the turn of the century, the Yellowstone Improvement Company (renamed the Yellowstone Park Association) upgraded the park's accommodations, with a new luxury hotel at Old Faithful as the main focus. Designed by the Chicago architect Robert Reamer, the Old Faithful Inn combined a rustic style with luxurious appointments, defining a new type of "grand hotel" appropriate for wilderness settings, a formula that would be widely copied in other national parks. When the new hotel was completed in 1904, visitors could ride the NP spur line directly to the park's northern entrance and transfer to coaches for a six-day circuit of the park's major attractions, staying at a comfortable hotel each night. The tour had a regimented quality to it, routing visitors to each of Yellowstone's attractions in a prescribed order, but the convenience and comfort of these arrangements was obviously attractive to tourists, as the number of park visitors rose to more than fifty thousand annually by 1915.[32]

Not surprisingly, this programmed tourism in Yellowstone had its critics. Rudyard Kipling's distaste for the "Rayment" tourists was widely shared. Owen Wister (best known as the author of *The Virginian*), who toured Yellowstone several times in the 1880s and 1890s, always on horseback, poked fun at "citified" visitors who squealed with amazement at each new scene and stared at Wister and his companions as if they were part of the scenery. As early as the 1890s, there were those who criticized what they perceived as overdevelopment of Yellowstone, attacking rumored proposals to build a railroad through the park and construct an elevator at the Lower Falls. In 1896, Wister commented regretfully on the changes he had observed: More roads had been built, a new, bigger hotel had gone up at the Grand Canyon, and bears had discovered garbage piles around the hotels and campers with their stashes of food.[33]

The NP's development and promotion of Yellowstone established a model that was widely copied. The Great Northern Railway, which paralleled the NP along a more northerly route, attempted to compete with its rival line by promoting the mountains and glaciers of northwestern Montana, a region that first came to public attention in 1885 when the federal government sent George Bird Grinnell, an ethnologist and naturalist, to investigate conditions among the Blackfoot Indians. James J. Hill, president of the Great Northern, and his son Louis eagerly supported Grinnell's efforts to have the area designated a national park.

By the time Glacier National Park was authorized in 1910, the Great Northern was ready to develop and publicize it. Travelers could reach the park via railroad from either the east or the west. At the western entrance, a small hotel built in Swiss chalet style accommodated visitors overnight; the next morning, they could take a stagecoach to Lake McDonald, where launches waited to transport them to one of three hotels, including the three-hundred-room Glacier Hotel. A local concessionaire could arrange horseback tours lasting one to three days. There was another small hotel at the eastern gateway, while a chain of six tent camps—each with a large dining tent and smaller sleeping tents—was set up a day's horseback ride apart. The last of the camps was just six miles from the Glacier Hotel, making it possible for travelers to cross the entire park and leave from the opposite gateway.[34]

To promote the park, Louis Hill (who had taken over management of the company from his father) launched a massive publicity campaign with the slogan ''See America First.'' Although not the first to adopt this slogan, the Great Northern turned it into a company motto, printing it prominently on brochures and using it as the theme of a promotional trip to the park for reporters and public officials. This strategy was so successful that other companies and organizations copied it; the Northern Pacific, for example, used the slogan on its timetables. Reminiscent of arguments made by travel writers like Samuel Bowles and Charles Nordhoff, this new ''See America First'' campaign had none of the defensiveness of the earlier attempts to praise America by comparing it with Europe. Hill eschewed comparisons between Glacier's mountain scenery and the Alps, preferring instead to celebrate the regional Indian culture. Brochures and articles about the park featured pictures of men and women from the local Blackfoot tribe; in 1912, a delegation greeted reporters in a ceremony culminating with Hill's initiation into the tribe. In an even more dramatic stunt, Hill shipped a group of Indians to New York for the annual Travel and Vacation Show, where they camped out on the roof of a hotel and drew considerable attention from the press. Overall, the campaign to promote Glacier was remarkably successful. Upwards of six thousand tourists visited in 1912, far fewer than those attracted to Yellowstone, but three times the number who went to Yosemite.[35]

Following similar strategies, in the late 1880s the Canadian Pacific

Railway began promoting the Canadian Rockies, building luxury ho-
tels in locations that later became national parks, notably the Banff
Springs Hotel and Chateau Lake Louise in the Canadian Rockies.
The Northern Pacific and the Tacoma Eastern Railroad both ad-
vocated creating a national park around Mount Rainier; and the
Southern Pacific, which operated trains between Portland and Los
Angeles, began sponsoring tours to Crater Lake after it was desig-
nated a national park in 1902.[36]

As both regional and national railroad lines proliferated, the
Union Pacific, lacking a compelling scenic attraction along its route,
made a virtue out of its less interesting terrain by billing itself as
"the most direct route, being laid out along the line of least resistance," but also one that passed through "the parts of the West
richest in agricultural wealth and scenic beauty." An advertising
poster proclaimed it "the Great Central Short Line Between the Missouri River and the Pacific Coast." "What is the use of wasting your
time en route and your money on extra meals when it costs no more
to travel in the finest trains on a perfectly balanced road over a direct
route?" one advertisement asked.[37]

At the same time, the railroad undertook a program of expansion
to tap into the growing interest in less accessible scenic attractions.
In the late 1870s, for example, the UP acquired the Utah & Northern
narrow-gauge railroad, then under construction between Ogden and
western Montana, intending to build a branch line into Yellowstone
from the west. The company continued acquiring shares in regional
lines and began to compete directly with travel agents by offering its
own package tours. In 1903, the UP teamed up with the Chicago &
North Western Railroad to conduct tours of both Yellowstone and
Rocky Mountain national parks, and in 1908 the company finally
completed its own branch line to Yellowstone. Much later, in the
1920s, after Zion and Bryce canyons in southern Utah were designated national parks, the UP built a branch line to Cedar City, Utah,
operating bus tours from there to the two parks as well as to Cedar
Breaks National Monument and the North Rim of the Grand
Canyon. The railroad also built and operated hotels in the parks.[38]

But the Union Pacific's biggest advantage continued to be offering the most direct route to California, and much of its promotional

literature focused on the appeal of California itself. A series of pamphlets published in the early twentieth century, titled *California Calls You,* featured covers with a picture of a young woman sitting under a tree, gazing at mountains in the distance, and an opening paragraph asking "Did you ever listen to your own heart through a stethoscope? . . . Is it not true that one of the most constant longings would be found to be the desire to visit California?" Heavily illustrated with photographs, the booklets described favorite tourist destinations in detail and promoted the Union Pacific as the fastest and most reliable way to get there.[39]

In turn, the Southern Pacific promoted itself as the best way to see the sights within the state, and for good reason; by the late 1870s, the SP controlled 85 percent of the railroads in California. Perhaps more than any of its competitors, the Southern Pacific identified itself with California and recognized that promoting the state was essential to its growth. As its first public relations agent, the SP hired Benjamin C. Truman, whose credentials as a California booster were already well established with his book *Semi-Tropical California,* which touted the state as an agricultural paradise boasting a climate surpassing that of any European health resort. Truman's first assignment was promoting the Del Monte Hotel, but he went on to write a number of books under SP auspices, including a guide to California resorts accessible via the Southern Pacific and Central Pacific lines. The company also hired agents in cities throughout the United States and paid writers like Charles Nordhoff to mention the railroad and its subsidiary interests prominently in their books about California.[40]

The SP's boldest and most original promotion was the magazine *Sunset,* launched in 1898 as an altogether new concept in railroad public relations—an effort to promote the region served by the company's lines in a general way without making explicit claims for the railroad itself, distributed through hotels and YMCAs as well as SP passenger agents and railroad stations. *Sunset* would be "unbiased," without advertising, its editors claimed; the first issue carried an article titled "The Southern Pacific Company as a Bureau of Information," which argued that railroad companies had a responsibility to provide information about the regions through which their trains passed. In lieu of advertising, *Sunset* featured articles and short blurbs about such attractions as the Hotel Del Monte (owned, of course, by the SP), Yosemite, Santa Cruz, and Lake Tahoe, as well as a regular column called "Notes from the Resorts." Within a year, however, the no-advertising policy was dropped, and gradually the practice of free distribution was supplemented by mail subscriptions. By 1913, when the SP sold *Sunset*, it had been transformed from a loosely disguised promotional piece to a general magazine about the West, emphasizing but not limited to tourism.

The completion of SP's line to Los Angeles in 1876 made it easier for tourists to add southern California to their western itineraries, although the region continued to lag well behind San Francisco and the Monterey peninsula in popularity until the mid-1880s, when both the SP and the Atchison, Topeka & Santa Fe opened transcontinental services linking the East and Midwest with southern California. The two lines followed quite different routes—the Santa Fe crossed Kansas, southern Colorado, northern New Mexico, and Arizona, while the SP took a more southerly route from New Orleans—and targeted different geographical markets, with the Santa Fe focusing on the Midwest and the SP promoting its links with eastern lines to form a direct transcontinental route from the mid-Atlantic states. In addition, the SP's primary focus was on promoting tourism within California, while the Santa Fe launched efforts to interest tourists in the Southwest, making a virtue of its route through the high-altitude regions of northern New Mexico and Arizona (less snow in winter, cooler temperatures in summer) and eventually developing the area around the Grand Canyon. Even so, competition between the two lines resulted in a rate war in 1886 and 1887 that cut fares to as little as one dollar between the Missouri River and Los Angeles.[41]

Southern California businessmen and real estate developers took advantage of the greater accessibility provided by the newly completed transcontinental routes to promote tourism and settlement in their region. The Los Angeles Chamber of Commerce, which reorganized itself in 1888 (after disbanding during the recession of 1877), rapidly became the most active such organization in the country, creating a "California on Wheels" exhibit that toured the United

States over a two-year period. California boosters, including Southern Pacific, also sponsored exhibits at state fairs, trade shows, and world's fairs in Chicago, Atlanta, Omaha, St. Louis, and even Paris, pitching the region to both tourists and settlers.[42] Climate was always central to the pitch. Unlike northern California, where winters were temperate but summers could be cold, southern California was "the land of perpetual summer, where every month is June," in the words of a Santa Fe brochure. Promotional literature invariably portrayed Los Angeles and environs as a tropical paradise, filled with orange groves and flowers. Such publicity conveniently ignored the fact that most of southern California is a desert unless irrigated, choosing instead to make a virtue of the dry climate, advocating its benefits for invalids, especially those suffering from respiratory disease.

Luxury resort hotels went up throughout southern California in the 1880s and 1890s. One of the first, completed in 1885, was the Hotel Raymond in Pasadena, built by the Raymond & Whitcomb travel agency on land donated by the Santa Fe Railroad, which then built a station adjacent to the hotel. Similar luxury hotels followed, among them the Coronado in San Diego and the Arlington in Santa Barbara. By 1890, R&W brochures observed that first-class accommodations were available all over California, whereas just a few years earlier, the Hotel Del Monte had been the only luxury resort on the Pacific coast. Claiming that California now surpassed all other parts of the country and even the famous European resorts as the "sanitarium of America and the great winter resort of eastern people who desire to escape the rigors of the Atlantic Coast climate," R&W offered winter tours to southern California, in addition to its annual spring tours to Colorado, Yellowstone, and northern California.[43]

Despite the hype about southern California's climate, few visitors were disappointed. To walk through orange groves, plucking fruit at will, to sit outdoors and smell flowers in December seemed nothing short of miraculous to tourists from the East and Midwest. In language that outdid even the most gushing of the brochures, one visitor declared Pasadena "the most lovely spot on earth," while another called the countryside around Los Angeles "too utterly beautiful for anything but fairyland . . . warm, voluptuous, languishing beauty; air faint with odors of millions of sleepy flowers; a bewilderment of bloom and brightness; a veritable, wild garden."[44]

The SP also supported the creation of Yosemite National Park, even though it had no direct interest in the tourist concessions there (unlike the Northern Pacific and Yellowstone), and it would be years before the railroad built a spur line to the park entrance. First seen by white men in 1851, the Yosemite Valley very quickly became one of the West's most famous attractions, although its remote location kept the number of visitors at modest levels until well into the twentieth century. The first tourists to visit Yosemite, in 1855, were James Mason Hutchings, an Englishman who went to California in search of gold and stayed to become a journalist, and three of his friends, including Thomas Ayres, an artist. Hutchings included an article on Yosemite in the inaugural issue of his *Hutchings' California Magazine,* the first of his many books promoting settlement and tourism in California, while lithographs of Ayres's drawings appeared in East Coast magazines and newspapers in the late 1850s. Together with a famous article published in the *Boston Evening Transcript* by Thomas Starr King, a Unitarian minister who visited Yosemite in 1860, they put the Yosemite Valley on the western tourist's map.[45]

In 1864, after a group of Californians lobbied to preserve the valley, Congress passed the Yosemite Park Act stipulating that it and the Mariposa Grove be set aside for public use, administered by the state of California. At the time, however, only a small number of people made the arduous and expensive journey from San Francisco. Until the mid-1870s, the last one hundred miles or so could be made only on foot or horseback. Even after the first carriage roads were completed, a visit to Yosemite from San Francisco required three days of travel via train and stagecoach. Accommodations were primitive: two simple wood frame structures built in the late 1850s with small "bedrooms" separated by canvas sheets. The buildings were expanded and upgraded over the years—Hutchings bought one of them, known as the Upper Hotel, in 1864—and new hotels added, but until the late 1880s, when the first hotel with any pretensions to comfort was completed, a trip to Yosemite was "roughing it" indeed.

Those who made the effort, however, rarely complained. After a long ride over steep, rutted roads, the first views of the famous valley were so overwhelming that the discomforts of the journey receded quickly into the background. Nothing in the Alps could equal it, one traveler remarked; or, as Ralph Waldo Emerson put it, "this valley is the only place that comes up to the brag and exceeds it."[46]

Although the number of visitors to Yosemite was minuscule by modern standards—about twenty-five hundred a season in the 1880s, far fewer than the numbers who toured Yellowstone—many supporters of the region were concerned that it was becoming too commercialized, despite its status as a state preserve. Following the Yellowstone precedent, they sought to have the valley and the surrounding area designated as a national park. Among the leaders of the movement were John Muir, who first visited the valley in 1868 and spent much of his time living in the High Sierra, and Robert Underwood Johnson, the editor of *Century* magazine. Both were especially concerned about the prospect of uncontrolled development in the adjacent areas, which threatened forests and watershed lands, advocating a national park that would encompass a much larger area than the state-controlled park. Taking their cue from the Yellowstone case, they sought the support of the Southern Pacific. The bill to designate Yosemite a national park passed Congress in 1890, along with bills establishing Sequoia and General Grant National Parks (the latter now known as King's Canyon). A decade later, the SP backed the creation of Crater Lake National Park as well.[47]

Despite its interest in designating Yosemite as a national park, the SP did not follow the example of the Northern Pacific and become involved in park development, nor did it move immediately to build a rail link. Instead it was the regional Yosemite Valley Railroad that finally brought rail service to the park, completing a line from Merced to El Portal, at the western entrance, in 1907 and building a luxury hotel at the terminus. A YVR stagecoach carried visitors from El Portal into the valley itself. In 1909, the company arranged with the SP to link Los Angeles and El Portal; a year later, similar services were initiated from San Francisco.[48]

Curiously enough, the Grand Canyon, today one of the most popular national parks, was rarely visited until the first decade of the twentieth century. Little was known about the region until John Wesley Powell's two expeditions to the Colorado River in 1859 and 1871–72. Powell's work was well publicized, first in a series of articles in *Scribner's Monthly* in 1874–75 and subsequently in book form, but the sparsely settled region around the Grand Canyon remained inaccessible to ordinary travelers until the Santa Fe completed its line across Arizona in the mid-1880s. Even then, reaching the canyon itself was an all-day journey by stagecoach from Flagstaff or Ash Fork to the South Rim, where crude tent cabins offered the only accommodations.[49]

Rough traveling and primitive accommodations had not deterred visitors to Yosemite, which gained fame as a tourist attraction at a time when getting there was an expensive, uncomfortable expedition. But unlike Yosemite or the Colorado Rockies, the Grand Canyon was hidden away in a vast desert that held little appeal for nineteenth-century tourists. Nothing about the southwestern landscape resembled anything in their previous traveling experience, and it presented no handy comparisons like the "Switzerland" or "Italy" of America. The best Amy Bridges (traveling on a Raymond & Whitcomb tour in 1886) could say while visiting Santa Fe was that it was "nothing like New England." Recognizing this problem, the Santa Fe Railroad initially focused its efforts on winning a larger share of southern California–bound passengers by stressing the health advantages of its route as well as its superior service. With the slogan "Santa Fe all the way," the company billed itself as the shortest line from Chicago to southern California, and the only route under single management. Southern California boosters had already enjoyed considerable success in promoting their region as an ideal setting for invalids, superior even to the famous resorts of Switzerland and the Mediterranean; Santa Fe publicists played to this same market by emphasizing the temperate, dry air of the high desert country across northern New Mexico and Arizona. In its first effort to develop a resort in the Southwest, the company chose the area around Las Vegas Hot Springs in northeastern New Mexico, targeting health-conscious travelers.[50]

Not until the 1890s did railroad promoters look to the Grand Canyon as a potential new source of revenue. By then, the discovery of the remains of ancient civilizations in northern Arizona and New Mexico had increased the region's appeal by endowing it with a history stretching back well beyond the earliest European settlements in America. As the archaeological evidence demonstrated, the prehistoric peoples of the Southwest had created complex societies with a highly developed material culture, in some cases building multi-story stone masonry structures with dozens or even hundreds of rooms. Documenting the customs of native peoples of the region, as well as its geological history and natural features, was among the goals of Powell's second expedition down the Colorado. Primarily in response to his efforts, the U.S. government established a Bureau of Ethnography in 1879 and named Powell as its first director.[51]

These discoveries led many travelers to look more favorably on the human landscape of the Southwest, a shift that was especially apparent in the growing popularity of Santa Fe. While Amy Bridges had called Santa Fe "quaint and woebegone," with "queer low adobe homes—narrow streets full of strange things," and another Raymond & Whitcomb excursionist described the local population as "a rough looking people and said to be vicious and reckless," with "customs and habits of a primitive order," later visitors were more likely to praise the simple design and historic significance of the town's architecture—"a happy combination of Indian Pueblo and early Spanish style," as one man put it—and purchase Indian crafts to take home as souvenirs. Emily Post (best known as a writer of etiquette books) was astonished at seeing the cliff dwellings of the Southwest, a region she had expected to be like the Sahara Desert. Living in ignorance of these ancient cultures was like living in Cairo and never seeing the Pyramids, or in Italy and never visiting Pompeii, she thought. By the early twentieth century, a picture book called *The Great Southwest Along the Santa Fe,* published as a promotional brochure for the railroad, included photographs of the "Indian building" in Albuquerque, a museum and shop featuring local crafts; an old Spanish church in Ácoma, New Mexico; an inn built in the style of a Spanish hacienda; an Apache warrior on his horse; and, of course, views of the Grand Canyon. And a 1908 advertisement for the railroad highlighted three features of the southwestern route: "antiquities" (prehistoric cliff dwellings), "things unique" (the Petrified Forest), and "the biggest and most beautiful sight on earth" (the Grand Canyon).[52]

In the early 1890s, the Santa Fe Railroad moved to develop the Grand Canyon as a tourist destination, initially by taking over the stagecoach companies that provided the only transportation link between the main Santa Fe line and the South Rim. In the mid-1890s, Raymond & Whitcomb launched a three-day side trip to the canyon as part of its California tours. A private developer built the first hotel in 1897, a simple log-cabin affair overlooking the canyon, and several others followed by the end of the decade. Still, the journey remained arduous. Travelers had to ride for hours in a stagecoach over poor roads and put up with rustic accommodations. Around the turn of the century, however, this situation changed dramatically. The Santa Fe completed its spur line from Williams to the South Rim (at the location of the present-day Grand Canyon Village) in 1901, cutting travel time from about eleven hours to three, and shortly thereafter bought and renovated one of the small hotels overlooking the rim. With these changes, the railroad began to promote the canyon heavily, linking it with Yellowstone and Yosemite as one of the three great scenic attractions of the West and claiming that it was now the easiest of the three to reach.

Following the example of the Northern Pacific in Yellowstone, the Santa Fe set about turning the Grand Canyon into a luxury resort, working with its subsidiary, the Fred Harvey Company, which operated dozens of restaurants along the Santa Fe route as well as dining cars on the trains. The high quality of both food and service at the Harvey Houses had been a Santa Fe selling point since the late 1870s. In 1905 the two companies teamed up to open the El Tovar Hotel, which combined rustic architecture with a luxurious standard of service in a spectacular setting overlooking the canyon. The Harvey Company also built a museum and gift shop known as Hopi House adjacent to the hotel, featuring displays of Hopi and Navajo baskets, blankets, and other objects, as well as craft demonstrations and dance performances.[53]

The Santa Fe also improved roads and trails along the edge of the Grand Canyon (designated a national monument in 1908 and a national park in 1919). "All the descriptive superlatives in the language have been used,'' gushed one brochure, ''but the Grand Canyon has never been adequately described and never will be. It is the one thing that one must see to comprehend.'' The railroad capped its campaign with a lavish exhibit at the Panama-Pacific Exhibition in San Francisco in 1915—a six-acre model of the canyon and its environs, complete with miniature Pullman Palace cars that visitors could ride along the make-believe rim. Tourists could even descend a trail to the bottom of the ''canyon'' to stroll through an ''Indian village'' where Navajo and Hopi men and women imported from Arizona demonstrated handicrafts.54

BY THE END of the nineteenth century, with the completion of five major transcontinental rail lines and countless regional lines linking the major scenic attractions of the West, a journey across the continent was no longer quite the expensive, time-consuming expedition of twenty years earlier. As C. D. Irwin remarked at the beginning of his second cross-country tour, in 1885, the trip had become an ''old story,'' not at all like his first such journey when ''it seemed like undertaking an ocean voyage to start across the great plains, deserts and mountains to the Pacific coast.'' Nor was a western tour limited to the rich. Competition lowered fares at a time when economic growth gave more Americans the money and leisure to take pleasure trips. Railroad officials and others in the travel business came to realize, as one historian has written, that ''the great profits in the western tourist and vacation industry came not from serving squab to the few but from selling gasoline, hamburger sandwiches, and postcards to the many.''55

Railroad rate wars in 1886 and 1887, while damaging when they reached extremes, demonstrated the profitability of selling more tickets at lower prices. By the end of the 1880s, railroads were offering special fares for passengers traveling to conventions or expositions; in the first decade of the twentieth century, these fares were transformed into regular summer excursion rates designed to lure vacationing families. In addition to cheaper tickets, a new style of Pullman car, stripped of the wood paneling and luxurious appointments of the so-called Palace Cars, cut the cost of sleeping accommodations by nearly half. The new cars "have solved the problem of how to travel long distances comfortably and at minimum cost," the company's brochures claimed. Simpler in design than the older cars, they were nevertheless attached to the same fast trains, operated by the same company, and served by the same Pullman conductors and porters. As a further inducement, the railroad sponsored escorted tours using tourist sleepers, with "special attention given to ladies and children traveling without escort."[56]

New travel agencies also organized low-cost tours, aiming at the market a cut below the clients of Cook and Raymond & Whitcomb; Henry Gaze, one of Cook's chief competitors in Britain (and occasionally criticized by Cook for his low-budget tours), opened an office in New York in 1891, while several new American agencies were established beginning in the 1880s, among them A. Phillips & Co., Colpitts, and Ask Mr. Foster. The first Sunday newspaper travel sections were launched around the turn of the century, offering articles with a more practical bent than the literary essays of magazines like *Scribner's* and the *Atlantic Monthly,* which had been the main venue for American travel writing in the late nineteenth century.[57]

Throughout the West, new hotels and resorts catered to the traveler on a budget. On the Monterey Peninsula, tourists who couldn't afford the Del Monte Hotel might stay at the Pacific Grove Retreat, established by the Methodist Church in 1875. Several other budget resorts in California were also founded with religious or educational goals, among them Laguna Beach, which hosted the first California Chautauqua Assembly in 1884, Huntington Beach, founded in 1904, and Mount Hermon in the Santa Cruz Mountains (1905). National parks began to offer a more diverse array of accommodations as well. A Montana school superintendant named William Wylie set up a series of tent camps in Yellowstone, offering a seven-day tour (known as the "Wylie Way") for $35 at a time when the Yellowstone Park Improvement Company's six-day circuit cost $50. In Yosemite, David and Jennie Curry established a similar operation, featuring tent cabins with wooden platforms, a central dining room, and entertainment—which included a dance floor, swimming pool, campfire programs, and the nightly "firefall" created by pushing the embers of an enormous bonfire over the cliff at Glacier Point into the valley below. By 1910, Camp Curry accommodated about one third of all summer visitors to the park.[58]

Tent camps and cottage colonies had the advantage of low cost, but they also appealed to Americans who preferred casual camping over the formality and social conventions of large resorts. By the end of the nineteenth century, as the United States became more urban, and wilderness areas more accessible and therefore less threatening, many Americans wanted their vacations to provide an escape from the noisy, crowded conditions of city life, favoring quiet settings and vigorous outdoor activities over the socializing typical of the luxury resorts. Railroads began offering special campers' fares, provided pointers for inexperienced campers, and put together camping parties, although fixed routes and the logistical complications of carrying the baggage required for a camping vacation on a train made such trips cumbersome.[59] By the first decade of the twentieth century, however, travelers found in the automobile a means of transport ideally suited for getting away from civilization. Although automobile ownership remained a luxury until after World War I, a surprising number of travelers took to the roads before then, when "motors," as they were popularly called in the early years, were little more than carriages fitted with gasoline engines and many roads, especially west of the Mississippi, mere dirt tracks.

THE FIRST RECORDED transcontinental journey by automobile started as a gentlemen's bet and ended as a publicity stunt for the Winton Motor Carriage Company, one of the first American automobile manufacturers. Alexander Winton, a transplanted Scotsman who first experimented with gasoline-powered carriages in 1896 and began manufacturing the vehicles at a factory in Cleveland two years later, realized that selling such a revolutionary vehicle would take creative marketing. He drove one of his first cars from Cleveland to New York in 1897, a highly publicized ten-day journey that drew crowds all along the route. No amount of advertising could equal the publicity value of thousands of small-town Americans getting their first look at a "horseless carriage." Over the next several years, Winton and other automobile manufacturers sponsored races and hill-climbing contests to demonstrate their product's speed, power, and reliability to critics who refused to believe that these fragile machines—the early Wintons were simply carriages powered by two-cylinder, twenty-horsepower motors—could ever supplant horse-drawn conveyances. The boldest of these early tests, however, was inspired by an argument among a group of men dining at San Francisco's University Club in May 1903. Horatio Nelson Jackson, a wealthy young physician from Vermont, took exception to disdainful remarks that automobiles were useless as a means of long-distance transportation. After a heated argument, Jackson bet $50 that he could drive across the continent—a feat never before attempted, and one that he guessed would require anywhere from six weeks to six months.[60]

Jackson selected a 1903 model two-seat Winton touring car, recruited a mechanic, Sewall Crocker, to travel with him (a necessity on long automobile trips), sent his wife home on the train, and embarked five days later, equipped with spare parts, machinists' tools, two extra tires, plenty of tire-patching material, a shovel, block and tackle, twenty extra gallons of gas and five gallons of oil, several guns (for catching game and defending himself and his companion against outlaws), fishing rods, and waterproof sleeping bags. In Idaho the two men acquired a third passenger—a stray bulldog they named Bud, who stuck with them for the entire journey.

To avoid the desert heat, Jackson and Crocker chose a route through northern California and across Oregon, Idaho, Wyoming, Nebraska, and Iowa. Although the trip started out smoothly enough over the hard-packed clay and sand roads of California's Central Valley, by the time they reached the California-Oregon border, the two men had patched and repatched their tires so many times that they had to telegraph to San Francisco for replacements. At various points along the way they had to drag the car out of a streambed with the block and tackle, clean wet clay off the spokes of the wheels when the mud got so thick the wheels wouldn't move, and heave boulders off "roads" carved out of mountainsides. Between Oregon and Nebraska, the pair navigated mostly by compass. They hired a cowboy to guide them across Idaho, where they had only animal tracks to follow; in western Wyoming, where even the animal tracks disappeared, the car's wheels sank into soft sand, despite the ropes wrapped around the tires for extra traction. Along one stretch, Jackson and Crocker were reduced to spreading bundles of sagebrush several yards in front of the car, then driving it forward, picking up the bundles, and repeating the process over and over again.

Remarkably, they were able to buy gasoline in most villages along the route, although it was often exorbitantly expensive. Only once did they run out, in eastern Oregon, forcing Crocker to hike twenty-nine miles to the nearest settlement. The resourceful mechanic proved his value on more than one occasion, replacing worn wheel bearings with the bearings from a farmer's mowing machine and repairing a broken front axle with a length of iron pipe. On other occasions, the men had no choice but to wait for parts from the Winton factory in Cleveland. East of Cheyenne, with the mountains and the most desolate parts of the West behind them, the going got easier. They followed a stagecoach road across Nebraska and sped across Iowa, motoring from Omaha to Chicago in just two days.

In every village and hamlet along the route, the mud-caked Winton, its spare tires lashed to the front of the hood like oversized doughnuts, created a sensation. West of the Mississippi, many of the people they met had never seen an automobile. Some thought it was a small railroad engine that had somehow become disengaged from its cars. In Nebraska, a frightened farmer grabbed his wife and dove under his wagon for safety, while in another village Jackson and Crocker encountered a young boy who had ridden his horse sixty-eight miles to get his first glimpse of a car. In every town big enough to publish a newspaper, Jackson made headlines as "the mad doctor." City officials and automobile dealers hosted receptions in Omaha and Chicago. There could have been no better publicity for the Winton Company, which sent a delegation to meet Jackson and Crocker a few miles outside Cleveland and escort them into the city, where they were feted at yet another banquet. Company officials wanted to overhaul the car for the last third of its journey, but Jackson refused; he did not want to do anything that would make his trip appear to be a company-sponsored promotional tour. Already he and Crocker were being labeled as agents for the company, accused of trading cars along the route and covering part of the distance by train. The Winton Company posted a $10,000 reward, augmented by another $15,000 from Jackson himself, to anyone who could prove that the tour was anything other than what Jackson claimed it to be.

The two men and their dog continued with relative ease from Cleveland to New York, covering the last two hundred-plus miles in twenty-four hours and cruising into Manhattan unannounced at 4:30 A.M., sixty-three days and six thousand miles after leaving San Francisco. After a few days' rest, they cranked up the car again and drove to Jackson's home in Vermont (where, a few weeks later, he was arrested for exceeding the speed limit of six miles per hour). The Winton Company published Jackson's account of his journey under the title *From Ocean to Ocean in a Winton* and placed ads announcing the trip had been accomplished not in a specially equipped vehicle but in a perfectly ordinary Winton—suggesting, in short, that anyone could duplicate Jackson's cross-country tour.[61]

At least two other teams did manage to cross the continent by car that same year, one bettering Jackson's time by ten days and the other taking about a week longer, and automobile companies continued to promote recreational driving by sponsoring long-distance tours and races. One of the more unusual publicity schemes was the brainchild of the sales manager for the Maxwell-Briscoe Company, who recruited Alice Ramsey to become the first woman to drive across the continent. Ramsey, an avid "automobilist" (as the early aficionados of motor travel were called), handy with tools, and married to a man of modern views who didn't object to his wife taking off on a cross-country adventure, in turn recruited three friends to accompany her, including her two sisters-in-law. Proper spinsters in their forties, several years older than Ramsey, they surprised her by agreeing to the plan with enthusiasm. Unlike Jackson's tour, this trip was very clearly a company-sponsored project designed to generate publicity for Maxwell. The company paid for the car and all expenses, and hired the automobile editor for *The Boston Herald* to follow the women by train across the eastern part of the country, arriving a few hours ahead of them at each overnight stopping point to arrange for hotel accommodations.

With their escort and their Blue Books—state-by-state guides for motorists that provided detailed descriptions of roads, mileage between major towns, and basic information about each town—the first third of the journey proceeded smoothly, apart from occasional blowouts, minor breakdowns, and confusion created by the absence of road signs. (The Blue Book's directions relied on landmarks like houses and trees; Ramsey missed a turn in a sparsely populated section of western Pennsylvania because a yellow house at the turnoff had been repainted green.)

Beyond the Mississippi River, however, conditions deteriorated rapidly. Several days of spring rains turned Iowa's dirt roads into mud, slowing the pace to a crawl and taxing the Maxwell's engine to the point that it frequently overheated. Although the women were well prepared with tools and extra tires, their radiator's water ran out about a third of the way across the state. Ditches alongside the road were full to overflowing, but the women had failed to include buckets among their supplies. At this point, Ramsey's refined sisters-in-law thought of the cut-glass bottles, filled with perfumes and other toiletries, in their custom-made leather suitcases, and volunteered to use them to carry water from the ditches to the car's radiator. Ramsey, who had laughed to herself about the unsuitability of such elegant luggage on an adventure trip, was touched at her companions' readiness to sacrifice their fine things to the exigencies of the moment. Of course it took dozens of trips between ditch and car to refill the radiator, but finally they were on their way—although not for long.

About halfway across Iowa, on the advice of "J.D.," a Maxwell representative who intended to accompany the women across the middle part of the country (taking up where the *Herald* reporter had left off), Ramsey's companions boarded a train for Omaha with their luggage and some of the expedition's gear, leaving Ramsey and J.D. to continue by car in the expectation that a lighter load would make it easier to negotiate the muddy roads. Road conditions continued to deteriorate, however, so they headed for higher ground, aiming for Sioux City instead of Omaha. In Sioux City the weather was so bad that they were forced to stay put for several days, much to Ramsey's frustration; their luck would never change for the better, she began to think, until they got out of Iowa.

Reunited finally in Omaha, the group drove across Nebraska, blessedly free of mud but plagued with mechanical problems, including loose magneto screws, a broken spring in the brake pedal, and a broken rear axle. At Grand Island, one of the sisters-in-law bailed out and took the train to Cheyenne, escorted by J.D., who arranged for a mechanic to travel with the three remaining women. In Cheyenne, they were entertained by local Maxwell owners whose help proved invaluable because the roads in Wyoming, as Jackson had discovered, were hardly worthy of the name, and Blue Book guides were available only for states east of the Missouri River. The Cheyenne "Maxwellites," as Ramsey called them, arranged pilot cars to get the women across their state. In Salt Lake City, the Maxwell Company arranged for another scout to guide the women to Reno, where yet another led them on to Sacramento, following a sandy wagon trail over the Sierra. Despite the mud and mechanical breakdowns, Ramsey and her friends cut three weeks off Jackson's time, completing their journey in forty-one days.[62]

American companies were not alone in sponsoring publicity tours. In what was perhaps the most unusual automobile stunt of the early twentieth century, several European and American manufacturers sponsored an around-the-world race, starting from Paris, in 1908. Like Ramsey, Antonio Scarfoglio, driver of the one Italian vehicle (and the only participant who published an account of the journey), got mired in mud in Iowa, suffered mechanical failures in Nebraska, and met an enthusiastic welcome in Cheyenne—in his case, from the local Italian community. He also slogged through snow in upstate New York, met more mud in the Rockies (where the car sank up to engine level), and endured the deserts of southern California en route from Los Angeles to San Francisco. None of this even approached the challenge of crossing Siberia, however, where Scarfoglio and his companions intended to follow the tracks of the Trans-Siberian Railway but were forced to drive directly on the tracks for long stretches when severe flooding made the adjacent land impassable. The men used a portable telephonelike apparatus with a long pole that they attached to overhead telegraph wires to get information about approaching trains. Most of the time this worked, but once they had trouble getting the car off the tracks and came within one hundred

yards of a train before it stopped. A few miles farther on, they ran
out of oil and sent one member of the group to the next village to
get more. Hours later, he returned with the only thing he could find:
thirty small bottles of Singer sewing-machine oil.[63]

Unlike railroad publicity schemes, which promoted the West as a
means of expanding their business, automobile manufacturers and
related companies advertised their product, not the region. Railroads had expanded into the western states at a time when the region was thinly populated and seldom visited by tourists; for the
new routes to be successful, railroad companies had no choice but to
link their own expansion with that of the states through which they
passed. By the time automobiles came into use, however, the situation was quite different. It was no longer necessary to promote the
idea of travel or settlement in any particular part of the United
States; the automobile companies' challenge was to persuade traveling Americans to use cars instead of trains. But although
automobile company–sponsored tours were successful in garnering
immense publicity for the fledgling industry, and people like Jackson and Ramsey tended to play down the hardships of their journeys, long-distance automobile travel was not about to compete
seriously with the railroads until both machines and roads improved
dramatically.

The potential was obvious, however, to anyone who observed
what was happening in Europe, where automobiles were a popular
form of transport by the first decade of the twentieth century. Thomas Cook & Son offered its first tours by automobile (to Switzerland)
in 1900. Within a decade, nearly all the Baedeker and Murray guides
to Europe included sections offering advice to motorists—Baedeker's
1909 guide to northern France observed that "motoring enjoys an
enormous vogue in France" and that gasoline and mechanics
equipped to make repairs could be found in nearly every village—
while Michelin, the French tire company, began publishing a new
series of guides directed primarily to tourists traveling by automobile.
Eventually they would supplant the Baedeker and Murray handbooks as the most popular guides to Europe.[64]

In the United States, however, roads were much poorer than in
Western Europe, especially west of the Mississippi, with the result

that automobile travel took longer to catch on as a practical alternative to the railroad. While the industrialized nations of Europe had extensive networks of paved roads by the beginning of the twentieth century, only 7 percent of intercity roads in the United States were considered "improved," and nearly all of those were surfaced with gravel, sand, shell, or planks. A good rain turned most roads into quagmires, as Alice Ramsey and many other early motorists discovered to their dismay. Tire chains for slippery, muddy stretches and tools for leveraging cars out of deep ruts and potholes were standard equipment for the long-distance motorist. (Scarfoglio, accustomed to European roads, attributed the poor quality of roads in the United States to Americans' dependence on railroads; no one uses the roads, he observed, except the occasional farmer.) The economies of rail travel over long distances and the United States' long tradition of placing responsibility for road construction and maintenance on local jurisdictions provided little incentive for improvement until the 1890s, when pressure for better roads came from two very different quarters: farm organizations, which lobbied for better roads linking farms with market towns, and bicyclists.[65]

Invented in the 1860s in France and demonstrated at the 1867 Paris Exhibition, the bicycle became popular in the late 1880s, after the modern, low-wheeled style of bicycle was invented in England. Cycling organizations proliferated in the 1880s and '90s, in both Europe and America, taking as one of their major causes the construction of better roads. With support from both cyclists and farmers, the National League for Good Roads was established in 1892, and the Office of Road Inquiry created within the Department of Agriculture the following year. The automobile industry and the growing number of automobile enthusiasts added their weight, most notably with the creation of the American Automobile Association, in 1902. The AAA and the National Grange (then the major farm organization in the United States) sponsored a joint Good Roads Convention in 1907. Even the railroad companies brought some pressure to bear, believing that better roads would make it easier for potential passengers to reach railroad lines. Louis Hill enlisted the AAA as a partner with the Great Northern Railway when he launched his "See America First" campaign in 1912; the following year, he urged

Charles Glidden, a wealthy Bostonian and car enthusiast who organized an annual automobile tour in cooperation with the AAA, to bring his tour to Glacier National Park.[66]

These lobbying efforts achieved only limited results before World War I, however. By 1914, the mileage of surfaced roads was about double that of a decade earlier, but even so, 90 percent of American roads remained unimproved dirt. The first federal highway act, passed in 1916, provided the opening wedge in shifting responsibility for the nation's highways from local jurisdictions to state and federal governments; but the limited provisions of the bill, which authorized funds for improvement of existing rural roads, and the debate over its passage demonstrated the level of disagreement in Congress about the need for a national highway system and the federal government's responsibility for funding it. A substantial proportion of lawmakers still believed that rural roads should be designed primarily to serve the needs of farmers; one group of congressmen argued that "neither freight nor passengers will ever be carried long distances over roads as cheaply as they could be over railways, and it is an idle dream to imagine that auto trucks and automobiles will take the place of railways in the long-distance movement of freight or passengers." The debate was significant, because farmers wanted roads to market towns, which implied a spoke-and-wheel arrangement linking rural areas with regional centers, while long-distance freight and passenger traffic required roads connecting major towns and cities. It was not until the 1920s that the federal government passed legislation authorizing a national highway system to be built in part with federal funds.[67]

Given the intense debate about a nationally maintained highway system, it is hardly surprising that representatives of the automobile industry, not government, mounted the first effort to build a transcontinental highway. In 1911, Carl G. Fisher, an Indianapolis businessman and founder of the Prest-O-Lite Company, manufacturer of automobile headlights, proposed a plan for a coast-to-coast highway. (He also founded the Indianapolis Speedway and launched the annual five-hundred-mile race.) To fund his scheme, Fisher sought contributions from automobile manufacturers and related industries. Henry Ford refused to contribute, arguing that roads should be funded by taxes and that privately sponsored ventures would only reduce government incentives to build roads, but other industry leaders responded with enthusiasm. Henry Joy, president of the Packard Company, suggested lobbying Congress to protest the appropriation of more than a million dollars for a monument to Lincoln in Washington, when a more suitable memorial would be something useful— like a cross-country road. Joy's idea was hardly practical, but it inspired Fisher to call his proposed road the Lincoln Highway. Henry Joy became its primary organizer and fund-raiser. In 1913, the two men established the Lincoln Highway Association and mapped a route, roughly the same as today's Interstate 80, that would make use of existing roads as much as possible. The association worked with local governments to improve segments of the road that passed through their jurisdictions and put up red, white, and blue markers to guide motorists.[68]

In the spring of 1915, with most of the Lincoln Highway complete, the association issued its first guidebook, the *Complete Official Road Guide to the Lincoln Highway,* and launched a campaign to encourage Americans to take to the road. The guide claimed, with some justification, that the cross-country trip could now be made in a month—while automobile companies advertised, with less justification, that an auto trip was now the cheapest way to see the country—but the guide's list of recommended equipment indicated that crossing the country by car still amounted to a major expedition. The well-prepared motorist was advised to carry tire chains, tools, two jacks, two extra tire casings, four inner tubes, three spark plugs, eight feet of high-tension cable, a valve and spring, three gallons of oil, an ax, shovel, radiator connections, extra headlight bulbs, camping equipment, and a good supply of provisions, including canned food, bread, salt, pepper, rice, potatoes, evaporated milk, sugar, coffee, and tea.[69]

Among those who traveled over the Lincoln Highway in 1915 was Emily Post, veteran of several auto tours in Europe, including a trip from the Baltic to the Adriatic in 1898. More accustomed to the highways of Europe than of the United States, Post thought the new highway hardly lived up to its billing. "With such titles as 'Transcontinental' and 'Lincoln' put before it," she remarked, "you dream of a wide straight road like the Route Nationale of France, or state roads in the East, and you wake rather unhappily to the actuality of a meandering dirt road that becomes mud half a foot deep after a day or two of rain!'' While the Lincoln Highway guide claimed that, in dry weather, driving across Illinois, Iowa, and Nebraska compared favorably with traveling through southern France, the accounts of early motorists suggest that the weather was rarely dry across the middle part of the country, and driving across Iowa in the rain was torture, as Alice Ramsey and her friends had discovered. Post spent several days in small Iowa towns waiting for the roads to dry out, an easier if equally time-consuming approach to the problem of rain and mud.[70]

The Lincoln Highway may not have deserved its name—even the official guidebook admitted that a cross-country car trip remained ''something of a sporting proposition''—but with its distinctive red, white, and blue markers and its detailed mile-by-mile guidebook, the road made it possible for motorists with a sense of adventure and a reasonable amount of mechanical skill to traverse the country without the kind of special help given Ramsey or the hardships Jackson endured. It also inspired several other cross-country highway projects, including the Midland Trail from Washington, D.C., to Los Angeles and the National Old Trails Road between Baltimore and Los Angeles. By 1922, there were nine named transcontinental highways—most of them, like the Lincoln Highway, privately funded. The most famous of them all, Route 66, was laid out in 1926.[71]

There were other signs as well suggesting that the automobile would revolutionize the way Americans traveled. Thanks in part to Henry Ford's introduction of the Model T in 1909, which dramatically reduced the cost of automobile ownership, the number of cars registered in the United States skyrocketed from a mere 8,000 in 1900 to 500,000 in 1910 to 8 million, or about one car for every thirteen Americans, by 1920. The Lincoln Highway Association estimated that 25,000 cars traveled the road between the Missouri and California in 1915—probably an exaggerated estimate, but even half that would have been an astonishing number, considering the primitive state of automobile travel just a decade earlier.[72] And in the

national parks, the number of tourists arriving by car began to out-
pace those arriving by train within a few years after the parks were
first opened to automobiles. Although a handful of travelers had visited Yosemite and Yellowstone by car as early as 1901, official policy
subsequently prohibited automobiles in the western national parks,
partly out of concern for the wildlife. Mount Rainier was the first of
the western parks to rescind the ban, in 1908, followed by Crater
Lake in 1911, Glacier in 1912, Yosemite in 1913, and Yellowstone—
where lobbying from the Northern Pacific kept the automobile at
bay a bit longer—in 1915. By 1918, two out of three visitors to Yellowstone came by automobile. At Yosemite, where train service was
not so convenient as at Yellowstone, the figure was seven out of
eight.[73]

The appeal of the automobile was the freedom and flexibility it
offered—to reach places the railroads didn't go, to arrange one's own
itinerary and change it at will, to set one's own pace. The reliability
and speed of train travel, once hailed as progress, came to seem more
restrictive than liberating. The leisurely pace of auto travel became
a virtue, allowing one to observe the landscape closely rather than
attempt to absorb passing scenes through the window of a fast-
moving train.[74] For Edith Wharton, traveling in France in 1907, the
automobile brought back "the romance of travel," by "freeing us
from all the compulsions and contacts of the railway, the bondage
to fixed hours and the beaten track, the approach to each town
through the area of ugliness and desolation created by the railway
itself." She even made a virtue of her car's frequent mechanical
failures, for they provided an opportunity to savor small details of
the rural landscape.

In a curious twist on the sort of travel nostalgia that made some
people pine for horse and carriage in the era of the railroad, or sailing
ships in the era of steam, Wharton found in automobile travel "the
wonder, the adventure and the novelty which enlivened the way of
our posting grandparents." But unlike the Ruskins and Wordsworths
of earlier generations, who had fought railroads as a threat to older
and slower forms of travel, Wharton—and many other pioneer motorists—hailed the latest technology as a way of retreating from the

335

modern obsession with speed and schedules. For her the twentieth-century traveler had come full circle, from the grand tourists' leisurely, unplanned pace through ever-faster, more rigidly defined, and more precisely scheduled itineraries, back to something resembling the serendipity of eighteenth-century travel.[75]

EPILOGUE

IN ITS May 1913 issue, under the heading WHY SEE AMERICA? in inch-high block letters, *Travel* magazine urged its readers to pay more attention to their own country. Foreigners cherish their historic monuments and scenic wonders, the article observed, while most Americans don't even know about their own, equally marvelous, attractions—"an Egypt in our own southwest," "prehistoric ruins antedating the pyramids," not to mention unclimbed peaks in the Rockies and lakes more beautiful than those in the Scottish Highlands or the Italian Alps. A little over a year later, *Travel* reprinted the article, this time with a short introductory paragraph stating the obvious: War had closed Europe to travelers, perhaps for an extended period of time.[1]

If patriotism and curiosity were not enough to get Americans to "see America first," war left them no choice. The promotional campaigns launched by railroads and other western business interests had encouraged millions of Americans to travel west by the first decade of the twentieth century, but it was the war in Europe, not

337

ingenious advertising, that finally guaranteed the success of the "See America First" campaign. Just as the French Revolution and the Napoleonic Wars forced British grand tourists to discover the possibilities of travel in their own country, World War I kept Europeans at home and forced Americans to make a virtue out of traveling in the Western Hemisphere.

The sponsors of the Lincoln Highway were quick to take advantage of restrictions on European travel to promote the idea of seeing America by automobile. Appealing to Americans' isolationism and sense of superiority over the warring nations of the Old World (the possibility of U.S. involvement in the war seemed remote to most Americans in 1914), Lincoln Highway boosters described the road as a "wonder-trail . . . running like a gleaming thread of gold from sea to sea, girding the continent with startlingly new and romantic values." A "consolation" to Americans cut off from Europe, the highway offered "an intimacy with their own America" that one could get only if freed from the speed and restrictions of the train. In short, a trip cross-country on the Lincoln Highway was "an inspirational course in Americanism." And the summer of 1915 would be "the greatest motor touring year" ever, highway promoters confidently asserted, as thousands of Americans were expected to take to the roads. The reasons? The war, of course, but also improvements in roads and cars, the cumulative effects of the "See America First" campaign, and, finally, San Francisco's Panama-Pacific International Exposition, set to open in February 1915 and expected to draw as many as 10 million visitors.[2]

Beginning with the Crystal Palace exhibition in 1851, the major world's fairs never failed to draw enormous crowds, and the Panama-Pacific Exposition was no exception despite what might have seemed, to some, its rather distant location. If anything, the Exposition's backers underestimated its drawing power; by the time it closed in December, nearly 19 million people had passed through its gates. One of the largest world's fairs ever mounted, it followed closely, if on a grander scale, the model of earlier expositions in celebrating industrial technology and material prosperity. It also observed the tradition of recent U.S.-sponsored world's fairs in commemorating an event of major historical significance: in this case, the opening of the Panama Canal. If previous fairs had taken as their *raison d'être* the anniversaries of important past events—American independence (Philadelphia, 1876), Columbus's discovery of the Americas (Chicago, 1893), and the Louisiana Purchase (St. Louis, 1904)—the Panama-Pacific Exposition celebrated history-in-the-making.[3]

For decades, visionaries had dreamed of linking Atlantic and Pacific with a canal across Central America. For North American commercial interests, such a canal would have the same economic significance that the Suez had for Europe: It would provide a faster, easier, safer route to Asian markets. For dreamers, the Panama Canal had symbolic meaning as well. By bridging the Americas and joining the world's two great oceans, it provided the last important link in a global transportation network. In an era that equated technology with progress, when many believed that the free flow of people and goods would strengthen ties among nations, the Panama Canal represented both the power of technology and a hope for world unity. So it was sadly ironic that the first ship steamed through the Canal on August 3, 1914, the same day that Germany declared war on France. By the time of the Canal's official opening on August 15, public attention throughout the world was riveted on the unfolding war in Europe. Years in the planning and construction, the Panama Canal opened to little fanfare, with few of the invited dignitaries in attendance and newspaper coverage relegated to back pages.[4]

In San Francisco, plans for the celebratory fair went forward, however, despite rumblings that such an event would be inappropriate in time of war. In the end, Britain and Germany opted not to build national pavilions, but otherwise the Exposition went on as planned. This was not especially surprising, for the fair's purpose was to celebrate the Pacific and the American West as much as the Canal. In the minds of the local promoters, it was also intended to demonstrate San Francisco's remarkable recovery from the devastating earthquake and fire of April 1906 (and incidentally to encourage further investment and settlement in California). In competing for the privilege of hosting the fair, San Francisco businessmen had played heavily on the importance of the Panama Canal in opening the Pacific to travel and commerce, and on their city's significance as the largest port on the American side of the Pacific.[5]

Less than two years after city fathers launched their bid to host the Exposition, much of San Francisco was leveled by the combined effects of earthquake and fire, raising doubts about the city's capacity to carry out its plans. When the fair opened, on schedule and on the lavish scale envisioned by the original promoters, guidebooks billed it as a tribute to San Francisco, "a phoenix risen from the ashes," as well as a "graphic record of the status of the World in 1915." In the tradition of previous expositions, the San Francisco fair celebrated progress and the conviction that advancing industry and technology would promote "that universal understanding which makes for international friendship." As one recent writer aptly put it, the Panama-Pacific Exposition was the last of the nineteenth-century world's fairs. What set it apart from its predecessors was not any sense of impending change, but the efforts of its promoters to persuade the world that the future lay in the West, on the shores of the Pacific.[6]

The fair's organizers called it the "Dream City"—a takeoff on the "White City" of Chicago's World Columbian Exposition in 1893, but appropriate under the circumstances. To Laura Ingalls Wilder, visiting from Missouri (years before she became famous for her "Little House" books), it was a "fairyland," the buildings all in pastel colors "blended into one perfect whole without a jar anywhere."[7] Today, when all that is left of the fair is the Palace of Fine Arts, magnificent in scale but a bit shabby at close range, it is hard to imagine the vast panorama of the Exposition, which covered 635 acres along the waterfront on what was then the northwestern edge of the city. Its layout followed the pattern of earlier fairs, with the main exhibits—those displaying the latest in industrial technology— arrayed in a group of buildings mainly neoclassical in design, clustered around a series of courtyards. The Tower of Jewels, an immense structure 432 feet high, covered with 102,000 pieces of faceted, colored glass backed with mirrors, dominated the central area and was visible across much of San Francisco. For R. L. Duffus, a San Francisco newspaper reporter, the tower "was a thing of magic.

The winds came in from the sea, and the bits of glass were hardly ever still; and the crowds stared and exclaimed, and nobody worried too much about the future." Looking at the tower, "sometimes it seemed that this Exposition, and its Tower of Jewels would stand forever, or at least until the whole earth had been converted to justice, freedom, and peace."[8]

When visitors tired of strolling through the formal exhibit halls, which included a Ford Motor Company assembly line that turned out a car every ten minutes and a working Underwood typewriter fifteen feet tall and twenty-one feet wide, they could head for the Joy Zone on the edge of the fair grounds, where monumental architecture and educational exhibits gave way to such fanciful displays as submarine rides, a moving panorama re-creating the battle of Gettysburg, the Santa Fe Railroad's model of the Grand Canyon, and a reproduction of Yellowstone's Old Faithful Inn, complete with fake geysers.[9] The most ambitious exhibit in the Zone, appropriately enough, was a massive replica of the Panama Canal. Passing through a giant arch with PANAMA CANAL emblazoned across the top, visitors entered an enormous auditorium sprawling over nearly five acres. In the center was a scale model of the Canal, exact in every detail—the chief architect of the Canal, George Goethals, had checked the design himself—down to the miniature ships operated by a system of magnets. A twelve-hundred-seat amphitheater revolved slowly around the model as spectators listened to a recorded narrative through telephone receivers installed at each seat.[10]

Perhaps the most popular attraction at the fair, however, was not the Canal, or the miniature railroads and mountains and geysers, or the other circus-style amusements of the Zone, but the daily display of the very latest in transportation technology. Nearly every afternoon, a tiny, single-engine airplane roared along the broad expanse of grass between the main buildings and the bay, taking off for a demonstration of loops and turns before a crowd of astonished spectators. In the early weeks of the fair, the pilot was Lincoln Beachey, famous as the first American to execute a complete loop in the air, a feat known as "looping the loop." A methodical man who analyzed the aerodynamics of his maneuvers, practicing over and over until he could predict how his plane would handle in a given situation,

Beachey was best known among professional aviators for solving the problem of how to pull a plane out of a spin, the most common cause of early crashes. (The answer was much the same as the strategy for handling a skidding car: Steer in the direction of the spin.) Beachey had retired from exhibition flying in 1913, in part because he felt responsible for the large number of young men killed while trying to imitate stunts he had pioneered, but he was persuaded to come out of retirement for the fair. Even his exceptional skill was no guarantee against disaster, however; just a few weeks into the fair, Beachey crashed and died when the wings of his plane collapsed.[11]

The Exposition's promoters quickly hired Art Smith, an ambitious twenty-one-year-old from Fort Wayne, Indiana, who had made a reputation doing exhibition flights all over the Midwest. In his five years of flying, Smith had his share of accidents, most dramatically when he and his fiancée decided to elope—her father didn't approve of aviation as a career—and ended up crashing in a cow pasture in southern Michigan. (They went on with the wedding anyway, swathed in bandages, in a bedside ceremony at the hotel where they were recuperating.) But Smith, like Beachey, was methodical in thinking through the scientific basis for every maneuver, and after some early brushes with disaster, he learned not to be drawn into flying under unsafe conditions. That and a certain amount of luck— he claimed that his mother's anguished prayers were all that had saved him from crashing in one of his early exhibitions—kept him alive through dozens of flights in 1915 and many years afterward.[12]

For most of the spectators watching Beachey and Smith, flying was a stunt—the more dips and loops and death-defying feats, the better. But for Smith and many other early aviators, "fancy flying," as the exhibition flights were called, was not mere entertainment but a way of pushing the limits of aviation technology, of learning more about how planes worked in order to make them better. In 1915, aviation was already far more advanced in Europe, where national governments were subsidizing the development of planes for use in war.[13] But the potential for aviation in peacetime was even greater, Smith believed, for the airplane not only covered distance faster than any other form of transportation, but made boundaries, whether geographical or political, irrelevant. Imagine how far fifteen miles was when the only way to get about was to walk, he asked, while now a fifteen-mile distance is nothing. In an airplane, he claimed, two hundred miles is equivalent to fifteen on the ground—a mere trifle—and the speed of air travel would only increase in the future, dwarfing the changes inspired by the invention of steamships and railroads.[14] In the manner of the more optimistic promoters of the Panama Canal, Smith saw in a shrinking world the key to peace among nations.

It was a vision shared by many others, especially in the United States, where the love affair with technology had a long history. Orville Wright, not one to make excessive claims for his invention— on at least one occasion he expressed doubts that planes would ever compete with trains or cars, or fly at speeds much faster than forty-five miles per hour—said in 1917 that airplanes would soon wipe out all motive for war by eliminating the geographical and political barriers between nations. Others predicted, in an argument foreshadowing claims for the deterrent value of nuclear weapons, that aviation would put a stop to war because only "fools" would fight when armies had planes as part of their arsenals. (On the other hand, there were many in Britain who had quite a different view of the airplane's potential, recognizing that their country's natural geographical barriers would no longer protect it from attack, a point of view expressed most chillingly in H. G. Wells's futuristic novel *The War of the Worlds.*)[15]

As misguided as these visionaries seem today, their optimism about the power of technology to promote world peace was hardly new. Early champions of the railroad in Europe, especially in France, had viewed it as a way of erasing class differences by improving mobility for workers, while Thomas Cook launched his career on the belief that travel would encourage mutual knowledge and understanding among people of different nationalities. Where Cook used the latest in transportation technology to take working people to the first world's fair in 1851, Smith—with the 1915 fair as his platform—looked beyond the war in Europe to argue that the airplane could be an instrument for bringing people together in time of peace. Soon, he believed, exhibition fliers like himself would be out of a job, as flying became an ordinary affair. It was always "thrilling" to go up in a plane, he observed, but before long it would be no more exciting than picking up the telephone. Within five years, he predicted, licenses to fly airplanes would be issued much like licenses to drive automobiles. Then, he added, "a change will begin in human life—a change so tremendous we can not even imagine it today."[16]

NOTES

PREFACE

1. Daniel Boorstin, "From Traveler to Tourist: The Lost Art of Travel,"
   in *The Image: A Guide to Pseudo-Events in America*, rev. ed. (New
   York, 1987), pp. 77–117; Paul Fussell, *Abroad: British Literary Traveling
   Between the Wars* (New York, 1980), pp. vii, 41; William W. Stowe,
   *Going Abroad: European Travel in Nineteenth-Century American Cul-
   ture* (Princeton, N.J., 1994), pp. 221–222.
2. Boorstin, op. cit., p. 85; Fussell makes this point as well, op. cit., p. 39.
   One of the earliest examples of the word *tourist* from the *Oxford English
   Dictionary* is "a traveller is nowadays called a tourist." For a particularly thoughtful analysis of the interplay between the notions of "traveler" and "tourist," and the history of what the author calls
   "anti-tourism" in Western culture, see James Buzard, *The Beaten Track:
   European Tourism, Literature, and the Ways to Culture, 1800–1918* (Oxford, 1993).
3. Quoted in Terry Caesar, *Forgiving the Boundaries: Home As Abroad in
   American Travel Writing* (Athens, Ga., 1995), p. 53.
4. Ian Ousby, *The Englishman's England: Taste, Travel, and the Rise of
   Tourism* (Cambridge, 1990), pp. 6–7. There are a number of books about
   what has come to be called the "golden age of travel," which is usually
   defined more or less as the period from the 1870s to World War II, thus
   beginning at the point when luxury trains and so-called "grand hotels"

first made luxury travel possible, and ending with the beginning of commercial airplane travel on a large scale. See, for example, Alexis Gregory, *The Golden Age of Travel, 1880–1939* (New York, 1991); H. B. Morrison, *The Golden Age of Travel: Literary Impressions of the Grand Tour* (New York, 1951), and Harold Darling, *Bon Voyage! Souvenirs from the Golden Age of Travel* (New York, 1990).

CHAPTER I: YOUNG GENTLEMEN ON TOUR

1. Among recent writers on travel, both Dennis Porter and Eric J. Leed discuss Boswell at some length; Porter argues that he was quite typical of eighteenth-century grand tourists. Porter, *Haunted Journeys: Desire and Transgression in European Travel Writing* (Princeton, 1991), esp. pp. 30–31; Leed, *The Mind of the Traveler: From Gilgamesh to Global Tourism* (New York, 1991), pp. 265–268.

2. *Boswell in Holland, 1763–1764,* ed. Frederick A. Pottle (New York, 1952), p. 1; Frederick A. Pottle and Chauncey B. Tinker, *A New Portrait of James Boswell* (Cambridge, Mass., 1927), pp. 46–52.

3. Alexander Boswell to James Boswell, August 10, 1765, in *Boswell on the Grand Tour: Italy, Corsica, and France, 1765–1766,* ed. Frederick A. Pottle and Frank Brady (New York, 1955), p. 211; *Boswell on the Grand Tour: Germany and Switzerland, 1764,* ed. Frederick A. Pottle (New York, 1953), p. 90.

4. *The Englishman's Fortnight in Paris* (London, 1777); J.A.R. Pimlott, *The Englishman's Holiday: A Social History* (London, 1947), pp. 69–71; Christopher Hibbert, *The Grand Tour* (London, 1987), pp. 235–237; Porter, *Haunted Journeys,* p. 27.

5. Geoffrey Trease, *The Grand Tour* (London, 1967), pp. 154–155, 179–180; Tobias Smollett, *Travels Through France and Italy* (London, 1766), pp. xx–xxi; *Correspondence of Thomas Gray,* ed. Paget Toynbee and Leonard Whibley, 3 vols. (Oxford, 1935), Vol. 1, p. 99.

6. Jeremy Black, *The British and the Grand Tour* (London, 1965), pp. 1–5; Hibbert, *Grand Tour,* p. 39.

7. Jane Robinson, *Wayward Women: A Guide to Women Travellers* (Oxford, 1990), pp. 32–34; Introduction to Johann Wolfgang von Goethe, *Italian Journey,* trans. W. H. Auden and Elizabeth Mayer (New York, 1962), pp. xii–xv.

8. Philip Thicknesse, *Useful Hints to Those Who Make the Tour of France* (London, 1768), p. 116; Porter, *Haunted Journeys,* p. 19; John Pemble, *The Mediterranean Passion: Victorians and Edwardians in the South* (Oxford and New York, 1987), pp. 96–99; Paul Fussell, *Abroad: British Literary Traveling Between the Wars* (New York, 1980), pp. 73–76.

9. Thomas Nugent, *The Grand Tour,* 4 vols. (London, 1749). On the changing interest in Italy and France, see Trease, *Grand Tour,* pp. 22, 129; Maxine Feifer, *Tourism in History: From Imperial Rome to the Present* (New York, 1986), p. 79; E. S. Bates, *Touring in 1600*

(London, 1987), pp. 111–112; Hibbert, *Grand Tour*, pp. 16–17; John Stoye, *English Travellers Abroad, 1604–1667: Their Influence in English Society and Politics* (London, 1952), pp. 24–25, 120–121; James Howell, *Instructions for Forraine Travel* (London, 1642), pp. 18–19, 26–29.

10. Quoted in Paul Franklin Kirby, *The Grand Tour in Italy, 1700–1800* (New York, 1932), p. 6.

11. Hibbert, *Grand Tour*, pp. 36–37; *The Autobiographies of Edward Gibbon*, ed. John Murray (London, 1897), pp. 135–136; *Boswell...Italy*, pp. 116–117. On the general connection between education and pleasure in motivating the grand tour, see Charles L. Batten, *Pleasurable Instruction: Form and Convention in Eighteenth Century Travel Literature* (Berkeley, Calif., 1978).

12. Goethe, *Italian Journey*, pp. 88, 110, 316–317.

13. See, for example, Thomas Martyn, *A Gentleman's Guide in His Tour Through France* (London, 1787), and John Moore, *A View of Society and Manners in Italy*, 2 vols. (London, 1792).

14. William Edward Mead, *The Grand Tour in the Eighteenth Century* (Boston, 1914), pp. 29–30; Hibbert, *Grand Tour*, pp. 41–44; Black, *British and the Grand Tour*, pp. 6–8.

15. Smollett, *Travels*, pp. 9, 114.

16. Pemble, *Mediterranean Passion*, pp. 33–34; Hibbert, *Grand Tour*, pp. 113–114; Black, *British and the Grand Tour*, pp. 88–92; Trease, *Grand Tour*, pp. 7–8.

17. Hibbert, op. cit., p. 33; Martyn, *Gentleman's Guide*, pp. vii–xv; G. R. DeBeer, *Early Travellers in the Alps* (London, 1930), p. 5.

18. Gray, *Correspondence*, Vol. 1, p. 101; *Boswell...Germany*, p. 50.

19. Young, quoted in Hibbert, *Grand Tour*, p. 46; Smollet, *Travels*, p. 66.

20. Goethe, *Italian Journey*, p. 110.

21. Martyn, *Gentleman's Guide*, pp. xv–xvii, 11; Hibbert, *Grand Tour*, pp. 45–46; Smollett, *Travels*, pp. 64–66; Constantia Maxwell, *The English Traveller in France, 1698–1815* (London, 1932), pp. 22–27, 34; Pemble, *Mediterranean Passion*, pp. 20–21.

22. Gray to Ashton, April 21, 1739, *Correspondence*, Vol. 1, p. 105; Thicknesse, *Observations on Customs and Manners of the French Nation* (1766), p. 32, and *A Year's Journey Through France*, 2 vols. (1777), Vol. 2, p. 153; Walpole quoted in Hibbert, *Grand Tour*, pp. 62–63.

23. Hibbert, op. cit., p. 64.

24. Howard C. Rice, Jr., *Thomas Jefferson's Paris* (Princeton, N.J., 1976), pp. 14–20, 37–42.

25. R. S. Lambert, *The Fortunate Traveller: A Short History of Touring and Travel for Pleasure* (London, 1950), p. 48; Hibbert, *Grand Tour*, p. 59; Smollett, *Travels*, pp. 33, 44–45; Young, quoted in Eric Newby, *A Book of Travellers' Tales* (New York, 1987), p. 136; Thicknesse, *Journey Through France*, Vol. 2, p. 98.

26. Hibbert, op. cit., pp. 60–62.

27. Gibbon, *Autobiographies*, p. 125; Thicknesse, *Observations on...the*

French Nation, pp. 35–36, 57–58; Gray, *Correspondence*, Vol. 1, pp. 105–107; Smollett, *Travels*, p. 46; Hibbert, op. cit., pp. 75–76.

28. Smollett, op. cit., p. 44; Johnson quoted in Hibbert, ibid., p. 54; Thicknesse, *Journey Through France*, pp. 92–100. On general reactions to Paris, see also Hibbert, pp. 59–63; Maxwell, *English Traveller in France*, pp. 39–44.

29. Gray, *Correspondence*, Vol. 1, p. 105; Smollett, *Travels*, pp. 52–55.

30. Hibbert, *Grand Tour*, pp. 78–87; *Boswell . . . Germany*, pp. 43–46; Pottle and Tinker, *Portrait of Boswell*, pp. 151–153.

31. *The Letters and Works of Lady Mary Wortley Montagu*, ed. Lord Wharncliffe, 2 vols. (London, 1893), Vol. 2, pp. 257–258; *Boswell . . . Germany*, p. 202.

32. Hibbert, *Grand Tour*, p. 195; *Boswell . . . Germany*, pp. 279–294.

33. Rousseau had not settled in Môtiers by accident. In the 1750s and early 1760s he had lived in Paris, where he published three of his most famous works, *La Nouvelle Heloïse*, *Emile*, and *Le Contrat Social*, all in the period 1761–62. Because of its unorthodox statements about religion (which, in fact, had a profound influence on Boswell), *Emile* drew the wrath of French authorities. The book was banned and an order issued for Rousseau's arrest. He fled to Switzerland, only to be driven out again, and finally retreated to Neuchâtel, which was not at that time part of Switzerland but under the control of Prussia.

34. *Boswell . . . Germany*, pp. 218–225.

35. DeBeer, *Early Travellers in the Alps*, p. 12; Hibbert, *Grand Tour*, pp. 91–95; Martyn, *Gentleman's Guide*, pp. 1, 5, 20–22; Black, *British and the Grand Tour*, pp. 18–20.

36. Trease, *Grand Tour*, p. 183; *Boswell . . . Italy*, pp. 22–23; Gray, *Letters*, November 7, 1739, p. 126.

37. Gray to West, November 16, 1739, *Correspondence*, Vol. 1, p. 128; Gray to his mother, December 19, 1739, op. cit., p. 134; Joseph Addison, *Remarks on Several Parts of Italy . . . in the Years 1701, 1702, 1703* (London, 1718), p. 350. The distaste for mountains had deep roots in European folklore and religious beliefs. Traditional theology, going back to Augustine, held that God had produced the irregular and barren features of the earth after the original creation, in his wrath at Adam's fall; thus it was possible to believe in the perfection of God's creation while abhorring some of the earth's physical formations, which were intended to be ugly and horrifying. According to popular mythology, mountains (and the Alps in particular) were home to fierce dragons, a belief that persisted in some quarters well into the seventeenth century. In 1706, a Swiss scientist published a book that included a catalogue of dragons, canton by canton, complete with illustrations. See Francis Gribble, *The Early Mountaineers* (London, 1899), pp. 14–16.

38. Smollett, *Travels*, pp. 114–115, 202–211.

39. Addison, *Remarks on . . . Italy*, pp. 1–7; *Boswell . . . Italy*, pp. 225–236.

40. Ibid., pp. 24, 31.

41. Black, *British and the Grand Tour,* p. 22.

42. Hibbert, *Grand Tour,* pp. 125–130, 135–136, 141–147; Goethe, *Italian Journey,* pp. 45, 83–84; *The Grand Tour of William Beckford,* ed. Elizabeth Mavor (Harmondsworth, 1986), p. 61.

43. Hibbert, op. cit., p. 141; Beckford, op. cit., p. 79.

44. Hibbert, op. cit., pp. 149–152; John Moore, *Society and Manners in Italy,* Vol. 2, pp. 390–391.

45. Beckford, *Grand Tour,* p. 110; Goethe, *Italian Journey,* pp. 115–116; Gibbon, *Autobiographies,* pp. 134–136; Addison, *Remarks on . . . Italy,* p. 207.

46. Montagu, *Letters,* Vol. 2, p. 208; Moore, *Society and Manners in Italy,* Vol. 1, p. 487.

47. Goethe, *Italian Journey,* pp. 136–138; *Boswell . . . Italy,* pp. 60–62; Beckford, *Grand Tour,* p. 113.

48. Hibbert, *Grand Tour,* pp. 177–180, 242–247; *Boswell . . . Italy,* p. 74.

49. Gray to West, April 16, 1740, *Correspondence,* Vol. 1, p. 148; *Boswell . . . Italy,* p. 72.

50. Walpole quoted in Newby, *Travellers' Tales,* p. 128; Addison, *Remarks on . . . Italy,* pp. 136, 138; Gray to West, April 16, 1740, *Correspondence,* Vol. 1, p. 148.

51. Addison, *Remarks on . . . Italy,* pp. 138–139; Beckford, *Grand Tour,* p. 113; Hibbert, *Grand Tour,* pp. 155–157.

52. Moore, *Society and Manners in Italy,* Vol. 2, pp. 147–158; Martyn, *Gentleman's Guide,* pp. 287–288; Goethe, *Italian Journey,* pp. 199, 312–317.

53. Goethe, op. cit., pp. 199–200, 319.

54. Moore, *Society and Manners in Italy,* Vol. 1, p. 362.

CHAPTER 2: TOURING IN SEARCH OF THE PICTURESQUE

1. *Boswell's Journal of a Tour to the Hebrides with Samuel Johnson,* ed. Frederick A. Pottle and Charles H. Bennett (New York, 1936), p. 3.

2. Ibid., p. 33.

3. On the "foreignness" of Scotland, Malcolm Andrews, *The Search for the Picturesque: Landscape Aesthetics and Tourism in Britain, 1760–1800* (Palo Alto, Calif., 1989), p. 201.

4. Boswell, *Tour to the Hebrides,* p. 3.

5. Ibid., p. 16.

6. Ibid., pp. 82–96; quote from p. 96.

7. Ibid., pp. 99–101; quote from p. 101.

8. Leslie Stephen, *The Playground of Europe* (London, 1871), p. 10; Boswell, *Tour to the Hebrides,* pp. 6, 30; quote from p. 30.

9. Johnson, *A Journey to the Western Islands of Scotland,* ed. J. D. Fleeman (Oxford, 1985), pp. 95–98.

10. Ibid., pp. 33–36.

11. Boswell, *Tour to the Hebrides,* p. 210.

12. Ibid., pp. 108, 46.

13. Johnson, *Scotland,* p. 55; Boswell, *Tour to the Hebrides,* p. 120.

14. Introduction to Johnson, *Scotland,* pp. xxxi–xxxv; Andrews, *The Search for the Picturesque,* p. 198; William Mavor, *The British Tourists* (London, 1798), Vol. 1, p. vii.

15. William Gilpin, *Observations Relative Chiefly to Picturesque Beauty, Made in the Year 1776, on Several Parts of Great Britain; Particularly the High-Lands of Scotland,* 2 vols. (London, 1789), Vol. 1, p. 209; Vol. 2, pp. 123–127.

16. William Gilpin, *Observations on the River Wye, and Several Parts of South Wales, &c., Relative Chiefly to Picturesque Beauty . . .* 2nd ed. (London, 1789), and *Observations on Several Parts of England, Particularly the Mountains and Lakes of Cumberland and Westmorland,* 3rd ed. (London, 1808).

17. Quoted in Andrews, *Search for the Picturesque,* p. 200.

18. Keith Thomas, *Man and the Natural World: Changing Attitudes in England, 1500–1800* (London, 1983), pp. 15–22.

19. Boswell, *Tour to the Hebrides,* p. 331.

20. Christopher Hussey, *The Picturesque* (New York, 1927), pp. 55–60; Elizabeth Manwaring, *Italian Landscape in Eighteenth-Century England* (New York, 1925), pp. 175–176; Andrews, *Search for the Picturesque,* pp. 109–110. Oceans evoked similarly fearful reactions, and for similar reasons; see Alain Corbin, *The Lure of the Sea: The Discovery of the Seaside in the Western World, 1750–1840,* trans. Jocelyn Phelps (Berkeley and Los Angeles, 1994), pp. 3–6.

21. Thomas, *Man and the Natural World,* pp. 212–213.

22. C. Cambry, *Voyage Pittoresque en Suisse et en Italie,* 2 vols. (Paris, 1801), p. 77.

23. Quoted in John Julius Norwich, *A Taste for Travel* (New York, 1985), p. 7.

24. *Letters of William and Dorothy Wordsworth,* ed. E. DeSelincourt, *The Early Years, 1787–1805,* rev. Chester L. Shaver (Oxford, 1967), p. 37.

25. Gilpin, *Picturesque Beauty,* Vol. 1, p. 50.

26. Arthur Young also used the term while traveling in the Lake District in the 1760s; see Manwaring, *Italian Landscape,* p. 168.

27. Antoine Nicolas Dezallier d'Argenville, *Voyage Pittoresque de Paris, ou Indication de tout ce qu'il y a de plus beau dans cette grande Ville, en Peinture, Sculpture, et Architecture,* 4th ed. (Paris, 1765); G.M.A. Brune, *Voyage Pittoresque et sentimental dans plusieurs provinces occidentales de la France* (London, 1802); Th. de M. de Rouvrois, *Voyage Pittoresque en Alsace* (Mulhouse, 1844); C. de Lambertie, *Voyage Pittoresque en Californie et au Chili* (Paris, 1853). On Gilpin's chauvinism, see Edward J. Nygren with Bruce Robertson, *Views and Visions: American Landscape Before 1800* (Washington, 1986), pp. 18–19.

28. Ann Bermingham, *Landscape and Ideology: The English Rustic Tradition, 1740–1860* (Berkeley and Los Angeles, 1986), pp. 33, 57–58; David Manning, "The Visual Arts," in *Eighteenth-Century Britain*, Vol. 5 of *The Cambridge Cultural History of Britain*, ed. Boris Ford (Cambridge, 1992), p. 144.

29. Manwaring, *Italian Landscape*, p. 169.

30. Joseph Addison, *Remarks on Several Parts of Italy . . . in the Years 1701, 1702, 1703* (London, 1718), p. 350; Arthur Humphreys, "The Arts in Eighteenth Century Britain," in *Eighteenth-Century Britain*, p. 44; Hussey, *The Picturesque*, p. 87; Manwaring, op. cit., p. 175.

31. Hussey, op. cit., pp. 53–60; Manwaring, op. cit., p. 17; Ian Ousby, *The Englishman's England: Taste, Travel, and the Rise of Tourism* (Cambridge, 1990), p. 146.

32. Cambry, *Voyage Pittoresque en Suisse*, p. 185.

33. Wordsworth, *Letters, The Early Years*, p. 35.

34. Bermingham, *Landscape and Ideology*, p. 84. Uvedale Price published a book attempting to distinguish among the picturesque, sublime, and beautiful: *An Essay on the Picturesque Compared with the Sublime and the Beautiful . . .* (London, 1794–98). Arthur Young, *A Six Months' Tour Through the North of England* (London, 1770), p. 119; Dorothy Wordsworth, *Journals*, ed. E. DeSelincourt, 2 vols. (1941), Vol. 1, pp. 223–224.

35. D. Wordsworth, *Journal of a Tour to the Continent*, op. cit., Vol. 2.

36. Arnold Lunn, *Switzerland and the English* (London, 1944), pp. 32–47; Paul P. Bernard, *Rush to the Alps: The Evolution of Vacationing in Switzerland* (New York, 1978), pp. 18–22, 87–88.

37. Cambry, *Voyage Pittoresque en Suisse*, p. 13; Arnold Lunn, *Switzerland*, pp. 66–68, and *A Century of Mountaineering, 1857–1957* (London, 1957), pp. 28–29.

38. Andrews observes that the "divinization" of nature was even more pronounced in Britain than elsewhere, perhaps as a consequence of greater urbanization and industrialization; *Search for the Picturesque*, p. 153.

39. "Ode to the Sun," 1776, quoted in Andrews, op. cit., p. 153.

40. Esther Moir, *The Discovery of Britain: The English Tourists, 1540 to 1840* (London, 1964), pp. xiv, 37, 129; quote from p. 37. See also Marjorie Nicolson, *Mountain Gloom and Mountain Glory: The Development of the Aesthetics of the Infinite* (Ithaca, N.Y., 1959), p. 76, on the remoteness of this region.

41. Thomas West, *A Guide to the Lakes in Cumberland, Westmorland, and Lancaster* (London, 1778).

42. Gray, "Tour of the Lakes," in ibid., pp. 359–364; quotes from pp. 360, 364.

43. Andrews, *Search for the Picturesque*, p. 158; Manwaring, *Italian Landscape*, pp. 182, 194–195.

44. Young, *Travels*, pp. 150–151, 163–164.

45. Quoted in Andrews, *Search for the Picturesque*, p. 175; Nicolson, *Mountain Gloom*, p. 69.

46. Young, *Travels*, p. 126.

47. [William Combe], *The Tour of Doctor Syntax in Search of the Picturesque: A Poem*, 3rd ed. (London, 1813); Moir, *Discovery of Britain*, pp. 139, 147–149; Nicolson, *Mountain Gloom*, pp. 110–111; Jane Austen, *Northanger Abbey*.

48. William Hutchinson, *An Excursion to the Lakes in Westmorland and Cumberland . . .* (London, 1776), pp. 66–67; Nicolson, *Mountain Gloom*, pp. 105–106; Ousby, *Englishman's England*, pp. 150–151; quote from Ousby.

49. Ousby, op. cit., pp. 172–173; Andrews, *Search for the Picturesque*, pp. 153–154; Introduction to William Wordsworth, *A Guide Through the District of the Lakes in the North of England* (London, 1951).

50. Ousby, op. cit., p. 179; W. Wordsworth, op. cit., pp. 69–83; also Moir, *Discovery of Britain*, pp. 155–156, notes that Wordsworth wanted to encourage a simpler, less programmed approach to seeing the lakes.

51. Letter to Isabella Fenwick, August 2, 1848, *The Letters of Mary Wordsworth, 1800–1855*, ed. Mary E. Burton (Oxford, 1958), p. 299; Ousby, op. cit., p. 180.

52. *Atlantic Monthly*, October 1895, pp. 514–515.

53. Andrews, *Search for the Picturesque*, p. 200.

54. Mrs. S. Murray Austin, *A Companion and Useful Guide to the Beauties of Scotland, and the Hebrides, to the Lakes of Westmorland, Cumberland . . .* , 3rd ed., 2 vols. (London, 1810), Vol. 1, pp. 41, 60–61. On the conditions of travel in general, see Andrews, op. cit., p. 22; James Holloway and Lindsay Errington, *The Discovery of Scotland: The Appreciation of Scottish Scenery Through Two Centuries of Painting* (Edinburgh, 1978), p. 103; John Stoddart, *Remarks on Local Scenery and Manners in Scotland*, 2 vols. (London, 1800).

55. Gilpin, *Picturesque Beauty*, Vol. 2, p. 111; Stoddart, *Manners in Scotland*, pp. x–xi.

56. Andrews, *Search for the Picturesque*, p. 206.

57. Ibid., pp. 213–217.

58. D. Wordsworth, *Journals*, Vol. 1, pp. 264, 286. On routes through northern Scotland, see Holloway and Errington, *Discovery of Scotland*, p. 57. On encounters with the Highlanders, see D. Wordsworth, p. 257, and Stoddart, *Manners in Scotland*, p. 249; on travel in northern Scotland generally, see Andrews, *Search for the Picturesque*, p. 204.

59. [William Combe], *The Tour of Doctor Prosody in Search of the Antique and Picturesque Through Scotland, the Hebrides, the Orkney and Shetland Isles* (London, 1821).

60. Holloway and Errington, *Discovery of Scotland*, p. 71.

61. See, for example, William Preston, who used the first canto as "the programme of our route," *The Reminiscences of William C. Preston*, ed. Minnie Clare Yarborough (Chapel Hill, N.C., 1933), pp. 44–45; also

Harriet Beecher Stowe, *Sunny Memories of Foreign Lands* (Boston, 1854), Vol. 1, Chapters 2–3; William Cullen Bryant, *Letters of a Traveller* (New York, 1871), p. 184; and Bayard Taylor, *Views A Foot, or Europea Seen with a Knapsack* (New York, 1902), p. 29, who called Scott's descriptions "wonderfully exact." On Scott's popularity in general, see Holloway and Errington, *Discovery of Scotland*, p. 109.

62. Quoted in Holloway and Errington, op. cit., p. 103.

63. John F. Sears, *Sacred Places: American Tourist Attractions in the Nineteenth Century* (New York, 1989).

64. Bryant, *Letters of a Traveller*, p. 184.

CHAPTER 3: THE GRAND TOUR REVISITED

1. Hugh Tregaskis, *Beyond the Grand Tour: The Levant Lunatics* (London, 1979), pp. 66–105.

2. Marianne Baillie, *First Impressions on a Tour upon the Continent* (London, 1819), p. 33; Byron quoted in the Introduction to *The Italian Journal of Samuel Rogers,* ed. J. R. Hale (London, 1956), p. 60; John Pemble, *The Mediterranean Passion: Victorians and Edwardians in the South* (Oxford and New York, 1987), pp. 1, 7, 39; James Fenimore Cooper, *Gleanings in Europe: Italy* (Albany, N.Y., 1981), p. 23.

3. Pemble, *Mediterranean Passion,* p. 77; James Fenimore Cooper, *Gleanings in Europe: France* (Albany, N.Y., 1983), p. 46; Foster Rhea Dulles, *Americans Abroad: Two Centuries of European Travel* (Ann Arbor, Mich., 1964), p. 27.

4. Dennis Porter makes the point that, beginning around the turn of the century, the grand tour ceased to be primarily educational in purpose, as travel simply for the sake of pleasure became broadly acceptable. He cites Byron as one of the exemplars of this new style of travel in *Haunted Journeys: Desire and Transgression in European Travel Writing* (Princeton, N.J., 1991), pp. 125–126.

5. Richard Boyle Bernard, *A Tour Through Some Parts of France, Switzerland, Savoy, Germany and Belgium During the Summer and Autumn of 1814* (London, 1815), p. 65; Harold Perkin, *The Origins of Modern English Society, 1780–1880* (London, 1969), pp. 3–4; Douglass C. North, *The Economic Growth of the United States, 1790–1860* (Englewood Cliffs, N.J., 1961), pp. 27, 68–81.

6. Quoted in Pemble, *Mediterranean Passion,* p. 1.

7. Dulles, *Americans Abroad,* p. 28.

8. Geoffrey Trease, *The Grand Tour* (London, 1967), p. 233.

9. Dulles, *Americans Abroad,* pp. 26–27, 43; George R. Taylor, *The Transportation Revolution, 1815–1860* (New York, 1951), pp. 112–117.

10. Philip S. Bagwell, *Britain and America, 1850–1939: A Study of Economic Change* (London, 1970), pp. 41–43, 48–49; Wolfgang Schivelbusch, *The Railway Journey: The Industrialization of Time and Space in the Nineteenth Century* (Berkeley, Calif., 1986), p. 7; J.A.R. Pimlott,

The Englishman's Holiday: A Social History (London, 1947), p. 75; W. T. Jackman, *The Development of Transportation in Modern England* (London, 1966), pp. 285–302; 310–311, 314; Ian Ousby, *The Englishman's England: Taste, Travel, and the Rise of Tourism* (Cambridge, 1990), pp. 9–10.

11. Fernand Braudel, *The Identity of France*, Vol. 1: *History and Environment*, trans. Siân Reynolds (London, 1989), pp. 113–115.

12. Mariana Starke, *Travels on the Continent, Written for the Use and Particular Information of Travellers* (London, 1820), Vol. 1, pp. 6, 51, 69–71, and *Information and Directions for Travellers on the Continent of Europe* (London, 1839), p. 39; Baillie, *First Impressions*, pp. 216–217.

13. *The Roads and Railroads, Vehicles, and Modes of Travelling, of Ancient and Modern Countries* (London, 1839), pp. 196–197.

14. Pemble, *Mediterranean Passion*, p. 22; see also The Countess of Blessington, *The Idler in France*, 2 vols. (London, 1842), Vol. 1, pp. 359–360, 385–389.

15. Benjamin Silliman, *A Visit to Europe in 1851*, 2 vols. (New York, 1854), Vol. 1, p. 241; also Cooper, *Italy*, pp. 55–57; Dickens, *Pictures from Italy* (New York, 1988), pp. 49–52.

16. John Murray, *A Hand-Book for Travellers in France* (London, 1843), pp. xxiv–xxv; Cooper, *France*, p. 58; Frances Trollope, *A Visit to Italy*, 2 vols. (London, 1842), pp. 3–5.

17. William Hazlitt, "Notes of a Journey Through France and Italy" in *The Collected Works of William Hazlitt*, ed. A. R. Waller and Arnold Glover, 12 vols. (London, 1903), p. 184.

18. William Preston, *The Reminiscences of William Preston*, ed. Minnie Clare Yarborough (Chapel Hill, N.C., 1933), p. 52.

19. For example, see John Murray, *A Hand-Book for Travellers in Switzerland and the Alps of Savoy and Piedmont* (London, 1838), pp. xii–xvi, and *The Tourist in Europe: or A Concise Summary of the Various Routes, Objects of Interest, &c.* (New York, 1838), p. 37.

20. *The Journal of John Mayne During a Tour on the Continent*, ed. John Mayne Colles (London, 1909), pp. 128, 150. Dickens and Trollope also recommended using vetturini in preference to posting.

21. Lady Sydney Morgan, *France in 1829–30*, 2 vols. (London, 1830), Vol. 1, pp. 19–22; Cooper, *Italy*, p. 20; Pemble, *Mediterranean Passion*, p. 106.

22. Bayard Taylor, *Views A Foot*, p. 316.

23. Morgan, *France in 1829–30*, Vol. 1, pp. 13, 19–22. Trollope notes addition of carpets also.

24. Starke's first book was titled *Travels in Italy, Between the Years 1792 and 1798 . . .* (London, 1802). The first edition of her work published by Murray was titled *Travels on the Continent . . .;* subsequent editions were titled *Information and Directions for Travellers . . .* (see above, note 12, for full citations).

25. Thomas Martyn, *A Gentleman's Guide in His Tour Through France* (London, 1787).

26. Starke, *Travels on the Continent*, pp. 47–48.

27. Samuel Smiles, *A Publisher and His Friends: Memoir and Correspondence of the Late John Murray* (London, 1891), p. 460; J. G. Ebel, *Manuel de Voyageur en Suisse*, 3rd French ed. (Paris, 1816); Introduction to Murray, *Hand-Book for ... Switzerland.*

28. John Murray, *A Hand-Book for Travellers to the Continent* (London, 1836), p. iii.

29. Herbert Warren Wind, "Profiles: The House of Baedeker," in *The New Yorker*, September 22, 1975, pp. 50–52. See also W. G. Constable, "Three Stars for Baedeker," *Harper's*, April 1953, pp. 76–83, and Arthur J. Olsen, "A Tour of Baedeker," *The New York Times Magazine*, November 29, 1959.

30. Murray, *The Tourist in Europe*, Preface.

31. John Murray, *A Hand-Book for Travellers to Denmark, Norway, Sweden, and Russia* (London, 1839), pp. iii–iv.

32. Wind, "House of Baedeker," p. 58.

33. Dulles, *Americans Abroad*, pp. 63–64.

34. Pierre C. Couperie, *Paris Through the Ages: An Illustrated Atlas of Urbanism and Architecture*, trans. Marilyn Low (New York, 1971), n.p.

35. Morgan, *France in 1829–30*, Vol. I, p. 5.

36. Gautier quoted in Donald J. Olsen, *The City As a Work of Art: London, Paris, Vienna* (New Haven, 1986), p. 34. On postwar Paris, see Murray, *Hand-Book for ... France* (1843); Morgan, op. cit., Vol. I, pp. 5, 16, 28–29; Hazlitt, "Notes of a Journey," p. 155; Frances Trollope, *Paris and the Parisians in 1835* (New York, 1936), pp. 77, 132–137, 187–188; Bryant, *Letters of a Traveller*, p. 219; Baillie, *First Impressions*, pp. 34, 46–47; *Journal of John Mayne*, pp. 48, 155; Bernard, *A Tour Through ... France*, pp. 20–22.

37. Germain Bazin, *The Louvre*, trans. M. I. Matin (New York, 1958), pp. 31–50.

38. Ibid., pp. 58–59.

39. The National Gallery in London was not established until 1824, moving to its present building in 1838. The British Museum dates back to 1759, but its collections consisted mostly of books and manuscripts until the early nineteenth century; its present building was completed in 1844.

40. Bazin, *The Louvre*, pp. 55–56.

41. Trollope, *Paris and the Parisians*, p. 39.

42. Introduction to Cooper, *France*, pp. xviii–xx. On the theater, see Morgan, *France in 1829–30*, Vol. I, pp. 73–76.

43. John Russell, *Paris* (New York, 1983), pp. 187–198.

44. *Galignani's New Paris Guide for ... 1844* (Paris, 1844), pp. 12–13; see also Russell, op. cit.

45. Emma Willard, *Journal and Letters from France and Great Britain* (Troy, N.Y., 1833), p. 62; Trollope, *Paris and the Parisians*, p. 247.

46. Cooper, *France*, pp. 47–48, 76–77, 90–91; Baillie, *First Impressions*, 41; Shepherd, 175; Caroline Kirkland, *Holidays Abroad* (New York, 1849), p. 75.

47. Taylor, *Views A Foot*, p. 436; Stowe, *Sunny Memories*, Vol. 2, p. 146; similar sentiments were expressed by John Overton Choules, *Young Americans Abroad; or, Vacation in Europe* (Boston, 1852), pp. 172–173; also Bryant, *Letters of a Traveller*, p. 12.

48. Hazlitt, "Notes of a Journey," pp. 98–99; see also Blessington, *Idler in France*, Vol. 1, pp. 21–24, and Trollope, *Paris and the Parisians*, p. 133.

49. Quoted in Dulles, *Americans Abroad*, pp. 39, 218.

50. Baillie, *First Impressions*, pp. 64–65, 68; Blessington, *Idler in France*, Vol. 1, pp. 150–155; [Charlotte Eaton], *Continental Adventures*, 3 vols. (London, 1826), Vol. 1, p. 34.

51. Eaton, op. cit., Vol. 1, p. 30; see also Baillie, *First Impressions*, p. 63.

52. Cooper, *Gleanings in Europe: Switzerland* (Albany, 1979), pp. 14–15; Eaton, op. cit., Vol. 1, pp. 94–95; see also *Journal of John Mayne*, p. 83; Baillie, *First Impressions*, p. 297.

53. The fascination with sites associated with writers continues today, as Paul Theroux observes in his recent travelogue *The Pillars of Hercules: A Grand Tour of the Mediterranean* (New York, 1995), p. 56.

54. Frances Trollope, *A Visit to Italy*, 2 vols. (London, 1852), Vol. 1, p. 7.

55. Johann Wolfgang von Goethe, *Italian Journey, 1786–1788*, trans. W. H. Auden and Elizabeth Mayer (New York, 1962), p. 88; Cooper, *Italy*, p. xx; Stendhal, *Rome, Naples, and Florence in 1817*, trans. Richard N. Coe (London, 1959), p. xiii.

56. On the appeal of the climate, see, for example, Blessington, *Idler in Italy*, Vol. 3, pp. 179–180.

57. Cooper, *Italy*, p. 21; Stendhal, *Rome, Naples*, pp. 2, 147–148.

58. Madame de Staël, *Corinne, or Italy*, trans. Avriel H. Goldberger (New Brunswick, N.J., 1987), pp. 135–136.

59. See, for example, Baillie, *First Impressions*, pp. 143, 162; Dickens, *Pictures from Italy*, p. 37.

60. For example, Catherine Maria Sedgwick, *Letters from Abroad to Kindred at Home*, 2 vols. (New York, 1841), Vol. 2, pp. 212–214.

61. Dickens, *Pictures from Italy*, pp. 23–24, 31–32; Baillie, *First Impressions*, p. 156.

62. The sense of Italy as a place of death and decline is a theme throughout Pemble, *Mediterranean Passion*.

63. [Boddington, Mary], *Sketches in the Pyrenees*, 2 vols. (London, 1837), Vol. 2, pp. 480–481.

64. Van Wyck Brooks, *The Dream of Arcadia: American Writers and Artists in Italy, 1750–1915* (New York, 1958), pp. 111–113.

65. See, for example, Blessington, *Idler in Italy*, Vol. 1, pp. 299, 389–393.

66. Cooper, *Italy*, p. 3.

67. Trollope, describing a party where the guests included British, French, Russians, and Germans but no Italians, remarked with annoyance that it was impossible to meet Italians in Italy; but most British visitors seemed quite happy to spend their time with their fellow countrymen: *A Visit to Italy*, Vol. 2, p. 154. On horse racing, see Taylor, *Views A Foot*, pp. 347–348.

68. Rome was even more influential among American artists; see William Vance, *America's Rome* (1989).

69. Sedgwick, *Letters from Abroad*, Vol. 2, pp. 142, 212–214; Trollope, *A Visit to Italy*, Vol. 2, pp. 161–163, 185, 262–263, 295; Dickens, *Pictures from Italy*, pp. 106–109; Hazlitt, "Notes of a Journey," p. 232.

70. Sedgwick, op. cit., Vol. 2, pp. 108, 150–151; Preston, "Reminiscences," p. 80; Hazlitt, op. cit., p. 232.

71. Dickens, *Pictures from Italy*, p. 141; Sedgwick, op. cit., Vol. 2, pp. 186–188, 219; Rogers, *Italy*, pp. 238–239.

72. Cooper, *Italy*, p. xxiii; Trollope, *A Visit to Italy*, Vol. 2, pp. 304–305; Rogers, op. cit., pp. 87–88.

73. Washington Irving, *Notes and Journal of Travel in Europe, 1804–05* (New York, 1920), Vol. 3, pp. 23–25; see also Sedgwick, *Letters from Abroad*, Vol. 2, p. 228.

74. Hazlitt, "Notes of a Journey," pp. 265–266; Blessington, *Idler in Italy*, Vol. 3, pp. 55, 68, 239; Trollope, *A Visit to Italy*, Vol. 2, pp. 22–23; Dickens, *Pictures from Italy*, p. 81.

75. Blessington, op. cit., Vol. 3, p. 139; Trollope, *A Visit to Italy*, Vol. 2, pp. 67, 80, 93–94; Dickens, op. cit., pp. 70–75.

76. Boddington, *Pyrenees*, Vol. 2, pp. 10, 208–211. Terry Caesar makes the point that, although tourists seem always to have criticized other tourists, the effort to find uncrowded places away from the usual tourist haunts does not appear to have been widespread until the late nineteenth century: *Forgiving the Boundaries: Home As Abroad in American Travel Writing* (Athens, Ga., 1995), p. 54.

77. William Makepeace Thackeray, "The Kickleburys on the Rhine," in *The Christmas Books of Mr. M. A. Titmarsh*, Vol. 12 of *The Works of William Makepeace Thackeray* (Philadelphia, 1876), p. 193; Brooks, *Dream of Arcadia*, p. 85; Introduction to Rogers, *Italy*, p. 61; Pemble, *Mediterranean Passion*, pp. 42–43; Blessington, *Idler in Italy*, Vol. 3, p. 67.

78. George Sand, *Lettres d'un Voyageur*, trans. Sacha Rabinovitch and Patricia Thomson (Harmondsworth, 1987), pp. 257–260.

79. Irving, *Travel in Europe*, Vol. 3, p. 128.

80. Ibid., pp. 103–104; Taylor, *Views A Foot*, p. 477; Sedgwick, *Letters from Abroad*, Vol. 2, p. 68; Charles Dudley Warner, *Saunterings* (New York, 1879), p. 57.

81. Frances Trollope, *Belgium and Western Germany in 1833*, 2 vols. (Brussels, 1834), Vol. 2, pp. 112–116; Dickens, *Pictures from Italy*,

p. 120; Blessington, *Idler in Italy,* Vol. 1, p. 21; Hazlitt, "Notes of a Journey," p. 89; Murray, *Hand-Book for... France,* pp. xxvii–xxviii.

82. Trollope, *A Visit to Italy,* Vol. 2, pp. 271–274; Introduction to Roger, *Italy,* p. 71.

83. Trollope, *A Visit to Italy,* Vol. 2, p. 272.

84. Frances Trollope, *The Robertses on Their Travels* (London, 1846); [Eaton], *Continental Adventures.*

85. Bernard, *A Tour Through... France,* pp. 66–67; Pemble, *Mediterranean Passion,* pp. 106–107.

86. H. J. Dyos and D. H. Aldcroft, *British Transport: An Economic Survey from the Seventeenth Century to the Twentieth* (Leicester, 1979), pp. 115–124, 129, 140; Bagwell, *Britain and America,* p. 92.

87. Henri Peyret, *Histoire des Chemins de Fer en France et dans le Monde* (Paris, 1949), pp. 33, 36–39; Roger Price, *The Modernization of Rural France: Communications Networks and Agricultural Market Structures in Nineteenth-Century France* (New York, 1983), pp. 208–209; Murray, *Hand-Book for... France,* p. xxvii; Alfred Cobban, *A History of Modern France* (Harmondsworth, 1957), pp. 165–166; Bagwell, *Britain and America,* p. 169; G. Freeman Allen, *Railways: Past, Present and Future* (London, 1982, 1987), pp. 32–33.

88. Murray, *A Hand-Book for... the Continent* (1850), p. 216; Allen, *Railways,* pp. 27–29; Nicholas Faith, *The World the Railways Made* (London, 1990), p. 27.

89. Dyos and Alden, *British Transport,* pp. 210–211; Schivelbusch, *Railway Journey,* pp. 33–34.

90. Bagwell, *Britain and America,* p. 107.

91. Ibid., pp. 108–109; Schivelbusch, *Railway Journey,* p. 72; Murray, *A Hand-Book for... the Continent,* pp. 97–98.

92. Edmund Swinglehurst, *The Romantic Journey: The Story of Thomas Cook and Victorian Travel* (New York, 1974), p. 22; Bagwell, op. cit., pp. 125–126; Peyret, *Histoire,* p. 31; Schivelbusch, op. cit., pp. 70–77.

93. Pimlott, *Englishman's Holiday,* pp. 91–93.

94. Wind, "House of Baedeker," p. 53; Kemble, quoted in Eric Newby, *A Book of Travellers' Tales* (New York, 1986), pp. 226–227.

95. Quoted in Schivelbusch, *Railway Journey,* pp. 57–58.

96. Ibid., pp. 11–12, 22–23; *The Collected Writings of Thomas De Quincey,* ed. David Masson (Edinburgh, 1890), Vol. 13, pp. 284–285; James Fenimore Cooper, essay in *The Home Book of the Picturesque: or, American Scenery, Art, and Literature* (New York, 1852; reprinted Gainesville, Fla., 1967), p. 65; James Holloway and Lindsay Errington, *The Discovery of Scotland: The Appreciation of Scottish Scenery Through Two Centuries of Painting* (Edinburgh, 1978), p. 103.

97. Quoted in Schivelbusch, op. cit., p. 61.

98. Arthur Sketchley, *Out for a Holiday with Cook's Excursion Through Switzerland and Italy* (London, 1870), p. 10; Stowe, *Sunny Memories,* Vol. 1, p. 42.

99. Schivelbusch, *Railway Journey,* pp. 64–66; Jack Simmons, *The Victorian Railway* (London, 1991), pp. 245–246; Faith, *World the Railways Made,* pp. 246–247.

100. James Walvin, *Leisure and Society, 1830–1950* (London, 1978), p. 15; Schivelbusch, op. cit., p. 42.

101. William Wordsworth, "Kendal and Windermere Railway. Two Letters Re-Printed from the Morning Post," London, 1845; in Vol. 3 of *The Prose Works of William Wordsworth,* ed. W.J.B. Owen and Jane Worthington Smyser, 3 vols. (Oxford, 1974), pp. 331–347.

102. *The Works of John Ruskin,* ed. E. T. Cook and Alexander Wedderburn (London, 1908), Vol. 34, pp. 140–141.

103. W. Wordsworth, "Kendal and Windermere Railway," p. 334.

CHAPTER 4: THE ''FASHIONABLE TOUR''

1. Charles Weld, *A Vacation Tour in the United States and Canada* (London, 1955), p. 2.

2. Introduction to Charles Dickens, *American Notes for General Circulation* (London, 1972), p. 11.

3. Elizabeth McKinsey, *Niagara Falls: Icon of the American Sublime* (Cambridge, 1985), p. 86.

4. James Fenimore Cooper, essay in *The Home Book of the Picturesque: or, American Scenery, Art, and Literature* (New York, 1852; reprinted Gainesville, Fla., 1967), pp. 52, 54, 69.

5. Edward J. Nygren with Bruce Robertson, *Views and Visions: American Landscape Before 1830* (Washington, 1986), p. 21.

6. Nathaniel Parker Willis, *Rural Letters* (New York, 1949), pp. iii, 1–2.

7. Bryant quoted in Hans Huth, *Nature and the American: Three Centuries of Changing Attitudes* (Berkeley and Los Angeles, 1957), pp. 36, 78; Nygren, *Views and Visions,* p. 40.

8. Theodore Dwight, *Travels in America* (Glasgow, 1848), p. 220; C. A. Goodrich, *The Family Tourist: A Visit to the Principal Cities of the Western Continent* (Philadelphia, 1948), p. vi.

9. Theodore Dwight, *Travels,* pp. 34–35. On early American travel in general, see John F. Sears, *Sacred Places: American Tourist Attractions in the Nineteenth Century* (New York, 1989), pp. 3–5; on European travelers in North America, see the Introduction to Dickens, *American Notes,* pp. 13–14, 20; Jane Mesick, *The English Traveler in America, 1785–1835* (New York, 1921); Max Berger, *The British Traveller in America, 1836–1860* (New York, 1943).

10. Isaac Weld, *Travels Through the States of North America and the Provinces of Upper and Lower Canada,* 2nd ed., 2 vols. (London, 1799), Vol. 1, pp. 47, 97; Timothy Dwight, *Travels in New England and New York,* ed. Barbara Miller Solomon (Cambridge, Mass., 1969), pp. 11–12. On the early conditions of travel, see also Basil Hall, *Travels in North America,*

in the Years 1827 and 1828 (Philadelphia, 1929), p. 63; Mesick, *English Traveler*, pp. 47–51, 55–60; Berger, *British Traveller*, pp. 44–45.

11. George R. Taylor, *The Transportation Revolution, 1815–1860* (New York, 1951), pp. 17–22.

12. *Sarmiento's Travels in the United States in 1847*, trans. Michael Aaron Rockland (Princeton, 1970), p. 220; Dickens, *American Notes*, p. 125.

13. *A Description of the Canals and Railroads of the United States* (New York, 1840).

14. Theodore Dwight, *The Northern Traveller; Containing the Routes to Niagara, Quebec, and the Springs, with the Tour of New-England, and the Route to the Coal Mines of Pennsylvania*, 2nd ed. (New York, 1826), pp. 50, 78–79; Frances Trollope, *The Domestic Manners of the Americans* (London, 1927), p. 326.

15. Taylor, *Transportation Revolution*, p. 84.

16. Charles Weld, *Vacation Tour*, p. 68; Dickens, *American Notes*, pp. 111–112; on rail travel in general, see Taylor, op. cit., pp. 74–84; John L. Stover, *The Life and Decline of the American Railroad* (New York, 1970), pp. 22–23.

17. Theodore Dwight, *Travels*, pp. 77–78; Washington Irving, essay in *Home Book of the Picturesque*, pp. 72–73; Cooper, in *Home Book*, p. 143.

18. On fares and schedules, see Taylor, *Transportation Revolution*, pp. 141–143, and *The Traveller's Guide: Through the Middle and Northern States, and the Provinces of Canada*, 5th ed. (Saratoga Springs, N.Y., 1833), pp. 120–121.

19. *Sarmiento's Travels*, pp. 136–138.

20. Berger, *British Traveller*, p. 26.

21. Nygren, *Views and Visions*, p. 210; on maps, see, for example, William Wade's *Panorama of the Hudson River from New York to Albany* (New York, 1845), and *Sarmiento's Travels*, pp. 137–138.

22. *The Traveller's Guide*, published in several editions between 1822 and 1840; the 4th edition was published under the title *The Fashionable Tour*.

23. On basic routes, see Sears, *Sacred Places*, pp. 4, 56; Mesick, *The English Traveler*, pp. 17–21; *Traveller's Guide*.

24. Marianne Finch, *An Englishwoman's Experience in America* (New York, 1969), p. 241; A. M. Maxwell, *A Run Through the United States*, 2 vols. (London, 1841), Vol. 2, p. 47; Dickens, *American Notes*, p. 25; Hall, *Travels in North America*, pp. 27–29, 185; Trollope, *Domestic Manners*, p. 323; Murray, *Travels in North America, 1834–1836* (New York, 1839), p. 62.

25. Trollope, *Domestic Manners*, pp. 323–324; Charles Dudley Warner, *Saunterings* (Boston, 1879), pp. 40–41; see also Charles Weld, *Vacation Tour*, pp. 362–363; Finch, op. cit., p. 241; Maxwell, op. cit., Vol. 2, p. 47; Sears, *Sacred Places*, p. 60; Harriet Martineau, *Retrospect of Western Travel*, 2 vols. (London, 1838), Vol. 1, p. 43.

26. Irving, in *Home Book of the Picturesque*, pp. 71–72; Hall, *Travels in North America*, p. 46; *Traveller's Guide*, pp. 133–134; Sears, *Sacred Places*, p. 67; Martineau, *Western Travel*, Vol. 1, p. 58.

27. Hall, op. cit., pp. 53–54; Sears, op. cit., p. 66; *Traveller's Guide*, pp. 133–134; Theodore Dwight, *Travels*, pp. 238–239.

28. Horace Sutton, *Travelers: The American Tourist from Stagecoach to Space Shuttle* (New York, 1980), pp. 14–15, 32.

29. Charles Weld, *Vacation Tour*, pp. 70–76.

30. Quoted in Huth, *Nature and the American*, pp. 106–107; Murray, *Travels in North America*, p. 65.

31. Isaac Weld, *Travels Through the States*, Vol. 2, pp. 112–133; Timothy Dwight, *Travels*, pp. 52–63; Charles Weld, *Vacation Tour*, p. 171; Sears, *Sacred Places*, p. 12.

32. Dickens, *American Notes*, pp. 242–244; Charles Weld, op. cit., p. 166; Trollope, *Domestic Manners*, p. 335; Lydia Sigourney, *Scenes in My Native Land* (Boston, 1845), p. 15. On the concept of visitors as pilgrims, see Sears, op. cit., pp. 5, 12; Nathaniel Hawthorne, "My Visit to Niagara," in *The Centenary Edition of the Works of Nathaniel Hawthorne*, ed. William Charvat et al., 20 vols. (Columbus, Ohio, 1962), Vol. 2, p. 283; on Niagara as a sublime and religious experience, see Sears, op. cit., pp. 14–15; Jeremy E. Adamson, *Niagara: Two Centuries of Changing American Attitudes* (Washington, 1985), p. 14; Barbara Novak, *Nature and Culture: American Landscape Painting, 1825–1875* (New York, 1980), pp. 7–8.

33. Hawthorne, op. cit., p. 281; Maxwell, *United States*, pp. 260–261; Murray, *Travels in North America*, Vol. 2, p. 70; Dickens, op. cit., pp. 242–244; Trollope, op. cit., p. 357.

34. Sears, *Sacred Places*, p. 15; *Picturesque America*, 2 vols. (New York, 1872–74), Vol. 1, p. 434; Trollope, op. cit., p. 337; Hawthorne, op. cit., p. 285; Margaret Fuller, *Summer on the Lakes in 1843* (Boston and New York, 1844), p. 11.

35. Sigourney, *Native Land*, p. 18; Hawthorne; op. cit., p. 285.

36. Willis, *Rural Letters*, pp. 4–5; Finch, *An Englishwoman's Experience*, p. 366; Charles Weld used similar language in *Vacation Tour*, p. 177.

37. Willis, op. cit., pp. 27–28, 72; Finch, op. cit., pp. 367–368; *Sarmiento's Travels*, p. 224.

38. Sears, *Sacred Places*, pp. 17–23; Nygren, *Views and Visions*, p. 204.

39. Tocqueville, quoted in Adamson, *Niagara*, p. 117. On arguments about development at Niagara, see, for example, Charles Weld, *Vacation Tour*, p. 169; Sigourney, *Native Land*, p. 10; Murray, *Travels in North America*, Vol. 2, p. 327; Adamson, p. 118.

40. Hall, *Travels in North America*, pp. 83–84; Nygren, *Views and Visions*, p. 204; Timothy Dwight, *Travels*, pp. 172–173. The tension between nature and technology in American history has been the subject of several important books, notably Leo Marx, *The Machine in the Garden: Technology and the Pastoral Ideal in America* (New York, 1964).

41. Adamson, *Niagara*, pp. 51, 97.

42. Ibid., pp. 122–123.

43. Dickens, *American Notes*, p. 75.

44. Ibid., pp. 81–94.

45. Sears, *Sacred Places*, pp. 87–92; Murray, *Travels in North America*, p. 66; on prisons, David J. Rothman, *The Discovery of the Asylum: Social Order and Disorder in the New Republic*, rev. ed. (Boston, 1990) pp. 79–83.

46. Charles Weld, *Vacation Tour*, pp. 50–53; on Lowell, see also Finch, *Englishwoman's Experiences*, pp. 40–41; Dickens, *American Notes*, p. 120. On Boston in general, see Dickens, pp. 75–77; Barbara Leigh Smith Bodichon, *An American Diary, 1857–8*, ed. Joseph W. Reed, Jr. (London, 1972), pp. 4–5; Finch, p. 185; Charles Weld, pp. 29–63; *Sarmiento's Travels*, p. 226.

47. Murray, *Travels in North America*, pp. 312–313.

48. Sears, *Sacred Places*, p. 191; *Traveller's Guide*, pp. 75–86.

49. Dickens, *American Notes*, pp. 163–164; Theodore Dwight, *Travels*, pp. 23–25; Trollope, *Domestic Manners*, pp. 180–181.

50. Theodore Dwight, op. cit., pp. 23–25, 29; Dickens, op. cit., pp. 163–164.

51. Charles Weld, *Vacation Tour*, pp. 196, 240–248.

52. Ibid., pp. 189–196, 199.

53. Dickens, *American Notes*, pp. 207, 210–212.

54. Ibid., pp. 220–228.

CHAPTER 5: TRAVELING WITH THE MILLIONS

1. J.A.R. Pimlott, *The Englishman's Holiday: A Social History* (London, 1947), p. 90; Philip S. Bagwell, *Britain and America, 1850–1939: A Study of Economic Change* (London, 1970), p. 127; Jack Simmons, *The Victorian Railway* (London, 1991), p. 292; *Excursionist*, April 7, 1860. The Midland Counties Railway served the area bounded by the cities of Rugby, Birmingham, Nottingham, Derby, and Matlock.

2. John Pudney, *The Thomas Cook Story* (London, 1952), pp. 52–62, 73–79; Edmund Swinglehurst, *The Romantic Journey: The Story of Thomas Cook and Victorian Travel* (New York, 1974), pp. 28–30; *Excursionist*, July 9, 1872. Hereafter, all dates refer to the *Excursionist* unless otherwise noted.

3. April 7, 1860, and July 9, 1872; Edmund Swinglehurst, *Cooks Tours: The Story of Popular Travel* (Poole, 1982), p. 17.

4. April 7, 1860.

5. Piers Brendon, *Thomas Cook: 150 Years of Popular Tourism* (London, 1990), pp. 40–41.

6. July and August 1854.

7. Pudney, *Thomas Cook Story*, pp. 22–48.

8. July 19 and 21, 1851.

9. June 1851; Swinglehurst, *Romantic Journey,* pp. 34–35; Pudney, *Thomas Cook Story,* pp. 100–104.

10. May 31, 1851.

11. June 21, July 19, July 21, 1851.

12. May 31, 1851; Brendon, *Thomas Cook,* p. 59.

13. Swinglehurst, *Cooks Tours,* pp. 32–33; Pudney, *Thomas Cook Story,* pp. 108–109.

14. August 6 and 20, 1855; June 4, 1856; Pudney, op. cit., pp. 112–113; Swinglehurst, *Cooks Tours,* p. 38.

15. June 25, 1858; July and August 1854; June 4 and July 18, 1856.

16. July 18, 1856; September 22, 1855.

17. June 4, 1856.

18. June 1854.

19. May 26, 1859; June 13, 1860.

20. April 27, 1861.

21. June 5, 1861.

22. July 26 and August 9, 1862; May 7 and September 30, 1863; June 24, 1872.

23. September 30, 1863.

24. June 6, 1853; July 9, 1872.

25. May 7 and 15, 1863.

26. June 6 and 18, 1863.

27. August 6, 1863; Jemima Morrell's account of her trip to Switzerland, typescript, Thomas Cook Archives (hereafter TCA), pp. 11–15.

28. William Morrell to his father, July 10, 1863, TCA.

29. Jemima Morrell's account, pp. 6, 8; William Morrell to his father, July 3, 1863, TCA.

30. May 15 and August 28, 1863.

31. April 25, June 6, August 2, 1864.

32. June 24, 1872; "Diary of a Trip to Switzerland and Italy with Cook's Party," typescript, September and October 1864, TCA.

33. February 1, 1867; Pudney, *Thomas Cook Story,* pp. 146–147; Swinglehurst, *Romantic Journey,* p. 108.

34. July 11, 1863; April 25, 1864.

35. June 6, 1864; April 3, 1865.

36. August 23, 1869.

37. June 24, 1865.

38. Swinglehurst, *Romantic Journey,* pp. 116–121; Brendon, *Thomas Cook,* p. 2; June 20, 1868.

39. Swinglehurst, *Cooks Tours,* pp. 114–115; July 29, 1875, and May 1, 1876.

40. May 1, 1866; Swinglehurst, *Cooks Tours,* p. 65.

41. June 7, 1872.

42. August 28, 1863; Swinglehurst, *Cooks Tours,* pp. 174–179; Brendon, *Thomas Cook,* p. 185.

43. *Blackwood's Magazine,* Vol. 97 (February 1865), pp. 230–233; *Saturday Review* article reprinted in *Excursionist,* March 17, 1877.

44. Edmund Yates, "My Excursion Agent," in *All the Year Round* (1864); September 18, 1865; May 21, 1872.
45. September 21, 1872; May 1, 1865.
46. Ruskin quoted in Simmons, *Victorian Railway*, p. 199; *Cornhill Magazine*, Vol. 20 (1869), pp. 209–211.
47. Arthur Sketchley, *Out for a Holiday with Cook's Excursion Through Switzerland and Italy* (London, 1870), pp. 7–8, 136.
48. Arthur Sketchley, *Mrs. Brown on the Grand Tour* (London, 1870), p. 7.
49. May 22, 1865. Thomas died in 1892 and John Mason in 1900. J.M.'s three sons continued the business until 1928, when they retired and sold out to the Compagnie Internationale des Wagons-Lits of Belgium. After World War II, the firm was acquired by a group of British railway companies. It was nationalized, along with the railroads, in 1948, but later returned to private ownership. It is today the largest travel agency in the world.

CHAPTER 6: TRAVELING IN STYLE

1. Piers Brendon, *Thomas Cook: 150 Years of Popular Tourism* (London, 1990), pp. 182, 188; Neil Harris, "On Vacation," in Architectural League of New York and Gallery Association of New York State, *Resorts of the Catskills* (New York, 1979); *Scribner's Magazine* 7 (January–June 1890), pp. 789–790; 3 (January–June 1888), pp. 481–488.
2. Eric Hobsbawm, *The Age of Empire, 1875–1914* (New York, 1987), pp. 9–10.
3. Harold Perkin, *The Origins of Modern English Society, 1780–1880* (London, 1969), pp. 134–138; Jack Simmons, *The Victorian Railway* (London, 1991), pp. 290–292; Geoffrey Best, *Mid-Victorian Britain, 1851–1875* (London, 1971), pp. 1–3, 205–207; Hobsbawm, op. cit., pp. 35–36; Thompson, F.M.L., ed., *The Cambridge Social History of Britain, 1750–1950*, Vol. 2: *People and Their Environment* (Cambridge, 1990), pp. 147–148, 280–287.
4. John Pemble, *The Mediterranean Passion: Victorians and Edwardians in the South* (Oxford, 1987), pp. 18, 26–27; John Murray, *A Handbook for Travellers in France* (London, 1870), p. xv, *A Handbook for Travellers in Southern Italy* (London, 1883), pp. xlii–xliii, and *A Handbook for Travellers in Central Italy* (London, 1892), xi–xii; Alexis Gregory, *The Golden Age of Travel, 1880–1939* (New York, 1991), pp. 43–46; G. Freeman Allen, *Railways Past, Present and Future* (London, 1982), p. 97; Hobsbawm, op. cit., p. 13; Nicholas Faith, *The World the Railways Made* (London, 1990), p. 28; Ludwig Pauli, *The Alps: Archaeology and Early History*, trans. Eric Peters (London, 1984), p. 236.
5. Baedeker, *Southeastern France, including Corsica: Handbook for Travellers* (Leipsig, 1898), p. xvi; Simmons, *Victorian Railway*, pp. 37–40, 183–190, 299, 345–346; David S. Landes, *Revolution in Time: Clocks and the Making of the Modern World* (Cambridge, Mass., 1983),

p. 286; Michael Barsley, *The Orient Express: The Story of the World's Most Fabulous Train* (New York, 1967), pp. 70–74; George Behrend, *Luxury Trains from the Orient Express to TGV* (New York, 1982), p. 37; Gregory, *Golden Age,* p. 75.

6. Gregory, op. cit., pp. 199–200; *Scribner's* 9 (April 1891), pp. 400–418; Foster Rhea Dulles, *Americans Abroad: Two Centuries of European Travel* (Ann Arbor, Mich., 1964), pp. 43–47, 102; John Maxtone-Graham, *The Only Way to Cross* (New York, 1978), pp. 5–8; Charles E. Lee, *The Blue Riband: The Romance of the Atlantic Ferry* (London, 1930), pp. 27, 32, 50–55, 64–65, 81–88, 231.

7. Baedeker, *Southeastern France,* p. xv; Murray, *Handbook . . . to France* (1870), p. xviii; Pemble, *Mediterranean Passion,* pp. 27–28.

8. Charles Dickens, *American Notes for General Circulation* (London, 1972), pp. 53–54.

9. *Scribner's* 9 (April 1891), pp. 407–408; 18 (June 1879), p. 309; Maxtone-Graham, *Only Way to Cross,* pp. 46–47.

10. Brian Morgan, ed., *The Great Trains* (New York, 1973), p. 28; G. Freeman Allen, *Luxury Trains* (New York, 1979), p. 11.

11. Behrend, *Luxury Trains,* pp. 12–13; Gregory, *Golden Age,* pp. 46–48.

12. Allen, *Railways,* p. 122; Gregory, op. cit., pp. 46–48; Behrend, op. cit., pp. 12–14; Allen, *Luxury Trains,* p. 10.

13. Allen, *Railways,* pp. 122–125; Allen, *Luxury Trains,* pp. 16–17.

14. Behrend, *Luxury Trains,* p. 17.

15. Allen, *Railways,* p. 128.

16. Behrend, *Luxury Trains,* pp. 16–19; Gregory, *Golden Age,* pp. 50–54; Allen, *Luxury Trains,* pp. 19–20.

17. Behrend, op. cit., p. 30.

18. Edmond About, *De Pontoise à Stamboul* (Paris, 1884), pp. 5–6, 12–14, 27–30, 39, 54–67; Henri Stefan Opper de Blowitz, *Une Course à Constantinople* (Paris, 1884), p. 77; Behrend, op. cit., pp. 30–36; Allen, *Luxury Trains,* p. 20; Allen, *Railways,* pp. 130–131; Gregory, *Golden Age,* pp. 119, 136.

19. Gregory, op. cit., p. 119.

20. Behrend, *Luxury Trains,* pp. 10–12, 47–49; Allen, *Luxury Trains,* pp. 11–12, 21–27; Baedeker, *Southern France . . . : A Handbook for Travellers* (Leipsig, 1914), p. xiii.

21. Dulles, *Americans Abroad,* pp. 106–107; Murray, *Handbook . . . to Central Italy* (1892), p. 3; Murray, *Handbook . . . to Southern Italy* (1883), p. 76; Gregory, *Golden Age,* p. 75; Simmons, *Victorian Railway,* pp. 37–40.

22. Gregory, op. cit., pp. 75–76; Hugh Montgomery-Massingbird, *The London Ritz: A Social and Architectural History* (London, 1980), p. 25; Willi Frischauer, *The Grand Hotels of Europe* (New York, 1965), passim; Morgan, *Great Trains,* p. 189; George Behrend, *The History of Wagons-Lits, 1875–1955* (New York, 1959), p. 12; Martin Meade, Joseph Pritchett, and Anthony Lawrence, *Grand Oriental Hotels* (New York, 1987), p. 92.

23. Marie Louise Ritz, *César Ritz: Host to the World* (Philadelphia, 1938), pp. 17–29, 46–47, 55, 61–70; Frischauer, *Grand Hotels*, pp. 24–30; Gregory, *Golden Age*, p. 76.

24. Ritz, op. cit., pp. 71–73, 88, 94, 104, 113–114, 123–125.

25. Ibid., pp. 143–145, 151–152, 160–161, 171; Gregory, *Golden Age*, p. 78.

26. Ritz, op. cit., pp. 175–176, 228–231, 286–287; Montgomery-Massingbird, *London Ritz*, pp. 22, 25; Gregory, op. cit., p. 78.

27. Montgomery-Massingbird, op. cit., p. 27; Ritz, op. cit., pp. 175–176; Gregory, op. cit., p. 80.

28. Maxtone-Graham, *Only Way to Cross*, pp. 88–97; Gregory, op. cit., p. 172.

29. Baedeker, *Italy: Handbook for Travellers* (Leipsig, 1909), p. xvii, and *Southeastern France* (1898), p. xvi; see also Murray, *Handbook . . . to Central Italy* (1892), p. xiv.

30. *Scribner's* 7 (January–June 1890), p. 790.

31. Pemble, *Mediterranean Passion*, p. 40; Patrick Howarth, *When the Riviera Was Ours* (London, 1977), p. 16; C. Graves, *The Royal Riviera* (London, 1957), pp. 23, 37–41.

32. Howarth, op. cit., pp. 31–32, 36; Pemble, op. cit., pp. 45–46, 101; Graves, op. cit., pp. 60–62; Gregory, *Golden Age*, p. 94.

33. Graves, op. cit., p. 76.

34. Howarth, *Riviera*, p. 69; Graves, op. cit., p. 79.

35. Howarth, op. cit., pp. 53, 58, 62–65; Pemble, *Mediterranean Passion*, pp. 43–44; Murray, *Handbook . . . to France* (1870), pp. 539, 545–547; Baedeker, *Southeastern France* (1898), 256–262.

36. Baedeker, *Southern France* (1914), pp. 59, 68–69; James Henry Bennett, *Winter and Spring on the Shores of the Mediterranean: or, The Riviera, Mentone, Italy, Corsica, Sicily, Algeria, Spain, and Biarritz, As Winter Climates*, 4th ed. (New York, 1870).

37. Pemble, *Mediterranean Passion*, pp. 47–48.

CHAPTER 7: THE ''PLAYGROUND OF EUROPE''

1. John Murray, *A Hand-Book for Travellers in Switzerland and the Alps of Savoy and Piedmont . . .* (London, 1838), pp. iii, xv.

2. Leslie Stephen, *The Playground of Europe* (London, 1871).

3. Paul Bernard, *Rush to the Alps: The Evolution of Vacationing in Switzerland* (New York, 1978), pp. 43–55.

4. Ibid., pp. 94–95; Murray, *Hand-Book for . . . Switzerland*; G. R. DeBeer, *Early Travellers in the Alps* (London, 1930), pp. 4–6.

5. Murray, op. cit. (1856 edition), pp. xvi–xxvii; Bernard, op. cit., p. 95; H. G. Senn, *La Suisse et le Tourisme* (Lausanne, 1918), pp. 71–72; Nicholas Faith, *The World the Railways Made* (London, 1990), pp. 63–64.

6. Bernard, op. cit., pp. 95–96, 102; Eric Hobsbawm, *The Age of Empire*,

1875–1914 (New York, 1987), p. 13; Senn, op. cit., p. 73.

7. Bernard, op. cit., pp. 13, 17, 90, 102.

8. Senn, *La Suisse,* pp. 74, 79; listings in Murray, *Hand-Book for . . . Switzerland,* various editions.

9. Amelia Edwards, *Untrodden Peaks and Unfrequented Valleys* (Boston, 1987), pp. 221–223; Murray, *Hand-Book for . . . Switzerland* (1838), pp. xxxi–xxxiii; C. E. Montague, in Eric Newby, *A Book of Travellers' Tales* (New York, 1986), p. 169.

10. Quoted in Bernard, *Rush to the Alps,* p. 178.

11. Ibid., pp. 128–133.

12. Ibid., pp. 135–136.

13. Ibid., pp. 137–138.

14. *Scribner's Monthly* 16 (September 1878), pp. 641–642; Bernard, op. cit., pp. 139–144, 166.

15. Edwards, *Untrodden Peaks,* pp. xxix–xxx.

16. Ibid., pp. 3–4.

17. Ibid., pp. 47, 65–66, 132–133.

18. Ibid., pp. xxxi, 202, 212–223.

19. Stephen, *Playground of Europe,* pp. 47–48.

20. Edith Wharton, *Italian Backgrounds* (New York, 1989), p. 5.

21. Mrs. Henry Freshfield, *Alpine Byways, or Light Leaves Gathered in 1859 and 1860, by a Lady* (London, 1861), pp. 140–142.

22. Arnold Lunn, *The Swiss and Their Mountains: A Study of the Influence of Mountains on Man* (London, 1963), p. 108.

23. Claire Engel, *A History of Mountaineering in the Alps* (London, 1950), pp. 96, 100; Arnold Lunn, *A Century of Mountaineering* (London, 1957), p. 33.

24. Bernard, *Rush to the Alps,* p. 37; J. Monroe Thorington, *Mont Blanc Sideshow: The Life and Times of Albert Smith* (Philadelphia, 1934), passim; Arnold Lunn, *The Exploration of the Alps* (New York, n.d.), pp. 119–123; Engel, op. cit., pp. 108–109.

25. Bernard, op. cit., p. 38; Arnold Lunn, *Exploration of the Alps,* pp. 111–114; Edward Whymper, *Scrambles Amongst the Alps* (Salt Lake City, 1986), p. 9; Arnold Lunn, *Century of Mountaineering* pp. 31–32, 38–39, 48.

26. Arnold Lunn, *Century of Mountaineering,* pp. 86–88; Hobsbawm, *Age of Empire,* p. 181.

27. Arnold Lunn, *Century of Mountaineering,* pp. 42–44, 98–103; Engel, *Mountaineering in the Alps,* pp. 120–122, 147–148; W.A.B. Coolidge, *The Alps in Nature and History* (London, 1908), p. 240.

28. Arnold Lunn, *Century of Mountaineering,* pp. 98–100; *Alpine Journal* 62 (1957), p. 44; 32 (1919), pp. 343–346.

29. Francis Gribble, *The Early Mountaineers* (London, 1899), pp. 240–247; *Alpine Journal* 62 (1957), p. 44; biographical information on LeBlond from Jane Robinson, *Wayward Women: A Guide to Women Travellers* (Oxford, 1990), pp. 20–21.

30. Gribble, op. cit.; Engel, *Mountaineering in the Alps,* p. 158; Mrs.

H. W. Cole, *A Lady's Tour Round Monte Rosa; with Visits to the Italian Valleys* . . . (London, 1859), pp. 6–9.

31. Verena Gurtner, *Jungfrau Express: With the Jungfrau Railway Up to the Glaciers,* 7th ed. (Zurich, 1986), pp. 12, 25–30, 40.

32. Charles Dudley Warner, *Saunterings* (Boston, 1879), p. 70. Zermatt is first included in Murray's guides in the late 1870s; see, for example, the 1879 edition of *Hand-Book for . . . Switzerland.*

33. Bernard, *Rush to the Alps,* pp. 101–102; Cole, *A Lady's Tour,* pp. 27–30.

34. Cole, op. cit., pp. 12–14; Murray, *Hand-Book for . . . Switzerland* (1856), p. xiii; Freshfield, *Alpine Byways,* p. 169.

35. Whymper, *Scrambles Amongst the Alps,* pp. 36, 40.

36. Arnold Lunn, *Century of Mountaineering,* pp. 51, 58–59; Whymper, op. cit., pp. 9, 12–18, 35.

37. See, for example, Freshfield, who talks about meeting Tyndal in Breuil in *Alpine Byways,* p. 169; Whymper, op. cit., p. 156.

38. Whymper, op. cit., pp. 193–206; Arnold Lunn, *Century of Mountaineering,* p. 54.

39. Ronald Clark, *The Day the Rope Broke: The Story of the First Ascent of the Matterhorn* (New York, 1965), p. 190; Bernard, *Rush to the Alps,* p. 42.

40. Even today, it can still be a dangerous climb. In the first month of the summer season in 1990—the 125th anniversary of Whymper's ascent—ten people were killed on the mountain, eight of them on the same ridge where Whymer's companions fell. Recent fatalities have all been people who went up the mountain without guides; Zermatt guides claim they have not had a fatal accident in forty years. *The New York Times,* August 12, 1990.

41. Warner, *Saunterings,* p. 59.

42. Bernard, *Rush to the Alps,* pp. 119, 136, 139, 169; Willi Frischauer, *The Grand Hotels of Europe* (New York, 1965), pp. 205–211.

43. Henry S. Lunn, *How to Visit Switzerland,* 3rd ed. (London, 1896), p. 3, and *Round the World with a Dictaphone* (London, 1928), pp. 11–12, 21–26, 41–45, 53–54; Bernard, op. cit., p. 123.

44. Henry Lunn, *How to Visit Switzerland,* p. 3.

45. Bernard, *Rush to the Alps,* p. 124; Henry Lunn, *Round the World,* pp. 67–69.

46. Henry Lunn, op. cit., pp. 68–69; Arnold Lunn, *The History of Skiing* (London, 1927), p. 33.

47. Arnold Lunn, *Century of Mountaineering,* pp. 142–144; Mrs. Fred Burnaby, *The High Alps in Winter or, Mountaineering in Search of Health* (London, 1883).

48. Bernard, *Rush to the Alps,* pp. 120–122.

49. Ibid., pp. 120–122; Henry Lunn, *Round the World,* p. 70; Arnold Lunn, *History of Skiing,* pp. 20–22, 30–32.

50. Senn, *La Suisse,* pp. 123–132.

51. Bernard, *Rush to the Alps,* pp. 169–170.
52. *Scribner's Monthly* 16 (September 1878), pp. 639–651.

CHAPTER 8:   THE GRAND TOUR MOVES EAST

1. Rodney Searight, *The Middle East: Watercolours and Drawings by British and Foreign Artists and Travellers, 1750–1900* (London, 1971), p. 163; Amelia Edwards, *A Thousand Miles Up the Nile* (London, 1877), p. 1. For a detailed discussion of Edwards, see Billie Melman, *Women's Orients: English Women and the Middle East, 1718–1918* (Ann Arbor, Mich., 1992), pp. 254–275.

2. James C. Simmons, *Passionate Pilgrims: English Travelers to the World of the Desert Arabs* (New York, 1987), pp. 15–38.

3. Quoted in ibid., p. 19.

4. Brian M. Fagan, *The Rape of the Nile: Tomb Robbers, Tourists, and Archaeologists in Egypt* (New York, 1975), pp. 66–77; Neil Asher Silberman, *Digging for God and Country: Exploration in the Holy Land, 1799–1917* (New York, 1982), pp. 12–17; Simmons, op. cit., pp. 254–275; Albert Hourani, *A History of the Arab Peoples* (Cambridge, Mass., 1991), pp. 265–268; Edward Said, *Orientalism* (New York, 1979), pp. 80–88.

5. Silberman, op. cit., p. 19.

6. Ibid., pp. 18–22; Simmons, *Passionate Pilgrims,* pp. 254–275.

7. Simmons, op. cit., pp. 39–82; see also Virginia Childs, *Lady Hester Stanhope: Queen of the Desert* (London, 1990), and *Memoirs of the Lady Hester Stanhope, as Related by Herself in Conversation with Her Physician* (London, 1845).

8. Peter A. Clayton, *The Rediscovery of Ancient Egypt: Artists and Travellers in the Nineteenth Century* (London, 1982), pp. 31–42, 47.

9. Ibid., p. 46.

10. Said, *Orientalism,* pp. 158–160.

11. Silberman, *Digging for God and Country,* pp. 37–45.

12. Said, *Orientalism,* pp. 171–175.

13. John Pemble, *The Mediterranean Passion: Victorians and Edwardians in the South* (Oxford, 1987), p. 58; William H. Bartlett, *The Nile Boat; or Glimpses of the Land of Egypt* (London, 1849), *Forty Days in the Desert, on the Track of the Israelites,* 5th ed. (London, 1862), and *Walks Around the City and Environs of Jerusalem* (London, 1844); Clayton, *Rediscovery of Ancient Egypt,* pp. 49–50.

14. Alexander Kinglake, *Eothen: Trace of Travel Brought Home from the East* (Oxford, 1982), pp. 3–5, 78–79.

15. Quoted in Simmons, *Passionate Pilgrims,* pp. 37–38.

16. Sir Gardiner Wilkinson, *Modern Egypt and Thebes,* 2 vols. (London, 1843), Vol. 1, pp. 1–6; John Murray, *Hand-Book for Travellers in Egypt; Including a Description of the Course of the Nile to the Second Cataract,*

Alexandria, Cairo, the Pyramids, and Thebes, the Overland Transit to India, the Peninsula of Mount Sinai, the Oases, &c. (London, 1847), pp. x, 8; Karl Baedeker, *Handbook for Travellers: Palestine and Syria* (Leipsig, 1894), pp. 7–8; Pemble, *Mediterranean Passion*, pp. 23–25.

17. Wilkinson, *Modern Egypt*, pp. 23, 53–55.

18. Ibid., pp. 14, 85–88.

19. Shirley H. Weber, *Voyages and Travels in the Near East During the 19th Century* (Princeton, N.J., 1953); Lucie Duff-Gordon, *Letters from Egypt (1862–1869)* (London, 1969), p. 142; her source was one of the local consular agents, who had been looking after tourists for thirty years; Pemble, *Mediterranean Passion*, p. 47.

20. Edwards, *A Thousand Miles Up the Nile*, pp. 1, 2, 600; Charles Dudley Warner, *My Winter on the Nile* (Boston, 1882), p. 25.

21. Warner, op. cit., p. 30; Harriet Martineau, *Eastern Life, Past and Present*, 3 vols. (London, 1848), Vol. 1, p. 5; Florence Nightingale, *Letters from Egypt: A Journey on the Nile, 1849–1850* (London, 1987), p. 22; Charles G. Leland, *The Egyptian Sketch Book* (New York, 1874), p. 32.

22. Martineau, *Eastern Life*, Vol. 1, p. 5; Wilkinson, *Modern Egypt*, pp. 96–97.

23. Nightingale, *Letters from Egypt*, pp. 21, 23; Warner, *Winter on the Nile*, p. 30.

24. John Lloyd Stephens, *Incidents of Travel in Egypt, Arabia Petraea, and the Holy Land*, ed. Victor W. von Hagen (Norman, Okla., 1970), p. 4; Martineau, *Eastern Life*, Vol. 1, p. 7; J. E. Plummer, "Up the Nile, 1862–1863," typescript in Thomas Cook Archives, pp. 2–3; Gustave Flaubert, *Flaubert in Egypt: A Sensibility on Tour*, trans. and ed. Francis Steegmuller (Chicago, 1979), pp. 25, 29.

25. Nightingale, op. cit., pp. 29, 31; Wilkinson, *Modern Egypt*, pp. 175–176.

26. Martineau, op. cit., Vol. 2, pp. 116–117; Herman Melville, *Journal of a Visit to Europe and the Levant, October 11, 1856–May 6, 1857*, ed. Howard C. Horsford (Princeton, 1955), p. 114; Warner, *Winter on the Nile*, p. 50; Edwards, *A Thousand Miles Up the Nile*, p. 5.

27. Warner, op. cit., p. 51; Duff-Gordon, *Letters from Egypt*, p. 44; Martineau, op. cit., Vol. 2, p. 116.

28. William Makepeace Thackeray, *Notes of a Journey from Cornhill to Grand Cairo* (London, 1888), p. 303; Martineau, op. cit., Vol. 2, p. 117.

29. Warner, *Winter on the Nile*, p. 51; Wilkinson, *Modern Egypt*, pp. 301–302.

30. Duff-Gordon, *Letters from Egypt*, pp. 48, 133, 171; Nightingale, *Letters from Egypt*, pp. 188–192; Martineau, *Eastern Life*, Vol. 2, p. 122; Thomas Appleton, *Nile Journal* (Boston, 1876), p. 44.

31. Martineau, op. cit., Vol. 2, p. 187; for a more positive view of the Copts, see Stephens, *Incidents of Travel*, p. 120; Leland, *Egyptian Sketch Book*, p. 94; Duff-Gordon, *Letters from Egypt*, pp. 171–173.

32. Duff-Gordon, op. cit., p. 171.

33. Melman, *Women's Orients*, pp. 59–76, 99–136.

34. Edwards, *A Thousand Miles Up the Nile,* p. vi; Murray, *Hand-Book for*
. . . Egypt, p. 122; Edward L. Wilson, "The Modern Nile," in *Scribner's*
Monthly (September 1887), pp. 260–261.

35. Martineau, *Eastern Life,* p. 19.

36. Edwards, *A Thousand Miles Up the Nile,* pp. 15–17.

37. Wilkinson, *Modern Egypt,* Vol. 1, pp. 1, 213; Stephens, *Incidents of*
Travel, pp. 134–135; Duff-Gordon, *Letters from Egypt,* p. 51.

38. Nightingale, *Letters from Egypt,* pp. 90–91; Martineau, *Eastern Life,* Vol.
1, p. 120.

39. Nightingale, op. cit., p. 100; Martineau, op. cit., Vol. 1, pp. 101–104.

40. Martineau, op. cit., Vol. 1, p. 113.

41. Ibid., Vol. 1, p. 126; Melville, *Journal of a Visit,* p. 116; Duff-Gordon,
Letters from Egypt, p. 47; Nightingale, *Letters from Egypt,* p. 187; Edwards, *A Thousand Miles Up the Nile,* pp. x–xi, 160–161, 449–451.

42. Edwards, op. cit., pp. 449–452. Edwards was so taken with her brief experience as an archaeologist and so concerned about the need to excavate
and preserve sites properly before it was too late that she wrote several
newspaper and magazine articles after returning to England, publicizing
the deteriorating state of Egyptian antiquities and embarked on a letter-
writing campaign to prominent public figures in an effort to raise money
to excavate and restore the monuments. Over the next decade, the developing field of Egyptology would replace fiction writing as her primary
occupation. In 1882, she helped establish the Egypt Exploration Fund,
an organization devoted to organizing and funding archaeological excavations; in 1889–90, she went on a lecture tour of the United States to
raise money for the fund. See Introduction to her *Untrodden Peaks and*
Unfrequented Valleys (Boston, 1987), pp. xvii–xviii, and Fagan, *Rape of*
Egypt, pp. 316, 322–323, 329.

43. Nightingale, *Letters from Egypt,* pp. 63, 113–114.

44. Appleton, *Nile Journal,* pp. 64, 80–81; Martineau, *Eastern Life,* Vol. 1,
pp. 84, 87; Warner, *Winter on the Nile,* p. 167.

45. Warner, op. cit., p. 194; Martineau notes that there were six boats, five
English and one Russian, op. cit., p. 284.

46. Nightingale, *Letters from Egypt,* pp. 137–138; Warner, op. cit., pp. 175–
178; Appleton, *Nile Journal,* pp. 216–217; Edwards, *A Thousand Miles*
Up the Nile, p. 53.

47. Warner, op. cit., pp. 175–176; Appleton, op. cit., pp. 133–134.

48. Duff-Gordon, *Letters from Egypt,* pp. 74, 285; Leland, *Egyptian Sketch*
Book, p. 87; Baedeker, *Palestine and Syria,* p. 16.

49. Appleton, *Nile Journal,* p. 37; Martineau, *Eastern Life,* Vol. 1, p. 20; Vol.
2, pp. 177–179; Stephens, *Incidents of Travel,* pp. 20–21.

50. Appleton, op. cit., p. 38.

51. John Murray, *A Hand-Book for Travellers in Syria and Palestine* (London), p. 67. All of that area collectively referred to as "the Holy Land"
by nineteenth-century travelers was then part of the Ottoman Empire.
The modern nations of Syria, Lebanon, Israel, and Jordan were collec-

tively known as Syria throughout the century; that portion approximately corresponding to modern Israel and the western part of Jordan was commonly called Palestine. "Lebanon" referred to the mountainous area just north of Palestine, corresponding roughly to the southern portion of the modern country of that name.

52. See, for example, Ida Pfeiffer, *Visit to the Holy Land, Egypt, and Italy,* trans. H. W. Dulcken (London, 1852), pp. 251–252.

53. Baedeker, *Palestine and Syria,* pp. xi–xii.

54. By the end of the nineteenth century, several carriage roads crossed northern Palestine running east-west, from Jaffa and Haifa on the coast to Nablus and Nazareth inland, and the first railroads were under construction; but the great north-south valley from the Dead Sea north to the Sea of Galilee, one of the most popular routes among tourists, had no roads suitable for wheeled vehicles; ibid., pp. xix, 212, 239.

55. Guidebooks cautioned tourists against patronizing the "khans," or inns, located along the major desert routes as well as in larger towns, as they were said to be plagued by fleas and other "vermin." For those who had no alternative, Baedeker's guide advised pulling up the straw matting on the floor, beating it thoroughly, sweeping the floor, and then sprinkling it with water. In the area around Jerusalem, travelers could stay at hospices maintained by priests and monks of the Roman Catholic, Greek Orthodox, and Russian Orthodox churches, which were likely to be cleaner if spartan. Although intended primarily for pilgrims of their respective faiths, the hospices were open to all. See Franklin Walker, *Irreverent Pilgrims: Melville, Browne, and Mark Twain in the Holy Land* (Seattle, 1974), pp. 20–23; Melville, *Journal of a Visit,* pp. 124–125; Baedeker, op. cit., pp. xx–xxiv.

56. Murray recommended traveling "light"; *Syria and Palestine,* p. 7; Mark Twain, in Daniel M. McKeithan, *Traveling with the Innocents Abroad: Mark Twain's Original Reports from Europe and the Holy Land* (Norman, Okla., 1958), pp. 182, 187; William Prime, *Tent Life in the Holy Land* (New York, 1865), pp. 29–32.

57. Wilkinson, *Modern Egypt,* Vol. 2, pp. 396–398; Murray, *Syria and Palestine,* p. xli.

58. Murray, *Syria and Palestine,* p. xlvi; Prime, *Tent Life,* p. 114; for a counter example, see Martineau, *Eastern Life,* Vol. 3, p. 46.

59. Pemble, *Mediterranean Passion,* pp. 58, 185–187; Benjamin Dorr, *Notes of Travel in Egypt, the Holy Land, Turkey, and Greece* (Philadelphia, 1856), pp. 169–170; also Pfeiffer, *Visit to the Holy Land,* p. 102; Mark Twain, in McKeithan, *Traveling with the Innocents Abroad,* p. 266, and quoted in Dewey Ganzel, *Mark Twain Abroad: The Cruise of the "Quaker City"* (Chicago, 1968), pp. 246–247; Martineau, *Eastern Life,* Vol. 3, p. 53.

60. Ganzel, op. cit., pp. 265, 292; Prime, *Tent Life,* pp. 59–60.

61. Baedeker, *Palestine and Syria,* pp. ix, 20.

62. Ibid., p. 21.

63. Martineau, *Eastern Life*, Vol. 3, pp. 54, 162–163; *Excursionist*, October 21, 1869, and July 7, 1870; Twain, in McKeithan, *Traveling with the Innocents Abroad*, pp. 278–280; Pfeiffer, *Visit to the Holy Land*, p. 115.
64. Twain, in McKeithan, pp. 228, 288.
65. Martineau, op. cit., Vol. 3, p. 219; *Excursionist*, October 21, 1869; Twain, in McKeithan, p. 251.
66. Murray, *Syria and Palestine*, pp. 6, 316.
67. Twain, in McKeithan, pp. 221, 254.
68. Alexis Gregory, *The Golden Age of Travel, 1880–1939* (New York, 1991), pp. 154, 159.
69. "Diary of Cook's First Tour to Egypt and Palestine—1869," typescript, Thomas Cook Archives.
70. "Diary of Cook's First Tour," p. 21; *Excursionist*, May 3 and 15, 1869; Swinglehurst, *The Romantic Journey: The Story of Thomas Cook and Victorian Travel* (New York, 1974), p. 74.
71. *Excursionist*, July 1, 1869; Baedeker, *Palestine and Syria*, p. xi.
72. *Excursionist*, May 3 and June 1, 1869; Warner, *Winter on the Nile*, p. 117.
73. Piers Brendon, *Thomas Cook: 150 Years of Popular Tourism* (London, 1991), pp. 122, 129; John Edward Rodhouse to his brother Charles, November 24, 1874, Thomas Cook Archives.
74. John Pudney, *The Thomas Cook Story* (London, 1952), pp. 194–195; *Excursionist*, November 12, 1889; *Cook's Guide to Egypt*, 1897, Thomas Cook Archives; Douglas Sladen, *Egypt and the English* (London, 1908), pp. 414, 426, 430; Brendon, op. cit., p. 233.
75. Pudney, *Thomas Cook Story*, pp. 184, 212–223; Pemble, *Mediterranean Passion*, p. 47.
76. Brendon, *Thomas Cook*, pp. 189–194; Silberman, *Digging for God and Country*, p. 163.
77. Gregory, *Golden Age*, p. 156; Martin Meade, Joseph Pritchett, and Anthony Lawrence, *Grand Oriental Hotels* (New York, 1987), p. 24; *Cook's Guide to Egypt*, p. 14; *Excursionist*, November 12, 1889.
78. Pemble, *Mediterranean Passion*, p. 247; Gregory, op. cit., pp. 156, 164.
79. Pemble, op. cit., p. 47; William Makepeace Thackeray, *The Kickleburys on the Rhine*, in *The Christmas Books of Mr. M. A. Titmarsh*, Vol. 12 of *The Works of William Makepeace Thackeray* (Philadelphia, 1876), p. 165; *Atlantic Monthly*, March 1882, p. 368.

CHAPTER 9: AROUND THE WORLD

1. Ida Pfeiffer, *A Lady's Journey Round the World* (London, 1851).
2. Quoted in Valerie J. Fifer, *American Progress: The Growth of the Transport, Tourist, and Information Industries in the Nineteenth-Century West Seen Through the Life and Times of George A. Crofutt, Pioneer and Publicist of the Transcontinental Age* (Chester, Conn., 1988), p. 188.

3. Mignon Rittenhouse, *The Amazing Nellie Bly* (New York, 1956), pp. 13, 19, 39, 51.

4. New York *World,* November 14, December 8 and 12, 1889; also several other articles throughout December and January.

5. *World,* December 24, 1889, and January 26, 1890.

6. Piers Brendon, *Thomas Cook: 150 Years of Popular Tourism* (London, 1991), p. 150.

7. *Excursionist,* June 24, 1872; Cook's articles for *The Times,* reprinted in *Excursionist,* April 1873.

8. *Excursionist,* November 24, 1873, August 18, 1874, American edition, February 1890; Brendon, *Thomas Cook,* p. 152.

9. Mark Twain, *Following the Equator: A Journey Around the World* (New York, 1989, orig. published 1897), pp. 57–59; C. D. Irwin, "Letters of a Globe Trotter," Vol. 3, June 20, 1885, Huntington Library; *Excursionist,* November 24, 1873, American edition, February 1890; *A Souvenir of the Trans-continental Excursion of Railroad Agents, 1870* (Albany, N.Y., 1871).

10. *A Sketch of the Route to California, China and Japan, via the Isthmus of Panama* (San Francisco, 1867).

11. W. G. Beasley, *The Rise of Modern Japan* (London, 1990), pp. 27–34.

12. Ibid., pp. 38–39; Mitsuru Hashimoto, "Collision at Namamugi," *Representations* 18 (Spring 1987), pp. 69–89; Peter Duus, *The Rise of Modern Japan* (Boston, 1976), pp. 65–72; Hugh Cortazzi, *Victorians in Japan: In and Around the Treaty Ports* (London, 1987), pp. 93, 137, 169, 179.

13. Cortazzi, op. cit., pp. 54, 86–88, 90; *Excursionist,* American edition, July 1891.

14. Cortazzi, op. cit., pp. 223, 227; John Murray, *A Handbook for Travellers in Central and Northern Japan,* 2nd ed. (London, 1884), pp. 24–25; Irwin, "Letters of a Globe Trotter," Vol. 1, November 22, 1885.

15. Cortazzi, op. cit., p. 205; Murray, op. cit., p. 23.

16. Quoted in Cortazzi, op. cit., p. 166.

17. Ibid., pp. 145–146, 179, 188; *Excursionist,* American edition, October 1891; Irwin, "Letters of a Globe Trotter," Vol. 1, November 22, 1885.

18. Murray, op. cit., pp. 19–20.

19. Ibid., pp. 23–25; Irwin, "Letters of a Globe Trotter," Vol. 1, November 22, 1885; Isabella Bird, *Unbeaten Tracks in Japan* (Boston, 1987, orig. published 1880), pp. 36–37; Cortazzi, *Victorians in Japan,* pp. 247–251; *Excursionist,* American edition, July 1891.

20. Katharine S. Baxter, *In Beautiful Japan: A Story of Bamboo Lands* (New York, 1904), pp. 123–124; Irwin, "Letters of a Globe Trotter," Vol. 1, November 22, 1885; Murray, *Handbook for Northern Japan,* pp. 21–22; Bird, op. cit., pp. 36–37, 43–45, 49, 85–88.

21. Irwin, op. cit., Vol. 1, November 16, 1885; Baxter, op. cit., p. 157. E. A. Gordon, *"Clear Round!" Of Seeds of Stories from Other Countries, Being a Chronicle of Links and Rivets in This World's Girdle* (London, 1893), pp. 120–121, 178.

22. Irwin, op. cit., Vol. 1, November 16, 1885.

23. Baxter, *In Beautiful Japan*, p. 163; Irwin, op. cit., Vol. 1, November 16, 1885; *Excursionist*, American edition, July 1891; Bird, *Unbeaten Tracks in Japan*, pp. 15–16.

24. *William H. Seward's Travels Around the World*, ed. Olive R. Seward (New York, 1873), p. 100; Gordon, *Clear Round!*, p. 179; Irwin, op. cit., November 16, 1885; Bird, op. cit., p. 80; Baxter, op. cit., p. 195.

25. Cortazzi, *Victorians in Japan*, pp. 264–272; Seward, *Travels*, p. 103; Irwin, op. cit., November 29, 1885.

26. Duus, *Modern Japan*, pp. 85–90; "Sights in and Around Yedo," *Scribner's Monthly* 3 (January 1888), pp. 132–142.

27. Cortazzi, *Victorians in Japan*, pp. 86–88; Bird, *Unbeaten Tracks*, p. 11; Irwin, "Letters of a Globe Trotter," Vol. 1, November 29, 1885; *Excursionist*, American edition, August 1891; Baxter, *Beautiful Japan*, p. 352; Gordon, *Clear Round!*, p. 129.

28. Seward, *Travels*, pp. 107–112; *Excursionist*, American edition, April 1873; Irwin, op. cit., Vol. 1, December 12, 1885; Gordon, op. cit., p. 265.

29. Gordon, op. cit., pp. 276–281; Anna D'A[lmeida], *A Lady's Visit to Manila and Japan* (London, 1863), p. 186; Irwin, op. cit., December 12, 1885; Seward, op. cit., pp. 111–112; *Excursionist*, American edition, December 1891.

30. John Murray, *A Handbook for India; Being an Account of the Three Presidencies . . . Intended as a Guide for Travellers, Officers, and Civilians . . .* (London, 1859), and *A Handbook for Travellers in India and Ceylon* (London, 1891); Martin Meade, Joseph Pritchett, and Anthony Lawrence, *Grand Oriental Hotels* (New York, 1987), pp. 18–21.

31. Murray, *Handbook for India* (1891), pp. xv–xvi; Frank G. Carpenter, *From Bankok to Bombay: Siam, French Indo-China, Burma, Hindustan* (New York, 1924), p. 168; Robert Palmer, *A Little Tour in India* (London, 1913), pp. 40–41; Gordon, *Clear Round!*, pp. 323–324; Irwin, "Letters of a Globe Trotter," Vol. 2, February 22, 1886.

32. Irwin, op. cit., March 6, 1886.

33. *Excursionist*, April 21 and December 12, 1881.

34. Ibid., December 12, 1881.

35. Ibid.; Brendon, *Thomas Cook*, pp. 205, 210–211.

36. Brendon, op. cit., pp. 205–209; *Excursionist*, October 10, 1887, and August 11, 1888; 1914 brochure on tours in India, Burma, and Ceylon, in Thomas Cook Archives.

37. E. Warren Clark, *From Hong-Kong to the Himalayas: or, Three Thousand Miles Through India* (New York, 1880), p. 142; Irwin, op. cit., Vol. 2, January 26, 1886.

38. Clark, op. cit., p. 142; Twain, *Following the Equator*, p. 345.

39. Irwin, "Letters of a Globe Trotter," Vol. 2, February 4, 1886; Twain, op. cit., p. 484.

40. Cook, letter to the *The Times* in *Excursionist*, February 15, 1873; Sidney and Beatrice Webb, *Indian Diary*, ed. and introduced by Niraja Gopal Jayal (Delhi, 1987), p. 55; Irwin, op. cit., February 6, 1886; Twain, op. cit., pp. 549–581.

41. Twain, op. cit., p. 397; Gordon, *Clear Round!*, pp. 367–368; John Matheson, *England to Delhi: A Narrative of Indian Travel* (London, 1870), pp. 99–101; Palmer, *A Little Tour*, pp. 95, 113; Webbs, *Indian Diary*, pp. 19–20.

42. Cook's fifth letter to *The Times*, reprinted in *Excursionist*, American edition, April 1873; Matheson, op. cit., pp. 99, 310; Palmer, op. cit., pp. 95, 152, 178; Webbs, op. cit., p. 19.

43. Palmer, op. cit., pp. 97, 178; Cook's fifth letter; Webbs, op. cit., p. 19; Matheson, op. cit., pp. 103–105; Clark, *Hong Kong to the Himalayas*, p. 198.

44. Seward, *Travels*, p. 357.

45. Webbs, *Indian Diary*, pp. 75–87; Palmer, *A Little Tour*, pp. 53–54.

46. Pfeiffer, *A Lady's Journey*, pp. 94–95; Webbs, op. cit., p. 91; for a similar attitude, see Irwin, "Letters from a Globe Trotter," Vol. 2, January 12, 1886.

47. See, for example, Irwin, op. cit., Vol. 1, December 21, 1885, and January 4, 1886; Gordon, *Clear Round!*, pp. 297–300.

48. Twain, *Following the Equator*, pp. 339–340; Irwin, op. cit., January 12, 1886; Gordon, op. cit., pp. 307–315; *Excursionist*, American edition, April 1873; Meade et al., *Grand Oriental Hotels*, pp. 26–27.

49. Maugham, *Gentleman in the Parlour: A Record of a Journey from Rangoon to Haiphong* (New York, 1989, orig. published 1930), pp. 201, 222, 287–289; Seward, *Travels*, p. 287; Carpenter, *A Little Tour*, pp. 3–13, 36–37. On Java, see Seward, p. 338; and Irwin, op. cit., Vol. 1, December 26, 1885.

50. Brendon, *Thomas Cook*, p. 213; *Excursionist*, February 1, 1889, and March 1, 1890; on interest in exotic destinations, see frequent articles in *Century* and *Scribner's Monthly*, e.g., on South Africa, Arabia, the Arctic, Cambodia, overland across Asia, China, Siam, the Masai region of Africa, the Sierra Madre, and Bokhara; and in the *Atlantic Monthly*, on crossing Russia by rail, the Galápagos, the Grand Canal of China, Africa, and a series on remote parts of Japan.

51. On Cooks' Japanese tour, see Brendon, op. cit., p. 152; 1909 brochure on China and Japan, in Thomas Cook Archives.

CHAPTER 10: SELLING THE AMERICAN WEST

1. Rudyard Kipling, *From Sea to Sea: Letters of Travel* (New York, 1913), p. 194.

2. Ibid., pp. 436–454.

3. Ibid., pp. 56–60.

4. Ibid., pp. 67–68, 73–74, 96–97.

5. Ibid., p. 116.

6. Mark Twain, *The Innocents Abroad*, first published in 1869, and *Roughing It* (Berkeley and Los Angeles, 1972, orig. published 1872).

7. Twain, *Roughing It*, pp. 48, 60; see also Samuel Bowles, *Across the*

Continent: A Summer's Journey to the Rocky Mountains, the Mormons, and the Pacific States (Springfield and New York, 1866), pp. 9, 20. Twain recalled passing a group of Mormon emigrants who had taken eight weeks to cover a distance the mail coach traversed in eight days, pp. 64, 70.

8. Anne F. Hyde, *An American Vision: Far Western Landscape and National Culture, 1820–1920* (New York, 1990), p. 108; train fare was about $300 first-class, plus the cost of a sleeping compartment.

9. Ibid., p. 108.

10. Samuel Bowles, *The Switzerland of America: A Summer Vacation in the Parks and Mountains of Colorado* (Springfield, Mass., Boston, and New York, 1869), *Our New West: Records of Travel Between the Mississippi River and the Pacific Ocean . . .* (Hartford, 1869), p. 131, and *Across the Continent,* pp. 30–31.

11. In addition to the titles cited above, Bowles published *The Pacific Railroad—Open: How to Go, What to See* (Boston, 1869). For biographical information on Bowles, see Stephen G. Weisner, *Embattled Editor: The Life of Samuel Bowles* (Lanham, Md., 1986).

12. Earl Pomeroy, *In Search of the Golden West: The Tourist in Western America* (New York, 1957), pp. 32–34; Bowles, *Our New West,* pp. vi–vii, 329. The guidebook writers George Crofutt and Henry T. Williams also called Colorado the Switzerland of America; see, for example, Williams, *The Pacific Tourist. Adams & Bishop's Illustrated Transcontinental Guide of Travel, from the Atlantic to the Pacific Ocean* (New York, 1884), p. 77.

13. Charles Nordhoff, *California: For Health, Pleasure, and Residence* (New York, 1872), p. 11; John Erastus Lester, *The Atlantic to the Pacific: What to See and How to See It* (London, 1873), p. 182.

14. Hyde, *An American Vision,* pp. 87, 96.

15. *A Souvenir of the Trans-continental Excursion of Railroad Agents, 1870* (Albany, 1871); Hyde, op. cit., pp. 96–97; Carlos Schwantes, *Railroad Signatures Across the Pacific Northwest* (Seattle, 1993), pp. 81–82.

16. Pomeroy, *Golden West,* p. 32; for general information on the transcontinental trip, see Pomeroy, pp. 6–7, 32–34, 43; Hyde, op. cit., pp. 107–109; C. D. Irwin, "Letters of a Globe Trotter," Vol. 3, May 23, 1885, ms. in Huntington Library; Williams, *Pacific Tourist,* pp. 5–7.

17. Valerie J. Fifer, *American Progress: The Growth of the Transport, Tourist, and Information Industries in the Nineteenth-Century West Seen Through the Life and Times of George A. Crofutt, Pioneer and Publicist of the Transcontinental Age* (Chester, Conn., 1988), pp. 16, 146–151, 170–181; Hyde, op. cit., p. 120.

18. Fifer, op. cit., pp. 14, 182–188, 247–248. The Appleton and Rand McNally guides were both published in 1871. Among the books modeled on Crofutt's were *Guide to the Great West,* published in 1871 by a man who had worked with Crofutt on his 1870 edition. In an attempt to compete, Crofutt enlarged his guide, doubling the number of illus-

trations, but by the 1880s he turned his attention to other ventures, including his newspaper, *Crofutt's Western World,* which he had launched in 1871, and a series of regional guides.

19. Schwantes, *Railroad Signatures,* pp. 81–82, 113; some other examples include Robert E. Strahorn, *To the Rockies and Beyond, or a Summer on the Union Pacific Railway and Branches* (Omaha, 1878); C. A. Higgins, *New Guide to the Pacific Coast; Santa Fe Route* (Chicago and New York, 1894), and *To California and Back* (Chicago, 1893).

20. Hyde, *An American Vision,* pp. 148–52; Fifer, *American Progress,* pp. 248–253; Williams, *Pacific Tourist,* p. 75; A. A. and C. W. Butler, "Colorado Outings," July 21, 1898, ms. in Huntington Library.

21. Hyde, op. cit., pp. 161–166.

22. Fifer, *American Progress,* p. 301.

23. *A Trip to Colorado and California,* Raymond & Whitcomb brochure, 1881; Pomeroy, *Golden West,* p. 14; Fifer, op. cit., p. 293; Amy Bridges, "Journal Kept on a Raymond Excursion from Boston to California and Return, 1886–87," ms. in Huntington Library. (Raymond & Whitcomb and railroad promotional brochures are all from the Bancroft Library, University of California, Berkeley, unless otherwise noted.)

24. Fifer, op. cit., p. 280; *Across the Continent by the Scenic Route,* Denver & Rio Grande brochure, ca. 1885.

25. *Around the Circle,* Denver & Rio Grande brochure, first published 1892; subsequent editions up to 1913; Fifer, op. cit., pp. 321–322.

26. Schwantes, *Railroad Signatures,* pp. 57, 74, 77; Fifer, op. cit., pp. 240–243.

27. Aubrey L. Haines, *The Yellowstone Story,* 2 vols. (Yellowstone National Park, 1977), Vol. 1, p. 135; Alfred Runte, *National Parks: The American Experience* (Lincoln, Neb., 1979), pp. 33–36, and *Trains of Discovery* (Niwot, Colo., 1990), pp. 15–19.

28. Hyde, *An American Vision,* p. 246; Richard A. Bartlett, *Yellowstone: A Wilderness Besieged* (Tucson, Ariz., 1985), pp. 45–50, 128–129; Haines, *Yellowstone Story,* Vol. 2, pp. 32–33; Piers Brendon, *Thomas Cook: 150 Years of Popular Tourism* (London, 1990), p. 178.

29. Hyde, op. cit., pp. 246–251; Haines, op. cit., Vol. 1, p. 272.

30. *The Land of Geysers,* Northern Pacific Railway brochure, 1907; *Alice's Adventures in the New Wonderland,* Northern Pacific brochure, 1880s.

31. *The Northern Pacific Railroad: The Wonderland Route to the Pacific Coast,* Northern Pacific brochure, first published 1885; Runte, *Trains of Discovery,* p. 22; Schwantes, *Railroad Signatures,* p. 113.

32. Hyde, *An American Vision,* pp. 253–258, 262, 267; *The Land of Geysers.*

33. Paul Schullery, ed., *Old Yellowstone Days* (Boulder, Colo., 1979), pp. 65–67, 75, 76–78, 148.

34. *See America First; Glacier National Park,* Great Northern Railway brochure, 1910.

35. Hyde, *An American Vision,* pp. 281–285; Schwantes, *Railroad Signatures,* p. 211; Runte, *Trains of Discovery,* p. 33. On the "See America

First'' campaign, see also Schwantes, pp. 115, 184, 212; Bartlett, *Yellowstone*, p. 73; *Travel* magazine, cover, March 1915, and advertisement in December 1914 issue.

36. Schwantes, op. cit., p. 210; W. Kaye Lamb, *History of the Canadian Pacific Railway* (New York, 1977), pp. 143, 182, 273, 320.

37. *California Calls You*, Union Pacific Railroad brochure, p. 37; Santa Fe Railroad poster, in Huntington Library; *Sunset* 9 (November 1902).

38. Haines, *Yellowstone Story*, Vol. 1, p. 255; Maury Klein, *Union Pacific: Birth of a Railroad, 1862–1893* (New York, 1987), pp. 354–356; Schwantes, *Railroad Signatures*, p. 209; *Across the Continent* brochures; Runte, *Trains of Discovery*, p. 44.

39. *California Calls You* brochures.

40. *Semi-Tropical California* (San Francisco, 1874); *Tourists' Illustrated Guide to the Celebrated Summer and Winter Resorts of California Adjacent to and upon the Lines of the Central and Southern Pacific,* (San Francisco, 1883); see also *From the Crescent City to the Golden Gate via the Sunset Route of the Southern Pacific Company* (New York, 1886); Hyde, *An American Vision*, pp. 164–165; Fifer, *American Progress*, p. 299.

41. Judith W. Elias, *The Selling of a Myth: Los Angeles Promotional Literature, 1885–1915,* M.A. thesis, California State University Northridge, 1979, copy in Huntington Library, p. 48; *California Tourist Sleeper,* Santa Fe Railroad brochure, ca. 1906; Fifer, op. cit., p. 288.

42. Fifer, op. cit., p. 325; Elias, op. cit., pp. 55–56.

43. Elias, op. cit., p. 35; *Winter Trips 1890–91*, Raymond & Whitcomb brochure.

44. Stephen Merritt, *Ocean to Ocean! Or Across and Around the Country. Being an Account of the Raymond and Whitcomb Pacific, North West and Alaska Excursion of 1892*, ms. in Huntington Library, p. 3; Mary E. Blake, *On the Wing: Rambling Notes of a Trip to the Pacific,* 3rd ed. (Boston, 1883), p. 87.

45. Orsi, " 'Wilderness Saint' and 'Robber Baron' '': The Anomalous Partnership of John Muir and the Southern Pacific Company for the Preservation of Yosemite National Park,'' *The Pacific Historian* XXIX (1985), pp. 136–156; Hutchings's books include *Scenes of Wonder and Curiosity in California* (San Francisco, 1860), *In the Heart of the Sierras* (Oakland, 1886), and *Hutchings' Tourist Guide to the Yosemite Valley and the Big Tree Groves for the Spring and Summer of 1877* (San Francisco, 1877). See also Hyde, *An American Vision*, p. 48.

46. Merritt, *Ocean to Ocean!*, p. 4; *Hutchings' Tourist Guide*, p. 4; Emerson quoted in Stanford E. Demars, *The Tourist in Yosemite, 1855–1985* (Salt Lake City, 1991), p. 31.

47. On the history of Yosemite in general, see Alfred Runte, *Yosemite: The Embattled Wilderness* (Lincoln, Neb., 1990), pp. 10–30, 45–55; Demars, op. cit., pp. 9–10, 15–17, 31, 43–48; Shirley Sargent, *Yosemite and Its Innkeepers* (Yosemite, 1965), pp. 12–15; Hans Huth, *Yosemite: The*

Story of an Idea (Yosemite, 1984), p. 28; Margaret Sanborn, *Yosemite: Its Discovery, Its Wonders, and Its People* (Yosemite, 1989), pp. 78–94, 199–200; Pomeroy, *Golden West*, pp. 150; Hyde, *An American Vision*, pp. 47–50; Orsi, "Wilderness Saint," p. 137. On Sequoia, see Lary M. Dilsaver and William C. Tweed, *Challenge of the Big Trees* (Three Rivers, Calif., 1990).

48. Runte, *Trains of Discovery*, pp. 50–53.

49. William Goetzmann, Foreword to Frederick S. Dellenbaugh, *A Canyon Voyage: The Narrative of the Second Powell Expedition* (Tucson, Ariz., 1988, orig. published 1908), pp. xvii–xviii; John Wesley Powell, *The Exploration of the Colorado River and Its Canyons* (New York, 1961, orig. published 1895); Hyde, *An American Vision*, pp. 269–270; Foreword to George W. James, *The Grand Canyon of Arizona* (Boston, 1910).

50. Bridges, *Journal Kept on a Raymond Excursion*, December 9, 1886; Augustus F. Tripp, *Notes of an Excursion to California in the Winter and Spring of 1893*, Vol. 2, p. 10, ms. in Huntington Library.

51. Hyde, *An American Vision*, pp. 212–213; Goetzmann, Foreword to *Canyon Voyage*, p. xxiv.

52. Bridges, *Journal Kept on a Raymond Excursion*, December 15, 1886; Tripp, *Notes of an Excursion*, Vol. 2, p. 11; Hyde, op. cit., p. 214; Blake, *On the Wing*, pp. 71–76; Emily Post, *By Motor to the Golden Gate* (New York, 1916), p. 155; Hyde, op. cit., pp. 212–213; Pomeroy, *Golden West*, pp. 37–40.

53. Hyde, op. cit., pp. 268–278; Runte, *Trains of Discovery*, p. 33; on the Fred Harvey Company, see Nicholas Faith, *The World the Railways Made* (London, 1990), p. 256; Fred Harvey, *The Great Southwest Along the Santa Fe* (Kansas City, 1914), pp. v, 15; Keith L. Bryant, *History of the Atchison, Topeka and Santa Fe Railway* (New York, 1974), p. 118. An immediate success with visitors, the El Tovar was, as one guidebook put it, "more like a country club than a hotel . . . it is a village devoted to the entertainment of travelers" (James, *Grand Canyon*, p. 17).

54. Harvey, *Great Southwest*, p. 15; Hyde, op. cit., p. 278; *The People's Easy Guide of the Panama-Pacific International Exposition* (San Francisco, 1915), pamphlet in Bancroft Library; Robert Rydell, *All the World's a Fair: Visions of Empire at American International Expositions, 1876–1916* (Chicago, 1984), pp. 227–228.

55. Irwin, "Letters of a Globe Trotter," Vol. 3, May 23, 1885; Pomeroy, *Golden West*, p. 113; on the growth in middle-class vacations, Neil Harris, "On Vacation," in Gallery Association of New York State, *Resorts of the Catskills* (New York, 1979), pp. 101–104.

56. Pomeroy, op. cit., pp. 122–123; Fifer, *American Progress*, p. 327; *California Tourist Sleeper Excursions*, Santa Fe Railroad brochure, ca. 1909, pp. 2–3.

57. Fifer, op. cit., pp. 331–335; Harris, "On Vacation," p. 102.

58. Pomeroy, *Golden West,* p. 113; Harris, op. cit., p. 103; Haines, *Yellowstone Story,* Vol. 1, p. 134; Bartlett, *Yellowstone,* p. 54; Demars, *Tourist in Yosemite,* pp. 66–68.

59. Demars, op. cit., pp. 56–58; Hyde, *An American Vision,* pp. 216–217; Roderick Nash, *Wilderness and the American Mind,* 3rd ed. (New Haven, Conn., 1982), pp. 143–156; Jackson Lears, *No Place of Grace: Antimodernism and the Transformation of American Culture, 1880–1920* (New York, 1981), p. xv; Fifer, *American Progress,* p. 333.

60. Drake Hokanson, *The Lincoln Highway: Main Street Across America* (Iowa City, Iowa, 1988), p. xvi; Pomeroy, *Golden West,* p. 125; John A. Jakle, *The Tourist: Travel in Twentieth-Century North America* (Lincoln, Neb., 1985), p. 105; Ralph W. Hill, *The Mad Doctor's Drive* (Brattleboro, Vt., 1964), pp. 5–7.

61. Hill, op. cit., passim. Jackson donated his car to the Smithsonian in 1944.

62. Alice Huyler Ramsey, *Veil, Duster, and Tire Iron* (Covina, Calif., 1961); see esp. pp. 1–7, 16–17, 25–26, 41–42, 61–69, 80.

63. Antonio Scarfoglio, *Round the World in a Motor-Car,* trans. J. Parker Hayes (London, 1909), pp. 29–32, 80, 89–101, 152, 246, 266.

64. Brendon, *Thomas Cook,* p. 249; Baedeker, *Northern France: Handbook for Travellers* (Leipzig, 1909), *Southern Italy: Handbook for Travellers* (Leipzig, 1912), and *Northern Italy: Handbook for Travellers* (Leipzig, 1913); Jakle, *The Tourist,* p. 102.

65. Scarfoglio, *Round the World,* pp. 38–39; John B. Rae, *The Road and Car in American Life* (Cambridge, Mass., 1971), pp. 27–32.

66. James J. Flink, *The Automobile Age* (Cambridge, Mass., 1988), p. 4; Rae, op. cit., pp. 30–33, 35.

67. Rae, op. cit., pp. 36–37; Flink, op. cit., pp. 169–170. Although total highway mileage increased only slightly during the 1920s, surfaced road mileage doubled. Even so, as late as 1945, only slightly more than half of all U.S. roads were surfaced, and "surfaced" still meant, more often than not, gravel or soil rather than macadam, concrete, or some other form of pavement; see Rae, pp. 38, 65–68.

68. Rae, op. cit., p. 36; Hokanson, *Lincoln Highway,* pp. 5, 9–12, 75.

69. Lincoln Highway Association, *The Complete Official Road Guide of the Lincoln Highway* (Detroit, 1916), p. 19.

70. Post, *By Motor to the Golden Gate,* p. 67; *Road Guide . . . Lincoln Highway,* p. 13. On Post's trip, see also Hokanson, *Lincoln Highway,* pp. 23–29.

71. *Road Guide . . . Lincoln Highway,* p. 13; Hokanson, op. cit., pp. 20, 95; Susan Croce Kelly and Quinta Scott, *Route 66: The Highway and Its People* (Norman, Okla., 1988).

72. Rae, *Road and Highway,* p. 50; Jakle, *The Tourist,* pp. 121, 154; "The Lincoln Highway," *Travel,* March 1915, p. 30; *Road Guide . . . Lincoln Highway,* pp. 13–14; Hokanson, op. cit., p. 26.

73. Hyde, *An American Vision,* pp. 297–298; Sargent, *Yosemite,* p. 43; De-

mars, *Tourist in Yosemite*, p. 84; Runte, *Yosemite*, pp. 155–158; on early cars in Yosemite, see William A. Clark, "Automobiling in the Yosemite Valley," *Overland Monthly*, August 1902, reprinted in *Yosemite* 57:4 (Fall 1995), pp. 2–5.

74. Warren J. Belasco, *Americans on the Road: From Autocamp to Motel, 1910–1945* (Cambridge, Mass., 1979), pp. 21–25, 42–44.

75. Edith Wharton, *A Motor Flight Through France* (New York, 1909), p. I, 35.

EPILOGUE

1. *Travel*, October 1914, unpaginated.

2. "The Lincoln Highway—A National Road," *Travel*, February 1915, p. 26.

3. Robert W. Rydell, *All the World's a Fair: Visions of Empire at American International Expositions, 1876–1916* (Chicago, 1984), p. 209; Louis C. Mullgardt, "The Panama-Pacific Exposition of San Francisco," *The Architectural Record* XXXVII (March 1915), p. 193. For comparison, the Philadelphia exposition of 1876 drew almost 19 million visitors; Paris (1889), 32 million; Chicago (1893), 27.5 million; Paris (1900), 48 million; and St. Louis (1904), 19.7 million. In terms of physical size, the Chicago fair was about the same size as San Francisco; St. Louis, at about double the size, was the only fair that was significantly larger. See Burton Benedict, *The Anthropology of World's Fairs* (London and Berkeley, Calif., 1983), p. 31.

4. David McCullough, *The Path Between the Seas: The Creation of the Panama Canal, 1870–1914* (New York, 1978), pp. 608–610.

5. *Why? Where? When? How? The Celebration Is to Take Place*, promotional brochure (San Francisco, 1913). All Exposition promotional literature is from the Bancroft Library unless otherwise noted. On planning for the fair, and competition with other cities, see Rydell, *All the World's a Fair*, pp. 214–217.

6. *Why? Where? When?*; Benedict, *World's Fairs*, p. 60.

7. *West from Home: Letters of Laura Ingalls Wilder to Alamanzo Wilder, San Francisco 1915*, ed. Roger Lea (New York, 1974), p. 35.

8. R. L. Duffus, *The Tower of Jewels: Memories of San Francisco* (New York, 1960), p. 104.

9. Burton Benedict, M. Miriam Dobkin, and Elizabeth Armstrong, *A Catalogue of Posters, Photographs . . . from San Francisco's Panama-Pacific International Exposition of 1915* (Berkeley, Calif., 1982), n.p.; *The People's Easy Guide of the Panama-Pacific International Exposition* (San Francisco, 1915); Rydell, *All the World's a Fair*, pp. 227–228.

10. *The Panama Canal at San Francisco* (San Francisco, 1915).

11. Harry Bruno, *Wings over America: The Inside Story of American Aviation* (New York, 1942), pp. 55–58.

12. Art Smith, *Art Smith's Story: The Autobiography of the Boy Aviator . . .*, ed. Rose Wilder Lane (San Francisco, 1915).

13. Ibid., p. 90. France led the world in 1914 with 1,500 army and 1,000 privately owned planes; Germany had 1,000 army and 450 private craft, while Britain was just beginning to build a fleet, with 82 planes. The United States, still three years away from entering the war, had just 17 military airplanes, 6 owned by the army and 11 by the navy; see Bruno, *Wings over America,* pp. 83–84.

14. Smith, op. cit., pp. 3–4.

15. The editor of an American aviation magazine wrote, in 1938, that World War I would be the last great war in history because airplanes would soon put an end to the motives for war; see Joseph J. Corn, *The Winged Gospel: America's Romance with Aviation, 1900–1950* (New York, 1983), pp. 37–44.

16. Smith, *Art Smith's Story,* p. 3. Five years proved to be a generous estimate. The first commercial passenger airline service, between London and Paris, was launched in September 1919; see Kenneth Hudson, *Air Travel: A Society History* (Totowa, N.J., 1972), pp. 11–13.

A NOTE ON SOURCES

THE MOST IMPORTANT sources for this book include accounts
of journeys written by individual travelers, guidebooks, and promotional literature produced by the travel industry, mainly railroads
and travel agencies. I have used mostly printed books and pamphlets.
The exceptions are the materials included in the Archives of Thomas
Cook Ltd. and manuscript accounts of travelers in the Huntington
library. The Cook Archives include the *Excursionist,* the promotional newspaper published continuously from 1851; promotional
brochures; guidebooks produced by the Cook company; and accounts
of travelers on Cooks' excursions. Railroads and travel agencies produced promotional brochures and posters by the thousands. They
were, of course, not intended to be preserved as historical documents,
but many have survived in various collections. I have used materials
in the Bancroft and Huntington libraries in addition to those in the
Thomas Cook Archives.

What follows is not intended to be an exhaustive bibliography of
works used in writing this book; detailed references are included in

the notes to each chapter. Rather, I have attempted to provide a brief survey of books for the reader who wishes to know more about the subject without combing through the notes.

There are a number of general histories of travel, most of them quite superficial in their treatment of the subject. They include Maxine Feifer, *Tourism in History: From Imperial Rome to the Present* (New York, 1986); R. S. Lambert, *The Fortunate Traveller: A Short History of Touring and Travel for Pleasure* (London, 1950); Horace Sutton, *Travelers: the American Tourist from Stagecoach to Space Shuttle* (New York, 1980); Geoffrey Hindley, *Tourists, Travellers and Pilgrims* (London, 1983); and Winfried Löschburg, *A History of Travel* (London, 1979). Eric J. Leed provides a much more sophisticated survey, focusing on the intellectual significance of travel, in *The Mind of the Traveler: From Gilgamesh to Global Tourism* (New York, 1991).

Much recent work on travel has focused on travel literature as a means of understanding the cultural meaning of travel. Paul Fussell's *Abroad: British Literary Traveling Between the Wars* (New York, 1980) is a pioneering example of the genre. More recent works include Dennis Porter, *Haunted Journeys: Desire and Transgression in European Travel Writing* (Princeton, 1991); William W. Stowe, *Going Abroad: European Travel in Nineteenth-Century American Culture* (Princeton, 1994); James Buzard, *The Beaten Track: European Tourism, Literature, and the Ways to Culture, 1800–1918* (Oxford, 1993); and Terry Caesar, *Forgiving the Boundaries: Home As Abroad in American Travel Writing* (Athens, Ga., 1995).

For readers who want to sample a range of travel literature, several good anthologies are available, among them Paul Fussell, ed., *The Norton Book of Travel* (New York, 1987); John Julius Norwich, ed., *A Taste for Travel* (New York, 1985); and Eric Newby, ed., *A Book of Travellers' Tales* (New York, 1987). There are two collections specifically of writings by women travelers: Mary Morris, *Maiden Voyages: Writings of Women Travelers* (New York, 1993), and Jane Robinson, *Unsuitable for Ladies* (Oxford, 1994).

The study of women travelers has become a growth industry in recent years. Dea Birkett, *Spinsters Abroad: Victorian Lady Travellers* (Oxford, 1989), and Dorothy Middleton, *Victorian Lady Travellers* (London, 1965), offer rather broad treatments of nineteenth-century

British women travelers. Jane Robinson's *Wayward Women: A Guide to Women Travellers* (Oxford, 1990) is a valuable reference work providing brief descriptions of four hundred women who published travel accounts in English. There are a number of biographies of women travelers, including Katherine Frank, *A Voyager Out: The Life of Mary Kingsley* (Boston, 1986), and Virginia Childs, *Lady Hester Stanhope: Queen of the Desert* (London, 1990). Virago and Beacon presses have reissued a number of travel accounts written by women in the nineteenth century. Recent scholarship on women travelers has tended to analyze their experiences through the lens of feminist theory and literary criticism; see, for example, Billie Melman, *Women's Orients: English Women and the Middle East, 1718–1918* (Ann Arbor, Mich., 1992), and Sara Mills, *Discourses of Difference: An Analysis of Women's Travel Writing and Colonialism* (London and New York, 1991).

Probably more has been written about the grand tour than about any other single topic in travel history. Among the best works on the eighteenth-century grand tour are two by Jeremy Black, *The British and the Grand Tour* (London, 1965) and *The British Abroad: The Grand Tour in the Eighteenth Century* (New York, 1992), and Christopher Hibbert, *The Grand Tour* (London, 1987). On Continental travel before the eighteenth century, see John Stoye, *English Travellers Abroad, 1604–1667: Their Influence in English Society and Politics* (London, 1952; rev. ed. New Haven, 1992), and E. S. Bates, *Touring in 1600* (London, 1987).

On Continental travel in the nineteenth century, see especially John Pemble, *The Mediterranean Passion: Victorians and Edwardians in the South* (Oxford, 1987). Foster Rhea Dulles provides a useful survey of Americans traveling in Europe, in *Americans Abroad: Two Centuries of European Travel* (Ann Arbor, Mich., 1964). There are a number of general works on the so-called "golden age of travel" (ca. 1870s–1930s), of which the most serious is Alexis Gregory, *The Golden Age of Travel, 1880–1939* (New York, 1991), which is especially valuable for its excellent illustrations.

On travel in Britain, see Ian Ousby, *The Englishman's England: Taste, Travel, and the Rise of Tourism* (Cambridge, 1990); Malcolm Andrews, *The Search for the Picturesque: Landscape Aesthetics and*

Tourism in Britain, 1760–1800 (Palo Alto, Calif., 1989); Esther Moir, *The Discovery of Britain: The English Tourists, 1540 to 1840* (London, 1964); and James Holloway and Lindsay Errington, *The Discovery of Scotland: The Appreciation of Scottish Scenery Through Two Centuries of Painting* (Edinburgh, 1978). Paul Bernard's *Rush to the Alps: The Evolution of Vacationing in Switzerland* (New York, 1978) is a fascinating history of travel in Switzerland; for an entertaining contemporary account, see Leslie Stephen, *The Playground of Europe* (London, 1871).

On travel in the Middle East, see James C. Simmons, *Passionate Pilgrims: English Travelers to the World of the Desert Arabs* (New York, 1987); Brian M. Fagan, *The Rape of the Nile: Tomb Robbers, Tourists, and Archaeologists in Egypt* (New York, 1975); Neil Asher Silberman, *Digging for God and Country: Exploration in the Holy Land, 1799–1917* (New York, 1982); and Peter A. Clayton, *The Rediscovery of Ancient Egypt: Artists and Travellers in the Nineteenth Century* (London, 1982). On Japan, Hugh Cortazzi, *Victorians in Japan: In and Around the Treaty Ports* (London, 1987), provides a useful survey.

There are several excellent works on travel in the United States. John F. Sears, *Sacred Places: American Tourist Attractions in the Nineteenth Century* (New York, 1989), analyzes popular tourist attractions of the early to mid-nineteenth century. Anne F. Hyde's *An American Vision: Far Western Landscape and National Culture, 1820–1920* (New York, 1990) is an excellent treatment of the development of tourism in the western states. On publicizing the West, see Carlos Schwantes, *Railroad Signatures Across the Pacific Northwest* (Seattle, 1993), and Valerie J. Fifer, *American Progress: The Growth of the Transport, Tourist, and Information Industries in the Nineteenth-Century West Seen Through the Life and Times of George A. Crofutt, Pioneer and Publicist of the Transcontinental Age* (Chester, Conn., 1988). John A. Jakle, *The Tourist*, surveys American travel in the twentieth century. On British travelers in North America, see Jane Mesick, *The English Traveler in America, 1785–1835* (New York, 1921), and Max Berger, *The British Traveller in America, 1836–1860* (New York, 1943).

INDEX